PHILIPPA
OF
HAINAULT

About the Author

Kathryn Warner holds a BA and an MA with Distinction in Medieval History and Literature from the University of Manchester, and is the author of biographies about Edward II and his queen Isabella. Kathryn has had work published in the *English Historical Review*, has given a paper at the International Medieval Congress, and appeared in a BBC documentary.

PHILIPPA
OF
HAINAULT

MOTHER OF THE
ENGLISH NATION

KATHRYN WARNER

AMBERLEY

First published 2022

Amberley Publishing
The Hill, Stroud
Gloucestershire, GL5 4EP

www.amberley-books.com

British Library Cataloguing in Publication Data.
A catalogue record for this book is available from the British Library.

ISBN 978 1 3981 1089 2 (paperback)
ISBN 978 1 4456 6280 0 (ebook)

Typesetting by Aura Technology and Software Services, India.
Printed in the UK.

Contents

Genealogical Tables

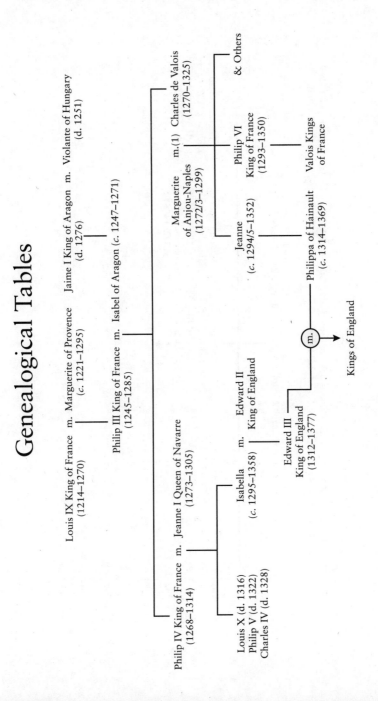

Jan Count of Hainault   m.   Philippa of Luxembourg   Charles de Valois   m.   Marguerite of Anjou-Naples
and Holland (d. 1304)   (d. 1311)   (1270–1325)   (1272/3–1299)

Willem Count of Hainault & Holland   m.   Jeanne de Valois (c. 1294/5–1352)
(c. 1286/7–1337)

Margaretha	Johanna	Philippa	Willem Count of	Jan I (d. 1316)
(1310–1356) m.	(c. 1311/2–1374)	(c. 1314–1369)	Hainault & Holland	Lodewijk (1325–27)
Ludwig of Bavaria	m. Wilhelm	m. Edward III	(c. 1317–1345)	Jan II (b. & d. 1327)
(Holy Roman Emperor)	Duke of Jülich	King of England	m. Johanna of Brabant	Isabella (c. 1323/4–1361)
(1282–1347)			(1322–1406)	
				Agnes (d. 1326/7)
				Sibilla?

Ludwig the Roman	Gerhard	→
Wilhelm	Wilhelm	
Albrecht	Elisabeth	
Otto	(Others)	
Margarethe		
Anna		
Elisabeth		
Beatrix		

Dramatis Personae

Philippa of Hainault (b. *c.* 1314), queen of England, lady of Ireland, duchess of Aquitaine, countess of Ponthieu and Chester: third or perhaps fourth daughter of Willem, count of Hainault and Holland, and Jeanne de Valois; marries Edward III, king of England, on 24 or 25 January 1328

Willem (b. *c.* 1286/7), count of Hainault, Holland and Zeeland, lord of Friesland: third but eldest surviving son of Jan, count of Hainault and Holland (d. 1304), and Philippa of Luxembourg (d. 1311); Queen Philippa's father

Jeanne de Valois (b. *c.* 1294/5), countess of Hainault, Holland and Zeeland: second daughter of Charles de Valois, count of Valois (1270-1325), the second son of King Philip III of France, and his first wife Marguerite of Anjou-Naples (1272/3-1299), eldest daughter of Charles II 'the Lame', king of Naples; sister of Philip VI, king of France from 1328; Queen Philippa's mother

Margaretha of Hainault (b. 1310), Holy Roman Empress, queen of Germany and Italy, duchess of Bavaria: Philippa's eldest sister; marries Ludwig von Wittelsbach of Bavaria, king of Germany and later emperor, in February 1324; has ten children, including Margarethe, Anna, Beatrix, Ludwig the Roman, Wilhelm, Albrecht and Otto; inherits the counties of Hainault and Holland on the death of her younger brother Willem in 1345

Johanna of Hainault (b. *c.* 1311/12), countess and later duchess of Jülich, countess of Cambridge; Philippa's other elder sister, the second daughter of Count Willem and Jeanne de Valois; marries Wilhelm, heir to the county of Jülich, in February 1324; her children include Elisabeth of Jülich, countess of Kent, Gerhard, count of Berg and Ravensberg, and Wilhelm, duke of Jülich

Sibilla? (alive 1319?), **Agnes** (b. *c.* late 1310s or early 1320s), and **Isabella** (b. *c.* 1323/24?) of Hainault: Queen Philippa's other sisters; Isabella is the youngest daughter of Willem and Jeanne, marries the brother of the marquis of Namur in 1354 but has no children; Sibilla, if she exists, is probably older than Philippa and dies young; Agnes is younger than Philippa and dies young in or before 1327

Willem (b. *c.* 1317), count of Hainault, Holland and Zeeland, lord of Friesland: Philippa's younger brother, their father's heir, and the only son of Willem the elder and Jeanne de Valois who survives childhood; marries Johanna of Brabant (b. 1322) but has no surviving children, and his eldest sister Empress Margaretha is his heir

Jan (d. 1316 in infancy), **Lodewijk** (1325-27) and another **Jan** (b. and d. 1327) of Hainault: Philippa's other brothers, who all die young

Jan van de Poel, Jan Aelman, Jan van Dolre, Jan Zuurmond, Claas van de Gheijne, Willem, Aleide, Elisabeth of Holland and possibly **Matilde de Luwembergh**: illegitimate children of Willem the elder (b. *c.* 1286/7), count of Hainault and Holland; Queen Philippa's half-siblings. Elisabeth of Holland (d. 1375) moves to England and is a nun of Stratford-le-Bow; Aleide is a nun of Leeuwenhorst; Matilde is abbess of Nivelles

Ludwig of Bavaria, also often called Ludwig von Wittelsbach (b. 1282): Holy Roman Emperor, king of Germany and Italy, duke of Bavaria: son of Ludwig 'the Strict', duke of Bavaria, and Melchilde von Habsburg; marries Beatrix of Świdnica (d. 1320) in 1308 and Philippa's eldest sister Margaretha in 1324

Wilhelm (b. *c.* 1299/1300), count and later duke of Jülich, made first earl of Cambridge by Edward III in 1340: son of Gerhard of

Jülich and Elisabeth of Aarschot; marries Philippa's second sister Johanna in 1324; his younger brother **Walram von Jülich** is elected archbishop of Cologne in 1332

Edward III (b. 13 November 1312), king of England, lord of Ireland, duke of Aquitaine, count of Ponthieu, earl of Chester: eldest child of Edward II and Isabella of France; becomes king of England in January 1327 after his father's forced abdication; known as 'Edward of Windsor' before his accession; betrothed to Philippa of Hainault in August 1326, and marries her in January 1328

Edward II (b. 1284), king of England, son of Edward I (d. 1307) and Leonor of Castile (d. 1290): Edward III's father; forced to abdicate his throne to his son in January 1327, reportedly dies at Berkeley Castle in September 1327 and buried in Gloucester that December; rumours spread in and after 1329 that he is in fact alive

Isabella of France (b. *c.* 1295), queen of England, daughter of Philip IV of France (d. 1314) and Jeanne I, queen of Navarre (d. 1305): marries Edward II of England in 1308, Edward III's mother and Queen Philippa's mother-in-law; sister of Louis X (d. 1316), Philip V (d. 1322) and Charles IV (d. 1328), kings of France and Navarre; first cousin of Philip VI, king of France

Thomas of Brotherton, earl of Norfolk (1300-38) and **Edmund of Woodstock**, earl of Kent (1301-30): half-brothers of Edward II and uncles of Edward III. Edmund's son John (b. 1330) marries Philippa's niece Elisabeth of Jülich in 1348, and his daughter and ultimate heir Joan (b. 1326/7) marries Philippa's eldest son, Edward of Woodstock, in 1361

John of Eltham (b. 1316), earl of Cornwall: younger son of Edward II and Isabella of France, and Edward III's only brother; never marries and has no children

Eleanor of Woodstock (b. 1318), countess and later duchess of Guelders: elder daughter of Edward II and Isabella of France, and sister of Edward III; marries Reynald of Guelders in 1332; her children are Reynald (b. 1333) and Eduard (b. 1336), both dukes of Guelders

Joan of the Tower (b. 1321), queen of Scotland: Edward III's other sister; marries David Bruce (b. 1324), son and heir of Robert I, king of Scotland, in 1328; he succeeds as David II of Scotland in 1329; they have no children and his heir is his half-nephew Robert Stewart

Hugh Despenser ('the Younger') (b. *c.* 1288/9), lord of Glamorgan: powerful nephew-in-law, chamberlain and probably lover of Edward II; son of Hugh Despenser the Elder (b. 1261), earl of Winchester; enemy of Queen Isabella and Edward of Windsor; married to Edward II's niece Eleanor de Clare (b. 1292)

Roger Mortimer (b. *c.* 1286/8), lord of Wigmore, first earl of March in 1328: powerful favourite of Queen Isabella, and her co-ruler between 1327 and 1330 during Edward III's minority; married to Joan Geneville (b. 1286) since 1301; his eldest son Edmund dies in 1331 and his heir is his grandson Roger (b. 1328), second earl of March

Charles IV (b. 1294), king of France and Navarre: third and youngest son of Philip IV (d. 1314); brother of Isabella, queen of England, and uncle of Edward III; succeeds his brother Philip V in 1322; marries 1) Blanche of Burgundy in 1308, 2) Marie of Luxembourg in 1322, and 3) Jeanne of Evreux in 1324

Charles de Valois (b. 1270), count of Valois, Anjou, Maine, Alençon, Perche and Chartres, titular Latin Emperor of Constantinople: second son of Philip III of France (d. 1285) and his first wife Isabel of Aragon (d. 1271); brother of Philip IV, uncle of Charles IV and of Isabella, queen of England, and great-uncle of Edward III; married to 1) Marguerite of Anjou-Naples (d. 1299), 2) Catherine de Courtenay, heiress of the Latin Empire of Constantinople (d. 1307), and 3) Mahaut de Châtillon (d. 1358); father of Jeanne de Valois, countess of Hainault, and Queen Philippa's maternal grandfather

Marguerite of Anjou-Naples (1272/3-1299), countess of Anjou and Maine: eldest daughter of Charles II 'the Lame', king of Naples (1254-1309), and Marie of Hungary (*c.* 1255-1323); sister of Charles Martel, king of Hungary, Robert 'the Wise', king of Naples, Philip of Taranto, despot of Romania, and others; granddaughter of Erzsébet the Cuman, queen of Hungary and Croatia (d. 1290); Queen Philippa's maternal grandmother

Philip de Valois (b. 1293): eldest son of Charles de Valois and his first wife Marguerite of Anjou-Naples; becomes King Philip VI of France in 1328, first of the Valois kings who rule France until 1589; married to Jeanne of Burgundy (b. *c.* 1293) and secondly to Blanca or Blanche of Navarre (b. 1330/31); Queen Philippa's maternal uncle

John II (b. 1319), duke of Normandy, king of France 1350 to 1364: son of Philip VI and Jeanne of Burgundy; Queen Philippa's first cousin; marries Bonne, née Jutta, of Bohemia (1315-49), and secondly Jeanne, countess of Auvergne (1326-60)

Charles V (b. 1338), king of France 1364 to 1380: eldest son of John II and Bonne of Bohemia; marries Jeanne de Bourbon; his younger brothers are Louis, duke of Anjou (b. 1339), John, duke of Berry (b. 1340) and Philip, duke of Burgundy (b. 1342)

Jeanne II (b. 1312), queen of Navarre: daughter and only surviving child of Louis X, king of France and Navarre (d. 1316); niece of Charles IV and of Isabella, queen of England, and first cousin of Edward III of England; becomes queen-regnant of Navarre in 1328; her son and heir is **Carlos II 'the Bad'** (b. 1332, r. 1349-87)

Alfonso XI (b. 1311), king of Castile and Leon, two of the four Spanish kingdoms; married to Maria of Portugal (b. *c.* 1313) but has many children with his mistress Leonor Guzman

Pedro 'the Cruel' (b. 1334), king of Castile and Leon: son and heir of Alfonso XI and Queen Maria; betrothed to Philippa and Edward III's second daughter Joan in 1348; succeeds his father as king in 1350 and marries Blanche de Bourbon, one of Queen Philippa's first cousins, in 1353

Enrique of Trastamara (b. 1334): eldest surviving son of Alfonso XI of Castile and his mistress Leonor Guzman; half-brother and enemy of Pedro 'the Cruel'; later King Enrique II of Castile and Leon

Constanza (b. *c.* 1354) and **Isabel** (b. *c.* 1355) of Castile: daughters of Pedro 'the Cruel' and his mistress Maria de Padilla, legitimised after the death of Pedro's queen Blanche de Bourbon in 1361;

they marry Queen Philippa's sons John of Gaunt and Edmund of Langley after Philippa's death

Afonso IV (b. 1291), king of Portugal from 1325; his eldest daughter Maria (b. *c.* 1313) marries Alfonso XI of Castile and is the mother of Pedro 'the Cruel', and his youngest daughter Leonor (b. *c.* 1328) is proposed as a bride for two of Queen Philippa's sons but marries Pedro IV of Aragon

Otto (b. 1301), duke of Austria, and his son **Friedrich** (b. 1327), betrothed to Philippa's second daughter Joan in 1335

John III (b. 1286), duke of Brittany, a great-grandson of Henry III, king of England (d. 1272); and his niece **Jeanne de Penthièvre** (b. *c.* 1319), countess of Blois and claimant to the duchy of Brittany

Robert of Artois (b. 1287): count of Beaumont-le-Roger and claimant to the county of Artois; married to Jeanne de Valois (b. 1304), second daughter of Charles de Valois and his second wife Catherine de Courtenay, half-sister of Philip VI and of Jeanne de Valois, countess of Hainault and Holland; Queen Philippa's uncle by marriage

Guy de Châtillon, count of Blois, married to Philippa's aunt Marguerite de Valois, and their sons **Louis**, count of Blois, killed at the battle of Crécy in 1346, and **Charles** (b. 1319), count of Blois, married to Jeanne de Penthièvre

Jan van Beaumont (b. *c.* 1288/90): younger brother of Willem, count of Hainault and Holland; married to Marguerite, countess of Soissons; Queen Philippa's uncle

John de Montfort (b. *c.* 1295), half-brother of John III of Brittany, and claimant to the duchy; his son **John de Montfort** the younger (b. 1339), later Duke John IV of Brittany, who marries Philippa's daughter Mary of Waltham in 1361; and his daughter **Jeanne de Montfort**, the 'damsel of Brittany'

Henry of Luxembourg (*c.* 1275-1313), Holy Roman Emperor, a first cousin of Philippa's father Willem, count of Hainault and Holland; Henry's son **Johann 'the Blind'**, king of Bohemia

(b. 1296); Johann's son **Karl IV** (b. 1316), Holy Roman Emperor; Johann's daughter **Bonne/Jutta** (b. 1315), duchess of Normandy, mother of Charles V of France; and Henry's brother **Balduin** (b. *c*. 1285), archbishop of Trier and one of the seven Electors

Robert I (Robert Bruce), king of Scotland (b. 1274, r. 1306-29), and his son and heir **David II** (b. 1324), who marries Edward III's sister Joan of the Tower (b. 1321) in 1328

Edward of Woodstock (b. 1330), prince of Wales and Aquitaine, duke of Cornwall, earl of Chester: eldest child of Queen Philippa and Edward III; heir to the English throne; marries his cousin Joan of Kent in 1361

Isabella of Woodstock (b. 1332): eldest daughter of Queen Philippa and Edward III; betrothed many times before marrying Enguerrand (or Ingelram) de Coucy in 1365; has daughters Marie (b. 1366) and Philippa (b. 1367/8)

Joan of Woodstock (b. 1334): second daughter of Queen Philippa and Edward III; betrothed to Friedrich of Austria in 1335 and Pedro of Castile; dies in the south of France in the summer of 1348 on her way to marry Pedro

William of Hatfield (b. and d. 1337), **Blanche of the Tower** (b. and d. 1342) and **William of Windsor** (b. and d. 1348): children of Queen Philippa and Edward III who die young

Lionel of Antwerp (b. 1338), first duke of Clarence, earl of Ulster: third but second surviving son of Queen Philippa and Edward III; marries 1) Elizabeth de Burgh, countess of Ulster, in 1342, and 2) Violante Visconti in 1368

John of Gaunt (b. 1340), second duke of Lancaster, earl of Richmond, titular king of Castile and Leon: fourth but third surviving son of Queen Philippa and Edward III; marries 1) Blanche of Lancaster in 1359, 2) Constanza of Castile in 1371, and 3) Katherine Swynford in 1396

Edmund of Langley (b. 1341), first duke of York, earl of Cambridge: fifth but fourth surviving son of Queen Philippa and Edward III; marries 1) Isabel of Castile in 1372, and 2) Joan Holland in 1393

Mary of Waltham and **Margaret of Windsor** (b. 1344 and 1346): fourth and fifth, and youngest, daughters of Queen Philippa and Edward III; both marry, but die childless in their teens

Thomas of Woodstock (b. 1355), first duke of Gloucester, earl of Buckingham: seventh but fifth surviving son of Queen Philippa and Edward III, and their twelfth and youngest child; marries Eleanor de Bohun, co-heir of the earldoms of Hereford, Essex and Northampton

Philippa of Clarence (b. 1355), countess of March and Ulster: only child and heir of Lionel of Antwerp and Elizabeth de Burgh; Queen Philippa's eldest legitimate grandchild; marries Edmund Mortimer in 1358

Henry of Lancaster (b. 1280/81), earl of Lancaster and Leicester: second son and ultimate heir of Edward I's brother Edmund of Lancaster (d. 1296) and Blanche of Artois (d. 1302), dowager queen of Navarre; first cousin of Edward II and uncle of Queen Isabella; great-uncle of Edward III; grandfather of Elizabeth de Burgh, countess of Ulster (b. 1332)

Henry of Grosmont (b. *c*. 1310/12): only son and heir of Henry of Lancaster; marries Isabella Beaumont in 1330; earl of Derby 1337, earl of Lancaster and Leicester 1345, earl of Lincoln 1349, and first duke of Lancaster 1351; father-in-law of John of Gaunt

Maud (b. 1340) and **Blanche** (b. 1342) of Lancaster: daughters and co-heirs of Henry of Grosmont; Maud marries Queen Philippa's nephew Wilhelm of Bavaria in 1352 and Blanche marries Philippa's third son John of Gaunt in 1359

Eleanor of Lancaster (b. *c*. 1316/18): fifth of the six daughters of Henry, earl of Lancaster, and sister of Henry of Grosmont; marries 1) John, Lord Beaumont (b. 1317) in 1330 and 2) Richard Fitzalan (b. *c*. 1313), earl of Arundel, in 1345; a friend of Edward III and Queen Philippa

Elizabeth de Burgh (b. 1332), countess of Ulster: daughter and heir of William de Burgh, earl of Ulster (1312-33) and Maud of Lancaster (b. *c*. 1310/12), third of the six daughters of Henry, earl of Lancaster (b. 1280/81); marries Queen Philippa's second son

Lionel of Antwerp in 1342; their daughter and heir is Philippa of Clarence, countess of March and Ulster (b. 1355)

Joan of Kent (b. 1326/27), countess of Kent in her own right: daughter and ultimate heir of Edward III's uncle Edmund of Woodstock, earl of Kent; marries Sir Thomas Holland (d. 1360) then Philippa's eldest son Edward of Woodstock in 1361; mother of Philippa's grandsons **Edward of Angoulême** (b. 1365) and **Richard of Bordeaux**, later King Richard II (b. 1367)

John of Kent (b. 1330); earl of Kent: posthumous son and heir of Edmund of Woodstock, and Edward III's first cousin; marries Queen Philippa's niece **Elisabeth of Jülich** in 1348 but dies childless in 1352, leaving his sister Joan as his heir; Elisabeth outlives him by almost sixty years and dies in 1411

Humphrey de Bohun, earl of Hereford and Essex (b. 1307) and his brother **William de Bohun**, earl of Northampton (b. *c.* 1309): grandsons of Edward I, and first cousins of Edward III

William Montacute (b. *c.* 1301), earl of Salisbury: friend of Edward III; married to **Katherine Grandisson**; their son and heir **William** (b. 1328) marries Edward I's granddaughter Joan of Kent (supposedly a bigamous marriage as she later claimed that she had already wed Thomas Holland)

Margaret of Norfolk, also sometimes called Margaret Marshal (b. *c.* 1322), countess of Norfolk in her own right: daughter and ultimate heir of Edward III's uncle Thomas of Brotherton, earl of Norfolk; marries 1} John, Lord Segrave (1315-53) and 2) Walter, Lord Manny or Mauny, a Hainaulter knight who comes to England with Queen Philippa

Laurence Hastings (b. 1321), earl of Pembroke, and his son and heir **John Hastings** (b. 1347), who marries Queen Philippa's youngest daughter Margaret of Windsor (b. 1346) in 1359

Roger Mortimer (b. 1328), second earl of March: grandson and heir of Roger Mortimer (1286/7-1330), first earl of March; marries **Philippa Montacute** (b. *c.* early to mid-1330s), sister of William (b. 1328), earl of Salisbury; their son and heir is **Edmund Mortimer**

(b. 1352), third earl of March, who marries Queen Philippa's granddaughter Philippa of Clarence (b. 1355) in 1358

Ralph Stafford (b. 1301), earl of Stafford; **Robert Ufford** (b. 1298), earl of Suffolk; **William Clinton** (b. *c.* 1304), earl of Huntingdon; **John Neville of Hornby**: friends and allies of the king

Thomas Beauchamp, earl of Warwick (b. 1314); **Richard Fitzalan**, earl of Arundel (b. *c.* 1313); **John de Warenne**, earl of Surrey (b. 1286); **John de Vere**, earl of Oxford (b. *c.* 1312); **Hugh Audley**, earl of Gloucester (b. *c.* 1291/93): some of the other English earls of Edward III's reign

1

The Hainault Family

Edward III, king of England, was fifteen years old at the time of his wedding in York on 24 or 25 January 1328, and Philippa of Hainault, his bride, was perhaps fifteen months or so younger and, according to one chronicler, about to turn fourteen. Although their marriage was to endure for more than four decades and would prove to be a most happy and successful one that produced a dozen children, it could hardly have begun in a more unromantic fashion. Edward's mother Queen Isabella had arranged her son's marriage with Philippa's father Willem, count of Hainault in 1326 so that he would provide ships and mercenaries for her to invade her husband Edward II's kingdom in order to bring down the man she loathed above all others, Edward II's adored chamberlain and perhaps lover Hugh Despenser the Younger. Just a month before his wedding to Philippa, Edward III had attended the funeral of his deposed, disgraced and possibly murdered father, the former king, at St Peter's Abbey in Gloucestershire. Whether intentionally or not, Edward III and Philippa of Hainault married on his parents' twentieth wedding anniversary, and on the first anniversary of the young Edward's reign as king of England.

Philippa of Hainault accompanied her husband abroad on many of his military and diplomatic missions; the couple hated to be apart for long and spent as much time together as they possibly could. Despite Philippa's decades-long marriage to one of medieval England's most famous and successful kings, there has only ever been one full-length biography of her, published by

Blanche Christabel Hardy in 1910 and titled *Philippa of Hainault and Her Times*. In addition, two chapters in Agnes Strickland's nineteenth-century work *The Lives of the Queens of England* cover the basics of Philippa's life, and Lisa Benz St John's 2012 book *Three Medieval Queens* examines the lives of Philippa and her two predecessors as queen of England.

Edward III and Philippa of Hainault shared a set of great-grandparents, King Philip III of France (born 1245) and his half-Spanish and half-Hungarian first wife, Isabel of Aragon (born *c.* 1247). On 11 January 1271 in the southern Italian town of Cosenza in the province of Calabria, the pregnant Queen Isabel was thrown from her horse while returning to France from Tunis with her husband and the rest of the French royal family. Her father-in-law King Louis IX had sailed there before his planned second crusade to the Holy Land, and died of the dysentery which decimated his army days after his arrival and without setting eyes on the Holy Land again. The French royal family trailed slowly home, and were resting in southern Italy when Isabel had her accident. The young queen died of her injuries on 28 January 1271, and her unborn child with her. She had been queen-consort of France for a mere five months following the death of Louis IX and the accession of her husband Philip III on 25 August 1270.

Isabel of Aragon, only about twenty-three years old at the time of her death, left two small sons. The elder was the future King Philip IV of France, who was born sometime in 1268 and who had four surviving children: three kings of France and Navarre, and the queen-consort of England. Edward III of England was Philip IV's grandson. Philip III and Isabel of Aragon's younger son was Charles de Valois, born on 12 March 1270, who became count of Valois, Anjou, Maine, Alençon, Perche and Chartres, and who was Philippa of Hainault's maternal grandfather. Valois married his cousin Marguerite of Anjou-Naples on 16 August 1290 when he was twenty. She was born in 1272 or 1273 and brought him the counties of Anjou and Maine in north-western France as her dowry and as part of her inheritance from her father Charles II 'the Lame' (d. 1309), king of Naples and Albania and a scion of the French royal family.[1]

Via her grandmother Marguerite of Anjou-Naples and Marguerite's mother Marie of Hungary, Philippa of Hainault was the great-great-granddaughter of István (or Stephen) V, king of Hungary and Croatia, and his queen Erzsébet (or Elizabeth) the Cuman, who had been born into a shamanistic people of the Eurasian steppes who fled into Hungary in the 1230s and 1240s to escape the invasions of the Mongols, and settled there. Erzsébet was the daughter of the Cumans' khan or chieftain, whose name was probably either Seyhan or Köten (or Kötöny). She converted to Christianity before her marriage to István and took the Christian name of Erzsébet; her birth name is not known, and she may have chosen her new name in honour of Saint Erzsébet of Hungary (1207-31), her husband István's aunt, a member of the Hungarian royal family who was canonised four years after her death. Erzsébet the Cuman and István V's third daughter Marie of Hungary, who was born around 1255 and became queen of Naples and Albania via her marriage to Charles II 'the Lame', lived until 1323, about nine years into the lifetime of her great-granddaughter Philippa of Hainault.

Philippa's maternal grandmother Marguerite, countess of Anjou, Maine and Valois, died at the end of 1299, twenty-four years before the death of her mother Marie of Hungary. Marguerite's widower Charles de Valois, brother of the then reigning king of France, Philip IV, married again twice, and his second marriage to Catherine de Courtenay made him emperor of the Latin empire of Constantinople, albeit in name only. Valois's three marriages all produced children, mostly daughters who married into several royal and noble families; Charles de Valois is sometimes known as the Grandfather of Europe. His eldest son Philip de Valois became the first of the Valois kings of France in 1328, and thus Charles founded a dynasty which would rule France until 1589, when King Henri III died without children and was succeeded by the first of the Bourbon kings of France, Henri IV. Philippa of Hainault's mother Jeanne de Valois was the second daughter of Charles de Valois and his first wife Marguerite of Anjou-Naples. The couple's first daughter Isabelle was born in 1292, and their first son, King Philip VI of France, in 1293. Jeanne therefore was probably born in 1294 or 1295. Three more children – Marguerite, countess of Blois; Charles, count of Alençon (b. 1297); and Catherine (b. 1299), who died in infancy – followed Jeanne before Countess Marguerite's premature death on the last day of the thirteenth century, aged twenty-six or twenty-seven.

It is possible that Jeanne, the third Valois child, and Marguerite, the fourth, were twins, and their mother Marguerite of Anjou-Naples must have died as a result of childbirth after she bore her sixth child Catherine, who did not live long after her birth. Jeanne and her siblings gained a stepmother fourteen months after their mother's death when Charles de Valois married Catherine de Courtenay, heiress of Constantinople, on 28 February 1301. Catherine was the mother of four of their half-siblings, and died in October 1307 in her early thirties. Valois's third and much younger wife Mahaut de Châtillon (b. *c.* 1293), daughter of the count of Saint Pol, gave Valois another four children between about 1309 and 1318. Otherwise, almost nothing is known of Jeanne de Valois's childhood or where and with whom she grew up, though later evidence suggests that she maintained an excellent relationship with her brother King Philip VI, who was close to her in age.

She is also known to have kept in touch with her other full brother Charles of Alençon and with her younger half-sister and namesake Jeanne de Valois (b. 1304), and the siblings exchanged books.[2] Their elder sister Isabelle, who married the heir to the duchy of Brittany, died at the age of seventeen in 1309, leaving Jeanne as Charles de Valois's eldest surviving daughter.[3]

Jeanne de Valois married very young: her wedding took place at Chauny in Picardy, northern France on 19 May 1305, when she was probably only about ten and cannot, even if she was a twin of her eldest sister Isabelle, have been more than thirteen. Even if her wedding did take place when she was under twelve, the marriage would certainly not have been consummated until she was twelve or older, and Jeanne may have remained in her native France until she was old enough to cohabit with her husband. Her bridegroom, Philippa of Hainault's father, was Willem of the house of Avesnes, count of Hainault and Holland, born in about 1286 or 1287 and in his late teens at the time of his wedding. Willem inherited the counties of Hainault and Holland from his father Jan II, who died in September 1304 a few months before Willem's wedding. For the first fifteen or sixteen years of his life, Willem had not expected to succeed his father as he had two older brothers, but Jan the eldest was killed at the Battle of the Golden Spurs in 1302 (two of their brothers-in-law also died there) and Hendrik the second son died in 1303. Willem and Jeanne de Valois's wedding had been arranged in May 1303, two years before it took place.[4]

Philippa of Hainault came from a long line of counts of Hainault, Holland, Luxembourg and Flanders on her father's side. She was presumably named after her paternal grandmother Philippa of Luxembourg, countess of Holland, and perhaps also in honour of her maternal uncle Philip de Valois. In English documents of the fourteenth century, the queen's name was always spelt 'Philippe', 'Phelippe' or 'Phelipe'; very confusingly as Philippe is the male form of the name Philip in modern French, and the fourteenth-century *Brut* chronicle written in Middle English calls her *Philipp* and *Quene Phelip*. Chronicler Jean Froissart, who knew the queen personally, called her *madame Phelippe de Haynau*, 'my lady Philippa of Hainault.'[5] In fourteenth-century English, 'Phelip' was the usual spelling of the male form of the name as well, and it appears to have been a genderless name, both in English and French; the *Brut* chronicle also refers to Philippa's uncle Philip VI of France as 'Phelip', and Froissart calls both Philippa and Philip VI 'Phelippe'. In modern Flemish, the queen is called Filippa van Henegouwen ('of Hainault'), and she is sometimes also known as Philippa of Avesnes, the name of her dynasty.

Given that Philippa's mother was the granddaughter, niece and (from 1328) sister of kings of France, granddaughter of the king of Naples and Albania, niece of the kings of Hungary, Aragon, Naples, Majorca and Sicily and the half-sister of two empresses, marrying the count of Hainault and Holland was perhaps not a very brilliant match for Jeanne de Valois. Still, she and Willem seem to have formed a happy and solid partnership, despite his constant unfaithfulness and numerous bastards, and there is evidence that Jeanne was extremely close to her daughters by Willem. The couple would be married for thirty-two years.

The fourteenth-century county of Hainault bordered the kingdom of France and covered the area of the modern Belgian province of Hainaut and part of the modern French department of Nord. Despite its closeness to the kingdom of France, geographically, culturally and linguistically – Philippa's native language was probably French though she was surely fluent in Flemish (or Dutch) as well – when Philippa was born Hainault was part of the territories of the Holy Roman Empire, and the emperor was the count's overlord. Hainault's main town was Valenciennes, where Philippa may have been born, which lies on the River Scheldt and is nowadays in the Nord department very close to the Belgian border. The historic county of Holland, also ruled by Philippa's father, lies in the modern-day Netherlands, and is now divided into two provinces called North and South Holland (Amsterdam is situated in North Holland). Holland was also part of the Holy Roman Empire in the fourteenth century and was separated geographically from the county of Hainault by the large duchy of Brabant, whose capital was Brussels. Willem, count of Hainault and Holland was also count of Zeeland, an area that more or less corresponds to the province of Zeeland in the south-west of the modern Netherlands, and lord of Friesland or Frisia, a coastal territory now in the north of the Netherlands and also including a small part of northern Germany. Shortly before Philippa was born, the Holy Roman Emperor and overlord of Hainault, Holland and Zeeland was Henry of Luxembourg, who died in August 1313 and was a first cousin of her father Willem. Henry's successor as emperor was the German who in 1324 married Philippa's eldest sister, Margaretha: Ludwig von Wittelsbach, duke of Bavaria and count palatine of the Rhine.

Although one could describe Philippa of Hainault as merely the daughter of a man who ruled several small counties on the edge of north-west Europe, in fairness to her this would be to underestimate her – and their – importance. The patchwork of counties and duchies in the Low Countries, northern France and western Germany – Hainault, Holland, Brabant, Flanders, Guelders, Artois, Saint Pol, Luxembourg, Namur, Picardy, Cleves, Jülich and so on – were England's main trading partners, and were both wealthy and far more influential than one might imagine from their tiny size. Philippa's father ruled lands which were 'situated on the broad highways of the world's commerce, the Rhine, Meuse, the Scheldt, the Zuider Zee, and the North Sea'.[6] In the 1290s King Edward I of England married two of his daughters into this part of the world, to the count of Holland and the duke of Brabant, and in 1332 Philippa's husband Edward III, Edward I's grandson, married his sister Eleanor to the count (later duke) of Guelders.[7]

In addition, via Jeanne de Valois, Philippa was born into a powerful network of relatives that stretched across Europe. She was descended from emperors of Byzantium and Nicaea, kings of France, Aragon, Naples, Sicily, Hungary and Croatia and from the Turkic peoples of the Eurasian steppes. Philippa's eldest sister Margaretha was the Holy Roman Empress, queen of Germany and Italy and duchess of Bavaria, and her niece Beatrix was queen of Sweden. Her aunts included another Holy Roman Empress and a titular empress of the Latin empire of Constantinople. One of her uncles became king of France. Philippa of Hainault was descended from Harold Godwinson, the last king of Anglo-Saxon England, killed at the battle of Hastings in 1066. Harold's daughter Gytha of Wessex married Vladimir Monomakh, grand prince of Kievan Rus, and Gytha and Vladimir's granddaughter Euphrosyne of Novgorod and her husband King Géza II of Hungary were Philippa's ancestors. Philippa was also descended from King Stephen of England (reigned 1135-54), grandson of William the Conqueror. Stephen's great-granddaughter, Mathilde of Brabant, countess of Holland (d. 1267) was Philippa's great-great-grandmother. Stephen had been succeeded on his death in 1154 not by his own son but by Henry II, son of his cousin and enemy the Empress Maud, and Henry II was the ancestor of all the subsequent kings of England. Philippa of Hainault's marriage to Edward III brought King Stephen's bloodline back into the English royal family.[8]

Given Jeanne de Valois's youth at the time of her marriage in 1305, she is unlikely to have given birth before 1309/10 when she was fifteen or so. She and Count Willem had nine or ten children, four sons and five or six daughters; establishing the exact number of children, their birth order and the date of birth of their daughter Queen Philippa is tricky. Margaretha must have been their eldest daughter and was almost certainly the eldest child overall. She inherited the counties of Hainault and Holland on the death of her younger brother Willem, named after their father, in 1345. Margaretha was born on 24 June 1310 or 24 June 1311, almost certainly the former, when her mother was probably about fifteen or sixteen. Queen Philippa's date of birth is often given nowadays as 24 June 1314, but in fact we do not know the date, or even the correct year of her birth, for certain.[9] This date seems to be a modern misunderstanding: Philippa's sister Margaretha's date of birth wrongly assigned to Philippa, coupled with an assumption that Philippa was born in 1314. The Flemish chronicler Jean Froissart, who knew the queen well in later decades, says that she was 'almost fourteen years old' (*sus le point de quartorze ans*) when she married Edward III on 25 January 1328, which would place her date of birth in about late January or February 1314. Froissart, however, also says wrongly that she and Edward married in 1327 and that the king was seventeen at the time of his wedding. He was actually fifteen, born on 13 November 1312. Froissart is often an unreliable source and was not even born until the late 1330s, but given the evidence we have, placing Philippa's date of birth in 1314 does in fact seem reasonable. She became pregnant for the first time in September 1329, so is unlikely to have been born later than 1314 or early 1315. A date of birth in *c.* late January, February or perhaps March 1314, if Froissart is correct on this point, would make her about fifteen months younger than her husband.

Jean Froissart gives the names of Philippa and her sisters in what appears to be birth order: Margaretha, Philippa, Johanna and Isabella (in the original spelling of his French text, *Margerite, Phelippe, Jehanne et Ysabiel*). This order, although often repeated since, is incorrect, and also misses out one or two of the Hainault sisters. The second eldest daughter of Willem of Hainault and Jeanne de Valois was not Philippa but Johanna, as the Brederode chronicle states on several occasions, calling her the *secunda filia*, 'second daughter.'[10] The eldest Hainault sister Margaretha married Ludwig von Wittelsbach of Bavaria in Cologne on 26 February 1324, when she was probably thirteen years and eight months old. Born in 1282, Ludwig was almost three decades her senior, and indeed was a few years older than her parents as well.

The second Hainault sister Johanna married Wilhelm, born in *c.* 1299/1300 and heir to his father Gerhard's county of Jülich, also in Cologne on 26 February 1324. There was a double wedding of the two Hainault sisters and their German bridegrooms. Johanna of Hainault's marriage in February 1324, almost four years before her sister Philippa married Edward III of England, also indicates that she was older than Philippa. If Philippa were the second daughter, as almost invariably stated, it would have made little sense to skip over her and marry the third daughter to Wilhelm of Jülich instead. Willem, count of Hainault, and Gerhard, count of Jülich, had arranged the marriage of their children Johanna and Wilhelm on 24 June 1317. The two men jointly wrote a document in French, witnessed by the teenaged Duke John III of Brabant and Count Reynald I of Guelders and his son, among others, detailing the dowry in Jülich that would be given to Johanna of Hainault after her marriage. Count Willem had travelled to Cologne to discuss the matter with Gerhard. The two men's agreement stated that Wilhelm of Jülich and Johanna's wedding would take place as soon as 'the damsel Johanna (*demizele Jehane*) has come to the age when she may marry'. The age for a young noble girl to be considered old enough to marry and cohabit (rather than going through the wedding ceremony but remaining with her family, as was most probably the case with Jeanne de Valois in 1305) was usually twelve, and there is evidence that Johanna did not return to Hainault with her parents but remained in Germany with her new husband. She is extremely unlikely to have been less than twelve years old when she married on 26 February 1324, and it is virtually certain, therefore, that she was born before 26 February 1312.[11]

Johanna of Hainault's eldest son, Gerhard of Jülich, named after his paternal grandfather the count of Jülich, was almost certainly born no later than 1326 or 1327, further evidence that she herself can hardly have been born later than 1311 or early 1312. There is no doubt that Johanna was older than her sister Queen Philippa. As Margaretha and Johanna married on the same day, it is even possible that they were twins. Margaretha of Hainault's eldest child, Margarethe of Bavaria, may have been born as early as April 1325, fourteen months after the wedding to Ludwig von Wittelsbach in Cologne and about two months before Margaretha of Hainault herself turned fifteen. Her second child, Anna of Bavaria, was probably born in 1326, and her third, Ludwig 'the Roman,' in May 1328.

Margaretha and Johanna of Hainault, and their mother Jeanne de Valois, were all remarkably young mothers; Jeanne became a grandmother several times over in 1325/27 when she was only in her early thirties, and several of her grandchildren were older than her own youngest child, who was born in late 1327. Philippa of Hainault herself bore her first child, Edward of Woodstock, in June 1330 when she was most probably sixteen, perhaps only fifteen.

Between 1318 and 1321, Count Willem of Hainault and Holland was involved in negotiations with King Edward II of England regarding a possible future marriage between one of Willem's daughters and Edward's son and heir, Edward of Windsor, the future Edward III. Although Edward III later married Philippa, she was not the Hainault daughter in question at this time, as is sometimes assumed. A marriage between England and Hainault was on the cards sometime before 10 December 1318, when Edward II asked Pope John XXII to issue a dispensation for his son Edward and Willem of Hainault's eldest daughter Margaretha to marry, on the grounds of consanguinity (they were second cousins, both great-grandchildren of Philip III of France and Isabel of Aragon).[12]

To complicate matters, however, there was apparently another Hainault sister, Sibilla, who on 2 November 1319 was named as the potential future bride of Edward of Windsor, not Margaretha, in various letters sent by Edward II. Either Sibilla had been substituted for her sister, or this was an error by Edward II's clerk, who carelessly named the count of Hainault as 'Robert' instead of Willem in the letters. The count of nearby Flanders was called Robert, so probably the clerk mixed up the names, and might have made another error regarding the correct name of Willem's daughter.[13] On 9 November 1320, in a further letter about the potential betrothal of Edward of Windsor, Margaretha was again named as the future bride, though a frustrated Edward II merely referred to 'your daughter,' unnamed, in yet another letter to Count Willem about the matter on 30 March 1321.[14] Edward II was still evidently keen on the alliance well over two years after it was first proposed, but Willem had for some reason grown cold on the idea. The king of England gave up and began negotiating with King Jaime II of Aragon (born 1267, reigned 1291-1327) for a match for his son with one of Jaime's daughters – negotiations which ultimately proved unsuccessful. Margaretha of Hainault lost out on marriage to the future king of England, but ultimately made an even more splendid match by marrying an emperor. Count Willem of Hainault had probably betrothed his second daughter Johanna into Jülich in 1317 rather than her elder sister because he was hoping to make a much grander match for his eldest daughter, and certainly succeeded in this endeavour.

Sybil or Sibilla was often used as a pet name for women and girls named Isabella in the fourteenth century, rather than being an independent name. Philippa of Hainault certainly had a sister named Isabella, but she must have been considerably younger than Philippa, as she married the count of Namur's son Robert, who was born in about 1323 or 1326. Robert is unlikely to have married a girl born before the early 1320s, as the age gap would have been considered too great given that it would have limited the number of the couple's fertile years together (and indeed the couple did not marry until 1354, when they were both about thirty). Isabella is most unlikely to have been the girl mentioned by Edward II's clerk in 1319. This Sibilla may therefore have been yet another Hainault sister, unless she only existed as an English clerk's error, and if she existed, she must have died as a child or adolescent as she does not appear again in any other known source of the period and did not marry. It seems probable therefore that Philippa of Hainault had two or three older sisters, Margaretha, Johanna and perhaps Sibilla, as well as a much younger sister Isabella, born in the 1320s. There was also a sister called Agnes, who died as a child sometime before November 1327 and about whom almost nothing is known. Agnes was probably a few years younger than Philippa, born around the late 1310s or early 1320s.

The first son of Willem of Hainault and Jeanne de Valois was named Jan after Willem's father, and died in infancy in 1316. His date of birth is not known; he may have been older than his sister Philippa and born *c.* 1312/13, or younger, perhaps 1315 or 1316, so died when an infant or newborn. The second brother, called Willem after their father, was born around 1317, and succeeded the elder Willem as count of Hainault and Holland in 1337. He was certainly some years younger than Philippa, and perhaps came after Philippa and Jan and before Agnes in the birth order of the Hainault children. Willem the younger was the only one of the four Hainault sons who lived into adulthood, and married Johanna of Brabant (b. 1322), the eldest child and ultimate heir of Duke Jan III of Brabant, but had no surviving children with her. The third Hainault son, Lodewijk, was born in August 1325 and died shortly before 17 October 1327 when his funeral took place. Jeanne de Valois gave birth to her fourth son and youngest child, another Jan, shortly before Christmas 1327, around the time that her third (or fourth?) daughter Philippa set off for England to marry the king and when Jeanne already had several grandchildren from her eldest two daughters, Margaretha and Johanna, in Germany.

Little Jan the youngest Hainault child lived only for a few days, and his elder brother Lodewijk seems to have been ill for all his sadly short life: his mother Jeanne bought numerous medicines for him and went on pilgrimages to pray for a cure.[15] The Dutch or Flemish name Lodewijk is Louis in French and Ludwig in German, so Jeanne de Valois presumably named her third son either after her great-grandfather King Louis IX of France (d. 1270), or after her German son-in-law Ludwig of Bavaria, who had married Jeanne's daughter Margaretha eighteen months before little Lodewijk of Hainault was born. In total there were nine or possibly ten Hainault siblings, of whom Jan, a second Jan, Agnes, Lodewijk and, if she existed, Sibilla, died young. Willem the younger and Isabella both lived into adulthood and married, but Queen Philippa and her older sisters Margaretha, Holy Roman Empress, and Johanna, countess and later duchess of Jülich, were the only three of the Hainault siblings who had surviving children (or rather, surviving legitimate children; their brother Willem left at least two illegitimate sons when he died, and also had a legitimate son with Johanna of Brabant who died in infancy).

As well as Philippa's eight or nine full siblings, she had at least eight half-siblings, her father's illegitimate children born to a succession of mistresses. The names of three of his mistresses are known: Trude, Alida and Doedijn. Count Willem had six acknowledged illegitimate sons, four of whom he named Jan after his father, one who was called Willem after himself, and the sixth was named Claas. The count also had at least two and perhaps three acknowledged illegitimate daughters, all of whom entered the religious life. One was Aleide, and she was named as a nun of Leeuwenhorst in 1332.[16] A Matilde de Luwembergh, who was elected abbess of Nivelles (a town which now lies in the modern Belgian province of Walloon Brabant) in 1351, was also said to have been Count Willem's daughter, though other sources indicate that she may have been one of his sisters or half-sisters.[17]

Finally, an Elisabeth of Holland, 'bastard sister' of Queen Philippa, is mentioned in the English chancery rolls in August 1367 when Edward III granted her twenty pounds a year from the English exchequer at Philippa's request. The king bought 'Lady Elizabeth de Holand, sister of our said consort' twelve ells of black cloth when she attended the queen's funeral in early 1370.[18] Elisabeth of Holland wrote her will in England in September 1375, and was a nun of Stratford-le-Bow. She called herself 'sister of the lady Queen Philippa', and left a gold ring to Philippa's youngest child, Thomas of Woodstock, and a silver ring to Edward III's first cousin Margaret Marshal, countess of Norfolk. It seems that Philippa's second son Lionel of Antwerp and his wife Elizabeth de Burgh, countess of Ulster, visited Elisabeth at her convent in September 1356.[19] Elisabeth of Holland must have followed her half-sister to England and decided to settle there, and evidently was well-known to several of Philippa's relatives and her husband the king. At least one of Philippa's illegitimate half-brothers was known to her eldest son Edward of Woodstock: in 1349 when he was nineteen, Edward gave a horse to 'Sir John, bastard brother of the lady queen'.[20] It is not clear which of Philippa's four half-brothers named Jan this refers to – Jan van de Poel, Jan Aelman, Jan Dolre or Jan Zuurmond, or perhaps yet another illegitimate son of Count Willem called Jan who does not otherwise appear on record – but evidently one of them had travelled to England and was known there to Philippa's family.

It is unclear what kind of relationship, if any, Philippa had with her many illegitimate siblings, but as her father openly acknowledged them as his children, she must at least have been aware of them as she grew up, and perhaps all Willem's children, legitimate and illegitimate, were raised and educated together. Count Willem himself had at least five half-siblings, his father Count Jan's illegitimate children, as well as his eight legitimate full siblings.[21] Willem's older full sister Alix, or Alicia of Hainault, married into England; she wed the widowed and decades-older

Roger Bigod, earl of Norfolk and earl marshal of England (*c.* 1245-1306), in June 1290, but they had no children, and Countess Alix died in 1317, more than ten years before her niece Philippa of Hainault herself moved to England.

In 1319, King Edward II sent Walter Stapeldon, bishop of Exeter, to the county of Hainault to continue the ongoing negotiations for the future marriage of his son and heir Edward of Windsor (born in November 1312 and then not quite seven years old) to one of Count Willem's daughters. In his register which still exists today, Stapeldon wrote an extremely detailed and now famous description of the girl being proposed as the future Edward III's bride, which has often been assumed to have been a description of Philippa. As she was not the girl under discussion in 1319, however, the text is far more likely to have been a description of Margaretha, or even of the shadowy Sibilla.

To complicate matters still further, however, a later fourteenth-century hand wrote in the margin next to Stapeldon's description in his register that the girl in question was indeed Philippa. As the negotiations of 1318 to 1321 mentioned Margaretha and Sibilla but never Philippa, this seems most unlikely; yet as the marginal comment was written in the fourteenth century probably by Stapeldon's successor as bishop of Exeter, John Grandisson (d. 1369), who knew Queen Philippa personally, it cannot be discounted entirely. Then again, one might argue that Bishop Grandisson many years later was unaware or had forgotten that any of Philippa's sisters had ever been considered as his king's bride, and therefore automatically but wrongly assumed that the description of a girl of Hainault being proposed as Edward of Windsor's future wife must have been referring to Philippa.

The girl was well-loved (*bien ame*) by both her parents and by their household, Walter Stapeldon wrote, as far as he had been able to determine. The bishop added that her mother had informed him the girl would turn nine on the next feast of the Nativity of St John the Baptist, which is 24 June. It is unclear when exactly in 1319 he wrote this description – though almost certainly earlier in the year rather than later – so that the next 24 June might fall either in 1319 or in 1320, and therefore the girl was born either on or around either 24 June 1310 or 24 June 1311. This is nowadays usually assumed to be Margaretha's date of birth, and 1310 seems the more probable year, as she seems to have given birth to her eldest child in April 1325, more likely when fourteen going on fifteen, not thirteen going on fourteen. The 24th of June 1310 or 1311 is incredibly unlikely to be Queen Philippa's date of birth. As she was at least the third and perhaps fourth or fifth child of her parents and as Jeanne de Valois's own probable date of birth in about 1294 or 1295 makes it improbable that she had children earlier than 1309/10 when she was about fifteen; it would be impossible to fit Philippa's older siblings (certainly Margaretha and Johanna, perhaps also Sibilla and Jan) into the timeframe. The 24th of June is now often given as Philippa's date of birth in 1314, but it would be quite a coincidence if she had exactly the same birthday as her eldest sister Margaretha, and there is no reason to think that she did. This date, 24 June 1314, was also the day on which her future husband's father King Edward II famously lost the battle of Bannockburn to King Robert Bruce of Scotland, and it would also seem rather a large coincidence if Philippa of Hainault was born on that particular date. Perhaps the chronicler Jean Froissart was correct in stating that Philippa was 'almost fourteen' when she married on or around 25 January 1328, and was therefore born in late January, February or March 1314.

The poor girl whom Walter Stapleton saw in 1319, whoever she was, was examined and described minutely, as one might look over a horse one wished to purchase. Even the girl's nostrils, ears and chin did not escape attention: the first were 'a little large' and the latter two 'quite beautiful'. Her lower lip was fuller than her upper one, and some of her teeth were not too white. She was generally 'well-formed', was 'neither too big nor too small for her age', had a 'clean head' and 'quite beautiful' hair, *entre bloy et brun*. The word *brun* means brown, and *bloy* in the fourteenth-century dialect of French used by the English elite sometimes meant 'blue' but also meant blonde or tawny or golden.[22] Blonde or tawny or golden seems by far the likeliest interpretation of *bloy*. If Stapeldon had meant that the girl he saw had dark brown, almost black hair, or 'between blue-black and brown' as his statement has often been translated, he had several perfectly good Anglo-Norman words at his disposal to express the concept of very dark brown or almost black, and it seems most unlikely that he would have described the girl's hair as 'blue'. Hence the phrase *entre bloy et brun* means 'between blonde and brown'.

By far the most famous parts of Bishop Stapeldon's description are the following: the girl's eyes were deep and brown and a little black, she was 'brown of skin all over' (*brune de qui reyn par tut*), and her nose was smooth and even, but broad at the tip and somewhat flattened. This description is the main basis for a bizarre modern belief that Philippa of Hainault may have been of partly African ancestry. A few years ago, she appeared on a website titled '100 Great Black Britons' and was featured in an article about George III's queen, Charlotte of Mecklenburg-Strelitz (1744-1818) in *The Guardian* in 2009 titled 'Was this Britain's first black queen?' The article stated that Philippa 'may have had African ancestry'.[23] A book self-published in 2007 claims that Philippa's six greats grandmother, the mother of her five greats grandmother the Byzantine empress Euphrosyne Doukaina Kamatera, was Ethiopian. Euphrosyne's father was the Byzantine aristocrat Andronikos Doukas Kamateros, and although the identity of his wife is unknown it is virtually certain that she was also a Byzantine aristocrat, not Qirwerne, princess of Ethiopia, as claimed. No real evidence is cited.[24]

In the same sentence as his description of her skin, Bishop Walter Stapeldon said that the girl he met 'much resembles her father' (*molt resemble au pere*). As Count Willem was of entirely Northern European ancestry going back many generations, we can be sure that he was not black and cannot have had African facial features. And hair 'between blonde and brown' sounds typically European. Philippa's dozen children were not physically described in their lifetimes, so it is difficult to evaluate Philippa's appearance based on her children's, but her grandson Richard II, king of England (b. 1367) had fair hair and pale skin. Philippa's nephew Wilhelm of Bavaria (1330-89), second son of her eldest sister Margaretha who is extremely likely to have been the young girl described by Walter Stapeldon in 1319, was said by chronicler Jean le Bel (who probably saw him in person) to be tall and 'swarthy', but le Bel did not claim that Wilhelm looked anything but European.[25] None of Philippa's numerous relatives who came from the same bloodlines – and they were indeed numerous, as her grandmother Marguerite of Anjou-Naples was the second of fourteen children and her siblings married and had children all over Europe – were ever said to have black skin or African facial features.

Philippa and her siblings did have ancestors from the south of Europe but some generations back on their mother's side, which might have made their skin look comparatively 'brown' to an Englishman like Bishop Walter Stapeldon. It might also simply mean that the little girl was tanned. The Hainault sisters carried the blood of their great-great-grandmother Queen Erzsébet of Hungary and Croatia, whose shamanistic Cuman ancestors inhabited a vast territory in modern-day Kazakhstan, Russia and Ukraine. The Cumans fled into Hungary from the advancing Mongolians in and after the 1230s but were not themselves Mongolian, and came from nowhere near Africa. Erzsébet's father Seyhan or Köten, Philippa of Hainault's great-great-great-grandfather, was the Cumans' chieftain, but although the identities of Erzsébet's mother and other ancestors are not known, the Cuman people are believed to have been predominantly fair-haired, fair-skinned and blue-eyed. They cannot possibly have passed on African ancestry or African facial features to their descendants.[26] It is, however, interesting to note that Queen Philippa was descended from Erzsébet the Cuman in the direct female line (Erzsébet – Marie of Hungary – Marguerite of Anjou-Naples – Jeanne de Valois – Philippa of Hainault), so she carried Erzsébet's mitochondrial DNA. Philippa's English children, therefore, including the great warrior Edward of Woodstock and the famous military leader, statesman and lover John of Gaunt, also carried the mtDNA of a nomadic tribe of the Eurasian steppes who practised shamanism. So did Philippa's uncle and her husband's adversary, Philip VI of France, the son of Marguerite of Anjou-Naples and therefore also a descendant of Erzsébet the Cuman in the female line.

The part of Europe where Philippa of Hainault grew up was not, as sometimes claimed in support of her alleged African ancestry, ever ruled by 'Moors', as the Muslim rulers of part of the Iberian Peninsula from the 700s to the 1400s are sometimes called. Besides, the Moors (i.e. the Umayyad and Almohad caliphates and the Nasrid dynasty, rulers of much of the Iberian Peninsula for hundreds of years) came from Arabia and North Africa, not sub-Saharan

Africa. The word 'Saracen' was often used in fourteenth-century England to describe people from Arabia or North Africa, or simply for Muslims more generally, and had anyone noted that Queen Philippa or members of her immediate family looked as though they had non-European ancestry, this word was available for chroniclers to use. They did not. It seems vanishingly unlikely that in all the forty years Philippa lived in England, when she was seen by countless thousands of her husband's subjects and by the monks and royal clerks who wrote chronicles, that someone would not have remarked on her looks and pointed out if she had been in any way not of conventionally European appearance. They did not.

Philippa's eldest child, Edward of Woodstock, prince of Wales, is known to posterity as the 'Black Prince', a fact which has also been used in support of the notion that Philippa had African ancestry. This nickname, however, first appeared in print in a book published in 1568, Richard Grafton's *Grafton's Chronicle, or the History of England*, and was picked up and used by Shakespeare in his play about Henry V (reigned 1413 to 1422) some decades later.[27] Edward of Woodstock was born in 1330 and died in 1376, and the nickname is certainly not contemporary and cannot be used as evidence that anyone who saw him thought he was black-skinned or of African origin. The nickname does not appear in any fourteenth-century chronicle or other source, though by the sixteenth century it appears that several writers wrongly believed it to be a traditional appellation for Philippa's eldest son. In his own lifetime the prince of Wales was known as 'Edward of Woodstock', as it was the custom for fourteenth-century English royalty to be called by their places of birth; Edward's four younger brothers also were Lionel of Antwerp, John of Gaunt, i.e. Ghent, Edmund of Langley, and Thomas of Woodstock. The '100 Great Black Britons' website which claims that Philippa of Hainault was a black queen of England in the Middle Ages also states Edward of Woodstock was 'called black when he was very small' and that the French called him *le Noir*, 'the Black,' in his own lifetime. Although no source is cited for the statement, the quotations come from a 1688 biography of Edward III and Edward of Woodstock by Joshua Barnes, but no evidence is cited in support of these claims either by Barnes himself or by the website.

Philippa of Hainault was a European woman and emphatically not of African ancestry, and absolutely no-one in her own lifetime or long afterwards claimed otherwise, either about her or about any of her relatives and descendants. The effigy on her tomb in Westminster Abbey shows that she had become plump at the end of her life in 1369, but given how many children she bore, and that she spent the last few years of her life in physical pain and almost immobile, that is not surprising. Otherwise it is difficult to say much about her physical appearance except that she may have resembled her sister described in 1319 and had dark blonde or light brown hair, dark brown eyes and skin which tanned easily.

For his part, her husband Edward III stood five feet ten and a half inches, according to the life-size effigy of him made after his death in 1377.[28] He was several inches shorter than his grandfather Edward I (1239-1307): an examination of the king's remains in the late eighteenth century revealed that Edward I stood six feet two inches. Edward III and Philippa of Hainault's grandson Richard II (1367-1400) was six feet. The English royal family was certainly above average height for the era. The idea that Philippa's third (but second surviving) son Lionel of Antwerp, who was born in 1338 and died in 1368, was extremely tall – close to seven feet – is often repeated, and comes from the fifteenth-century chronicle of John Hardying. Hardyng was born *c.* 1378, about ten years after Lionel's death, and his claim is not supported by other evidence.

Meeting Edward

Little is known of Philippa of Hainault's childhood. She was probably old enough to be aware of her father Willem's ongoing conflicts with his neighbour Robert, count of Flanders, which persisted for much of the 1310s. Edward II of England tried to mediate between the two counts, though himself came into conflict with Willem over his failure to deal justly with some of his own subjects who robbed men from Hainault in England.[1] The reign of the English king lurched from disaster to disaster, most of his own making. He married Jeanne de Valois's first cousin Isabella of France, daughter of Philip IV of France and Queen Jeanne I of Navarre (d. 1305), and the sister of Louis X, Philip V and Charles IV, on 25 January 1308, and their eldest child the future Edward III was born at Windsor Castle in November 1312. Three more children, John of Eltham, Eleanor of Woodstock and Joan of the Tower, followed. Philippa was surely also aware of the negotiations with England for the marriage of one of her sisters to Edward of Windsor in the late 1310s and early 1320s, and of the visit of Bishop Walter Stapeldon to her home and his scrutiny of her sister.

Philippa's paternal grandparents Jan I and Philippa of Luxembourg, count and countess of Hainault, died in 1304 and 1311 before she was born, and her maternal grandmother Marguerite of Anjou-Naples died in 1299; Charles de Valois was the only one of her grandparents still alive at the time of her birth. Valois's elder brother King Philip IV of France died on 29 November 1314 after a hunting accident, aged forty-six, probably a few months after Philippa of Hainault was born. Philippa's mother Jeanne's first cousin Louis, already king of Navarre in northern Spain as his inheritance from his mother, succeeded his father as Louis X of France. Louis died in June 1316 and his brother and successor Philip V died five and a half years later, both of them leaving only daughters, and Philip IV's youngest son Charles IV thus succeeded his brothers as king of France and Navarre in January 1322.

Philippa of Hainault's great-grandmother Marie of Hungary, dowager queen of Naples and Albania, the last surviving child of Erzsébet the Cuman (d. 1290) and the mother of Marguerite of Anjou-Naples, died on 25 March 1323 when Philippa was probably nine years old, having outlived nine of her fourteen children. (Marie's brother-in-law the Byzantine emperor Andronikos Palaiologos, widower of her sister Anna, lived even longer, and died in 1332 in his early seventies.) It is doubtful whether Philippa of Hainault ever met Queen Marie, but she must have been aware of the redoubtable old lady, and of the extensive family network she had been born into. In the same year as Marie's death Philippa's father Willem finally reached a settlement with his neighbour Robert, count of Flanders.

Philippa spent an itinerant childhood and adolescence, as was always the case for royal and noble households of the fourteenth century. She and her family travelled frequently between their territories of Hainault and Holland and spent much time at Valenciennes in Hainault and at The Hague and Dordrecht in Holland. Her family also regularly spent time at the French court in and around Paris 125 miles from Valenciennes, and were often visited by the royalty and nobility of France and the Low Countries. In 1319 when Philippa was about five, for example, Jeanne de Valois's uncle Louis, count of Evreux, the younger half-brother of the late Philip IV of France and Charles de Valois, visited them at The Hague (Louis of Evreux died later that year). The same year, the Hainault family also received Mahaut, countess of Artois in her own right and countess of Burgundy by marriage, and mother-in-law of the then king of France, Philip V.

In 1320 the young king of Bohemia, John or Johann of Luxembourg (born in 1296 and known to history as Johann 'the Blind'), came to stay with them.[2] Johann was Philippa's second cousin, and would die at the battle of Crécy in 1346, the great victory of Philippa's husband Edward III and her eldest son over the king of France and his allies. Johann's sister Marie of Luxembourg married King Charles IV of France in September 1322, and was crowned queen of France in Paris on 15 May 1323. Also in May 1323, Johann of Luxembourg's little son Charles or Karl – the boy's name was originally Wenzel, but he changed it in honour of his godfather and uncle Charles IV of France – married in Paris. Born in May 1316, Karl had just turned seven at the time of his wedding, and his bride was Blanche de Valois, who was a half-sister of Philippa of Hainault's mother Jeanne de Valois but was born in *c.* 1317 and was thus about three years younger than Philippa herself. The Hainault family probably travelled to Paris to attend the coronation of Queen Marie and the wedding of Marie's nephew Karl to Countess Jeanne's little half-sister. As of 1315, Count Willem and Countess Jeanne owned their own house in Paris, the Hotel *Ostriche* (which means 'Austria', not 'ostrich'; *Autriche* in modern French), and Jeanne's accounts reveal that she sometimes stayed there.[3]

When they were not receiving guests, the Hainault court entertained themselves with various forms of gaming, for example playing at dice and at tables, and Philippa and her siblings were encouraged to participate. Her brother Willem (born *c.* 1317) was often given small change for gambling, and doubtless she was too.[4] Nothing is known of Philippa's education, but there is much evidence that books were prized at her parents' court, and Willem and Jeanne sometimes sent men to Paris to purchase books for them. In 1311 some years before Philippa was born, Willem owned nineteen books including two Arthurian tales, one about Merlin and the other about Lancelot, and plenty of religious tomes. Some of Count Willem's books cost a great deal of money, and the three most valuable were the book about Lancelot and two parts of a Bible in French. In March 1328, Willem and Jeanne purchased a manuscript of an untitled romance in Paris.[5] Religious instruction would have formed a large part of Philippa of Hainault's upbringing, and as she founded a college at the University of Oxford via one of her clerks in 1341, she clearly placed a high value on education.

Philippa almost certainly travelled to the German city of Cologne in February 1324 to attend the double wedding of her older sisters

Margaretha and Johanna, when she was nine or ten, Margaretha thirteen and Johanna probably twelve (unless she was Margaretha's twin). Margaretha's new husband Ludwig von Wittelsbach of Bavaria was almost forty-two at the time of the wedding, born on 1 April 1282, and had children from his first marriage to the Polish-German noblewoman Beatrix of Świdnica or Schweidnitz (d. 1320), who were close in age to his second wife Margaretha of Hainault. Ludwig von Wittelsbach is often called Louis or Lewis in English, and *Ludwig der Bayer* or 'Ludwig the Bavarian' in German. He had been engaged for some years in a long and bloody struggle for control of Germany and the rest of the Holy Roman Empire with his cousin Friedrich *der Schöne*, Frederick 'the Handsome', duke of Austria and Styria, and Ludwig was to emerge victorious. At the time of his wedding to Margaretha, Ludwig had been 'King of the Romans', i.e. king of Germany, for ten years jointly with his cousin and rival Friedrich, and alone since defeating Friedrich at the battle of Mühldorf am Inn in September 1322. At the time of his wedding to Margaretha of Hainault, Ludwig was still keeping his cousin captive in Trausnitz Castle, one of the great strongholds of his family the Wittelsbachs in Bavaria. Margaretha's mother Jeanne de Valois was opposed to the marriage of her barely pubescent daughter to a man almost three decades her senior who already had half a dozen children, and was worried about the potential conflicts of interest between her future son-in-law Ludwig and her uncle Robert 'the Wise', king of Naples – Marie of Hungary's third son and one of the many siblings of Jeanne's late mother Marguerite of Anjou-Naples – in Italy. Margaretha's father Count Willem pushed ahead with the match anyway.[6] Jeanne's misgivings can only have been compounded later in 1324 when Pope John XXII excommunicated her new son-in-law, and over the next few years attempted to belittle him by referring to him simply as 'the Bavarian'.[7] John XXII and Ludwig would remain at loggerheads for most of the remaining ten years of the pope's life.

Two months after the wedding of Philippa of Hainault's sister to Ludwig of Bavaria, Pope John sent letters to Edward II of England – whatever his many other faults, Edward was known to be a loyal son of the Roman Church – fuming that Ludwig was a 'heretic and idolater' who had done him 'injuries'.[8] One of Ludwig's allies against the pope was the English Franciscan friar William Ockham (born *c.* 1287) from Surrey, after whom Ockham's or Occam's Razor is named. In 1326, Ockham declared one of John XXII's teachings to be heretical, and fled from the papal court in Avignon to join Ludwig. John ordered his arrest.[9] In 1328 and recently crowned as emperor, Ludwig issued a decree declaring the pope deposed on the grounds of heresy.

Johanna of Hainault's new husband Wilhelm was heir to his father Gerhard's county of Jülich, which was later raised to a duchy by the emperor Ludwig of Bavaria and nowadays lies partly in the German state of North Rhine Westphalia and partly in the Limburg province of the Netherlands. Jülich is called Gulik in Dutch, Juliers in French and sometimes in English, and in Wilhelm and his father's letters of the 1320s and 1330s was spelt *Guylghe* or *Guleche*. In the fourteenth century the duchy of Jülich was, like the counties of Hainault and Holland, part of the Holy Roman Empire.[10] One of Wilhelm's younger brothers, Walram von Jülich, whom Queen Philippa must have met on occasion, was elected archbishop of Cologne in early 1332. As one of the seven powerful Electors who dominated German politics, Archbishop Walram spent time with Philippa's husband Edward III in the town of Koblenz in 1338 when the English king met the emperor and the Electors.

Wilhelm of Jülich himself, born around 1299/1300, was a few years older than his new wife Johanna of Hainault and in his mid-twenties when he married, so the age difference between them was not nearly as great as between Ludwig von Wittelsbach and Johanna's sister Margaretha. Johanna, however, seems to have found married life and moving away from her parents and her home painful and difficult, and she was, after all, probably barely even pubescent at the time of her wedding. In February 1326 two years after she married Wilhelm of Jülich, she returned to Hainault on a visit and stayed with her mother Jeanne until at least the end of May 1326. In 1329, five years after her wedding and when she already had several children, Johanna was still very dejected, homesick and missing her parents, and her mother hastened to visit her, taking many presents. Johanna was ill again in June 1331, possibly from the stress of living away from home and her family, and her mother demonstrated her anxiety over her daughter's condition.[11] Jeanne de Valois and

Johanna of Hainault visited England soon afterwards and spent time with Queen Philippa and Edward III, a visit perhaps intended to help Johanna recuperate from her recent illness. Jeanne also kept in touch with her eldest daughter Margaretha, and in November 1325 paid a messenger called Andries van Leids for taking her messages and presents to Margaretha. Andries was present with Margaretha and Ludwig of Bavaria in Rome in 1328 when they were crowned emperor and empress, and presumably sent reports back to Jeanne of her daughter's welfare.[12]

This all surely reveals that, despite the loss of at least four of their siblings in childhood and their father's mistresses and eight or more illegitimate offspring, the Hainault children had grown up in a happy and affectionate family environment. Jeanne de Valois has been described as 'a woman of strong maternal feeling [who] never lost interest in the welfare of her children and near relatives.'[13] The experiences of the Hainault sisters and their mother also demonstrate, however, how women born into royal and noble families in the late thirteenth and early fourteenth centuries were thrust into the roles and responsibilities of adulthood at a very young age. Jeanne de Valois had lost her mother when she was no more than five years old, married when she was probably little more than ten, and gave birth for the first time at about fifteen or sixteen. Both Jeanne's eldest daughter Margaretha of Hainault, and her third daughter Philippa's sister-in-law Eleanor of Woodstock, duchess of Guelders, became pregnant by their decades-older husbands and gave birth when they were still only fourteen.

Philippa's father Count Willem was still in Cologne on 1 March 1324, a few days after the double wedding of his two eldest daughters, when he sent a letter, in French, to Edward II of England. Willem, perhaps rather unnecessarily and boastfully, pointed out to Edward that he was 'with the king of the Romans' (the king of Germany, i.e. Ludwig of Bavaria) when he dictated the letter. Relations between Willem and Edward II had cooled considerably since they discussed a possible marriage between their children in the late 1310s and beginning of the 1320s. Edward complained that some of Willem's men had robbed ships belonging to merchants of Great Yarmouth, and that the indignant English merchants called the Hainault men 'evil-doers'. Willem countered that 'many of his people of Holland and Zealand have been robbed in the king's country, and he has often written to the king for restitution, but the king has done nothing. If the king will act, he will act.'[14]

Willem did tell Edward that he would deal with the matter when he returned home, and duly wrote again to the king on 17 April 1324 ('the Tuesday after Easter') and again on 3 June, the feast of Pentecost, regarding the matter, but the damage had already been done. Willem's displeasure with Edward II would lead to him forming an alliance with Edward's queen Isabella, his wife's first cousin, in 1326, and would lead to Edward's downfall and to the marriage of Willem's daughter Philippa to Edward of Windsor against Edward II's wishes. Edward II arranged a meeting in London between Willem's representatives and his own on 14 January 1326, but nobody from Hainault turned up. Edward wrote to Willem again in May that year informing him that a group of pirates from Hainault had attacked an English ship off the coast of Zeeland, stolen its cargo and killed its sailors. He had heard, he said, that the attack took place on Willem's order but that he found this hard to believe, 'since he cannot recollect that he has offended the count or his men contrary to justice in any way.' Although Edward professed that he would be displeased at the breaking of the peace between England and Hainault, Willem was not interested in reconciliation, and later in 1326 openly demonstrated his hostility towards the English king.[15]

Another important wedding took place at the French court five months after the double wedding of the Hainault sisters and their German husbands. Philippa of Hainault almost certainly attended the nuptials of her mother's cousin King Charles IV of France and his third wife, fourteen-year-old Jeanne of Evreux, at Annet-sur-Marne twenty miles east of Paris on 5 July 1324. Jeanne of Evreux was one of the daughters of Louis, count of Evreux (1276-1319), younger half-brother of Charles IV's father Philip IV, and she was thus the first cousin both of her husband and of Jeanne de Valois, countess of Hainault. Count Willem of Hainault purchased large quantities of velvet from Italian merchants in Paris for himself, his wife and their children, surely including Philippa, when they attended Charles and Jeanne's wedding.[16]

Charles IV's second wife, Marie of Luxembourg, sister of Johann 'the Blind', king of Bohemia, had died in March 1324 only ten months after her coronation as queen of France when she gave birth to a premature son who also died. His first wife Blanche of Burgundy had been imprisoned for adultery in 1314 and their two children died young. (Blanche was still alive in 1324, but had been in prison for ten years and would die there in 1326.) Charles IV turned thirty in June 1324 and was desperate for a son to succeed him, probably the reason he married one of his first cousins, which was not nearly as common among northern European royal families of the early fourteenth century as it became in later centuries, within months of his second wife's death. Jeanne of Evreux was not crowned as queen of France until almost two years after her wedding, on 11 May 1326.

It is possible that the Hainault family including Philippa travelled to Paris again on this occasion to attend the coronation, though there is no record of it. Then again, Philippa's soon-to-be fiancé Edward of Windsor certainly attended Queen Jeanne's coronation with his mother the queen-consort of England, and there is no record of him on the official livery list (the attendees for whom cloth was purchased) either. Probably the Hainault family were deemed wealthy enough to purchase their own cloth.[17]

In late 1325 came another visit to the French court for Philippa, then probably aged eleven. Her grandfather Charles, count of Valois, was now fifty-five and was dying, and his eldest surviving daughter Jeanne de Valois wished to spend time with him before he passed away. The reigning king of France, Charles IV, had succeeded his brother Philip V in early 1322 when Philip died at the age of thirty, leaving four daughters but no sons. Their eldest brother Louis X died in 1316 leaving only one surviving daughter, Jeanne II of Navarre, who became queen-regnant of Navarre in 1328 when she was sixteen but who, as a female, had no claim to the French throne. Until Charles IV and his third wife Jeanne of Evreux had a son, the heir to the throne of France was his uncle Charles de Valois, and after him, Valois's eldest son Philip (b. 1293), Philippa of Hainault's maternal grandfather and uncle.

Jeanne de Valois took her eldest unmarried daughter Philippa with her on the visit to France. To console her son Willem, who was about eight years old and was left behind in Hainault, the countess bought him some toys: bows and arrows, hobby-horses and wooden swords. In November 1325, young Willem had also been provided with a *layette* in which to keep his books, further evidence of how the Hainault court placed a high value on education and reading.[18] Also left behind in Hainault were Philippa's little brother Lodewijk, who had been born four months before, and her younger sisters Isabella and Agnes, if Agnes was still alive. Jeanne and Philippa left Valenciennes on Sunday, 1 December 1325 and travelled the 125 miles to Paris, where they arrived on the 6th; they stayed with the bishop of Cambrai on the first night of their journey, and he bore the costs. During the visit, Philippa must have met some of her numerous French relatives, perhaps including her mother's half-sister Catherine de Valois, titular empress of Constantinople in her own right as her inheritance from her mother, Charles de Valois's late second wife Catherine de Courtenay, and also princess of Achaea (in Greece).[19]

On Monday 9 December at Le Perray-en-Yvelines near Rambouillet, about thirty miles from Paris, Philippa and Jeanne visited Charles de Valois, the only one of her grandparents Philippa ever met. He died a week later. Valois was survived by his third and much younger wife Mahaut de Châtillon, eleven living children – eight of them daughters – and numerous grandchildren. (Two of his eight daughters were named Jeanne, Philippa's mother the countess of Hainault and the wife of Robert of Artois, and three were named Isabelle after the mother who died when Valois was a few months old, Isabel of Aragon.) His body was taken from Le Perray for burial in Paris, and Jeanne and Philippa went to Bourg-la-Reine, now a suburb of southern Paris, to watch the funeral cortège pass on 20 December. Valois was buried at the convent of the Jacobins, which was suppressed in 1790 at the time of the French Revolution, and his tomb and effigy are now in the basilica of Saint-Denis with his father Philip III, his mother Queen Isabel, his brother Philip IV, his nephews Louis X and Philip V, and countless other French royals.

Jeanne and Philippa spent Christmas 1325 in Paris, and probably stayed at the Hotel *Ostriche*, which Jeanne and her husband owned. By early January 1326 they were back in Hainault, staying again with the bishop of Cambrai for one night during the journey home. Philippa was reunited with her father Count Willem at Valenciennes on Saturday, 4 January 1326, and her mother's account refers to the presence in the town of 'my lord, my lady and their child' (*mesires, medame et leur enfant*). On 11 and 12 January 1326, Willem, Jeanne and their family were visited in their Hainault town of Mons by the duchess of neighbouring Brabant, Marie of Evreux, elder sister of the teenaged queen-consort of France, Jeanne of Evreux.[20] King Edward II of England, meanwhile, had given a generous gift of four pounds to the messenger who brought him news on 28 December of Charles de Valois's death.[21] Edward II was no friend of Valois, who was said by one chronicler to have 'pursued the English with an inveterate hatred' when his brother Philip IV went to war against Edward's father Edward I in 1294, and who had invaded Edward II's land of Gascony during the War of Saint-Sardos between England and France in the summer of 1324.[22]

Then again, Charles de Valois had tried to bury the hatchet with England and with Edward II specifically at the beginning of 1324, when he proposed two marriages for Edward's daughters, Eleanor of Woodstock (b. June 1318) and Joan of the Tower (b. July 1321). For one of the girls, he suggested his grandson John (b. 1319, later duke of Normandy and King John II of France), son of his eldest son Philip de Valois, and for the other he suggested his own youngest child Louis, count of Chartres (b. *c.* 1318), fourth child and only son of his third wife Mahaut de Châtillon.[23] In the end, nothing came of these proposed marriages, and Louis of Chartres was to die in childhood in 1328.

These weeks in Paris at the end of 1325 were almost certainly the first occasion when Philippa met her future husband Edward of Windsor, duke of Aquitaine, count of Ponthieu and earl of Chester, and his French mother Isabella, sister of Charles IV, first cousin of Jeanne de Valois and queen of Edward II. Isabella had arrived in her homeland in March 1325, sent by her husband and Pope John XXII to negotiate a peace settlement between Edward II and Charles IV, who had gone to war in the summer of 1324. Isabella did so successfully, but subsequently showed no signs of wishing to return to England and to Edward, who was infatuated with his powerful chamberlain Hugh Despenser the Younger, a man Isabella loathed.

Edward II sent his son Edward of Windsor (who turned thirteen on 13 November 1325) to France on 12 September 1325 to pay homage to his uncle Charles IV for the lands which the English Crown ruled in France. These were the small county of Ponthieu in northern France that Edward II had inherited from his mother, and more importantly, the territory of Gascony in the south-west, which was all that remained of the great duchy of Aquitaine that Edward II inherited from his father Edward I and ultimately from his great-great-grandmother Eleanor of Aquitaine (d. 1204). By early December 1325, when Philippa and her mother arrived in Paris, Isabella had publicly stated that she would not return to her husband unless he expelled his beloved Hugh Despenser from his court. She declared that she felt herself in physical danger from her husband's powerful friend (who may have been his lover) and that she felt like a widow mourning for the end of her marriage because an intruder had come between herself and her husband and had broken their marriage bond. The queen was also furious that her husband had seen fit to treat her as an enemy alien when he went to war against her brother and had confiscated all her lands in England in September 1324, an act for which the queen blamed Hugh Despenser the Younger. To prove the truth of her statement that she grieved for the death of her marriage, the queen of England took to wearing widow's clothes.

This was how Philippa saw her future mother-in-law for the first time. A woman and a queen refusing to return to her husband was scandalous, and in early 1326 Isabella made matters far worse by beginning an alliance with Edward II's enemies, the men he called the 'Contrariants', English baronial rebels who had fled from their homeland in and after 1322. Chief among them was the baron Roger Mortimer of Wigmore in Herefordshire (born around 1286 or 1288), who had been imprisoned in the Tower of London in February 1322 after he and his uncle Roger Mortimer, lord of Chirk, took part in a baronial uprising against Edward II and Hugh Despenser. Mortimer of Wigmore escaped from the Tower on 1

August 1323 and made his way to the continent to join his allies, other Contrariants who had evaded execution or imprisonment and had fled abroad. (His uncle Mortimer of Chirk was to die in prison in the Tower of London in August 1326.) At some point in late 1325 or early 1326, Roger Mortimer of Wigmore and the other English exiles, who considered him their leader, appeared at the French court. Queen Isabella, recognising that Mortimer alone had the ability, ruthlessness and will to help her rid herself of the hated Hugh Despenser and his father the earl of Winchester, and having sworn to bring Despenser down, took him and the other Contrariants as her allies.

Isabella dined with her uncle Charles de Valois on 16 October 1325 two months before his death, and probably on other occasions afterwards as well, though her itinerary no longer survives after mid-November when her furious husband Edward II cut off her funding on learning that she had issued an ultimatum and would not return to him unless he sent his beloved Despenser away.[24] At some point in December 1325, Queen Isabella must also have met her cousin Jeanne de Valois and Philippa of Hainault. Isabella had a powerful weapon in her hands, which she intended to use to her own advantage to force her husband to expel Hugh Despenser from his side and to restore the lands he had confiscated from her in September 1324: custody of her adolescent son, heir to the English throne. Edward II had recognised the dangers of sending his son and heir to France in the autumn of 1325, and before Edward of Windsor's departure from Dover ordered the boy not to marry without his 'assent and command' and until he had returned to his father.[25]

With hindsight, his decision to send his heir to France, given that it was soon to result in his forced abdication, seems incredibly foolish; but in 1325 Edward II had backed himself into a corner where every option available to him was fraught with danger. Someone, either he or his son, simply had to travel to France and pay homage to Charles IV as their overlord for the lands they held in France, or a large part of their inheritance would be lost to Charles and his descendants forever. After many weeks of agonising, reminded by Hugh Despenser that he, the widely detested royal favourite, would probably be killed in the king's absence if he left for France, Edward II decided that sending his son in his place was the best option.

Queen Isabella was well aware how she could use her son and his future marriage to force her husband to do what she wanted. Edward ignored her ultimatum and refused to send Hugh Despenser away from him as she had requested, and left her with no choice but to stay on the continent and seek allies to help her bring down the loathed Despenser. In an undated letter or proclamation sometime in or before December 1325, she swore to destroy him.[26] Precisely when she had first decided to act against the powerful favourite and by extension her husband, by using his son and heir, is a matter for speculation, but as Jeanne de Valois travelled to France alone with her daughter Philippa at the beginning of December it is possible that the two cousins had already discussed the possible marriage of their two children via messengers. Sometime that month, they surely discussed the possibility in person in France. Philippa's father Willem must have been aware of the idea, and approved. His daughter would be queen-consort of England, and the next ruler of that wealthy and powerful realm would be his grandson.

It would mean acting against the king of a sovereign nation, but Willem was angry with Edward II for failing to do justice to those men of Hainault who had been robbed in England, and threw in his lot with his wife's cousin. Willem was possibly already allied with Roger Mortimer and the other English exiles and rebels as early as October 1324, when Hugh Despenser knew or suspected that the English exiles on the continent and their forces would land in Norfolk or Suffolk in the east of England with the aid of the count of Hainault and the king of Bohemia, Johann the Blind, a French and Hainault ally and Charles IV's brother-in-law.[27]

Edward II wrote to his kinswoman Maria Díaz de Haro, lady of Biscay in northern Spain, on 1 January 1326, vehemently assuring her that his son was not going to marry in France. Just two days later, his certainty was given the lie by his pleas to the pope not to grant a dispensation for his son's marriage to any member of the French royal family without his consent. John XXII respected Edward's wishes, and did not grant the dispensation until late August 1327, seven months after Edward's deposition.[28] For rumours of Edward of Windsor's possible betrothal to have travelled from France to Spain and then to England by 1 January 1326 indicates that it must, at least unofficially, have taken place in early December 1325 at the latest. Edward of Windsor was in fact already betrothed to Leonor, sister of King Alfonso XI of Castile in Spain – Maria Díaz de Haro of Biscay was one of the regents for the fourteen-year-old Alfonso – but his mother Isabella ignored this.[29]

At New Year 1326, Philippa and her mother returned to Hainault, while Edward of Windsor and his mother remained at the French court for the time being. It is possible, though not certain, that Philippa and Edward met again at the coronation of Jeanne of Evreux as queen of France on 11 May 1326. Neither of them officially appears on the list of attendees for whom cloth was purchased, but Edward of Windsor was certainly present, as his father Edward II wrote to Charles IV on 19 June to complain that his wife Isabella had made their son appear in public at the coronation with his enemy Roger Mortimer. Pope John XXII in Avignon in the south of France was endeavouring, unsuccessfully, to reconcile the king and queen of England and sent envoys to both of them, but as long as Edward II refused to send Hugh Despenser away from him Isabella refused to return to him, and stayed in France under her brother's protection. She evidently found her opposition to her husband difficult, however: on 5 February 1326 she sent a letter to the archbishop of Canterbury explaining that she longed above all to return to Edward, whom she called her 'very dear and very sweet lord and friend', but did not dare because she felt herself in mortal danger from Hugh Despenser, whom she referred to as *nostre mauvoillant* or 'our evil-wisher'.[30]

At some point, the queen also told her chief ally Roger Mortimer that she had decided to go back to England and to her husband, but Mortimer, furious at the idea of losing his only chance of ever returning to his homeland and at the prospect of living as an impoverished and powerless exile on the continent for the rest of his life, threatened to stab her if she did so. There is no particular reason to suppose, contrary to popular modern myth, that the pair had become lovers and had fallen passionately in love and lust, and that Mortimer's threat to stab Isabella if she went back to Edward was the result of sexual jealousy. (Mortimer's wife Joan née Geneville, whom he had married in 1301 when they were both in their early or mid-teens, spent the period from early 1322 to late 1326 under house arrest in England as a result of her husband's rebellion against the king, and Edward II held some of their dozen children in captivity in various convents and at Windsor Castle.)

It is not impossible that Isabella and Mortimer fell in love or lust, but it is far more likely that they were merely political allies, at least at this point, though the relationship may have developed into something else later on. They both desired the downfall of Hugh Despenser the Younger, Isabella so that she could resume her position as Edward II's wife and queen and once more become the powerful politician, mediator and intercessor she had been until Despenser intruded into the royal marriage in and after 1322; and Roger Mortimer so that he could return to his homeland, family and lands. As long as Hugh Despenser was alive and in control of the English king and the English government, Mortimer would remain an exile on the continent separated from his family and deprived of his lands and income, and the same applied to the other English exiles. Separately, neither Queen Isabella nor the exiled Contrariants had any chance of bringing Hugh Despenser down, but together they had a much better chance. Edward II, highly dependent on Hugh Despenser and possibly infatuated with him, obstinately refused to send him away, even when faced with his wife threatening an invasion of his kingdom. So Isabella pressed on with her plans. Philippa of Hainault must have met Roger Mortimer when he travelled to her father's county sometime in 1326 to make arrangements for the invasion of Edward II's kingdom. Years later in England, she came to know him very well, probably far better than she had ever wished to know a mere baron, who by then had appointed himself ruler of her young husband's kingdom.

Sometime in the summer of 1326, Isabella and her son left Paris and travelled to Hainault, perhaps because Isabella's position at her brother Charles IV's court was becoming untenable. The later chronicler Jean Froissart, following the narrative of the more contemporary Liège chronicler Jean le Bel, gives a typically overblown and over-romanticised account of the queen of England's arrival in Hainault. Philippa's uncle Sir Jan van Beaumont, Count Willem's younger brother, supposedly promised to give the beautiful, tragic and weeping royal lady all possible support against her cruel enemies who were tormenting her and who had supposedly driven her from her rightful home. Froissart, le Bel and several other continental chroniclers operated under the incorrect assumption that Isabella and her son had been driven from England or had fled from there together in secret, after pretending to go to Canterbury on pilgrimage, and that the two spent years in involuntary exile on the continent. Sir Jan van Beaumont did indeed aid the queen by taking part in her invasion and in the deposition of her husband, but was given an almost absurdly large amount of cash for doing so, while Isabella herself had been sent to France by her husband to negotiate a peace settlement with her brother and could have returned to England any time she wished. She did not wish to because of her fear and loathing of Hugh Despenser the Younger, but her husband certainly did not banish her and their son. His surviving proclamations of 1326 make it clear that he ordered his wife and son to be treated with honour and respect if they returned to England, though his anger with Isabella is apparent from his references to her throughout 1326 as 'the king's wife'; he refused to acknowledge or use her rightful title of queen.

Edward II had written to his son on 18 March and 19 June 1326, ordering him home. In the letter of 18 March, the king addressed Edward of Windsor affectionately throughout as *Beaufuitz* or 'fair son', but by the time he dictated the letter of 19 June he had become frantic with worry, and ended the letter with what amounted to a threat. All correspondence between father and son ceased. Edward of Windsor's feelings about the whole situation are unclear; he was too young to be acting under his own agency and was being kept more or less as a prisoner by his mother and used as a weapon against his father whether he wished it or not. On the other hand, he loathed Hugh Despenser the Younger as much as everyone else did, and although he surely loved Edward II as a father and as a human being – whatever Edward II's faults, he was a good and loving father to his children – he was perhaps also rather ashamed of him as an unsuccessful ruler and war leader and as a lover of men. The young boy had been placed in an impossible situation by both his parents. When he was not even thirteen years old, his father had sent him to a country which, although it was ruled by his own uncle and was his mother's native land, had until very recently been at war with the boy's homeland; and his mother was now using him as a weapon against his father.

It was a terrible and tragic state of affairs, not least because Edward of Windsor must have been aware that whichever parent emerged victorious in their struggle, there was a very good chance that he would lose the other parent forever. If his mother's attempts to bring down Hugh Despenser the Younger were unsuccessful, she would not be able to go back to England and resume her marriage and her political position, but would have to remain at the French court, forever dependent on the goodwill of her brother Charles IV and his successors. If this occurred, Edward of Windsor would go back to his father, who was utterly furious with him, and nothing would change in the foreseeable future. The loathed Despenser would continue to dominate the English government and to be as powerful as ever, and Edward II was still only forty-two years old and was strong, fit and healthy, and there was every chance he would live for another twenty or twenty-five years (his father Edward I lived to be sixty-eight and his grandfather Henry III to be sixty-five). On the other hand, if Isabella defeated Despenser and her husband with her son at her side, Edward of Windsor would have publicly declared himself the enemy of his lord and father, to whom he owed obedience and allegiance, and would never be able to go back to him.

Possibly Edward of Windsor wished for his mother's success and for the downfall of Hugh Despenser, but such open rebellion against his own king and father must have sat uneasily with him. Edward II's letter to his son of 19 June 1326 ended with the harsh words that if Edward of Windsor continued in his wilful disobedience, his father would ordain that 'you will feel it all the days of your life.'[31] This was the last direct contact Edward of Windsor ever had with his father, as far as is known, and although the king's words would prove to be an empty threat, they may have caused the boy hurt and worry.

On 27 August 1326 in the Hainault town of Mons, Edward of Windsor, aged thirteen going on fourteen, and Philippa of Hainault, probably aged about twelve and a half, were betrothed. The boy swore an oath on the Gospels to marry *demiselle Phelippe*, 'the damsel Philippa', within two years, and promised that he would pay her father Willem a massive fine of £10,000 if he did not.[32] The engagement was not lawful, as Edward's legal guardian, his father the king of England, stood in firm opposition to it and did not give his permission or consent, and the boy was officially betrothed to Leonor, sister of King Alfonso XI of Castile. Young Edward was one of the most eligible bachelors in Europe, and earlier in 1326 King Afonso IV and Queen Beatriz of Portugal had written to Edward II expressing their desire for him to marry one of their daughters. The English king tactfully replied that although he was very keen to establish a 'treaty of perpetual friendship' between England and Portugal, his son was betrothed to the infanta of Castile and it was not 'fitting' for him to open negotiations with another kingdom regarding his son's future wife. Edward II added that if his son's marriage into Castile could not be completed for some reason, he would gladly begin discussions for Edward of Windsor's marriage to a daughter of the king and queen of Portugal instead, 'for the strengthening of peace and love' between the two kingdoms.[33] The king of England, although he admitted that his son was currently in France, did not mention that he had lost custody of the boy to his wife, or that there was a possibility of Isabella arranging their son's marriage into Hainault instead.

For the heir to the English throne to marry the eldest daughter of a king, as Edward II wished, might be deemed a far more appropriate match for Edward of Windsor than marrying the third daughter of a mere count. The Hainault alliance was a match which, for all Philippa's illustrious connections on her French mother's side, some people in and after 1326 might understandably have considered somewhat inadequate for someone of Edward of Windsor's rank. Edward's mother Isabella, however – herself the daughter of two sovereigns, a king of France and a queen-regnant of Navarre, and one of the most highly born queens of England in history – was less interested in finding a suitably royal wife for her son than in bringing down her husband's loathed favourite by any means necessary.

Jean Froissart states that Philippa of Hainault declared to him many years later that when she spent time with Edward of Windsor in her homeland in the late summer and early autumn of 1326, Edward preferred her and her company to that of any of her sisters, and chose her as his future bride over them. 'So I heard it from the good lady who became queen of England,' Froissart declared. Elsewhere, Froissart claims that Edward was asked which of Count Willem's three unmarried daughters he wished to marry, and he answered 'the youngest except one, who is called Philippa [*Phelippe*].'[34] (Who Froissart thought the other two unmarried Hainault daughters were is not clear; perhaps he meant Agnes and Isabella, though he does not mention Agnes on any other occasion, so perhaps he mistakenly believed that Johanna was not yet married.)

Froissart adds at this point that Edward 'always showed her [Philippa] more love than any of the others when he was in Hainault.' The Liège chronicler Jean le Bel, however, who spent time in England in 1327 with Philippa's uncle Sir Jan van Beaumont and whom Jean Froissart often used as a source, merely states that Count Willem was asked to 'send to the king one of his daughters' for Edward to marry. Despite his close association with the ruling family of Hainault and, later, with King Edward III (whom le Bel greatly admired), and despite being a source for many of Jean Froissart's narratives, apparently le Bel himself had never heard this particular story.[35]

The pleasant little tale that Edward chose Philippa of Hainault as his bride over her sisters has been repeated many times as though it is fact and as though Edward actually had a say in the matter. Philippa's older sisters Margaretha and Johanna had both been married for two and a half years at this point, and the shadowy Sibilla is likely to have died, assuming she ever existed at all and was not merely a clerical error in an English document of 1319. That left Philippa and her younger sister Isabella, who, given that she married a man born in the mid-1320s, is unlikely to have been much more than a toddler in August 1326. Jeanne de Valois, still only at the beginning of her thirties, gave birth to her two youngest sons Lodewijk and Jan in 1325 and 1327, and may have given birth to her youngest daughter Isabella *c.* 1323/24. There was another Hainault sister, Agnes, who is known to have died sometime before November 1327, and who was also much younger than Edward of Windsor and born probably in the late 1310s or early 1320s. Froissart was evidently unaware of her existence, and Philippa did not mention Agnes to him as one of the sisters Edward supposedly rejected in her favour. Agnes therefore was almost certainly already dead by August 1326. Even if she were still alive when Edward visited Hainault, she is unlikely to have been more than seven or eight years old and may only have been four or five. For the adolescent Edward of Windsor to prefer the company of a girl only about fifteen or so months his junior to that of one or two small children is hardly surprising, and he probably did not even meet Philippa's older sisters Margaretha and Johanna, as they lived in Germany. As the two were married, and Margaretha at least was already a mother by this time, it was irrelevant whether he preferred Philippa to them or not. Philippa was the oldest unwed Hainault sister and therefore was next in line to marry, and was by far the closest in age of the unmarried sisters to Edward of Windsor.

According to Froissart, Philippa burst into tears when Edward and his mother Queen Isabella left her homeland in September 1326, in the belief that she would not see him again. She was of course only twelve years old at most at the time, but even so, it is hard to imagine that she was as naïve, innocent and ignorant of what was going on around her as this tale of Froissart's suggests. It is also most unlikely that Philippa met Edward of Windsor for the first time when he and his mother arrived at her father's court sometime in the late summer of 1326, as has often been assumed. As previously noted, it is highly probable that they had already met at the French court in December 1325 when Philippa visited her grandfather Charles de Valois, Edward's great-uncle, and when their mothers almost certainly discussed their future marriage. The two perhaps met again in Paris in May 1326 at the coronation of Charles IV's queen Jeanne of Evreux.

Assuming Froissart recorded Philippa's words correctly, the queen was romanticising and viewing her past through rose-coloured spectacles later in life when she told him the story.

Either she had genuinely convinced herself that Edward had to choose between herself and her sisters and preferred her, or perhaps she felt she had to make up a sweet little tale because the true circumstances surrounding her betrothal could hardly have been less romantic. Choice did not come into it, on Philippa's side or Edward's, and the betrothal had nothing whatsoever to do with romance or with the whims and fantasies of adolescents. Given the enormous affection that later grew between the couple and the decades-long success of their marriage, it is of course not at all unlikely that they did indeed like each other very much and thoroughly enjoyed each other's company in 1326, but their betrothal was a hard-headed political decision by their parents. It came about because Philippa's future mother-in-law needed ships and mercenaries to launch an illegal invasion of a sovereign nation, so that she could destroy her husband's best friend or lover and was perhaps even contemplating the downfall of her husband as well, and was using Philippa's thirteen-year-old fiancé and his future marriage in an attempt to force his father to do what she wished. Philippa also conveniently forgot to mention to Jean Froissart that her fiancé was still officially betrothed to Leonor of Castile at the time that he allegedly chose her as his future bride. She may not have known of Edward's engagement in the summer of 1326 when he and his mother came to Hainault, but of course Edward of Windsor himself was certainly aware of it, and someone must have told Philippa about it in the years afterwards.

The English rhyming chronicler John Hardyng, who was born *c*. 1378, a good half a century later, added to the myths surrounding Edward of Windsor and Philippa of Hainault's betrothal. Hardyng wrote that Edward, after he became king of England in early 1327, sent an English bishop and several temporal lords to Hainault to choose a bride for him. The bishop and lords debated among themselves which of the daughters of the count of Hainault would be most suitable as a bride for their king, and chose Philippa because she had good wide hips and would bear sons, and because she was 'full feminine'.[36] This was written with more than a century of hindsight and in the knowledge that Philippa of Hainault did indeed bear Edward many sons, seven, of whom five survived infancy. Whether Philippa, at only twelve or thirteen years old, was already developed enough in 1326/27 to have 'good wide hips' and to look as though she might bear Edward many children seems doubtful. Again, Hardyng assumes that Edward of Windsor and his advisers were able to choose which Hainault daughter should marry the young king of England, a choice which in fact did not exist.

When Edward of Windsor, who by then had become King Edward III of England – or rather, someone acting on his behalf as he was still well underage – wrote to Pope John XXII about a dispensation for his marriage a year later on 15 August 1327, he only talked of 'a daughter' of Count Willem and did not mention Philippa by name. Likewise, when payments were made out of the English exchequer for the expenses of Edward and Philippa's wedding, she was referred to only as 'the daughter of the count of Hainault' and was not specifically named. Oddly enough, the chronicler Jean le Bel, who wrote a long account of Edward and Philippa's betrothal, never used her given name either; he always referred to her as 'the damsel in question', or 'the count's daughter', or, later, 'the young queen of England'. Another chronicler, Adam Murimuth, an English royal clerk, also simply called her 'the daughter of the count of Hainault' when writing about Philippa's marriage to Edward.[37]

Philippa in later years became Edward III's beloved wife, England's beloved queen and the beloved mother of a large number of children, and was a significant and influential figure in her own right, but as a twelve-year-old in 1326 she herself was not important except as her parents' daughter. Her marriage to Edward of Windsor would have gone ahead even if they had detested the very sight of each other. Had anything untoward happened to Philippa between her betrothal to Edward in August 1326 and their wedding in January 1328, he would have been married off to her toddler sister Isabella instead (Agnes, the next Hainault sister, had certainly died by early 1328 when Philippa's wedding to Edward went ahead). Had anything happened to both Philippa and Isabella of Hainault, Edward would almost certainly have been married to one of Count Willem's nieces, perhaps Sir Jan van Beaumont's daughter Johanna, to maintain the England-Hainault alliance. Had anything happened to King Edward III himself before the wedding, it is probable that Philippa would have had to marry his younger brother John of Eltham, born in August 1316 and the heir to the English throne between Edward III's accession in January 1327 and the birth of Philippa's eldest son in June 1330. This boy would have become King John II of England if Edward had died before he and Philippa had conceived a child. Queen Philippa's wish to draw a veil over all of this decades later, and to turn the harshly unromantic circumstances of her betrothal into a sweet and pretty fantasy, reveals much about her character.

Queen in Name Only

The papal dispensation for Edward and Philippa to wed, which was necessary as they were related in the third degree (i.e. second cousins), was issued on 30 August 1327, exactly a year after their betrothal and fifteen days after Edward wrote to John XXII requesting it. Unlike Edward, or whoever wrote the letter to the pope on his behalf, the pope actually referred to Philippa by her given name.[1] It is possible that John XXII issued the dispensation only reluctantly, fearing that Edward III's marriage to the sister-in-law of his greatest enemy, the German king and later Holy Roman Emperor Ludwig of Bavaria, might strengthen the ties between England and Ludwig.[2] By the time the dispensation was finally issued, Philippa's fiancé had been king of England for seven months. His mother's invasion of her husband's kingdom on 24 September 1326 had been highly successful, and just two months after her arrival she had Hugh Despenser the Younger grotesquely executed by hanging, drawing and quartering in Hereford. Despenser's father the earl of Winchester and Roger Mortimer's cousin and enemy, the earl of Arundel – and several other men who had the misfortune to be in the wrong place at the wrong time – had been executed as well.

Edward II's support simply collapsed, and whether Isabella and her allies had intended to overthrow him or not, it soon became clear that he could not continue as king. In January 1327 he was forced to abdicate in favour of his fourteen-year-old son, who succeeded as King Edward III and who was hastily crowned king of England at Westminster Abbey on 1 February 1327. Philippa's uncle,

Sir Jan van Beaumont, certainly attended the coronation, and may have personally knighted Edward III, though according to other evidence, this honour was given to Queen Isabella's uncle Henry of Lancaster, earl of Lancaster and Leicester. The young king's father, now merely Sir Edward of Caernarfon, was sent into reasonably comfortable captivity at Berkeley Castle in Gloucestershire in early April 1327, in the custody of Roger Mortimer's son-in-law Thomas, Lord Berkeley, and Berkeley's brother-in-law Sir John Maltravers. Such a thing had never happened in England before; although this would not be the last deposition or forced abdication of an English king – Queen Philippa's grandson Richard II would be the next, in 1399 – in 1327 it was a revolutionary act with no precedent.

Following a series of attempts by his supporters throughout 1327 to rescue him and perhaps restore him to the throne, news of Sir Edward of Caernarfon's death was taken to his son in Lincoln during the night of 23/24 September 1327, and was subsequently announced publicly. Contemporary chroniclers speculated wildly as to the cause of the former king's death at the age of only forty-three, coming up with strangulation, suffocation, grief, an unspecified illness, a fall, poison, natural causes, and, later, the mythical red-hot poker, which has, by dint of being luridly and revoltingly memorable, become the widely accepted tale of Edward II's demise. His death was at first presented as natural, though when his son Edward III overthrew his mother Isabella and Roger Mortimer three years later in 1330, the young king stated that his father had been murdered. Edward III never, however, stated exactly how his father had been killed, and rumour and speculation filled the information gap for many years to come (and indeed still do). Whatever truly happened to Edward II in September 1327 – and numerous influential men believed that he was alive in the late 1320s and early 1330s and acted on that belief – his funeral was held at St Peter's Abbey in Gloucester (now Gloucester Cathedral) on 20 December 1327. It took place in the presence of his son, now fifteen, his widow Isabella and her chief counsellor Roger Mortimer, his half-brother Edmund of Woodstock, earl of Kent, and much of the English nobility and episcopacy. What Philippa of Hainault thought about all this is a matter for speculation; she never met her husband's father and can only ever have heard reports of him from other people, whether accurate or not.

Philippa's father Count Willem held jousts at 's-Gravenzande a few miles south of The Hague in February 1327, which Philippa almost certainly attended; her brother Willem the younger, about nine or ten years old, received payments for his expenses incurred 'at the jousts' (given his youth, one assumes he was merely watching and not actually competing).[3] Sir Jan van Beaumont returned from England to Hainault in February 1327 to take part in the jousts, so would have been able to tell his niece the details of her fiancé's accession to the throne and all about his recent coronation, before he departed for the south of France to meet Queen Isabella's brother Charles IV (Jan went back to England later in the year after his French visit). Jeanne de Valois was at The Hague in May 1327 when she paid several minstrels who 'recited [verse] before my lady' there, and probably Philippa and her younger siblings were with their mother on this occasion and listened to the poetry.[4] The Hague was the residence which the count and countess, and their children, visited most often in their territory of Holland, and Philippa surely knew the town well.[5]

In 1327, Countess Jeanne was pregnant for about the ninth or tenth, and last, time. Philippa's brother-in-law Ludwig of Bavaria, meanwhile, was planning an invasion of Lombardy in Italy, and summoned his father-in-law Count Willem of Hainault and Holland and other noblemen of Germany and the Low Countries to Nuremberg to consult with them about his plans. Willem, preoccupied with other matters, failed to appear. Pope John XXII excommunicated Ludwig again on hearing of his intended invasion.[6] Ludwig and his wife Margaretha of Hainault, not quite seventeen years old, were crowned king and queen of Italy in Milan on 31 May 1327.

Philippa of Hainault must have been present at Le Quesnoy in Hainault on 4 August 1327, when Jeanne de Valois entertained envoys from England: Bartholomew, Lord Burghersh, Adam Orleton, bishop of Hereford, and Sir Hugh Audley, whom Edward III would make earl of Gloucester a few years later. A month after the envoys' visit, Pope John XXII wrote to Countess Jeanne stating that he would soon send to her the relics of her uncle Saint Louis (b. 1274), bishop of Toulouse – one of the many younger siblings of Jeanne's late mother Marguerite of Anjou-Naples – who had died in his early twenties in 1297 and whom John XXII had canonised in 1317.[7] In July 1335, Jeanne acquired a manuscript called the *Livre de Saint Loys*, 'the Book of Saint Louis', which either means her uncle Louis of Toulouse or her great-grandfather Louis IX, king of France (born 1214, reigned 1226-1270), who was canonised in 1297.[8] Philippa must have been raised to be well aware and proud of her saintly ancestor and relative.

Philippa was with her parents at Valenciennes in October 1327, and numerous important guests travelled there to join in the celebrations for her impending. Johann 'the Blind' of Luxembourg, king of Bohemia, was present, and so were Philippa's brother-in-law Wilhelm of Jülich with his father Gerhard, count of Jülich, and his younger brother Walram, future archbishop of Cologne (and, presumably, his wife Johanna, Philippa's older sister, unless she was too close to term to travel and had to be left behind in Jülich). Adolf, count of Berg, John, count of Namur – whose son Robert would marry Philippa's younger sister Isabella of Hainault – the burgrave of Voorne, and the bishops of Cambrai, Tournai and Arras, were other important guests keen to celebrate Philippa's forthcoming marriage. There was widespread joy and pride among Count Willem's subjects in Hainault, Holland and Zealand that their ruler was shortly to become the father-in-law of the king of England as well as of the German king, soon to become the Holy Roman Emperor. Roger Northburgh, bishop of Coventry and Lichfield, was empowered on 8 October to 'treat for a marriage between the king and Philippa' and to contract a marriage between them *per verba di presenti* when he visited Hainault; in short, the bishop conducted a proxy wedding.[9]

It was not all celebrations and festivities in the Hainault household, however, and the last three months of the year 1327 saw the deaths of two of Willem and Jeanne's children. In October, the same month as the joyous celebrations for her marriage, Philippa must have attended the funeral of her two-year-old brother Lodewijk, who had been unwell for most of his life. Her youngest brother, Jan, who bore the ill-fated name of his older brother who had died in 1316, also died soon after his birth around the time Philippa left Hainault in December 1327. She had lost yet another sibling, Agnes, as well, perhaps in 1326 or shortly before.

The Christmas festivities of 1327 must have been muted in the Hainault household. Little Jan had died, little Lodewijk had died, Agnes had died, Philippa had left home and gone to live in England permanently, and the only two of Jeanne de Valois's many children who remained in Hainault with her were Willem the younger, who was now about ten and was heir to the counties of Hainault and Holland, and Isabella, probably three or four years old. Even Jeanne's husband and brother-in-law Sir Jan van Beaumont were not present during the festive season, being on their way to England with Philippa. It is hardly surprising that the festive season of 1327 saw the arrival of several guests at the Hainault court, 'especially ladies and young ladies…to visit and console Madame'.[10] Jan, who was born and died in late 1327, was Jeanne de Valois's youngest child. Still only about thirty-two or thirty-three years old, married for twenty-two years and already a grandmother to Margarethe and Anna of Bavaria and Gerhard of Jülich, Countess Jeanne was to have no more children.

Froissart claims that Philippa of Hainault was Jeanne de Valois's favourite daughter: 'She loved her with all her heart, more tenderly than any of her [other] daughters.'[11] Even if Froissart made this up, as certainly seems possible given his track record of over-romanticising Philippa, it was surely very hard for Jeanne to experience yet another child leaving her so soon after the deaths of her two little sons, especially as she must have known that her young daughter was being sent into a very stressful situation in England. Philippa would marry a young man whose father had only recently died a sudden and obscure death and had perhaps been murdered, and Edward II's deposition and his son's subsequent accession to the throne in his father's lifetime were unprecedented in England and of dubious legality. During Edward III's minority, his kingdom was governed for him by his mother the dowager queen Isabella and her chief counsellor Roger Mortimer, also a legally questionable situation. It must have been upsetting for Philippa as well to have to leave her mother behind while Jeanne was grieving for the recent deaths of Lodewijk and Jan, in the knowledge that she might never see Jeanne again (though in fact her mother came to visit her in England at least twice over the next few years). The choice, however, was not hers to make, and there was nothing Philippa could do except go ahead with the wedding her father and mother-in-law had planned for her. Perhaps, at least, the prospect of seeing the handsome young Edward again and making a new life with him as queen of England was something she could eagerly anticipate. She did keep in touch with her parents after she arrived in her new home: at an unknown date in or after 1327, Willem sent his daughter a gift of a horse, a dog and two falcons, with a falconer to look after the birds. Philippa and Jeanne sent each other letters, and Philippa also wrote to her eldest sister Margaretha, and her second sister Johnna sent messengers to her with news. Countess Jeanne and her daughter Johanna would both visit Philippa in England in 1331.[12]

The thirteen-year-old Philippa left her homeland on 16 December 1327, four days before the former king Edward II's funeral in Gloucester. With her father Count Willem and his younger brother Jan van Beaumont, she sailed from the port of Wissant, and landed in Dover.[13] Philippa and her father were met there by the constable of Dover Castle, Bartholomew, Lord Burghersh, and the young knight Sir William Clinton, a close friend of the young king whom Edward III was to make earl of Huntingdon in 1337. Philippa had already met Lord Burghersh, one of the English envoys to Hainault a few weeks previously. The party reached London, where Philippa was 'joyfully received' by the inhabitants, a day or two before Christmas, and stayed at the Holborn palace of the bishop of Ely, John Hotham. From London, the Hainault party was escorted to York.[14] One young Hainaulter who accompanied Philippa to England and who stayed there for the remaining forty-five years of his life was Walter Manny or Mauny, who would become keeper of the queen's greyhounds, a great friend of Edward III and a Knight of the Garter, and who would marry Edward's first cousin the countess of Norfolk and become the father of the countess of Pembroke. Manny was probably about sixteen or seventeen when he arrived in England with Philippa in late 1327.

Roger Northburgh, bishop of Coventry and Lichfield, had acted as the liaison between England and Hainault and had travelled to Philippa's homeland to finalise all the wedding arrangements, and had taken part in a proxy marriage ceremony on 8 October 1327.

Northburgh was also part of Philippa's retinue when she and her father arrived in York on 23 January 1328. Evidently the people of England eagerly anticipated the arrival of their soon-to-be queen, as there is a reference to the 'much spoken of marriage'.[15] After the tyranny of Hugh Despenser the Younger's regime of the previous few years and the generally disastrous rule of Edward II since 1307, there must have been widespread excitement and optimism about the young king's accession and his impending wedding.

Philippa's wedding to Edward III took place in York, probably on 24 or 25 January 1328. Oddly, the exact date of the wedding is not completely certain, and fourteenth-century English chroniclers give a variety of dates, including as early as 4 January. The 25th of January, however, seems the most likely option. This was both the twentieth wedding anniversary of the young king's parents – Edward II and Isabella of France married in Boulogne, northern France on 25 January 1308 – and the first anniversary of Edward III's own accession to the throne: his reign officially began on 25 January 1327. The wedding ceremony was conducted by William Melton, archbishop of York, a former and future treasurer of England, and a man the young king trusted completely despite Melton's undying loyalty towards Edward II. Melton had refused to attend Edward III's coronation a year previously and had spoken out for Edward II at the parliament of January 1327 which forced his deposition, but Edward III, recognising Melton's worth and knowing that the archbishop would show him the same loyalty as he did his father, did not hold this against him. (Usually the wedding ceremony of the king of England would have been conducted by the archbishop of Canterbury, but Archbishop Walter Reynolds had died in November 1327, and although Simon Meopham had been elected to the position in December, he had not yet been consecrated by Pope John XXII in Avignon.)

Archbishop William Melton conducted the ceremony in his own apartments at his palace in York, and the royal clerk Nicholas Hugate had been sent there to supervise the preparation of the apartments and to make sure that they were suitably well-appointed for Edward and Philippa's wedding. The huge sum of £2,417 ten shillings and threepence was borrowed from the Italian bankers the Bardi to buy gold and silver jewels for Philippa for her wedding, which included the cost of transporting them from Paris, where they were purchased, to York. In addition, another £1,811 was recorded in the royal accounts under the heading 'Gifts' during the week of the royal wedding.[16]

A jousting tournament was held in York to celebrate the royal wedding, and Edward III, who, unlike his father, adored the sport and participated whenever he could, must have competed personally. Philippa gave her new husband a splendid wedding gift: an illuminated collection of texts for aspiring rulers, including the 'Book of Julius Caesar' and the 'Government of Kings'. She also gave him a book of music, featuring an image of Edward himself on the front cover holding a falcon. No doubt Edward III enjoyed and appreciated this splendid gift, but he was never a man to feel particularly sentimental about books and presents: the wedding gift was later broken up and given away piecemeal to bureaucrats and courtiers. He in turn may have given Philippa a wedding present which still exists: a tiny but lavishly decorated psalter in Latin, now held in the British Library in London (in fact, two psalters which once almost certainly belonged to Philippa still survive today).[17] The wedding festivities lasted for several days and there was lavish expenditure on gold and silver plate as well as on jewels, while cloth of gold was also purchased for Edward and Philippa's thrones.[18] Less happily, the 'poor people' of York presented two petitions in *c.* 1329/30, stating that numerous debts were still owed to them for items they had provided for the royal wedding, and that many traders were 'completely ruined' because they still had not been paid. Despite the traders' obvious misery, one of the petitions was turned down flat.[19] The tardy payments to the unfortunate and impoverished traders of York were not Philippa's fault, as she was little more than a child, and had no money with which to pay them anyway. Given the compassion she demonstrated on many occasions throughout her life, however, if she was aware of the financial hardship caused to the people who had provided the food, clothes, tableware, decorations and other items for her wedding, she was surely dismayed by the situation.

Philippa, who almost certainly was only thirteen going on fourteen in late January 1328, became queen-consort of England on marriage, and also held the titles lady of Ireland, duchess of Aquitaine, and countess of Chester and Ponthieu. The young girl would, however, have to wait for several years to gain her rightful position. Her mother-in-law Isabella of France had no intention of giving up any ground to her son's young wife, and Philippa was not even granted a proper income until April 1329, nor was she crowned as queen until February 1330, more than two years after her wedding. A coronation for her was vaguely planned in 1328, but never took place. It has been suggested by some modern writers that Philippa's coronation was delayed on the grounds of her youth, but Isabella of France had herself been crowned queen at Edward II's side on 25 February 1308 a month after their wedding. Isabella was then only twelve years old, even younger than Philippa, and no-one had suggested that her coronation should wait until she was older. Edward III's biographer Mark Ormrod has written of the remarkable 'infantilising of Queen Philippa' at the hands of her mother-in-law as a result of the dowager queen's 'increasingly obsessive efforts to maintain power and influence over the new regime'. The young king himself also came to feel infantilised, frustrated and suffocated by his mother in and after 1328, but for the time being there was nothing he could do about it.[20]

Isabella had granted herself an annual income of £13,333 on the day of her son's coronation in early February 1327, the largest income anyone in England except the kings received throughout the entire Middle Ages, and her chief counsellor Roger Mortimer also filled his coffers. Of the almost £80,000 left in Edward II's treasury at the time of his and Hugh Despenser's downfall at the end of 1326, a derisory £41 was left four years later when Edward III finally overthrew the pair. Even the £20,000 given to England by Robert Bruce in and after 1328, in return for England's recognition of him as king of Scotland, plus massive loans made to the English government by Italian bankers, merely fell into the bottomless pit of Isabella and Mortimer's greed and Edward III himself saw barely a penny of it. Isabella paid Philippa's uncle Sir Jan van Beaumont the astonishingly large sum of £32,722 between May 1327 and March 1328 in return for his aid and support during her invasion of England and its aftermath, while Philippa herself and her husband were embarrassed by their lack of money (and while the merchants of York waited in vain to receive the payment due to them for the items they had provided for the royal wedding).[21]

By 1330 Isabella had bankrupted her son's kingdom, and while she and Mortimer gorged themselves on money which by right was not theirs and wielded power which was also not rightfully theirs – neither of them was appointed to the regency council, which was meant to govern the kingdom during Edward III's minority – the young king and queen of England lived in humiliatingly straitened circumstances. The keeper of the king's great wardrobe threatened to resign in June 1330 because he had no money to purchase supplies for Edward's household.[22]

Despite the inauspicious beginning to their marriage, however, the young couple surely revelled in each other's company once they began to live together as husband and wife, perhaps in late 1328 or 1329. Edward found a loyal, devoted and supportive helpmate, and their long marriage would prove to be a most successful and contented one. Jean Froissart's statement that Edward chose Philippa as his wife over her sisters cannot have been true, but there is no doubt whatsoever that Edward III and Philippa of Hainault formed a close and happy marriage, and fell deeply in love. Philippa could hardly have been more different from her beautiful, clever and arguably manipulative mother-in-law Isabella. Edward III owed a great deal to his mother and knew it, though it is perhaps revealing that he formed such a close relationship with a woman who was Isabella's opposite. Whether the young couple consummated their marriage in 1328 is unclear. It may be that Philippa was considered too young to live with Edward just yet, and Froissart states that immediately after the royal wedding Philippa was removed from her husband's company and taken south to London.[23] She might not yet have begun her menstrual cycle or have become fertile when she married. She became pregnant in September 1329, twenty-one months after her wedding and when she was probably fifteen.

On 17 January 1328, just over a week before Philippa's wedding, her eldest sister Margaretha of Hainault and Margaretha's husband Ludwig of Bavaria were crowned Holy Roman Emperor and Empress at St Peter's Basilica in Rome. Usually only the pope could crown emperors and empresses, but John XXII (born Jacques Duèse) was based in Avignon in the south of France, not in Rome, and was a bitter enemy of Ludwig. As previously mentioned, Ludwig had declared John a heretic and the Antichrist, while John, for his part, spoke of the emperor derisively as 'the Bavarian'. The Roman senator Sciarra Colonna crowned the couple in John XXII's absence, and the pope excommunicated Ludwig yet again on hearing of his coronation. Ludwig responded by declaring John XXII deposed and installing a pliant anti-pope, Nicholas V (born Pietro Rainalducci), in Rome in his place. Margaretha of Hainault, still only seventeen years old, was pregnant with her third child and eldest son, who would be born in Rome on 7 May 1328 just days before her husband installed his anti-pope, and hence he was always known as Ludwig (or Louis) 'the Roman'. Philippa and Margaretha's father Count Willem did his best to mediate between his son-in-law and Pope John XXII in 1328 and on other occasions, but their vicious quarrel was not easily settled.[24]

Margaretha of Hainault's eldest child, Margarethe of Bavaria, born in 1325, married István of Hungary, duke of Slavonia and Transylvania, and her second child Anna was probably born in 1326. Anna followed in the footsteps of her maternal grandmother Jeanne de Valois, the dowager countess of Hainault after the death of Count Willem, by becoming a nun at Fontenelle Abbey near Valenciennes. Empress Margaretha and her husband left Rome on 4 August 1328, but spent the rest of that year and the whole of 1329 in Italy, finally returning to Germany in February 1330. By then, Margaretha was pregnant with Wilhelm, duke of Lower Bavaria, her fifth child and second son, born in May 1330. Her fourth child, Elisabeth, lady of Verona and countess of Württemberg, was born in Italy in 1329. After bearing five children in five years, Margaretha had a well-deserved break from pregnancy and childbirth for a few years after the birth of her son Wilhelm of Bavaria. Her next child, Albrecht, was not born until 1336, around the feast of All Saints, 1 November.[25]

On 1 February 1328 a few days after Edward III and Philippa's wedding, Edward's uncle King Charles IV of France died at the age of only thirty-three. Philip IV's sons did not live long: the eldest son Louis X died aged twenty-six and the second, Philip V, at thirty, though their sister Queen Isabella lived into her sixties.

Charles IV and his third wife Jeanne of Evreux had two daughters already, and Queen Jeanne was pregnant again when her husband died. All of France, and indeed Europe, waited with bated breath for the birth; if male, the child would become king of France the moment he drew breath. Charles's eldest brother Louis X had also left his widow Clemence of Hungary pregnant when he died in June 1316, and five months later she gave birth to a son, who immediately became King John I of France. The baby king died when he was five days old, however, and his uncle succeeded as King Philip V. Exactly two months after her husband's death, on 1 April 1328, the dowager queen gave birth to her third daughter, Blanche. As Charles IV and his brothers Louis X and Philip V had all left daughters but no surviving sons, the French throne passed to Philippa of Hainault's maternal uncle Philip de Valois, as the eldest son of Philip IV's brother Charles de Valois. He became King Philip VI, first of the many Valois kings who ruled France for the next 261 years.

Philip VI had no claim, however, to the small kingdom of Navarre in northern Spain, which had been united with the French throne since the marriage of Jeanne I of Navarre and Philip IV of France in 1284, and so it passed to sixteen-year-old Jeanne II, daughter and only surviving child of Philip IV's eldest son Louis X. Jeanne was married to her cousin Philip of Evreux, who, as the son and heir of Philip IV and Charles de Valois's younger half-brother Louis of Evreux (1276-1319), had a reasonable claim to the French throne himself. Jeanne II of Navarre and Philip of Evreux's son Carlos II 'the Bad', king of Navarre, born in 1332, would spend much of his life constantly switching sides between England and France, and was sometimes an ally of Philippa of Hainault's husband and eldest son and sometimes their enemy.

Edward III, as the only surviving grandson (besides his younger brother John of Eltham) of Philip IV, had a very strong claim to the French throne, but there was no chance whatsoever that the French would allow the king of England to become king of France as well. His mother Isabella, now the only surviving child of Philip IV, reacted with fury to the news of her cousin Philip VI's accession. As Edward III was duke of Aquitaine and count of Ponthieu as well as king of England, he now owed the ceremony of homage to Philip VI as his new overlord for his French territories, and would have to travel to France to do so. Isabella supposedly declared passionately that her son, who was the son of a king, would never do homage to the son of a mere count, but Edward had little choice; if he failed to do so, Philip VI would have the right to seize the duchy of Gascony and the county of Ponthieu permanently. Isabella sent a group of envoys to Paris to register her son's claim to the French throne as Philip IV's grandson.[26] For the time being, though, fifteen-year-old Edward III was powerless to act, and Philip VI was crowned king of France at Rheims on 29 May 1328. His sister Jeanne de Valois, countess of Hainault, with her husband Willem and Willem's brother Sir Jan van Beaumont, and Willem and Jan's kinsman the king of Bohemia, Johann of Luxembourg, were among the nobility of the Low Countries and Germany who attended.[27]

On the same day as her uncle Philip's accession to the throne of France, 1 April 1328, Queen Philippa was at the royal palace of Eltham in Kent, where she dictated a letter asking for a prisoner to be released.[28] It was standard for queens to intercede on behalf of petitioners, and Philippa's then twelve-year-old mother-in-law Isabella had done the same thing soon after her arrival in England in February 1308. A week after this, Philippa also asked for the release of Agnes of Penrith, who had been imprisoned for robbery in Yorkshire when she was under eleven years old. Three other grants and favours made 'at the request of Queen Philippa' are recorded in 1328 and 1329.[29] The girl, or young woman, was finding her feet in her new home and exercising a small measure of influence. However, she had no income of her own at all until 16 April 1329, fifteen months after her wedding, when she was finally granted an annual income of 1,000 marks or £666 from the Exchequer 'until some better provision be made for her estate'. On 15 May 1328, Edward III, or rather someone acting in his name, promised to assign Philippa lands as her dower within a year. This did not happen.[30] The money finally granted to her in 1329 was of course better than nothing, but it was not at all the same thing as being granted lands in her own right as she should have been.

Philippa did have her own household, including a treasurer, an usher of her chamber called John Dene who had previously worked for her parents-in-law, and Walter Wight, a valet of her 'cup-house'.[31] She also had damsels serving her – the title is an indication of rank, not of age – including one called Emma Prior, who had previously served Edward III's much older first cousin Eleanor de Clare (b. 1292), lady of Glamorgan, widow of Hugh Despenser the Younger. Emma was known by the nickname Emote or Emmote, an affectionate diminutive of her name. She had, rather curiously, already retired and been sent to a convent (as was usually the case with retired royal servants) in 1325, but must have decided to come out of her convent and serve the new queen.[32] Other damsels serving Philippa in the late 1320s and early 1330s were Joan Carru or Carew, Ida or Idonea Clinton, Margaret Peckebruge, Elena Mauley, and Amie Gaveston. Amie was the illegitimate daughter of Edward II's beloved favourite and probably his lover Piers Gaveston, earl of Cornwall, who had been beheaded in June 1312 by some of the king's disgruntled magnates five months before Edward III's birth. Queen Philippa's two ladies-in-waiting were named in June 1328 as the dowager countess of Pembroke, Marie de St Pol, and Lady Carew, and Philippa also had at least six and possibly eight clerks of her chapel by 1330.[33] One of her servants was called 'the holder of the queen's bridle'.[34]

Other than a handful of scattered references to her household, grants of land in 1330 and the five intercessions on behalf of others Philippa made, which are referenced above, the young queen does not appear on government record during the years of her mother-in-law's regime.[35] Although Philippa was the queen-consort of England, she was entirely overshadowed by the dowager queen Isabella for the first few years of her married life. She had rather more influence with Pope John XXII in Avignon and made various requests of him on behalf of herself and her household, which he granted, such as the right to choose her own confessor who might hear the confessions of her household, and the right to have a portable altar. Her confessor was Master Walter de Buxton, who had by 1343 had been succeeded by Master Simon de Nortwode or Northwood, and by 1361 by Master William de Polmorva.[36] John XXII wrote to Philippa on 7 August 1328 and again on the 27th of that month, congratulating her on her marriage and on becoming queen of England, and told her that it was 'her duty to assist the king, her husband, in defending the rights and liberties of the church, protecting the poor, and exercising herself in good works'. She was also exhorted to fulfil the duties of her position and to love her husband, advice which Philippa surely found easy to follow.[37]

Philippa does appear on record on 23 November 1328, when the mayor, sheriffs and aldermen of her husband's capital of London sent gifts to the young royal couple. The queen was presented with five carcasses of beef, price seventy-five shillings; twelve pigs, price forty-eight shillings; twelve pheasants, price forty-eight shillings; twelve swans, price sixty shillings; three stones of wax, price eleven pounds and nineteen shillings; two barrels of sturgeon, price six pounds; and three pike and three eels, price sixty-six shillings and eight pence. Edward III received exactly the same gifts, but at double the quantity; four barrels of sturgeon, twenty-four swans, six pike, six eels, and so on.[38]

In July 1328 the English regime made a treaty with Robert Bruce, king of Scotland, finally acknowledging him as the rightful king twenty-two years after his accession in 1306. The marriage of Robert's four-year-old son and heir David to Philippa's seven-year-old sister-in-law Joan of the Tower, youngest child of Edward II and Isabella of France, was arranged to cement the treaty. The child couple married immediately, and Joan was sent away to her new home in the northern kingdom. David and Joan became king and queen of Scotland, still aged only five and eight respectively, the following year when Robert Bruce died in his mid-fifties. Edward III was staunchly opposed to the treaty and to his sister's marriage, but for now, as he was still only fifteen years old, there was nothing at all he could do to prevent it. It must have been painfully apparent to Philippa of Hainault that her mother-in-law had no intention of letting go of power or of stepping back and allowing Philippa to become queen. Whatever the nature of Isabella's personal relationship with Roger Mortimer – whether they were lovers or merely close political allies – she allowed him to rule alongside her. At the Salisbury parliament of October 1328, Mortimer awarded himself the brand-new and grandiose earldom of March, i.e. earl of all the

English-Welsh borderlands. Although Philippa's twelve-year-old brother-in-law John of Eltham was made earl of Cornwall at the same time, an entirely uncontroversial appointment as he was the son and brother of kings, Mortimer's elevation seemed designed to provoke the great English magnates. They included Edward III's uncles the earls of Norfolk and Kent, who were Edward II's much younger half-brothers, and the young king's great-uncle Henry, earl of Lancaster and Leicester, a first cousin of the late Edward II and the uncle of Queen Isabella.[39]

Henry, earl of Lancaster, rebelled against the dowager queen and Mortimer at the end of 1328. He made a list of his grievances against their government, one of which stated that Philippa of Hainault 'ought to have her dowry on which to live without grieving the people', and that the king 'ought to have enough of his own to live fitly, without oppressing the people, together with treasure for defending his land and people if need arose'. The earl of Lancaster was in fact Edward III's legal guardian and was head of the regency council which was supposed to govern in the king's name, but was not allowed access to the young man or to wield any influence, while Isabella and Mortimer, never appointed to any official position, ruled the kingdom.

Someone, perhaps Roger Mortimer or the dowager queen, wrote a sarcastic reply to the earl of Lancaster in Edward III's name, declaring 'as regards the first point, namely, that he [Edward] ought to live of his own, that it was impossible for him to be any richer, since both he and his people were impoverished by the present disturbances, but if any man knew how to make him richer, it would give him and his advisers great satisfaction.'[40] Defensively, this same person or persons added, 'as regards the queen-consort's dowry, this ought not to be a reason for disturbance, since the matter concerned himself and her alone. It would not be an increased charge, and so he [Edward III] was willing that it should be done.' Roger Mortimer dealt with the earl of Lancaster's rebellion by taking an army to the earl's main base of Leicester at the beginning of 1329. He spent days sacking the town, which forced the earl to come to terms with his niece the dowager queen in mid-January. Henry of Lancaster and his allies had to acknowledge liability for massive and unpayable fines in the aftermath of his rebellion, a form of political blackmail also often utilised by Edward II and Hugh Despenser the Younger. The earl of Lancaster's rebellion had failed, and the regime of Queen Isabella and Roger Mortimer – by now grossly unpopular, even detested – continued. Any further opposition to them had to come from the young king himself; there was no-one else who could topple them.

The problem for Edward III, however, was that any action he took against them had to be entirely covert. He could hardly raise an army against his mother and her favourite without them noticing, and Mortimer kept spies in the young king's household, to Edward's utter fury: he later described himself as 'a man living in custody' during Mortimer's regime. The earl of Lancaster's failed rebellion had the unfortunate and unintended effect of making the young king even more dependent on Mortimer than he had been previously, and, as had happened with Edward II's powerful favourite Hugh Despenser the Younger during his period of power from about 1319 to 1326, private parties began to write to Roger Mortimer to seek his intervention in government.[41] Although he was never elected to an official position in Edward III's regency government, from early 1329 Mortimer came to wield more power than ever.

As yet unable to take overt action against Roger Mortimer, Edward III sent his good and loyal friend Sir William Montacute (born *c.* 1301) to Avignon with a letter for Pope John XXII sometime in 1329 or early 1330. This letter still exists, and contains an early extant example of a king of England's handwriting. Edward informed the pope that any future letters which contained the Latin words *Pater Sancte* or 'Holy Father' written in his own hand would come from himself, while any written in his name without those words were not sent from him but from those ruling his kingdom for him. He wrote out the words *Pater Sancte* to provide an example of his own handwriting.

Quietly, the young king also began to build up a small group of young knights he knew to be completely loyal to him, including his first cousins the twins Edward and William de Bohun (sons of Edward II's late sister Elizabeth, countess of Hereford), William Montacute, Ralph Stafford, Robert Ufford, William Clinton, and

John Neville of Hornby. In the meantime, Edward III and Queen Philippa had to continue to tolerate the ceaseless presence of Roger Mortimer, who dragged them off to Shropshire to attend the double wedding of two of his eight daughters, and who decided in 1329/30 that it was a fine idea to treat the young king as though he were his equal. Mortimer remained seated in Edward III's presence and even walked ahead of him, and this discourteous arrogant swagger infuriated the king and no doubt the queen as well.

4

Deposing the King of Folly

Edward III owed homage to his mother's cousin and Philippa's uncle Philip VI of France for his French territories. At noon on Friday, 26 May 1329, Edward departed from his kingdom and sailed to Wissant from Dover, leaving his twelve-year-old brother John of Eltham as nominal keeper of the realm. Philippa accompanied her husband through Kent before his departure, and in Canterbury Edward gave her a crown worth 200 marks.[1] On 6 June 1329 in the town of Amiens, in the presence of both kings' large retinues, Edward III knelt before Philip VI. The chamberlain of France (Sir Jean de Melun, viscount of Melun and lord of Tancarville) asked him if he became the liege man of the king of France in his capacity as duke of Aquitaine and as a peer of France. Edward answered simply, '*Voire*', 'Truly.' Philip took Edward's hands between his own and the two men kissed on the mouth to seal the ceremony. According to Froissart, three other kings were present in Amiens to meet Edward and to witness his homage ceremony: the king of Majorca, the king of Navarre, and the king of Bohemia.[2]

Queen Philippa remained in England and was soon reunited with her husband; Edward left France with what seems like undue haste, and was back in his kingdom on 10 June 1329 only four days after the homage ceremony. He held jousts at Canterbury, Dartford and Reigate that summer. During the Dartford tournament, the king had the good sense to dismount from an unruly horse that subsequently plunged headlong into the Thames, despite one of his knights trying to persuade him to remain on the animal as it would look bad for the king to change horses on the field. As he was dressed in heavy armour, the horse would have drowned him had he still been riding it.[3]

If anything had happened to the young king before he and Philippa conceived a child, Edward's brother John of Eltham, earl of Cornwall (who turned thirteen in August 1329) would have succeeded to the throne as King John II. This would have entrenched the dowager queen Isabella's power and considerably lengthened the period she would have been able to act as regent, and would have made Philippa's own position precarious and uncertain. She would, most likely, have been unceremoniously packed off back to her native Hainault once it had been ascertained that she was not pregnant, and her father would most probably have arranged another marriage for her. Days after his return to England in June 1329, Edward III sent men back to France to negotiate with Philip VI for his sister Eleanor of Woodstock (b. 1318) to marry Philip's eldest son, the future King John II of France (b. 1319) – a marriage first proposed by Philippa's grandfather Charles de Valois five and a half years previously – and for John of Eltham to marry Philip's daughter Marie. A few months earlier, Edward had sent men to Spain to negotiate a marriage for John of Eltham with Maria (b. *c.* 1318/20), daughter and heir of Juan *el Tuerto* or 'the one-eyed' (d. 1326), late lord of Biscay, and heir also of Juan's mother Maria Díaz de Haro (d. 1342), but none of these planned matches worked out and John was destined to die unmarried.[4]

Around mid or late September 1329, now probably about fifteen and a half years old – or just possibly, still only fourteen – Queen Philippa became pregnant. She and the king were in the west of England at the time; their child must have been conceived either in Gloucester, where Philippa's father-in-law Edward II was buried at St Peter's Abbey, or in Worcester. She and Edward III had spent 20 December 1328, the first anniversary of Edward II's funeral, in Gloucester, and now spent 21 September 1329, the second anniversary of Edward II's reported death at Berkeley Castle, also in Gloucester. Rumours had begun to circulate in England and Wales that Edward II was not dead at all, but alive and in captivity at Corfe Castle in Dorset. William Melton, archbishop of York, who had conducted Edward III and Philippa of Hainault's wedding in January 1328, was informed on 10 October 1329 that his friend the former king was alive. The archbishop sent a message to another devoted friend of Edward II: Donald, earl of Mar in Scotland, a nephew of King Robert Bruce, who had died a few months earlier. Donald of Mar promised to bring a huge army to England to secure Edward II's release, and Archbishop Melton was subsequently hauled before the court of King's Bench on a charge of treason, having invited a foreign army to England. Edmund of Woodstock, earl of Kent, the younger of Edward II's two half-brothers and thus Philippa's uncle-in-law, returned to England in early December 1329 after visiting John XXII in Avignon, supposedly (according to Kent's own testimony on the matter somewhat later) to inform the pope of Edward II's survival and to gain his support.

Philippa was present at a jousting tournament her husband held in Dunstable, Bedfordshire, on 20 October 1329, very soon after they conceived their first child. Almost certainly because of the young queen's pregnancy, the royal court spent the entire period from the end of October 1329 until the beginning of January 1330 at the castle of Kenilworth in Warwickshire (which belonged by right to Queen Isabella's out-of-favour uncle, Henry of Lancaster). This unusually long period spent at one castle, when it was the custom of the royal court to spend no more than a handful of days in one place, indicates that Philippa was tired, enduring a difficult first trimester, and perhaps suffering from sickness. The increasingly stressful situation she lived in – her mother-in-law and Roger Mortimer's stifling control of the English government, and now the awful possibility that her father-in-law was not dead after all and might be restored to his lost throne by powerful adherents – cannot have helped.

Edward III turned seventeen on 13 November 1329, about two months into Philippa's pregnancy. He must have been absolutely delighted at the news, though he was also living under great pressure. Edward's own attitude towards the notion that his father may not have been dead after all is difficult to ascertain, but he would never have been willing meekly to resign his throne to him. However much Edward III might have loved Edward II as a parent, he also knew what a disastrously inadequate ruler his father had been. Everyone knew that, but deposing a king and replacing him while he still lived had never previously happened in England, and plenty of people were deeply uncomfortable with the situation. There was still surprisingly widespread support for the former king across England and Wales. If it genuinely transpired that Edward II was not dead but hidden away somewhere, and that there had been a plot to keep him alive in secret while pretending to the kingdom at large – and perhaps even to Edward III himself – that he had died at Berkeley Castle in September 1327, influential men such as the earl of Kent, the archbishop of York and the mayor and bishop of London might demand the old king's restoration to the throne. The very real possibility of civil war reared its ugly head. And now the young queen was pregnant with the child who, if male, would become heir to the throne. The stakes could not have been higher.

Philippa of Hainault was finally given her first lands on 12 February 1330 a little over two years after her wedding, when she received the great lordship of Glamorgan in South Wales. It had been confiscated from Eleanor Despenser, niece of Edward II and widow of the executed royal favourite Hugh Despenser the Younger in late 1329, on the (rather peculiar and possibly fabricated) grounds that Eleanor had unlawfully removed jewels and other high-value items from the Tower of London. Eleanor, who had been abducted and forcibly married in early 1329 to her second husband William la Zouche, lord of Ashby in Leicestershire – yet another of the earl of Kent's adherents plotting the supposedly dead Edward II's release – was temporarily imprisoned at Devizes Castle in Wiltshire. Queen Philippa also received the Leicestershire manor of Loughborough, which had formerly belonged to Eleanor Despenser's executed father-in-law Hugh Despenser the Elder, earl of Winchester, and the enormous castle and town of Pontefract in Yorkshire. Pontefract should by right have gone to Henry, earl of Lancaster in 1327 as it had formerly been held by his brother Thomas, whose heir he was, but it was taken by his niece Queen Isabella. Isabella helped herself to Eleanor Despenser's manors of Tewkesbury (Gloucestershire) and Hanley (Worcestershire) in February 1330 as compensation for losing Pontefract to her daughter-in-law.[5]

Glamorgan was the first territory Philippa had ever held, but given her sense of fairness, the fact that it had been taken in very dubious circumstances from a noblewoman who was her husband's first cousin perhaps took some of the shine off the grant. Queen Isabella had come to England in 1326 supposedly to liberate the suffering people of England from the extortion and tyranny of Hugh Despenser the Younger, and now she and Roger Mortimer were behaving in remarkably similar ways. It was as though both of them were completely oblivious to what they were doing, and to what the consequences would be. Edward II and Despenser themselves had been equally blind.

It was scandalous that Philippa of Hainault was now pregnant with a child who, if male, would be the heir to the throne, but had not yet been crowned as queen of England, so her coronation was belatedly held at Westminster on 18 February 1330. The city of London contributed ten pounds, nineteen shillings and six pence to the cost of the coronation, and the money was paid out by the mayor, Simon Swanland.[6] (Although Edward III and his mother seem never to have discovered his involvement, Swanland was an important member of the ongoing conspiracy to free the former king, and was aiding the archbishop of York in the matter.) As Philippa was five months pregnant the ceremony was cut short so as not to tire her too much, though the young queen still took part in a long and splendid procession as she was led to the abbey between her husband's two uncles, the earls of Norfolk and Kent, who were riding palfreys. Both men, for some unexplained reason, were dressed as pages. As was the custom, Philippa stayed at the Tower of London the night before her coronation, and during her journey to the Tower wore a tunic of green velvet, very fine and expensive cloths of 'gold spinet' as her cloak, and furs of miniver – the extremely costly and luxurious white fur of the Baltic squirrel (given the date, 18 February, the weather was probably cold). On the day of her coronation she changed clothes no fewer than five times, and during the ceremony itself wore a lined tunic and a lined cloak of red and grey samite (silk interwoven with gold and silver threads). As Edward's biographer Ian Mortimer observed, Philippa's fabulously expensive clothes and astonishingly frequent changes of costume seem to have been done on purpose to make a point. Edward III and Philippa of Hainault later gained reputations for their incredible ostentation in dress, and this is an early example, during the period when Edward's mother was holding the purse strings and keeping the couple extremely short of money. In the early 1330s, as an example of her sartorial flamboyance, Philippa wore 'a hood made of brown scarlet [a type of rich cloth, not a colour] studded with 154 stars of pearls and trimmed with gold, each star being crafted out of seven large pearls with an especially large one at the top of each star' and 'a beaver-fur hat lined with velvet and adorned with white pearls and golden baboons'.[7] Not to be outdone, the dowager queen Isabella attended her daughter-in-law's coronation – she had stayed away from her son's two years before – and bought herself a new set of robes at her son's expense. The young couple retired to Windsor for several days after the ceremony, though even here they had no privacy from Roger Mortimer who insisted on accompanying them and, to rub salt into the wound, Edward lost at dice to his mother's powerful, overbearing and ubiquitous favourite.[8]

Finally, the young woman had been shown the respect she deserved, and officially crowned as queen. But unbeknown to Philippa, at her coronation her uncle-in-law Edmund of Woodstock, earl of Kent, was plotting secretly with his allies, and he met some of them at his manor of Kensington just before or afterwards.[9] The earl and his adherents made plans to free the former king Edward II from captivity at Corfe Castle in Dorset, where they had come to believe he was secretly being held years after his supposed death. William Melton, archbishop of York, was one of Kent's strongest supporters. As well as informing the Scottish earl of Mar of Edward II's survival, the archbishop sent a letter to his kinsman the mayor of London, Simon Swanland, informing him that Edward II was still alive and asking the mayor (a draper by profession) to provide clothes, shoes, belts, bags, cushions and other items for the supposedly dead former king. This letter, dated 13 January almost certainly in 1330, still exists, and is strong evidence that Edward II truly was alive more than two years after his funeral, or at the very least that a highly intelligent, educated and capable archbishop in his fifties had excellent reason to believe that he was. Hundreds of other men across England, Wales and Scotland believed the same thing.[10]

The earl of Kent was dramatically arrested at Winchester on 13 March 1330 during a parliament being held there. He confessed that he had been trying to free his half-brother, named many of his adherents, and claimed that Pope John XXII in Avignon was also supporting him in the matter. Kent, who was still only twenty-eight years old, was beheaded for treason in Winchester on 19 March, and his heavily pregnant widow Margaret Wake and their young children Joan and Edmund were imprisoned. Margaret gave birth to Kent's posthumous son, John, on 7 April; he would later marry Queen Philippa's niece.

What Philippa made of the earl of Kent's quick execution and his plot cannot be known. She was six months pregnant with the heir to the throne, and whatever affection she may have felt for the earl personally, any attempts to free Edward II and replace him on his lost throne would have been disastrous for her own position and status, and indeed extremely dangerous. Whether Edward II truly was still alive or not cannot be conclusively proved, but there is no doubt whatsoever that a sizeable group of influential men in 1329/30 acted as though they believed he was. A few years later an Italian nobleman and papal notary called Manuele Fieschi wrote a detailed letter to Edward III explaining how his father had escaped from Berkeley Castle in 1327 and ultimately made his way to a hermitage in Lombardy, Italy, via Corfe Castle in Dorset, Ireland, Avignon, Cologne and Milan. Peculiarly, there is much convincing evidence that Edward II died in 1327 but also much convincing evidence that he did not, and the truth of the matter may never be discovered. It may even be that Philippa herself was not sure whether her father-in-law was dead or not.

It must have been a frightening and stressful time for the young queen, and in the summer of 1330 some of the late earl of Kent's followers who had fled to the continent before and after Kent's execution plotted an invasion of England intended to bring down Isabella and Roger Mortimer. This planned invasion caused panic, and though ultimately it never took place, it reveals how deeply unpopular the ruling pair had become. Although the invasion was not aimed at Edward III personally but at his mother and Mortimer, a possible invasion of her husband's kingdom and the prospect of war must have been terrifying for the young Philippa. The number of the dowager queen Isabella's enemies on the continent grew ever larger. Even Roger Mortimer's first cousin Thomas, Lord Wake

(b. 1298), who had played a vital role in the downfall of Hugh Despenser the Younger and in Edward II's deposition in 1326/27, fled from England in 1330 before Mortimer could have him arrested. Many dozens of the late earl of Kent's followers who did not flee abroad were arrested and imprisoned, and their lands and goods were confiscated.

England, once again, seethed with unrest and rebellion as it had done for the last few years of Edward II's reign, and once again, a group of discontented rebels plotted the downfall of the regime. As Isabella and Roger Mortimer had done to Edward II and Hugh Despenser the Younger, their enemies were now doing to them. Mortimer used the lands and income of the late earl of Kent to benefit himself and his few remaining supporters, and strutted around as though he were the rightful king of England, dressed in 'wonder rich' clothes (as the *Brut* chronicle, written in Middle English, puts it). Mortimer was 'so full of pride' that people shook their heads and declared that 'his pride should not long endure.' His behaviour was by now so outrageous that even his own son Geoffrey Mortimer openly mocked him as the 'King of Folly'.[11]

Sometime before 10 May 1330, a messenger called Colard Maloysel travelled to England to bring Queen Philippa and Edward III the news that her sister Johanna had given birth. The king gave Maloysel twenty-five marks for the good tidings.[12] Johanna of Hainault and her husband Wilhelm of Jülich ultimately had half a dozen children: their elder son Gerhard became count of Berg and Ravensberg by right of his wife; a younger son, Wilhelm, his father's successor as duke of Jülich; and a daughter Elisabeth, in 1348 married Edmund of Woodstock's posthumous son and heir John, earl of Kent, and lived to a ripe old age in England, dying in 1411. Gerhard of Berg and Ravensberg would have been Wilhelm of Jülich's successor but died before his father, and was an ancestor of Louis XII of France (1462-1515) and of Henry VIII's fourth wife Anne of Cleves (1515-1557). Which one of the Jülich children was the infant born in 1330 is not clear; possibly Elisabeth, countess of Kent, or Richardis, countess of the Mark. Wilhelm of Jülich and Johanna of Hainault had become count and countess of Jülich in July 1328, six months after Philippa's wedding to Edward III, when his father Gerhard died, and Wilhelm's title would be upgraded to *Markgraf* ('margrave') in 1336 and upgraded again to duke in 1356.

Coincidentally, Philippa and Johanna's eldest sister Margaretha of Hainault, the Holy Roman Empress, also gave birth on 12 May 1330. It was her second son, another Wilhelm, a future duke of Lower Bavaria and count of Hainault and Holland, probably named in honour of his maternal grandfather Count Willem of Hainault. Empress Margaretha, not yet twenty years old in May 1330, had been married for six years and had already borne five children with another five to come (she bore her last in 1347, the year of her husband's death). Like his cousin Elisabeth of Jülich, Margaretha's son Wilhelm of Bavaria would also marry into England: in 1352, he wed Maud of Lancaster, a second cousin of Edward III and co-heir of the duke of Lancaster.

In Hainault, meanwhile, the delighted Jeanne de Valois, on hearing that her daughter in England and both her daughters in Germany were pregnant in 1330, declared that she 'may confidently hope that by the grace of the Almighty she will become the grandmother of kings.'[13]

Philippa and Edward III retired to the royal palace of Woodstock near Oxford at the end of March 1330. While there, the king spent the large sum of £240 on three coursers (horses) for himself, despite his embarrassing lack of money: Pomers, who was grey with a black head; Labryt, dappled with grey spots; and Bayard, a bright brown bay.[14] Even in the last few weeks of her first pregnancy, Queen Philippa had no escape from the constant presence of her mother-in-law Queen Isabella and Roger Mortimer, both of whom arrived at Woodstock at the end of March and remained there for the entire last trimester of Philippa's pregnancy.[15]

At Woodstock on Friday 15 June 1330, Queen Philippa gave birth to her first child. To the delight of herself, her husband and all his subjects (except perhaps Roger Mortimer), it was a boy, and he was named Edward after his father, grandfather and great-grandfather. Edward III had what he desperately needed, a son and heir, and now that he had secured the succession to his throne, he felt he could make a move against his mother and her favourite. His great-uncle Henry, earl of Lancaster, who had rarely been seen at court since the failure of his rebellion against Isabella and Mortimer at the end of 1328 and beginning of 1329, was at Woodstock on 8 June 1330 in anticipation of the birth. The earl granted an income of ten marks for life to Peter Eketon, the sergeant of the royal household who brought him news of the birth of Edward of Woodstock, the earl's great-great-nephew (as the great-grandson of Lancaster's older half-sister Jeanne I, d. 1305, queen-regnant of Navarre and queen-consort of France).[16] It is possible that the young king secretly took the earl's advice about ridding himself of Roger Mortimer, and that Henry offered his support.

Edward III himself gave an income of forty marks a year for life to his servant Thomas Prior 'for bringing the welcome news of the birth of Edward, the king's first-born son'.[17] As the king was also at Woodstock when his son was born, this was a generous amount to pay Prior for the simple task of walking from one part of the palace to another to tell him. Edward also promised to give the noblewoman Katherine Montacute née Grandisson, later countess of Salisbury and the wife of Edward's great friend Sir William Montacute, 500 marks 'for the welcome news'. Katherine finally received 200 marks of the payment five years later, and her closeness to the young queen is further revealed by her naming her third daughter Philippa; possibly the queen was the godmother of little Philippa Montacute, who was born sometime in the early or mid-1330s and later married Roger Mortimer's namesake grandson and heir (b. 1328).[18] Pope John XXII in Avignon in southern France had heard the news of Edward of Woodstock's birth by 19 July 1330, when he wrote to Philippa congratulating her.[19] The queen must also have sent messengers to her parents in Hainault and to her sisters Margaretha and Johanna in Germany with the joyous news of her child's birth.

Philippa and the king must have been absolutely overjoyed; Edward was still only seventeen and Philippa probably sixteen, and the young couple had already produced the future king of England. A household was set up for the little boy, and on 16 September the king assigned 500 marks a year for its expenses.[20] Edward II had made his son and heir earl of Chester in November 1312 when Edward of Windsor was only days old, and Edward III followed in his father's footsteps, granting his baby son the same earldom:

little Edward of Woodstock was referred to as 'earl of Chester' by January 1331.[21] Edward's nurse was called Joan of Oxford, and his rocker (the woman who rocked his cradle) Maud Plumpton.[22] Shortly after his son's birth, the king and his mother Isabella made a solemn pilgrimage to Gloucester and visited Edward II's tomb – whether they believed or knew he was in the tomb or not is a matter for speculation – and Edward III was back at Woodstock in time to attend Philippa's purification, a ceremony held forty days after childbirth. During this ceremony, Philippa wore purple or violet velvet robes embroidered with golden squirrels and furred with ermine and miniver, which, given that it was the middle of summer, must have been excessively hot.[23] Rather charmingly, the queen's accounts record the costs of repairing an embroidered bedspread in her chambers on the day of her purification after Edward of Woodstock's birth, because it had been torn and chewed by dogs.[24] It sounds as though Philippa was looking after a litter of puppies, who had perhaps been a gift to her from her husband.

Philippa was surely aware that a few weeks after her purification, in September 1330, her mother Jeanne de Valois, countess of Hainault and Holland, visited Paris and the court of her brother Philip VI, with whom she appears to have been very close. Jeanne ended up staying at the French court for seven months before returning to her husband's lands in April 1331, just months before she travelled to visit Philippa in England.[25] Countess Jeanne seems to have been very fond of her natal family and to have spent much time in her native France, and she was hugely popular in her husband's domains: one chronicler states that whenever Jeanne returned to the county of Holland from a visit to her daughter Johanna in Jülich, the whole population looked forward to her arrival and there was a festive atmosphere.[26]

On 19 October 1330, four months after the birth of his son, Edward III finally took action against his mother and Roger Mortimer, self-appointed earl of March. The king and a group of twenty or so young knights he knew to be completely loyal to him crept along a secret tunnel into Nottingham Castle and burst into the dowager queen's chambers, where they arrested the earl of March despite Isabella's screams to her son to 'have pity on gentle Mortimer' ('gentle' meaning that he was of noble birth, not a statement on his character). Mortimer was not in bed with Queen Isabella or in a private chamber alone with her, as sometimes assumed, but was holding a meeting with her and their few remaining allies, including his son Geoffrey Mortimer, the bishop of Lincoln, Henry Burghersh, and the knights Oliver Ingham and Hugh Turplington (the latter was killed defending Roger). Geoffrey Mortimer and Sir Oliver Ingham were also arrested but were soon freed, while the bishop of Lincoln, humiliatingly, had to be rescued after he tried to escape down a latrine shaft. The young king was persuaded by his great-uncle Henry, earl of Lancaster not to execute Roger Mortimer on the spot, and the royal favourite was taken to the Tower of London and walled up there for a few weeks until his trial before parliament. It is possible, indeed likely, that Henry of Lancaster played a greater role in the downfall of Isabella and Roger Mortimer than is visible from extant records, and certainly Edward III knew the wealthy earl was present at Nottingham with plenty of manpower to assist after his coup.

As for Queen Philippa, it is not clear whether she was at Nottingham when her mother-in-law and the endlessly overbearing earl of March were removed from power, but it is hard to imagine that she was anything but delighted about it. For the feast of All Saints on 1 November, less than two weeks after Isabella and Mortimer's downfall, Philippa sent agents to the great fairs of Boston and St Ives to purchase large quantities of fine Flemish and Italian cloth. At the feast the young queen wore expensive green Italian silk decorated with griffins' heads.[27] After years of penury enforced by her mother-in-law and Isabella's infantilisation of her and Edward, Philippa was determined to be a queen at long last, and to be seen to be a queen. In 1331, she had four crowns studded with rubies, emeralds and diamonds, and at the beginning of that year she spent over twenty-two pounds on a series of brooches, including two made of gold with diamonds and pearls.[28]

Pope John XXII in Avignon wrote to Philippa on 7 November 1330, asking her 'to insist with the king that in consideration of what his mother has done and suffered for him, his goodwill towards her should be restored.' The pope, deeply concerned about Queen Isabella in the aftermath of the king's coup, also wrote directly to Edward III expressing his discomfort that the king was failing to show signs of filial affection towards the dowager queen who had done so much for her son, and in fact he was so concerned about Isabella that he sent Edward a duplicate of this letter in case the first went astray. He begged the king to show mercy to Isabella so that he himself might find mercy on the day of judgement. John XXII, however, sent Edward yet another letter almost immediately afterwards, stating that he had been informed that he was now 'behaving with humanity and reverence to his mother'. Apparently somewhat troubled by events in England, John talked of 'the whirlwind excited in the realm' and of the way the king had, 'about the middle of the night, suddenly seized some princes and nobles of the realm, and imprisoned them'. The tone of the pope's letters to the young king and queen of England sounds as though he strongly disapproved of Edward's coup against his mother and Mortimer, and he sent yet more letters to Isabella's uncle, Henry of Lancaster, Edward's friend William Montacute, Simon Meopham, archbishop of Canterbury (d. 1333) and the bishop of Winchester (John Stratford, Meopham's successor as archbishop in 1333), requesting them to 'incline the king to clemency' towards those arrested.[29] On the other hand, John had kept faith with Edward, and never told Isabella that he and her son had devised a system whereby John would know whether letters sent in Edward's name were written by the king himself, or by Isabella or someone acting on her behalf.

The pope certainly believed that the young Queen Philippa had enough influence over her husband to be able to persuade him to treat his mother with kindness and clemency, and it was perhaps at the urging of Philippa and others, such as Henry of Lancaster and the king's close friend William Montacute, that Edward III treated his mother more leniently than he may have originally wished or intended to. His attitude towards the regime which had ruled his kingdom for the previous four years is apparent in the proclamation he ordered all the sheriffs of England to make on 4 November 1330, which referred to the 'oppressions, hardships or other grievances' caused to his subjects, and his anger about the way his mother and Mortimer had treated him during his minority is equally apparent in his statement that he had been 'like a man living in custody'.[30] Edward III's feelings about his mother Isabella may also be revealed in his statement eighteen years later in 1348 when founding a chapel dedicated to Saint Stephen at Westminster, when he referred to the Virgin Mary as a 'better mother'.[31] This may simply have been a statement on the king's veneration of the Virgin and not intended as a swipe at Isabella, but was still a rather remarkable comment to make in public.

Roger Mortimer, lord of Wigmore and first earl of March, was tried before parliament and hanged at Tyburn near London on 29 November 1330 on fourteen charges of appropriating royal power and of having the king's father killed. His ally Sir Simon Bereford was executed a few weeks later – somewhat mysteriously, as his role in the events of the previous few years is obscure – but no-one else suffered the ultimate penalty. Edward III left Mortimer's wife Joan née Geneville (Roger and Joan had been married for almost thirty years and had had a dozen children together) alone, and specifically ordered his men not to touch any of her belongings when they went to seize Mortimer's.[32] Having easily triumphed over his enemy, the young king showed a willingness to begin a new chapter and to forgive and forget the turbulent years of his father's reign and his mother's regime. All the men who had taken part in the earl of Kent's plot to free Edward II a few months previously were pardoned, restored to their lands and goods and invited back to England or released from prison, and the earl of Kent's infant son Edmund was restored to his rightful inheritance (the boy died in 1331, leaving his younger brother John as the Kent heir). The teenaged Richard Fitzalan, whose father the earl of Arundel had been unlawfully executed by Roger Mortimer and Queen Isabella in November 1326 for no better reason than Mortimer's hatred of him, was also restored to his rightful inheritance. Hugh Despenser the Younger's eldest son and heir Hugh, born in 1308 or 1309, was released from prison in July 1331 and was allowed to make a career in the retinues of the king and his younger brother John of Eltham, and Despenser and his younger brothers and nephews spent decades patiently restoring the family's fortunes.

Henry, earl of Lancaster and his followers were also forgiven for Lancaster's rebellion against Mortimer and Isabella in late 1328 and 1329, and were pardoned the massive debts they had been forced to acknowledge to the Crown in its aftermath. Edward III even wrote to the pope and the cardinals on several occasions promoting the canonisation of Henry's elder brother Thomas, executed by his cousin Edward II in 1322 – almost certainly not because Edward III believed that Thomas truly was a saint, but as a sign that the Lancasters had regained royal favour. For the rest of his reign, Edward III would demonstrate his lack of vindictiveness and his unwillingness to heap the sins of the father on the head of the son.

In later years he also restored the Mortimer family to royal grace, and would arrange the marriage of Roger Mortimer's great-grandson and heir Edmund (b. 1352) to his and Philippa's eldest granddaughter, an act which was to bring the Mortimers close to the throne in the late fourteenth century. As for the king's father Edward II, Edward III claimed at the parliament held in late 1330 that his father had been murdered, and accused a Somerset knight called Thomas Gurney (who had ridden to Lincoln in September 1327 to inform him of his father's death) and a man-at-arms called William Ockley of the deed. Both men were sentenced to death in absentia, but fled and were not executed. Whether Edward III really knew or believed that his father was dead cannot be known for sure, but accusing Roger Mortimer and other men of the murder of the former king sent out a strong message to his subjects that Edward II truly was dead, and would not come back to claim his throne.

The dowager queen Isabella was made to give up her appropriated lands and the absurdly high income of £13,333 she had awarded herself in 1327, immediately after the Nottingham coup. Her son allowed her a much more reasonable £3,000 a year, and later raised the amount to £4,500, the same sum she had received during her husband's reign. In public, at least, the dowager queen was presented as Roger Mortimer's victim, and all the ills and woes of the previous four years were heaped on Mortimer's head rather than hers. Isabella spent Christmas 1330 at Guildford in Surrey with her son, daughter-in-law and baby grandson Edward of Woodstock, and the king sent four men to the dowager queen's castle of Berkhamsted to bring her to him. Two of the men were his first cousins Edward and William de Bohun, who had helped him arrest Roger Mortimer at Nottingham, and a third was Mortimer's first cousin Thomas, Lord Wake, who had fled from England a few months previously after plotting with the earl of Kent against Mortimer and Isabella, and whom he had just pardoned and invited to return. The young king, therefore, seemingly made little attempt to spare his mother's feelings.[33]

Isabella of France was still only thirty-five years old at the end of 1330, and was to live for another twenty-eight years. Contrary to popular modern belief, she was not imprisoned at Castle Rising in Norfolk or forced into a nunnery, but lived a perfectly conventional life as a dowager queen for the best part of three decades, travelling round her estates, spending large sums of money on clothes and jewels, and entertaining numerous guests. By the early 1340s, after he had claimed the throne of France, Edward III began to show more public respect to his mother and began to visit her more often, and in the 1350s Isabella was, near the end of her long life, finally allowed once more to enjoy some measure of political influence.[34]

Although it is sometimes stated that the dowager queen had a breakdown or was seriously ill after Roger Mortimer's execution, there is no real evidence of this, although there are records of several payments to apothecaries after her downfall. Isabella did, however, spend a couple of years after her fall in seclusion, at her own manor of Berkhamsted and at Windsor. Whatever Edward III might have felt about his mother personally, she was royal and a crowned and anointed queen, and, importantly, she transmitted a strong claim to the French throne to him as the sole surviving child of Philip IV. It was therefore entirely in his own interests not to treat her too harshly, though one of Edward's biographers believes that the young king is unlikely to have had an affectionate relationship with his mother however much respect he might have accorded her in public, and 'could never quite free himself from the embarrassment of his parents'.[35] In the end, Philippa of Hainault only outlived her mother-in-law by eleven years and for the first thirty of the forty-one years of her married life Philippa was not the only queen in the country.

Shortly before Christmas 1330, Edward gave Philippa his houses at 'La Reol' in London to use for her wardrobe.[36] The first festive season which the young king spent in control of his own realm proved to be enormous fun, with indoor games and lots of jousting, and perhaps the royal couple were entertained by the elderly minstrel Robert 'the Fool'. He had often performed for Edward III's father and even for the young king's grandmother, Leonor of Castile, Edward I's first queen, who had died as far back as 1290, but was still in Edward III's retinue in the early years of his reign.[37] Other minstrels who performed for the royal couple at Christmas 1330 included Roger and Giles the trumpeters, Thomas the citole-player, John the harper and two named Mauprine and Cleys. Minstrels who were specifically said to be in the queen's household were John the psaltery player and Merlin the violist. Some years later Philippa also employed John de Mees of Lorraine and Peter of Burgundy as her court minstrels, and in the early 1360s a *giterner* or gittern-player (a stringed instrument) called Andrew Destrer of Bruges was a member of her household. Edward III himself retained about twelve to fifteen pipers, trumpeters and drummers as part of the royal household.[38] Philippa received some confiscated goods at Christmas 1330 which had belonged to the executed Roger Mortimer, including a *celure* (a canopy which hung over a bed or seat) of a fine rich material called sindon and 'powdered with black roses'. Suspending a cloth over one's head was a sign of honour and high status. Philippa also received twenty-four rugs that had belonged to the executed Mortimer.[39]

In late 1330, Edward III and Philippa of Hainault became the rightful king and queen of England at last, and Philippa could begin to enjoy the influence, wealth and patronage of which she had been deprived by her mother-in-law for almost three years. The future looked bright for the two teenagers, and for the realm which Edward III now began to govern in person.

Queen at Last

Just after Christmas 1330, Edward III granted Philippa the annual dower of £3,000 he had promised to provide at the time of their marriage and generously added another £1,000 on top, also annually. This income would come from her lands and the young queen was given, among many others, the manors of Isleworth, Stratfield Mortimer and Soham, the city and castle of Bristol, the town and castle of Knaresborough in Yorkshire, the towns and castles of Devizes and Marlborough in Wiltshire, and the royal Essex manor of Havering-atte-Bower. She was also allowed to keep the castle and town of Pontefract in Yorkshire, which by right should have belonged to the king's great-uncle Henry of Lancaster.

Philippa was now one of the wealthiest landowners in the country, though even her vast income proved to be 'not sufficient to maintain her household and for the expenses of her chamber' and was supplemented by a payment of 500 marks (£333) from the Exchequer in March 1333, a sum which 'the queen believes will meet the deficiency.' It did not, and in February 1334 she was granted another £200 annually.[1] Extravagant and incapable of living within her means, Philippa was given yet more grants from the Exchequer in January and February 1335 because her dower had 'proved inadequate to meet the expenses of her household' and because of the 'heavy charges she has to meet daily'.

The chancery rolls of the early to mid-1330s are full of references to Philippa being given £1,000 here, £500 there, another £2,000 here to pay off her debts, none of which ever seemed to suffice.[2]

She also borrowed large sums of money from the Italian banking firm the Bardi of Florence, and by January 1338 owed them more than £4,500 (in modern terms, this is a few million).[3] For the rest of her life Philippa demonstrated a complete inability to budget and economise and not to outspend her income, and was notoriously extravagant even by the standards of fourteenth-century royalty; though in fairness, the negligence and inefficiency of some of her officials compounded the problem. Over the years she received more grants of lands and money until she enjoyed an income of more than £7,000 a year, and even this was not enough. This was one thing, at least, she had in common with her mother-in-law Isabella, and as had happened with the dowager queen between 1327 and 1330, all the grants of money and loans made to Philippa merely fell into the bottomless pit of her debts. After Isabella had deliberately kept Philippa and Edward short of money for years, they both abandoned all fiscal checks and balances, though as Mark Ormrod has pointed out, much of Queen Philippa's excessive expenditure was used in the cause of supporting her husband's vision of courtly splendour, so perhaps she should not be blamed altogether for it.[4] Philippa was also a generous giver to charity and good causes, and the couple's large brood of children also necessitated great expense.

The household of Philippa's son Edward of Woodstock was attached to hers in 1331, and by 25 February 1331 she also had the official care of her twelve-year-old sister-in-law Eleanor of Woodstock, born in June 1318 and the elder daughter of Edward II and Isabella of France (Joan of the Tower, Edward III's other sister, had gone to live in Scotland in 1328 when she was only seven). A petition presented to Edward III and his council on Philippa's behalf sometime in the early 1330s pointed out that the lands granted to Philippa did not come close to giving her the income she had been promised and that she could not 'support the expenses of her household', a common theme which would arise again and again throughout Philippa's life, and especially in the early 1330s given that she had to look after her sister-in-law (called *madame dame Elianore*, 'my lady, Lady Eleanor') as well. According to the petition, Philippa could not even afford to buy food and clothes for herself and her household for the coming Christmas, and she was given fifty pounds for Eleanor of Woodstock's expenses.[5] To support the households of her son and her sister-in-law, Philippa was also granted 'the issues of the county of Chester'. By 6 March 1334, her second and third children, Isabella and Joan, were 'dwelling with her' as well, and she was given permission to 'order the household of the said earl [of Chester, her son Edward], Isabella and Joan at her will'.[6]

Philippa surrendered the lordship of Glamorgan given to her in February 1330 to her husband after her mother-in-law's downfall, and it was restored to its rightful owner Eleanor Despenser and her second husband William la Zouche on 8 January 1331.[7] Sometime shortly before her surrender of Glamorgan, evidently aware that she would have to give up the lordship as it had been seized unfairly, the canny young queen asked that before the lordship was handed over to Eleanor Despenser, she herself should receive surety that all debts owed to her from the few months of her possession of Glamorgan should be paid to her. In the same petition, she asked to retain possession of the county of Cheshire to maintain her son, which was duly granted, and to be given custody of the son and heir of the late Edmund of Woodstock, earl of Kent, executed in March 1330.[8] Kent's elder son Edmund died later in 1331, still only a young child, and therefore the earl's heir was his second son John, born on 7 April 1330 nineteen days after his father's execution. Edmund, earl of Kent also left a daughter, Joan of Kent, a much younger first cousin of the king, born in September 1326 or September 1327. Joan would, decades later, marry Philippa's eldest son.

In January 1331, Edward III sent envoys to France to discuss the 'mutual debts of the two kings' and 'all matters in dispute' with his mother's first cousin and his wife's uncle King Philip VI.[9] One of the men was his great-uncle Henry, earl of Lancaster and Leicester, firmly restored to royal favour after the removal of the dowager queen and the earl of March. Another envoy was Willem, count of Hainault and Holland, who was both Edward III's father-in-law and Philip VI's brother-in-law, and hence a very useful mediator.[10]

The young king himself secretly left England on 4 April dressed as a merchant and with only a small retinue, who included Henry of Lancaster's son and heir Henry of Grosmont (born *c.* 1310/12), and met Philip VI at Pont-Sainte-Maxence. The homage Edward had sworn in 1329 in his capacity as duke of Aquitaine and count of Ponthieu was deemed unsatisfactory in some way, and had to be repeated. The queen remained in England while her husband travelled to France again. On 15 April 1331 she was at Sturry in Kent, a manor belonging to the archbishop of Canterbury, where she made a payment to John the violist and his companions, who had performed for her a few days previously 'before the image of the Blessed Mary in the vault of Christ Church, Canterbury'.[11]

In the early 1330s, what comes across strongly is that Queen Philippa and Edward III were a happy young couple thoroughly enjoying themselves, and enthusiastically participating in different kinds of entertainment. Both of them owned chess sets and played chequers, and Philippa, as she generally did, ran up huge debts while gaming. Christmas at Edward's court especially was always a time of lavish festivities, masques, feasts and games. Hunting and falconry were traditional activities loved by the fourteenth-century nobility and royalty, and Edward III, somewhat unusually, also took up fishing in the 1340s.[12] Edward II had done the same in 1324/25 and perhaps in other years too, one of the few things Edward III had in common with his father.[13] Queen Philippa had grown up playing dice, board games and games of chance, and had plenty of opportunity to indulge in them in England as well. She possessed her own chess and chequers sets.[14] Musicians and other performers such as conjurors and acrobats were constantly in attendance at the royal court in the fourteenth century.

Both Edward and Philippa were conventionally devout, and Edward III inherited a large collection of holy relics from his father, his grandfather Edward I, and his mother Isabella when she died in 1358. Among many others, he owned a thorn from the Crown of Thorns, a fragment of the True Cross, the blood of St George, the blood and hair of St Stephen, a ring of St Dunstan, and the head of one of the eleven thousand virgins. All these precious items were kept under lock and key at the Tower of London.[15] Sometime before early 1336 Queen Philippa appears to have made a vow to go on pilgrimage to the Holy Land, to Rome, and to Santiago de Compostela. The pope gave permission for her confessor to commute the vows as the queen could not 'conveniently observe' them, though she was held to other vows of 'continence and chastity' which she had taken.[16] Philippa was also given papal permission to eat meat on days of fasting and abstinence, 'on the advice of her physician'. This may indicate that Philippa struggled with religious limitations on food during her many pregnancies or perhaps when she was menstruating, or may even indicate that she suffered from low blood sugar and that the problem was severe enough that she and her physician sought papal intervention.

Jeanne de Valois, countess of Hainault, and her son-in-law and her second daughter Wilhelm and Johanna, count and countess of Jülich, visited Philippa and Edward III in England in the late summer and early autumn of 1331. The king ordered eighty tuns of wine to be provided for the use of his mother-in-law and her household while they were in England, and gave £200 to William de Coleby, treasurer of Queen Philippa's household, for Jeanne's expenses in England.[17] Edward was adamant that his and Philippa's little son Edward of Woodstock would be well dressed to meet his grandmother, aunt and uncle, and purchased expensive cloth for him, and Philippa must have been delighted and proud to show off her son to her mother and her sister.

The summer of 1331 saw a great round of jousting tournaments held at Stepney, Cheapside, Dartford, Bedford and Havering, which the countesses of Hainault and Jülich must have attended in Philippa's company. In the procession before the tournament at Cheapside, which according to the *Anonimalle* chronicle was held between the cross at Cheapside and Soper Lane, each participant was accompanied by a noble lady wearing a red tunic and a simple white cap and led out by a silver chain. Edward III himself led out his sister Eleanor of Woodstock, who turned thirteen in June 1331. In pairs, a knight and his lady with her silver chain, they rode down Cheapside at Vespers (sunset) through cheering crowds. The knights wore masks and green tunics and cloaks lined with red and with red hoods; they were said to be 'dressed and masked like Tartars'. Behind them came over fifty squires, also masked, wearing white tunics with the right sleeves of green cloth embroidered with golden arrows. Twenty-six knights participated in the Stepney tournament, and the king and many of the great magnates led them through the city of London before it began.[18]

The entire summer of 1331 sounds like one joyous round of parties and fun, and must have been a great spectacle for a nation long starved of such splendid theatre during the troubled reign of the previous king and its aftermath. The king's father had banned jousting tournaments for most of his reign (though several famous ones took place in 1308 and 1309) as they provided a cover for armed men to assemble in large numbers and were thus considered too dangerous to permit to take place, and it was a long time since most knights had been allowed to participate in one or the general public had been able to watch them.

It was the first summer that Edward III spent in control of his own kingdom and when Philippa was accorded her rightful position as queen, and the young couple made the most of it. Tragedy almost struck, however, when the balcony or grandstand at the Cheapside tournament, stretching along the street, collapsed after dinner on the first day, and the young queen and other ladies – perhaps including her mother Jeanne and sister Johanna, and certainly her sister-in-law Eleanor of Woodstock – narrowly escaped with their lives. Some ladies and knights were seriously injured, and Philippa must have been badly shaken. The *Anonimalle* states that she and Eleanor of Woodstock were, by the grace of God, unhurt, but that Philippa's coronet came off her head and was damaged.[19] Despite her shock and despite the danger to her life, the queen interceded with her husband on behalf of the negligent carpenters who had constructed the grandstand, a typical example of the compassion, kindness, concern for others and instinctive mercy which Philippa would demonstrate throughout her life. Edward III listened to his wife and 'had peace and love proclaimed everywhere', and asked the queen to mount her palfrey and to ride up and down the lists, comforting the frightened and alarmed spectators. Philippa's reassurances calmed the situation down to the extent that overnight the grandstand was repaired and the tournament continued the next day. Philippa, presumably with her mother and sister, stayed in the home of Nicholas Farndon (d. 1334), an alderman, former mayor of London and a wealthy merchant, on Wodestret (Wood Street) during the tournament.[20]

Henry of Grosmont, only son and heir of Edward III's great-uncle Henry, earl of Lancaster and Leicester, and a man very close in age to the king, took part in the great tournaments of 1331, and several of his six sisters were among the spectators.[21] His father was now fifty years old and, according to two chroniclers, went blind sometime during or after 1330. Although Henry lived until 1345 when he was in his mid-sixties, he was unable to play much of a role in politics after the early 1330s, his visit to France in early 1331 being the last known occasion when he was able to travel abroad. Grosmont began to act in his father's stead. He had married Isabella Beaumont, second daughter of the French-born nobleman Henry, Lord Beaumont and his Scottish wife Alice Comyn, in the summer of 1330, and Blanche, the younger of Henry of Grosmont and Isabella Beaumont's two daughters, was to marry Philippa of Hainault's third son John of Gaunt. Henry of Grosmont was the epitome of fourteenth-century chivalry, an intelligent, thoughtful man, one of the greatest English military leaders of the century, and always a close ally and supporter of his cousin Edward III. Queen Philippa must have been hugely fond of him, as her husband certainly was. Other men close to the king in the 1330s were Sir William Montacute, probably the king's closest friend despite an age gap of almost a dozen years, the twins William and Edward de Bohun, who were sons of Edward II's sister Elizabeth and thus Edward III's first cousins, and the young knights Robert Ufford, William Clinton, John Neville and Ralph Stafford. William Montacute arranged and paid for the 1331 tournament of Cheapside, and Sir Robert Morley arranged the Stepney one, which was held just after Edward of Woodstock's first birthday.

The seventeen-year-old Queen Philippa attended a wedding in Lincolnshire on or a little before 14 July 1331, a wedding she had most probably arranged herself: her damsel Helen or Elena married Robert Maule or Mauley, and the queen gave twenty-six shillings and eight pence to her minstrel Mauprine and his unnamed companions who entertained the guests. The king and queen were in the city of Lincoln on 22 July, and Philippa paid five pence each to two female minstrels, Cecilia and Isabella Gerlond, who danced and performed acrobatics for her (they were called *saltatrices* or 'tumblers'). While Philippa and Edward were staying at Rockingham Castle, Northamptonshire on 23 August, two German minstrels, both called Hanekin, came to perform for them. One Hanekin came from Bavaria and the other was called 'Hanekin of Cologne', though he worked mostly in Hanover, and they were said to have travelled to England at the queen's behest. They had probably been recommended to her by one of her sisters Margaretha or Johanna, both resident in Germany. Hanekin of Cologne, a violist, was still in England on 22 October 1331. At Windsor, Hanekin gave the queen a present of a saddle, and she gave him a present of four pence in return – none too generous, given that the saddle must have cost Hanekin a good few shillings. Merlin the violist, named as a member of the queen's household in 1330, was also with Philippa and Edward at Rockingham Castle that August.[22]

Philippa became pregnant with her second child around September 1331, fifteen months after Edward of Woodstock's birth, probably while her mother Jeanne and sister Johanna were still in England and perhaps during the great tournament of Cheapside, which took place from 22 to 25 September after the king and queen returned to London from their journeys around Lincolnshire and Nottinghamshire. Countess Johanna also became pregnant at around the same time or a little earlier, perhaps while she and Wilhelm of Jülich were visiting England; Johanna announced the birth of a child sometime in the spring of 1332 or a little afterwards.[23] Edward III knew his wife was expecting on 30 November 1331, when he told the sheriff of Wiltshire to prepare the royal palace of Clarendon for the arrival of 'our dearest consort, who is pregnant'.[24]

Also in late November 1331, Edward III sent more men to 'treat with Philip, king of France, or his deputies, touching a journey to the Holy Land and other matters relating to that land'. At the same time, he told the envoys to negotiate a future marriage between his and Philippa's infant son Edward of Woodstock and Philip's daughter Jeanne.[25] Edward's children and Philip's children were very closely related, first cousins once removed, and the planned weddings never took place (though Edward of Woodstock ultimately ended up marrying a woman who was also his first cousin once removed).

The royal couple were together at Windsor Castle, Edward III's birthplace, in mid-November 1331 – including his nineteenth birthday, 13 November – and Edward left Philippa there for a few days while he travelled around other manors. On 17 November, Philippa gave her damsel Amie Gaveston various rents in the royal Essex manor of Havering-atte-Bower, one of the many manors the queen had been granted.[26] Presumably the queen was aware that Amie was the illegitimate daughter of the notorious Piers Gaveston, earl of Cornwall, the beloved companion and probably the lover of her husband's father Edward II. Gaveston had been murdered by some of the former king's disgruntled magnates in June 1312, when Queen Isabella was four months pregnant with Edward III.

Philippa and Edward spent Christmas 1331 at Wells in Somerset, and Philippa gave her husband a splendid gift at the beginning of 1332: a silver goblet enamelled with castles, ships and beasts on the outside and a great castle on the base of the inside, and a silver ewer enamelled with figures such as Julius Caesar, Charlemagne, Judas Maccabeus, and various figures from Arthurian legend including Lancelot and Arthur himself.[27] It was the custom at the royal English court in the fourteenth century to give and exchange gifts on 1 January, the Feast of the Circumcision, and Edward III gave Philippa an expensive sapphire set in a gold brooch.[28]

The queen cannot have met her father's older sister Alix or Alicia of Hainault, who moved to England in 1290 when she married Roger Bigod, earl of Norfolk (d. 1306) and died in 1317 when Philippa was probably only three years old, but evidently she knew exactly who Alix was. When she was about six months pregnant with her second child in March 1332, Philippa founded a chantry with three chaplains in Suffolk to celebrate divine service daily for Countess Alix's soul.[29]

In early May 1332, a few weeks before the queen was due to give birth to her second child, her sister-in-law Eleanor of Woodstock set off for Nijmegen for her wedding to Reynald II, count and later duke of Guelders (a territory nowadays in the Netherlands close to the German border). Reynald, with his father Count Reynald I (d. 1326), had been among the noblemen who witnessed the agreement between Philippa's father Willem of Hainault and Gerhard of Jülich for the marriage of their children Johanna and Wilhelm in 1317. Eleanor of Woodstock was accompanied to Nijmegen by a large retinue including her first cousins the de

Bohun twins Edward and William, Eleanor Despenser née de Clare, and Eleanor Despenser's second husband William la Zouche, and her eldest son Hugh 'Huchon' Despenser. Queen Philippa's squire Pamettus de Recte was another of those who accompanied Eleanor of Woodstock on her journey to Nijmegen.[30] Eleanor and her retinue arrived at the port of Sluis in the county of Flanders on 6 May and made their way to Nijmegen, where her wedding to the decades-older Count Reynald took place in late May 1332. As well as her noble attendants, Eleanor was accompanied by a crowd of minstrels: four women were paid in the port of Sluis for 'singing in the presence of the Lady Alianora' shortly after her arrival on the continent, a bagpiper performed for her, groups of minstrels danced for her on two occasions, and four minstrels came from as far away as Aragon in Spain.[31]

Peculiarly, according to the Fieschi Letter written to Eleanor's brother Edward III a few years later, Eleanor's supposedly dead father Edward II had also arrived at the port of Sluis sometime after late 1330, having left Ireland after the execution of Roger Mortimer. If this story is in any way true, it is not impossible that Edward II was in the same area of the continent around the same time as his daughter. The Fieschi Letter says that Edward II travelled from Sluis to Avignon to visit Pope John XXII, then travelled back up through France to the duchy of Brabant, where his nephew Jan III ruled and his sister Margaret the dowager duchess was still alive, and subsequently went on to the German city of Cologne. Supposedly he worshipped at the shrine of the Three Kings in Cologne, and one of Eleanor of Woodstock's attendants, William of Cornwall, made the same journey in May 1332.[32]

Eleanor of Woodstock was still three weeks short of her fourteenth birthday when she married Reynald, and her brother the king had arranged her marriage to the count in February 1332. Various abbeys and priories around England paid contributions towards the expenses of the wedding.[33] Reynald of Guelders was born around 1290 or 1295 and was thus not much younger than her father Edward II, and was a widower with four daughters. Eleanor's father had betrothed her to King Alfonso XI of Castile in 1324/25, but this did not work out, and in 1330 Edward III's government negotiated further possible matches for her with the future King John II of France (b. 1319) and secondly with the future King Pedro IV of Aragon (b. 1319), but these alliances also came to nothing.[34]

Eleanor of Woodstock should have been a queen in Spain or France and now was marrying a mere count in the Low Countries, a man who was decades older than her, and their marriage would prove to be an unhappy one; Reynald would allegedly try to repudiate Eleanor on the false grounds that she had leprosy. She gave birth to their first son, named Reynald after his father, a year after her wedding and before she turned fifteen, and her second, named Eduard after her own father, three years later. Eleanor had lived in her sister-in-law Philippa of Hainault's household since at least October 1330 when her mother Isabella fell from power, perhaps well before, and the two young women must have come to know each other very well. Philippa of Hainault was far luckier and far happier in her married life than her two English sisters-in-law Eleanor of Woodstock and Joan of the Tower, wife of King David II of Scotland, both of whom endured unhappy marriages.

Not long after Countess Eleanor's departure from England, sometime in May or June 1332 Queen Philippa and Edward III's second child and eldest daughter was born at the palace of Woodstock near Oxford, and was named after her paternal grandmother Isabella of France.[35] The child may have been a little premature and arrived unexpectedly, as the king had intended her to be born at the royal palace of Clarendon in Wiltshire, eighty miles from Woodstock.[36] Calling their daughter 'Isabella' does not signify anything important about Edward and Philippa's relationship with his mother or indicate that they were making a conscious effort to rehabilitate the dowager queen and her reputation. It was entirely conventional in the fourteenth century to name the first daughter after her paternal grandmother and the second daughter after the maternal grandmother, as Edward and Philippa did a couple of years later when they called their second daughter Joan after Jeanne de Valois. It says nothing about people's feelings or their personal relationships with their parents. Edward and Philippa also followed convention with their eldest two sons' names: their first son was Edward after Edward II, and their second was William of Hatfield, after his maternal grandfather Willem, count of Hainault.

There is no doubt at all that Philippa of Hainault had deep maternal instincts, and she and Edward III created remarkably close relationships with their children. They had seven sons, of whom five survived to adulthood, and the king remained on close and affectionate terms with all of them throughout his life. Given the frequent pattern of hostility and rebellion on the part of royal sons towards their fathers throughout the Middle Ages, for Edward III to retain the love and loyalty of all his sons until he died was a real achievement which should not be underestimated, and Philippa of Hainault was to a great extent responsible for the forging of affectionate ties between her husband and their children. (The often-repeated story, however, that Philippa eschewed the use of wet-nurses and breastfed her children herself is, however, untrue.)[37] Edward III adored his eldest daughter Isabella of Woodstock and was remarkably indulgent towards her, and a sad letter he sent to King Alfonso XI of Castile after his and Philippa's second daughter Joan died in her early teens on her way to marry Alfonso's son in 1348 leaves no doubt whatsoever as to the depth of his love for her. He also obviously adored his eldest son Edward of Woodstock, and – as with his eldest daughter Isabella – allowed him to remain unmarried until he was over thirty. He did not force either of his two eldest children into marriages. In an age when royal children were often betrothed in the cradle, married wherever it was convenient for their father's foreign policy and had little if any say in the selection of their spouses, the king's behaviour was truly remarkable.

As touched upon earlier, Queen Philippa the devoted wife and mother was also a dedicated fashionista. An account of her tailor William of London exists for the year 1332/33, and reveals much about the splendour of the queen's attire. For the feast of Pentecost on 7 June 1332, for example, she had three 'robes of five garments' and one of four garments, which meant a complete set of clothes including a tunic, overtunic and cloak. A few weeks later, for her purification or 'churching' ceremony after giving birth to her daughter Isabella of Woodstock, she had another 'robe of five garments' of velvet (which must have been very warm for the time of year, especially as all her clothes this year were lined with pure miniver fur).[38] After Philippa's purification of 1332, Edward III also gave her a set of clothes embroidered with the letters E and P and a set of hangings depicting sky and sea for her bed; the sky and sea hanging bore images of mermaids holding the arms of England and Hainault. The altars of the church in Woodstock where the ceremony took place were decorated with purple silk embroidered with birds, baboons and snakes.[39] The king borrowed money from a merchant called Anthony Bache to pay for items relating to the queen's purification, and ordered his treasurer and barons to pay him 'without delay' on 5 February 1333.[40] Edward III, inevitably, held a jousting tournament at Woodstock to celebrate Philippa's 1332 purification after little Isabella of Woodstock's birth, in which his household knights took part.[41] His cousin Henry of Grosmont, the greatest heir in the country, was with Edward and Philippa in the summer of 1332, and may have been little Isabella's godfather.[42] 'Isabella' was also the name of Grosmont's wife, and perhaps she was the royal infant's godmother as well. Henry of Grosmont made a special point in his will, decades later, of inviting Isabella of Woodstock to his funeral.

The queen was probably at Westminster in September 1332 where her husband held a short parliament. On 8 October Philippa and Edward arrived at the royal hunting lodge of Clipstone in Nottinghamshire. Here, the queen granted her valet William de Wight and his wife Elena some lands in the royal manor of Havering-atte-Bower, which belonged to her.[43] The queen's bedcover was repaired and lined with miniver in November 1332, apparently in expectation of a cold winter, and another entry in her accounts that year reveals that Philippa had curtains of purple sindon (fine linen cloth) around her bed and feather cushions.[44]

The royal couple subsequently travelled north and spent most of the last three months of 1332 and the first few months of 1333 in Yorkshire, mostly at Pontefract and Knaresborough, which also both belonged to the queen. Queen Philippa was at Pontefract with Edward on 12 February 1333, when she sent letters to the chancellor of England, John Stratford, appointing attorneys at the Exchequer. The attorneys were John de Hegham and Hugh de Glaunvyll or Glanville, who had organised the funeral of Edward II a few weeks before she arrived in England at the end of 1327. Another of her attorneys bore the excellent name of Ascolf or

Hasculph de Whitewell. At the same time, the king promised to pay over £2,200 to the Italian bankers the Bardi who had lent that sum to the ever-extravagant Philippa for her expenses.[45]

The king and queen were still at Knaresborough on 4 April 1333 when Philippa beseeched her husband to pardon a woman called Agnes of Scarborough. Agnes had stolen a surcoat or overtunic (an outer garment, sometimes sleeveless or with short sleeves) and three shillings in cash and had been sentenced to hanging for the theft by the steward and marshals of Edward III's household. On learning that Agnes of Scarborough was pregnant, Philippa begged her husband to show her mercy, and Edward III duly pardoned Agnes.[46] Philippa was to demonstrate similar concern for pregnant women sentenced to be executed for the rest of her life.

In or around April 1333, about ten months after the birth of Isabella of Woodstock, the royal couple conceived again: their third child and second daughter was probably born in January 1334, though the exact date is difficult to establish precisely and she may have been born at the end of 1333 or in early February 1334.

Edward III set out for the far north of England in May 1333, and took Philippa most of the way with him. The monks of Durham noted that the king and queen agreed to sleep apart when they were staying at the cathedral priory there, out of respect for its patron saint, the Anglo-Saxon Cuthbert (d. 687), a notable ascetic unfairly remembered as disliking women. Philippa had already entered the priory and had retreated to her chamber to rest when the monks informed the king that their patron saint had abhorred the presence of women and that the queen would therefore have to leave immediately. Whatever Philippa's private opinion of long-dead misogynistic saints who apparently despised half of humanity, she had no choice but to comply with the monks' wishes, and went to stay at the castle in Durham. She was supposedly in such haste to leave that she departed in her undergarments, and prayed that St Cuthbert 'would not avenge a fault which she had through ignorance committed'. That the royal couple were specifically noted as sleeping apart on this one occasion is yet another indication of their closeness, and on the rare occasions when Edward and Philippa were apart they sometimes exchanged hawks and horses, gifts which symbolised the means by which they could be reunited.[47]

Queen Philippa, in the first trimester of pregnancy, stayed at Bamburgh Castle throughout, a few miles to the south. One important royal ward with the queen at this time was twelve-year-old Laurence Hastings (b. March 1321), heir to his great-uncle Aymer de Valence's (d. 1324) earldom of Pembroke and to his late father Lord Hastings' (d. 1325) many lands. Laurence appears to have lived with Queen Philippa for most of the early 1330s: in late April 1333, Edward III sent a letter to Laurence's mother Juliana – now married to her third husband, the king's friend Sir William Clinton – asking her to look after her own son during Philippa's absence in the far north of England in the spring and summer of 1333, as 'the king does not wish the child to travel so far.'[48] There seems to have been a belief in the English royal family of the thirteenth and fourteenth centuries that the north of England was an unhealthy place for children. In 1290, Henry III's widow Eleanor of Provence (Edward III's great-grandmother) asked her son Edward I not to take his six-year-old son, the future Edward II, to the north when he travelled there, as the 'bad climate' would make the boy ill.[49]

Edward besieged the port of Berwick-on-Tweed, then in Scottish hands after being captured by King Robert Bruce in 1318, for most of May, the whole of June, and the first few days of July 1333. Berwick-on-Tweed, a vital port on the north-east coast on the border of England and Scotland, changed hands between the two kingdoms numerous times in the Middle Ages. Edward III's grandfather Edward I captured it in 1296, when he notoriously massacred many of the inhabitants, but Edward II lost it again to King Robert Bruce in 1318, and his attempt to win it back in September 1319 resulted in utter failure and he never tried again. It took him two months, but Edward III captured Berwick in July 1333, and shortly afterwards, the young king won a great victory over the Scots at the battle of Halidon Hill. Still only twenty years old – he turned twenty-one in November 1333 – Philippa of Hainault's husband had already proved his mettle as a battle commander.[50] The king found time in late July to remember his wife's condition, and ordered an Alexander le Porter to find comfortable and convenient transport for the pregnant queen. Edward also ordered the barons of the exchequer to order 'houses suitable for receiving Queen Philippa to be repaired' within the castle of York, which involved pulling down an 'old and ruinous house' on the south side of the castle and using the timber to build a new house for her on the north side.[51]

Far away in Ireland, the king's kinsman William de Burgh, earl of Ulster, was murdered by some of his own men on 6 June 1333 near Belfast, three months before he turned twenty-one (he was therefore officially still underage and the ward of Edward III, two months his junior). William left as his heir his only child, Elizabeth de Burgh, born on 6 July 1332 and eleven months old when her father was killed. Elizabeth's mother was Maud of Lancaster, third of the six daughters of Edward III's great-uncle Henry, earl of Lancaster and Leicester. Despite the close family relationship – William de Burgh's mother was Edward III's first cousin, so his daughter was a second cousin of the king and queen's children on both sides of her family – Edward decided that the tiny heiress one day would make an excellent wife for one of his sons. Not only would she inherit the earldom of Ulster, little Elizabeth was also heir to her wealthy paternal grandmother Elizabeth de Burgh the elder (b. 1295), who held a third of the earldom of Gloucester as her inheritance from her brother Gilbert, killed at the battle of Bannockburn in 1314. Edward III granted a generous annual income to the infant Elizabeth de Burgh and her widowed mother Maud of Lancaster, who returned to England within weeks of Earl William's murder. Little Elizabeth de Burgh remained in her mother's custody for the time being, though later would be cared for by Queen Philippa herself, and Edward III was her legal guardian, as was customary for the heir of a late tenant in chief, the important men and women of the realm who held lands directly from the king.[52]

The king and Philippa spent part of August 1333 back at Knaresborough Castle in Yorkshire. Philippa was now about four months pregnant. On 15 August the king announced his intention to go on pilgrimage, 'in fulfilment of a vow lately made by him', until Michaelmas, or 29 September. He ordered his household and Philippa's household to 'remain in certain places in England until his return'.[53] He was in Norfolk by 20 August and took the opportunity to pay a brief visit to his mother the dowager queen Isabella at her favourite residence of Castle Rising, not far from

King's Lynn, and almost certainly went to the great shrine of Our Lady at Walsingham. Probably in early September the king laid the foundation stone of Bisham Priory in Berkshire, founded by his great friend Sir William Montacute. At the end of that month, the king spent a few days at Waltham Abbey in Essex, though the occasion was a meeting of his great council rather than a spiritual retreat.[54]

Queen Philippa's mother Jeanne de Valois, countess of Hainault and Holland, visited England again in the autumn of 1333 and must have been delighted to see her daughter pregnant once more. Philippa paid for seven ships to bring Jeanne and her large retinue from Wissant to Dover on 23 September, and the countess left again on 13 October. The festive season of 1333 was spent at Wallingford, a few miles from Oxford and a castle where Edward III had spent much time in childhood. The king purchased fourteen hobby-horses for the Christmas and New Year games, which sounds like he, his retinue and the watching Queen Philippa must have had great fun.[55] Edward had recently turned twenty-one and thus had legally come of age, almost seven years after his accession to the throne, and had already proved himself as a warrior and as a leader. His son and heir was three years old and thriving, and his wife, not yet twenty years old, was pregnant with their third child. Times were good, and the future looked bright.

Building a Family

Probably in January or early February 1334, Philippa of Hainault and Edward III's third child and second daughter was born. They called her Joan, or Johane, or Johanne, as it was spelt in England in the fourteenth century. The name was the English form of Philippa's French mother's name Jeanne. The place of Joan's birth is not entirely certain; in November 1347 a royal clerk called her 'Joan of the Tower', though he was almost certainly mixing her up with her aunt, Edward III's youngest sibling the queen of Scotland (who was still only twelve years old in early 1334 though had been married and living in Scotland for five and a half years). Edward III was in Oxfordshire and Bedfordshire, not in or near the Tower of London, in January 1334 when his daughter was born. Two entries on the Patent Roll in April 1338 and May 1342 call her 'Joan of Woodstock' and given that Edward III stayed at the Oxfordshire palace of Woodstock from 11 to 13 January, was there again 30 January 1334 and spent much of the first two weeks of February 1334 there, it makes sense that Joan was born there.[1]

For one of Philippa's confinements, perhaps when she gave birth to Joan, the king ordered a bed of green velvet embroidered with gold sea sirens, carrying a shield with the arms of England and Hainault. He also bought her a white robe worked with pearls and a robe of velvet cloth embroidered with gold.[2] One of little Joan's attendants bore the unusual name of Lonota de Werthyngpole, another was Amy of Gloucester. Sometime before July 1337 she was placed in the official custody of the dowager countess of Pembroke, the king's second cousin, and a French noblewoman called Isabella de la Mote. For the time being, though, she remained with her mother: Edward III granted his wife all the issues of their son's earldom of Chester on 6 March 1334 'for the sustenance of Edward, earl of Chester, the king's first-born son, and of Isabella and Joan, the king's daughters'. Philippa was given permission to 'order the household of the said earl, Isabella and Joan as she will'.[3] The queen was churched or purified after Joan's birth on about 8 March 1334. If this took place forty days after childbirth, this would place the girl's birth around 27 January; if, as was sometimes the case with female children, it took place thirty days later, Joan was born around 6 February. Edward III was not present at Philippa's churching, being then in York.

Joan of Woodstock was only about eighteen months old in July 1335 when her father sent envoys to Otto, duke of Austria, to arrange her future marriage to Otto's son and heir Friedrich or Frederick. The king had not yet given up trying to find a bride for his younger brother, John of Eltham, earl of Cornwall, either, and sent envoys to the duchy of Brittany to negotiate a match between John of Eltham and Duke John III's niece Jeanne de Penthièvre at the same time.[4] Although Joan of Woodstock was sent to stay with her aunt the Empress Margaretha in Munich for a while, her planned Austrian marriage did not work out, and Friedrich died as a teenager in 1344. Another marriage for little Joan was on the table in April 1337, with Louis (b. 1330), son and heir of Louis, count of Flanders and a grandson of King Philip V of France via his mother. In November 1338, Edward III sent his brother-in-law Reynald II, count of Guelders, to negotiate a marriage between young Louis of Flanders and the English royal family, though on this occasion he offered his first daughter Isabella of Woodstock rather than his second. He pursued the Flanders marriage throughout 1339 and again in 1347, though ultimately the young Louis of Flanders married Margarethe of Brabant after the duke of Brabant abandoned his commitment to marry one or two of his children into the English royal family and allied with Louis's father, the pro-French count of Flanders, instead.[5]

Probably also in January 1334, though the date is not certain, the king held and took part in a jousting tournament at Dunstable in Bedfordshire. As Philippa most likely gave birth that month or in early February, it seems unlikely that she was personally present. Edward III fought incognito under the Arthurian name 'Sir Lionel' together with his younger brother John of Eltham, earl of Cornwall, now seventeen, their father Edward II's much younger half-brother Thomas of Brotherton, earl of Norfolk and earl marshal of England (born June 1300), and their first cousin Edward de Bohun (born *c.* 1309 or 1312/13), younger brother of the earl of Hereford.[6] Edward's kinsman Sir Hugh 'Huchon' Despenser (born 1308 or 1309), son and heir of the notorious Hugh Despenser the Younger whose brutal execution Edward had witnessed just after his fourteenth birthday in November 1326, was another of the many English noblemen and knights who jousted at Dunstable: a hundred and thirty-five in total. Two further jousting tournaments were held in 1334 in which the king personally participated, at Burstwick in Yorkshire in May, and at Nottingham in July.[7]

The king and queen spent the entire month of December 1334 at Roxburgh in Scotland, and the 'duke of Bavaria' – presumably a reference to Philippa's brother-in-law Ludwig of Bavaria, the Holy Roman Emperor – sent two minstrels there to perform for them. The two were called Tussettus of Swabia and Conpatus, and the nature of their performance is not recorded. A few weeks later, Philippa sent her violist Merlin, and two bagpipers called Barberus and Morlanus, to the continent to attend 'minstrel schools' there.[8] The extant household records of Philippa's mother-in-law Isabella of France reveals that there was also a 'school of minstrelsy' in London in the middle of the fourteenth century.[9]

Edward III held parliament at York in late May and early June 1335 – Philippa was there with him – and he and his army spent July and August 1335 on campaign in Scotland. His brother the earl of Cornwall went with him, as did Thomas Beauchamp, the twenty-one-year-old earl of Warwick, the earl of Surrey (b. 1286) and his nephew the earl of Arundel (b. *c.* 1313), and supposedly Henry of Lancaster and his son and heir Henry of Grosmont. Lancaster, now about fifty-five, was said by two chroniclers writing a few years later to have lost his eyesight some years before, though as he was summoned to a military campaign in 1335 this is perhaps rather unlikely. The chroniclers may have misdated the onset of the earl's blindness.[10]

Another man present on the Scottish campaign of 1335 was Queen Philippa's brother-in-law Wilhelm, count of Jülich. Wilhelm brought seven minstrels and heralds with him to England, one called Perotus de Insula and the other six unnamed in the extant records.[11] The *Anonimalle* chronicle says correctly, though also rather puzzlingly, that Wilhelm was married to 'the sister of the queen of Germany', Margaretha of Hainault, apparently failing to notice that Wilhelm's wife Johanna was also the queen of England's sister. Two years later, the author finally spotted a family connection, though he wrongly believed that Wilhelm was Philippa's uncle, and states that in 1337 Wilhelm of Jülich came to England again, this time with his brother Walram, archbishop of Cologne. The chronicler says that Guy, count of Namur, came to England in 1335 with eight knights and a band of armed men to aid Edward III against the Scots, and describes him as a cousin of Queen Philippa (Guy's younger brother Robert later married Philippa's youngest sister Isabella of Hainault). Philippa's uncle Philip VI of France and her kinsman Johann 'the Blind', king of Bohemia, by contrast, sent men and ships to the aid of King David II of Scotland, though Johann did send his minstrel Master John to Edward III with four swords and a pair of gloves as a gift for the English king.[12] The aldermen of London, meanwhile, spent six pounds and six shillings on an unspecified gift which they sent to 'our lord the count of Julers,' i.e. Wilhelm of Jülich, and another four pounds and sixteen shillings on a gift for the count of Namur.[13]

Another man who arrived in England in the early 1330s and offered his support to Edward III was the French nobleman Robert of Artois (b. 1287), count of Beaumont-le-Roger. In a typical example of the complicated royal inter-relationships of the era, Robert was both Edward III's second cousin and Queen Philippa's uncle-in-law: Artois's wife (b. 1304) was a younger half-sister of Philippa's mother the countess of Hainault, and confusingly was also called Jeanne de Valois. Robert had been embroiled in a decades-long vicious quarrel with his aunt Mahaut, countess of Artois in her own right, until Mahaut died in 1329. On the death of Mahaut's father, the count of Artois, in 1302, she had become countess of Artois in preference to her nephew Robert, only son of her late brother Philip (d. 1298). Robert claimed that as a grandson in the male line he had a better right to the county than a daughter, but he never managed to take Artois from his aunt. On Mahaut's death in 1329 the county then passed to Robert of Artois's cousin Jeanne of Burgundy, Mahaut's daughter and the widow of King Philip V of France, and on the dowager queen Jeanne of Burgundy's death in 1330 to her eldest daughter, another Jeanne (b. 1308). In his latest and desperate attempt to gain control of the county of Artois in 1331, Robert of Artois forged his late father Philip's will, but the deceit was discovered and the forger, a woman called Jeanne de Divion, burned at the stake. Robert fled from France, and his wife Jeanne de Valois was arrested by her own half-brother Philip VI. He imprisoned her and her children at Château Gaillard in Normandy in 1334, and she died there many years later in 1363 without ever regaining her freedom. Hardly surprisingly, Robert of Artois thereafter became a bitter enemy of his brother-in-law the king of France and transferred his allegiance to the king of England.

Sometime before 21 July 1335, Queen Philippa entrusted a merchant called John de Laundes with a gold ring, a 'velvet robe set with pearls' and other high-value jewels in her possession, and asked him to take them from York to London for her. While he was travelling between Ogerston and Weston in Huntingdonshire, the unfortunate John de Laundes was set upon by thieves, robbed, and killed. Most of the queen's precious items were stolen, though the thieves left some of them with John's body, perhaps being unable to carry them all. Edward III ordered a man called William le Ewer to hunt down and arrest the perpetrators, and to find the stolen jewels. Le Ewer's search proved unsuccessful, and three months later Philippa herself appointed Walter de Chesthunt and Peter de Laundes (presumably a relative of the murdered John) to find and recover her jewels and to arrest those responsible.[14]

Philippa and Edward III spent Christmas 1335 in Newcastle-upon-Tyne. The couple conceived their fourth child around April 1336, possibly while staying at the Tower of London or in one of the royal manors around London such as Havering-atte-Bower or Eltham. The queen was at the royal castle of Rockingham in Northamptonshire by early July 1336, while Edward III had set off for the north with his army on yet another campaign to Scotland.[15] While Edward was in Perth on 2 September 1336, an entry in the royal household records states that 'the lady queen held the hall of the king at Northampton. She called to the table the archbishop of Canterbury, seven bishops, eight barons and lords, thirty-eight knights and other great lords to consider the issue of Scotland.'[16] Whether or to what extent Philippa took part in the council meeting is not clear, but evidently she had the authority to summon it, a demonstration of the trust Edward III had in her. Medieval queens of England were never officially appointed as regents while their husbands were outside the realm, or when their sons were underage – even Queen Isabella was never officially appointed as her son's regent in 1327 or afterwards – but unofficially they could wield considerable influence. As her mother-in-law Isabella had also done during the reign of her husband Edward II, Philippa could act as an intercessor on behalf of others, and use her closeness to the king to request favours from him.

In early 1336, Edward III sent ambassadors to Germany and Austria to secure alliances with the Habsburg dukes, including Otto, duke of Austria, whose son and heir Friedrich's possible future marriage to Edward and Philippa's second daughter Joan of Woodstock was under discussion. Queen Philippa was able on this occasion to help in the negotiations, and as the sister-in-law of the German emperor and potential mother-in-law of Duke Otto, was well placed to wield influence with continental barons. In her correspondence on the matter, Philippa referred to her brother-in-law Ludwig of Bavaria by his correct imperial titles, even though he had been excommunicated several times and the pope refused to recognise his title of emperor. On 5 September 1336, Pope Benedict XII (who had succeeded John XXII at the end of 1334) wrote to absolve her of any blame punishable by excommunication for doing so.[17]

Philippa's brother-in-law John of Eltham, earl of Cornwall, died in September 1336 at the age of only twenty during Edward III's campaign in Scotland that year, still unmarried despite Edward's efforts over the years to arrange a good match for him. His mother Queen Isabella outlived him by more than twenty years. It is on record that Edward III suffered from nightmares after losing his only brother, and although one hostile Scottish chronicler suggests that the king stabbed John of Eltham to death, there is no reason at all to think that this is the case and every reason to reject the tale. For Edward, and no doubt also for Philippa of Hainault, John's early death was a tragic loss, and the king had 900 masses said for John's soul.[18]

Surviving Loss

The year 1337 proved to be a difficult one in many ways for Queen Philippa. Her brother-in-law John of Eltham was buried at Westminster Abbey on 13 January 1337 four months after his death, though whether the queen was able to attend is uncertain, given that she was either heavily pregnant or had just given birth. Edward III appears to have delayed his brother's funeral by some months so that he could attend in person.[1] John's tomb still exists in Westminster Abbey, surrounded by small statues of 'weepers' who represent John's family, one of them likely intended to be a depiction of Philippa herself and one of them certainly representing her mother-in-law Queen Isabella. In or before September 1337, the mayor, sheriffs and aldermen of London paid sixty shillings for three silk cloths 'for making an offering to the body of the earl of Cornwall'.[2] The cloths were probably intended to lie over John's tomb.

Sometime in January 1337 Queen Philippa gave birth to her fourth child and second son William at Hatfield in Hertfordshire, a manor that belonged to John de Warenne, earl of Surrey. The date of William's birth is not entirely clear; Edward III stayed at Hatfield from 28 January or slightly earlier until 2 February, though probably William was born nearer the beginning of January.[3] Although the birth of another son must have been a joyous occasion for both Philippa and Edward, tragedy struck when the little boy died at only a few weeks old at most, possibly days old. He was buried in distant York Minster on 10 February.[4] Philippa's purification took place on Sunday 16 February, probably forty or so days after she gave birth and after William of Hatfield was already dead and buried; it must have been a deeply sad occasion. In November 1345, Edward III, stating that his son William had died at the manor of Hatfield, asked thirteen monks to 'celebrate divine service daily' there for himself, Philippa, their children, the earl of Surrey (who owned the manor), and for the soul of little William.[5] Not only did the king and queen lose their second son in 1337, their first, Edward of Woodstock, was ill sometime in or around 1337 and must have caused his parents intense worry.[6] Fortunately, he recovered.

William of Hatfield was named after Philippa's father Willem, count of Hainault and Holland, and Willem died as well on 7 June 1337, the eve of the feast of Pentecost, aged about fifty. The count was buried on 16 June close to the high altar in the church of the Cordeliers in Valenciennes, his coffin draped with black sendal (expensive fine silk cloth), and in his will he left money to be paid out in alms to several dozen 'poor people' and servants of his who attended the funeral. They included Hanekin the messenger, Jakemin of the forge, Ghenekin of the wardrobe, Gosset and Renequin of the kitchen, Gillekin the butcher, Hemskin the page, Claisekin, Hemelrike, and 'the old clerk of the chapel'. Most of the names appear in a list of Willem's household members in 1335/36.[7]

Count Willem had dictated his will in his town of Valenciennes on 22 February 1336, so apparently had been ill for some time (in the fourteenth century, people generally only made their wills when they thought they might be dying), and he is known to have suffered badly from gout. The will was written in French, though some Dutch words such as *kierke* for 'church' crept into it, and the scribe who wrote it appears uncertain of French grammar, referring to Willem's daughters with the masculine *le* instead of the feminine form *la*. A similar occurrence of Dutch words creeping into a text written in French by a Hainaulter clerk occurs in the household account of Queen Philippa's brother Willem the younger in 1333, when he was about sixteen. The clerk recorded a payment *pour un esprevier Wuillaume reprins en la tune dune povre femme*, 'for one of Willem's sparrowhawks recovered in a poor woman's garden', where the entire sentence is written in French with the sole exception of the

Dutch word *tune* for 'garden' (modern Dutch: *tuin*).[8] On another occasion in 1328, Philippa's eldest sister Margaretha was referred to as *medame le royne*, 'my lady the queen' (of Germany) in one of her mother Jeanne's accounts, also with the male form *le* instead of the correct *la*, perhaps a further indication of the rather casual attitude towards correct French grammar among Hainaulter clerks.[9]

Other rather curious spellings in Count Willem's will of 1336 such as *chiertain* instead of the more standard *certein* ('certain') and *chiaus* for *ceaux* ('those') give some indication as to how Hainaulters, including presumably Queen Philippa, pronounced some French words with a 'sh' sound rather than the more standard 's'. The name of the town Valenciennes was often written 'Valenchiennes' or 'Valenchiènes' in the fourteenth century, also reflecting local pronunciation.[10] Philippa almost certainly grew up bilingual in French and Dutch (or Flemish), and perhaps also tended to mix words from both languages when she was speaking. She would have spoken French with her husband and family in England; whether or to what extent she learnt English is uncertain, though as she lived in England for more than four decades she presumably must have come to understand some, at least.

Willem referred to himself in his will by all his titles: count of Hainault, Holland and Zeeland, and lord of Friesland. He called his wife Jeanne 'Jehenne de Valoys', an interesting indication of how he and others in Hainault probably pronounced her given name. He also referred to Jeanne as 'our dear and beloved consort', left her numerous items including furniture and jewels, and made her his chief executor, an indication of his trust in her. Philippa appears as *no fille le* [sic] *royne d'Engletière*, 'our daughter the queen of England'.

Philippa's youngest sister Isabella (*Ysabiel*, as her name appears in the will) was probably only about twelve in early 1336 when her father made his will and was not yet married, and Willem declared that he intended her for the eldest son of Jan III, duke of neighbouring Brabant. (Isabella ultimately married the brother of the marquis of Namur, though not until 1354 when she was about thirty, and her intended fiancé Jan of Brabant married her cousin Marie de Valois and they both died young.)[11] All of Willem's living children, Margaretha, Johanna, Philippa, Willem the younger and Isabella, are mentioned in his will.

A poet called Jean de Condé, apparently the official court poet of the noble Hainault family, penned a eulogy in French to Count Willem shortly after his death. Condé called Willem the 'father of minstrels', an indication of how important music and performance were at the count's court, and mourned the loss of the brave, noble and powerful prince. He also composed a work collecting *Li Dis dou Boin Conte Willaume*, 'The sayings of the good Count Willem'. Countess Jeanne's status as the full sister of the king of France and her double royal descent from the royal families of France and Naples was acknowledged; evidently the countess's high birth and impressive connections were a matter of great pride at her husband's court. Willem's specifically using his wife's name, 'de Valoys', in his will also reveals his pride in her family connections.[12] Another eulogy for the count was written in French by Jean de la Mote, and two further contemporary poems, one in Flemish and one in Low German, were dedicated to Count Willem's memory. Jean de la Mote's poem was called *Li Regret Guillaume* and was dedicated to Queen Philippa and probably commissioned by her. De la Mote appears on record in England when he entertained Edward III, and presumably Philippa as well, at the palace of Eltham in 1343.[13] Philippa's father had ruled his counties for thirty-three years and a large number of his subjects would have been unable to remember a time before he had ruled over them.

Philippa's brother Willem junior, only survivor of their parents' four sons and probably about three years younger than Philippa, succeeded their father as count of Hainault and Holland, and had a magnificent marble sepulchre built for Count Willem in the church of the Cordeliers in Valenciennes the year after his death. It was decorated on all sides with the coats of arms of various members of the Hainault-Holland comital family, including the older Willem's great-uncle Wilhelm (d. 1256), king of Germany and count of Holland and Zeeland, and his great-great-grandfather Baldwin (d. *c.* 1205), count of Flanders and Hainault and first Latin emperor of Constantinople. Unfortunately, the church of the Cordeliers has long since vanished, and the burial sites of Willem and his eldest daughter the empress, also buried there in 1356, have been lost.

The younger Willem, twenty years old or thereabouts when his father died, was already married to the young Johanna of Brabant

(b. 1322), eldest child and ultimately the heir of Duke Jan III of Brabant after her three brothers died. A son, inevitably called Willem, died in infancy. They were to have no surviving children. Queen Philippa was probably at Fotheringhay in Northamptonshire, or somewhere close by, when she heard the sad news of her father's death; she was certainly at the castle of Fotheringhay on 3 June 1337.[14] Edward III was in the far north of his kingdom at the time that news of Willem's death must have reached England, on his way to Scotland with his army on his latest summer campaign there, so was not present to comfort her. The king had requiem masses performed for his father-in-law's soul when he heard the news of Willem's death.[15]

Philippa's widowed mother Jeanne de Valois, aged about forty-two or forty-three, became a nun at the Cistercian abbey of Fontenelle near the town of Maing, not far from her late husband's town of Valenciennes, a few months after losing Willem. (The abbey where Jeanne lived is often misidentified as a Benedictine convent in Normandy, formerly called the Abbey of Saint Wandrille, but now confusingly also called Fontenelle Abbey.) According to the chronicler Jean le Bel, she later became its abbess.[16] Jeanne de Valois's sister-in-law Johanna, one of Willem's many sisters, had also taken the veil there, and Jeanne's granddaughter Anna of Bavaria, Empress Margaretha's second daughter, followed in her footsteps and also became a nun at Fontenelle after she was widowed in late 1340 at the age of thirteen or fourteen (her husband Johann was barely eleven when he died).

For all that Willem of Hainault fathered at least eight or nine illegitimate children with three or more mistresses, there is every indication that his and Jeanne's marriage of more than thirty years had been a happy, affectionate and successful one. Jeanne's decision to retire from public life within months of her husband's death argues that she missed Willem greatly and did not wish to live in the secular world without him. She had already spent more time staying in abbeys in her native France and in her husband's territories than any other countess of Hainault and Holland throughout the entire Middle Ages, so apparently she enjoyed the atmosphere of religious houses.[17] At some point in *c.* 1337/38, soon after Jeanne entered the abbey of Fontenelle, she sent a medicinal treatise on the virtues of rosemary and cuttings of rosemary to her daughter Philippa in England, thus supposedly becoming the person responsible for introducing this Mediterranean plant to England. Much later in the fourteenth century, another treatise on rosemary written in English describes the one sent by Jeanne to her daughter as 'the litel boke that the Scole of Sallerne [school of Salerno] wroat to the Cuntasse of Henowd and sche sente the copie to her doughter Philip, the quene of England.'[18]

There was at least some good news for Queen Philippa in 1337. During the parliament held at Westminster that March, her husband created a new title for their eldest son Edward of Woodstock and made him duke of Cornwall. This was the first time any Englishman had held the title of duke, except that the kings of England had been dukes of Aquitaine in France since the middle of the twelfth century. Edward III also created a number of earls during the March 1337 parliament. His royal cousin Henry of Grosmont, born *c.* 1310/12 and heir to his aged father Henry's earldoms of Lancaster and Leicester, was made earl of Derby, and Hugh Audley (b. *c.* 1291/93), husband of the king's first cousin Margaret née de Clare, was made earl of Gloucester. Another royal first cousin, William de Bohun, younger brother and heir of the earl of Hereford, became earl of Northampton (Edward de Bohun, William's twin, had drowned in Scotland some years before or would probably also have been elevated to a title). Some of the king's greatest friends and supporters were raised to earldoms: William Montacute became earl of Salisbury, William Clinton earl of Huntingdon, and Robert Ufford earl of Suffolk. Another friend, Sir Ralph Stafford, later became the first earl of Stafford as well.

Sometime before December 1337, Queen Philippa spent the remarkably large sum of 2,000 marks or £1,333 6/- 8*d* on robes for herself and her son Edward of Woodstock, earl of Chester and now also duke of Cornwall, who turned seven on 15 June 1337. Philippa also borrowed another £450 from the Italian banking firm the Peruzzi sometime before October 1337, and the mayor and aldermen of London made her a gift of another 100 marks. At an uncertain date in the 1330s, the same people spent £7 on presents for Edward of Woodstock and Philippa's other children 'at the Feast of the Nativity' and on another occasion bought gifts for the royal children at a cost of £11. It is incredibly difficult accurately to assess how much this is today, but these were not cheap presents – the average wage for a labourer was about £3 a year.[19]

The most momentous event of 1337, however, was Edward III's open declaration of war on France and its king Philip VI, the war that much later would become known as the Hundred Years War, though of course no-one could possibly have guessed in the 1330s just how long it would last. At a meeting of the royal council in January 1337, Edward and his councillors discussed his dynastic rights to the French throne as the nearest male heir of his uncle Charles IV (d. 1328), and it was determined that according to civil law, unless Edward asserted his rights by his twenty-fifth birthday, he would lose them forever. His twenty-fifth birthday would fall on 13 November 1337. The king ordered the goods, chattels and lands of all French people living in England to be seized, though on 24 July 1337 he made an exception for Isabella, Lady de la Mote, and his kinswoman Marie de St Pol, dowager countess of Pembroke and the daughter of the count of St Pol in France, who were 'staying in the company' of his and Philippa's second daughter Joan of Woodstock and looking after the little girl.[20]

The causes of the Hundred Years War are of course enormously complex. Philip VI's confiscation of the duchy of Aquitaine in 1337, after Edward III refused to hand the renegade French nobleman Robert of Artois over to him as Philip had demanded, prompted the king of England to declare war on his wife's uncle. The origins of the conflict lay in the distant past, in the English kings' control of a sizeable area of France since the middle of the twelfth century, and the two kingdoms had often gone to war before 1337, most recently in 1324 when Edward III's uncle Charles IV invaded his brother-in-law Edward II's French territories after Edward failed to pay the requisite homage to Charles for them. Edward II's decision to send his adolescent son to France to pay homage to Charles in September 1325 in his place precipitated the crisis which put Edward III on the English throne. Edward III's grandfather Edward I had been at war with Philip IV of France for the second half of the 1290s, and the marriage of Edward III's parents was arranged in 1299 as a means of ending this particular war. Edward III's claiming of the French throne some decades later was an entirely unintended consequence of this marriage.

The dowager countess of Hainault, Jeanne de Valois, for all that she was veiled as a nun at Fontenelle Abbey in Normandy in and after late 1337, did her best to mediate between her brother Philip VI and her son-in-law Edward III, and to prevent war between them. Chronicler Jean le Bel calls her the 'sovereign of good ladies', and states that she frequently rode or travelled by carriage 'after her brother King Philip to see if she could intervene'. Jeanne's attempts, however, were unsuccessful, even though she 'often threw herself in tears at her brother's feet'.[21] (Probably, Jean le Bel did not intend the dowager countess's emotional and undoubtedly heartfelt interventions with Philip to appear as near-farcical as they unfortunately do in his account.)

Queen Philippa was at Westminster with her husband in August 1337 when she successfully requested a pardon for one Alice Wygodes, who had stolen several sheep in Essex when she was still underage and had been imprisoned until she was old enough to suffer the death penalty. The queen also asked her husband to pardon William Wit, who had stolen a horse and subsequently fled from the realm, and the king did so.[22] Edward III was planning a journey overseas by early September 1337, and wrote to the dukes of Austria, the brothers Otto and Albrecht, telling them that he would bring his daughter Isabella of Woodstock in his company, as well as the dukes' envoy Sir Heinrich Gasseler. Edward commented that the sea passage over the Channel was dangerous 'on account of pirates' and asked the dukes to excuse his, Gasseler's and Isabella's delay and that when they all arrived, they would 'complete the matters in treaty'.[23] It was in fact his second daughter Joan of Woodstock who had previously been betrothed into Austria, not her sister Isabella, so possibly this was an error by his scribes, or more probably, Edward had decided to substitute Isabella for Joan. He substituted Joan for Isabella when arranging a match with Pedro, heir to the Castilian throne, and Isabella for Joan in negotiations for a marriage into the county of Flanders.[24]

The royal couple were at the Tower of London in early October 1337, and the festive season of 1337/38 was spent at Guildford in Surrey and at the Tower. Edward and Philippa listened to two trumpeters called Gillet and Perott on the Feast of the Circumcision, 1 January 1338.[25] Queen Philippa, now perhaps recently turned twenty-four, became pregnant with her fifth child in around late February or early March: her third son would be born on 29 November 1338. Also in 1338, Philippa's godson Philip Beauchamp was born, and was given her name (as the name Phelip or Phelippe was given to both males and females in the fourteenth century) in her honour. Philip was the son of Sir Roger Beauchamp and his wife Sybil née Pateshull, whose wedding the king and queen had attended the year before; Edward III gave them seven cloths as a gift. Sybil was one of Philippa's attendants, and she and Edward surely had a hand in arranging her marriage to Roger Beauchamp. The queen's godson joined the Church when he was six years old in 1344, and his father Sir Roger became Philippa's steward in 1350 and after her death became the king's chamberlain.[26]

The effigy of Queen Philippa in the chapel of St Edward the Confessor, Westminster Abbey. She wears a reticulated head-dress, a cotehardie laced up the front with buttoned sleeves, and a long, narrow hip belt. (Copyright Dean and Chapter of Westminster; used with kind permission).

Above: Queen Philippa's tomb in Westminster Abbey, much vandalised and mutilated over the centuries; all but two of the numerous statuettes of her relatives as 'weepers' around the sides of the tomb have disappeared. (Copyright Dean and Chapter of Westminster; used with kind permission).

Below: Westminster Abbey, exterior. (Author's Collection)

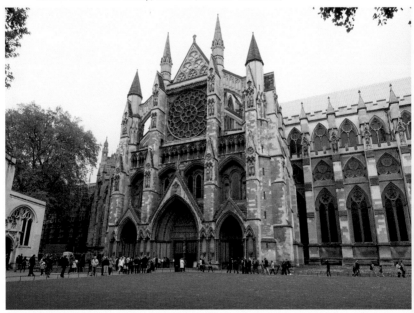

Above left: Philippa's mother Jeanne de Valois (c. 1294/5-1352), countess of Hainault, Holland and Zeeland. (Public domain)

Above right: Obverse of 1337 coin minted by Philippa's maternal uncle King Philip VI of France (b. 1293, reigned 1328-50), first of the Valois kings of France. (Public domain)

Below left: Philippa's father Willem (c. 1286/7-1337), count of Hainault, Holland and Zeeland and lord of Friesland. (Public domain)

Below right: Philippa's eldest sister Margaretha (1310-56), Holy Roman Empress, queen of Germany and Italy, duchess of Bavaria, countess of Hainault and Holland. (Public domain)

Guilielmus II Hanoniæ

Left: Philippa's brother Willem the younger (c. 1317-45), count of Hainault, Holland and Zeeland and lord of Friesland. (Public domain)

Below: Windsor Castle, Berkshire, birthplace of Philippa's husband on 13 November 1312, birthplace also of Philippa's tenth and eleventh children Margaret and William in 1346 and 1348, and the location of the queen's death on 15 August 1369. (A. L. Nieves on Flickr)

York Minster, where Philippa married Edward III on or about 25 January 1328, and where her fourth child and second son William of Hatfield was buried nine years later. (Author's Collection)

Queen's College, Oxford, founded in 1341 by Philippa's chaplain Robert of Eglesfield with her support and aid. (Fenlio)

The site of the abbey of Fontenelle, near Maing, northern France, where Philippa's widowed mother Jeanne de Valois was a nun from 1337 to 1352. Jeanne's granddaughter Anna of Bavaria, Philippa's niece, also became a nun there. Jeanne, Anna and Philippa's youngest sister Isabella of Hainault were all buried at Fontenelle. (Serge Ottaviani on Wikimedia Commons)

Saint-Géry Church in Maing, near Valenciennes. Jeanne de Valois was reburied here in September 2001 after her tomb was found at the former abbey of Fontenelle. (Georges Biron on Wikimedia Commons)

The church of San Pietro in Ciel d'Oro (St Peter in the Sky of Gold), Pavia, Italy; the original burial site of Philippa's son Lionel of Antwerp, who died in Alba on 17 October 1368 a few months after marrying into the Visconti family, lords of Milan and Pavia. (Courtesy of Alessandro Lupo of the Auramala Project in Pavia)

The ruins of Knaresborough Castle, Yorkshire, which belonged to Philippa and where she and Edward sometimes stayed. (Wikimedia Commons)

A seventeenth-century image of the interior of St Michael's Abbey in Antwerp, in modern-day Belgium, where Philippa gave birth to Lionel of Antwerp on 29 November 1338. The abbey was founded in 1124 and was demolished in 1831. (Public domain)

The tomb of Edward II depicted in the *Roman de Brut*. (Courtesy © The British Library Board)

Above: A fanciful but impressive engraving of kings Edward I, Edward II and Edward III by Dutch artist Hendrik Goltzius, 1584. Note the two crowns on Edward III's sword. (Courtesy Rijksmuseum)

Right: Sint-Baafskathedraal or St Bavo's Cathedral, Ghent, Belgium, formerly the Abbey of St Bavo, where Philippa gave birth to her sixth child and fourth son John of Gaunt on 6 March 1340. (Bvi4092 on Flickr)

A romantic image of Philippa interceding with Edward III on behalf of the burghers of Calais in 1347. (Public domain)

The city of Valenciennes, now in the Nord department of France near the Belgian border; possibly Philippa's birthplace, where her proxy wedding to Edward III took place in October 1327, and where her father Count Willem and eldest sister Empress Margaretha were buried in 1337 and 1356. (Wikimedia Commons)

A joust before Edward III from Froissart's Chronicles. The births of royal children during his reign were celebrated by extravagant tourneys. (Public domain)

The Dodenne Tower in Valenciennes, built by Philippa's nephew Albrecht of Bavaria (1336-1404), duke of Lower Bavaria, count of Hainault and Holland. (Public domain)

Nideggen Castle, now in North Rhine Westphalia, Germany, close to the Dutch border. The stronghold of the counts (later dukes) of Jülich, and where Philippa's elder sister Johanna, duchess of Jülich, spent much of her life. Johanna's husband Wilhelm extended the castle in the 1340s. (Wolkenkratzer on Wikimedia Commons)

Nideggen Castle. Wilhelm of Jülich and Johanna of Hainault were buried in the town of Nideggen below the castle in 1361 and 1374. (Bungert55 on Wikimedia Commons)

St Peter's Basilica, Rome, where Philippa's sister Margaretha and brother-in-law Ludwig of Bavaria were crowned Holy Roman Emperor and Empress on 17 January 1328, a few days before Philippa's wedding to Edward III. (Author's Collection)

Dom zu Unserer Lieben Frau, or the Cathedral of Our Dear Lady in Munich, Bavaria, burial place of Philippa's brother-in-law Ludwig, deposed Holy Roman Emperor, king of Germany and Italy and duke of Bavaria, in 1347. (Roman Sadovnikov on Flickr)

Above: Altenberg Cathedral, formerly Altenberg Abbey, in North Rhine Westphalia, Germany, burial place of Philippa's nephew Gerhard of Jülich, count of Berg and Ravensberg, after he was killed jousting in Düsseldorf in 1360. (Karl-Heinz Meurer on Wikimedia Commons)

Left: Lionel of Antwerp (1338-68), Philippa's third but second eldest surviving son. (Public domain; nineteenth-century drawing of his statuette on his father's tomb)

Right: John of Gaunt (1340-99), Philippa's fourth but third eldest surviving son. The portrait from the late sixteenth century is ascribed to a Dutch artist called Luca Cornelli, and may be a copy of an earlier portrait. (Public domain)

Below: Joao I of Portugal entertains John of Gaunt. (Harleain mss, from *John of Gaunt*, S. Armitage-Smith, 1905)

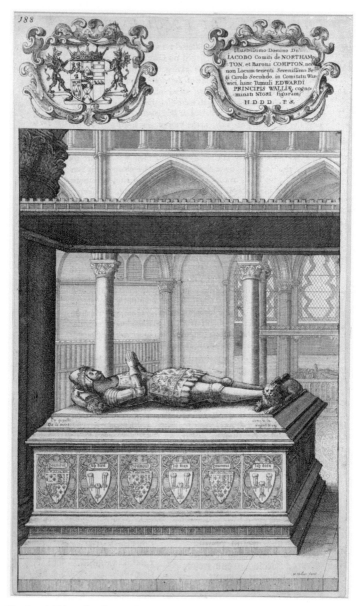

Tomb of Edward of Woodstock by Wenceslaus Hollar, 1677. (Courtesy Rijksmuseum)

A Long Sojourn Abroad

The 8th of March in an uncertain year, probably 1338, found Queen Philippa at the royal manor of Langley in Hertfordshire with her husband, when she sent a letter asking one Paul Montflour or Paolo Montefiore ('Paul Montflour' was the Anglicised form of his Italian name as written by English scribes) to attend diligently to her business and to prepare a passage for the king and herself overseas; they left England later that year. Philippa took a retinue of seventy-six people with her, and the king paid over £564 for the horses, plate, jewels and other items she took with her.[1] Her son Edward of Woodstock sent her a letter, or rather one of his clerks sent her a letter, dated at Kennington on 20 October, also in an uncertain year, perhaps 1338. The letter began:

> To my very dear and very dread lady and mother, I recommend me to your highness with all the reverences that I can and may, humbly requesting your blessing. My very dread lady, I am most greatly comforted to hear of your good health, which I pray to God that he may by his greatness grant you for a long time.[2]

Edward III and Queen Philippa spent most of the period from mid-July 1338 until the end of November 1340 outside England as Edward searched for allies on the continent against Philip VI and the French. It is significant that Edward took his queen with him during his long sojourn overseas: partly because he was surely unwilling to spend such a long time without his dear companion at his side, and also perhaps because he thought that Philippa, as the daughter and sister of counts of Hainault and Holland and the sister-in-law of the German emperor and of the count of Jülich, might smooth his path to making alliances with powerful men. Edward of Woodstock (who turned eight in June 1338) remained behind in England as nominal regent, but the royal couple took their two daughters Isabella and Joan, now six and four, with them. This says much about the royal couple's love for their children and their unwillingness to be separated from them, and stands in contrast to Edward III's grandparents Edward I and Leonor of Castile: when they spent over three years outside England in the late 1280s, they left all their children, including Edward III's father Edward of Caernarfon, behind in England.

Edward III and Queen Philippa, with their daughters and their retinues, sailed up the River Scheldt into the city of Antwerp on 22 July 1338, where a large crowd watched them disembark. The king, always a loving and generous father to his and Philippa's brood of children, gave Isabella and Joan a pair of decorated silver basins at this time.[3]

While the king and the pregnant queen of England were staying in Antwerp in July 1338, shortly after their arrival there, the house where they were staying caught fire and they and their households had to flee to safety. Edward and Philippa, rather embarrassingly, had to seek shelter at the abbey of St Bernard in their nightclothes.[4] Fire was of course not uncommon in an age when most buildings were made of wood. Edward III's father Edward of Caernarfon, as prince of Wales the year before his accession as Edward II, had to escape from Windsor Castle with his entire retinue in the middle of the night in April 1306 as flames swept through the castle, and in June 1313 Edward II saved his wife Queen Isabella's life when a fire broke out in the pavilion near Paris where they were staying during a long visit to Isabella's homeland. Edward rushed out into the street with his wife in his arms, both of them 'completely naked'.[5] The future Edward III, left behind in England while his parents travelled to France, was just seven months old at the time, and would have become king at that point had his father succumbed to the fire. Edward III's grandparents Edward I and Queen Leonor also escaped from a fire at Hope Castle in Wales on 27 August 1338, when Leonor was a few weeks pregnant with the future Edward II.[6]

A happier event occurred early in Edward III and Queen Philippa's stay in Antwerp, when they received a visit from Edward's sister Eleanor of Woodstock and her husband, Reynald II of Guelders.[7] Most probably, they had not seen Eleanor since her departure from England in May 1332, when she was not quite fourteen. Now she was twenty years old and the mother of two sons.

While Edward III was away from his kingdom, in August 1338, his last surviving uncle died: Thomas of Brotherton, earl of Norfolk and earl marshal of England, passed away at the age of thirty-eight. Thomas was the last surviving child of Edward I – unless the former king Edward II was still alive and at large on the continent somewhere – and was survived by his two daughters and co-heirs, Margaret (born *c.* 1322) and Alice (probably born *c.* 1324). Alice of Norfolk, tragically, would be beaten to death in late 1351 by her husband Edward Montacute, the earl of Salisbury's brother, and some of Montacute's retainers including a William Dunche of Bungay in Suffolk and Thomas, parson of Kelsale in the same county.[8] Alice's elder sister Margaret of Norfolk lived a remarkably long life and finally died in March 1399 well into her seventies, eighteen months after Edward III and Queen Philippa's grandson Richard II had made her duchess of Norfolk; she was the first Englishwoman to be made a duchess in her own right.

Philippa was in the second trimester of pregnancy when she and Edward sailed from England, and on 29 November 1338 gave birth to her fifth child and her third but second surviving son at the abbey of St Michael in Antwerp. The delighted Edward paid John de Bures £100 for bringing him news of his son's birth.[9] The king and queen gave their son the Arthurian name of Lionel, and he was always known in his own lifetime (and indeed still is today) as 'Lionel of Antwerp'. Edward III had called himself 'Sir Lionel' at the jousting tournament in Dunstable in 1334. Once he and Philippa had respectfully and conventionally named their two eldest sons after their fathers Edward II and Willem of Hainault, Edward III was free to choose the Arthurian name he clearly loved for his third, though it is perhaps interesting that none of Lionel's descendants themselves used the name for their sons (perhaps if Lionel himself had had sons, the name might have become more common, but he had only one daughter). Queen Philippa's biographer of the early twentieth century suggested that the name was, apart from its Arthurian associations, chosen to honour the people of Brabant, as the coat of arms of the duchy featured a yellow lion on a black background.[10] Lionel's name was usually spelt Lyonel or Lyonell in contemporary government records and he sometimes appears in the records of his father's government as 'Leo', which either represents the royal clerks getting his rather unusual name wrong, or perhaps was the pet name by which his family called him. The *Brut* chronicle calls him 'Sir Lyonell' or 'Sir Leonell', and Jean Froissart calls him 'Sir Lion'.[11]

In August 1339, Edward III gave the abbey and convent of St Michael in Antwerp the advowson (the right to put forward a candidate for a vacant ecclesiastical office) of a church in Northamptonshire 'in consideration of the long stay the king and Queen Philippa have made in the abbey and the great easements which they have had there, as well as of the fact that the king's son Lionel has been born there and baptised in the church of the abbey.'[12] According to the fifteenth-century chronicle of John Hardyng, in adulthood Lionel of Antwerp was extremely tall and some modern writers claim that he stood nearly seven feet, though as Hardyng was not born until *c.* 1378, ten years after Lionel's death, this statement should be treated with some caution.[13]

Some months before Lionel's birth, in late August and early September 1338, Edward III travelled south from Antwerp along the River Rhine deep into Germany. He took Philippa's brother-in-law Wilhelm, formerly count and now marquis of Jülich, with him, though the pregnant queen herself remained in Antwerp. She sent two of her minstrels, Lambert of Lorraine and John Cornmusere, with her husband, and they performed for him in a place his clerk recorded as 'Sensk', probably Sinzig near Remagen on the River Rhine.[14] Edward III and Wilhelm of Jülich passed through the city of Cologne, where Wilhelm's younger brother Walram ruled as archbishop, on 23 and 24 August. Pleased with the service and loyalty of his queen's brother-in-law, Edward III would make Wilhelm of Jülich the first earl of Cambridge, and promised him £1,000 of land in England annually; he may have done this as early as 1338, or at least had it in mind to do so. In May 1340 Edward acknowledged that he owed Wilhelm the staggeringly large sum of £30,000 in fees and war wages for the last few years. Edward courteously referred to Wilhelm as 'the king's brother'.[15]

Edward III took the time to worship at the shrine of the Three Kings (the Magi or Wise Men of the Gospels) in Cologne Cathedral in August 1338, and left a very generous donation there; he must have seen the magnificent golden casket housing the remains which had been made in 1191, and which stands in Cologne Cathedral to this day. Edward was certainly aware of a prophecy which began circulating in England around 1330 and was known as the Prophecy of the Six Kings, which stated that he was 'the boar who will come out of Windsor' and would have the heart and head of a lion, and would win fame as a great warrior and regain the lands lost by his ancestors. Furthermore, the prophecy stated Edward would one day be buried in Cologne Cathedral amongst the tombs of the Three Kings.[16] Edward duly promised in August 1338 that he would indeed be buried in Cologne, and might well have genuinely intended this to happen (or perhaps simply found it politically useful to claim that he did), though ultimately he was interred in Westminster Abbey in 1377 next to Queen Philippa, as per her dying wish.

During his stay in the city, Edward III dined one evening with the archbishop of Cologne, Walram von Jülich. He paid Walram's minstrels Konrad and Ancelin for entertaining him and Walram as they ate and talked together, presumably with Walram's brother Wilhelm also present.[17] Possibly Edward knew Walram quite well, as the *Anonimalle* chronicle says that the archbishop had travelled to see him in England the year before, in the company of his brother. On his journey through Germany, Edward passed through the lands owned by Wilhelm of Jülich. He probably spent time with his wife's sister Countess Johanna, and perhaps had the chance to visit Wilhelm's great hillside fortress of Nideggen in the Eifel.

In the town of Koblenz south of Cologne in early September, Edward met Philippa's brother-in-law Ludwig of Bavaria, who had convened a *Reichstag* there. A few weeks before Edward III met the emperor in Koblenz, Ludwig had sent a trumpeter called Konrad to perform for Edward and Philippa in Antwerp, and sent another eleven minstrels, including one called Master Ichell, to entertain Edward at his residence on the island of Niederwerth just outside Koblenz.[18] Six of the seven electors, the powerful politicians who elected the kings of Germany, were also in Koblenz, including the archbishop Walram von Jülich, and the archbishop of Trier, Balduin of Luxembourg (born *c.* 1285), a first cousin of Queen Philippa's late father. According to Froissart, Empress Margaretha was also in Koblenz, and piled Edward with splendid gifts on his departure 'for love of her sister, the queen of England'.[19] In probably the greatest diplomatic coup of his entire fifty-year reign, Edward III persuaded the emperor to ally with him against Philip VI and the French. Ludwig made the king of England a vicar of the Holy Roman Empire in a great ceremony held outside the *Kastorkirche* or Church of Saint Castor in Koblenz. This was a huge triumph for the English king, though the alliance would not last long, and only a year later Ludwig had evidently decided that Edward was a political liability and did his best to dismiss him as vicar of the Empire.[20] The emperor later allied with Philip VI against Edward.

A man referred to in Edward III's accounts as William *le Galeys*, 'the Welshman,' was brought to Edward III while the king was in Koblenz in early September 1338. The royal accounts state that William 'says that he is the king's father' and 'claims to be the king of England, father of the present lord the king'.[21] There is evidence, from the Fieschi Letter of *c.* 1338, addressed to Edward III by an Italian papal notary and future bishop called Manuele Fieschi, that Edward II had ultimately made his way to Italy after escaping from Berkeley Castle in September 1327 shortly before two men arrived there to murder him. The Fieschi Letter states that the former king landed at the port of Sluis sometime after the execution of Roger Mortimer in late 1330, travelled through France to visit Pope John XXII in Avignon, then travelled through the duchy of Brabant (where his sister Margaret, the dowager duchess, still lived) and visited the shrine of the Three Kings in Cologne Cathedral before setting off on the long journey south over the Alps to Milan and ultimately to the hermitage of Sant'Alberto di Butrio sixty miles south of Milan.

Whether Edward III knew it yet in August 1338 or not, he was following in his supposedly dead father's footsteps when he himself visited the shrine of the Three Kings, and it may be significant that according to the Fieschi Letter, Edward II passed through Cologne sometime in the early 1330s, around the time that Walram von Jülich, connected to Edward III via marriage, was elected the city's archbishop in January 1332. Edward II's route from Brabant to Cologne and then south to Milan would have taken him through territory ruled by Walram von Jülich's brother Wilhelm and by the nobly born and hugely influential archbishop of Trier, Balduin von Luxembourg, brother of the late emperor Henry of Luxembourg (d. 1313) and uncle of Henry's son Johann 'the Blind', king of Bohemia. Walram, Wilhelm and Balduin were with Edward III in Koblenz in early September 1338 when 'William the Welshman' was taken to meet the English king, and 'William' had been brought from Cologne to meet Edward III by an Italian sergeant-at-arms called Francekino Forcetti.

It is peculiar that Edward III had a man claiming to be his father brought to him at exactly the time that he was meeting some of the most powerful politicians in Europe and taking part in probably the most important negotiations of his entire long reign. If Edward merely wished to see the royal pretender to ascertain that he was not in fact Edward II or even just out of curiosity, he could have had the man brought to him at any time, and it is hard to imagine that Walram von Jülich and his brother Wilhelm and Balduin von Luxembourg were unaware that a man claiming to be Edward III's father passed through their territories in the early 1330s on his way to Italy, and again a few years later in the late summer of 1338. Balduin von Luxembourg was the ruler of Koblenz and can hardly have remained unaware of the presence of a man claiming to be the king of England's father in his own town.

The king's wardrobe accounts might indicate that 'William the Welshman' travelled to Antwerp when Edward III returned there, and if so, it is not impossible that this man met Philippa, then heavily pregnant with her son Lionel, and even that he spent Christmas 1338 with the royal couple a few weeks after Philippa gave birth on 29 November. If she did, and if this man was indeed Edward II still alive eleven years after his alleged death, this was the first and presumably the only occasion when Philippa had a chance to meet her father-in-law. This is the last reference to Edward II, or to a pretender claiming to be him, and after 1338 he disappears from history (although his widow Isabella and their son the king marked the anniversary of his supposed death on 21 September every year).

Ludwig of Bavaria sent his King of Heralds and piper, Ludekin, to entertain Philippa and Edward in Antwerp on Christmas Day, and on 28 December 1338, the feast of the Holy Innocents, the 'singing boys' of the local cathedral came to perform for the king and queen. Philippa's purification after Lionel's birth took place on 6 January 1339, the feast of the Epiphany. Her minstrel Luberkin performed for her, as did Ludekin the piper, who was still in the king and queen of England's company, and other unnamed minstrels sent by Edward III's brother-in-law Reynald II, duke (formerly count) of Guelders and Edward's cousin Jan III, duke of Brabant.[22]

Edward III and Queen Philippa were accompanied overseas in and after 1338 by a young couple they both liked very much, and who were both related to the king: John, Lord Beaumont, and his wife Eleanor of Lancaster (who was named at the top of the long list of people the queen took overseas in her retinue). John was born in 1317 as the son and heir of Henry, Lord Beaumont, a French nobleman by birth who died in early 1340 and who was a second cousin of Edward II. John's mother Alice Comyn was Scottish, one of the two nieces and co-heirs of John Comyn, earl of Buchan (d. 1308). John's wife Eleanor of Lancaster, born around 1316/18, was the fifth of the six daughters of the elderly earl of Lancaster and Leicester, and was one of the sisters of Henry of Grosmont. Eleanor became pregnant with her first child in early 1339, and she and John Beaumont made arrangements to return to England so that their child could be born there; English law at the time held that lands in England and Wales could only be inherited by people born within the allegiance of their king, that is, England itself, Wales, Ireland, Ponthieu or Gascony. In addition to this law, English landowners generally preferred their heirs to be born on their own estates so that the heir's birth there would be generally known to their tenants, and would not be questioned. Edward III and Queen Philippa, however, persuaded the Beaumont/Lancaster couple to remain with them in the duchy of Brabant and not to return to England for the birth, as they found their company 'greatly desirable'. Edward III further stated that Philippa found the young couple's presence of considerable comfort to her.[23]

John and Eleanor's son Henry Beaumont was duly born in Brabant in late 1339 or at the beginning of 1340. This birth outside the lands ruled by Edward III was to cause the boy problems ten years later when his grandmother Alice Beaumont née Comyn died and he should have been named as the heir to her lands. The jurors, however, ruled that as his father John Beaumont had died 'without an heir of his body born within the realm of England or the allegiance of the king of England,' the lands should pass instead to his uncle, John's younger brother Thomas. In February 1351, therefore, Edward III declared that Henry Beaumont and all other Englishmen 'born beyond the sea' should have the full right to their inheritances, and changed English law to accommodate them. Edward III had also stated in December 1340: 'taking into consideration that the said John [Beaumont] and Eleanor [of Lancaster] at the time of the conception and birth of the said Henry were cohabiting continually in Brabant in his company in marital intercourse, [he] reputes Henry to be their true and legitimate son.'[24] This gives some indication of the closeness between Edward III and Philippa and the young Beaumont/Lancaster couple. The king and queen also conceived a child some months after John and Eleanor conceived their son Henry: Philippa became pregnant for the sixth time around early to mid-June 1339, probably while she and the king were in Antwerp or Diest, not much more than half a year after the last time she had given birth. As two of their sons would be born abroad, this was also a reason for Edward III's change of the English law at the beginning of the 1350s.

Philippa kept herself informed of events in England during her long sojourn on the continent, and in August 1339 heard that a sergeant called Roger Mynot had stolen two horses, worth twenty marks, in Essex. Mynot was 'now vagabond in Essex … with the horses, asserting that they are the horses of Queen Philippa and that he is appointed to make purveyance for them and other horses of the queen, and is extorting money.' An indignant Philippa, furious that her good name was being used to steal and extort money and possessions, brought the matter to her husband's attention. Edward III appointed two men to arrest Mynot.[25]

Founding a College

Edward III was officially proclaimed king of France in the marketplace in the town of Ghent on 26 January 1340. He and the heavily pregnant Philippa, and their sons Edward of Woodstock and Lionel of Antwerp, had arrived in Ghent that day, accompanied by Edward's kinsmen and allies Reynald II of Guelders and Jan III of Brabant. The royal couple took up residence in the abbey of St Bavo, and a special guard was posted around the building to ensure their safety. According to Jean Froissart, Philippa had spent the winter of 1339/40 in the castle of Louvain (or Leuven in Dutch) in the duchy of Brabant, and was visited there by her brother Willem, count of Hainault and Holland, and their mother Jeanne de Valois, apparently given permission to leave the abbey near Valenciennes where she now lived. It is at this point that Froissart claims Jeanne de Valois loved Philippa 'with all her heart more tenderly than any of her [other] daughters' (*car elle l'amoit de tout son coer plus tenrement que nulles de ses filles*). Froissart adds that Willem's wife Johanna, future duchess of Brabant in her own right when her father died, also visited her sister-in-law Queen Philippa in Louvain that winter.[1]

On 6 March 1340 at the abbey of St Bavo in Ghent where she had lived for the previous few weeks, Philippa gave birth to her sixth child, John. John's father had returned to England some weeks before, but the queen was too heavily pregnant to be able to accompany her husband, and Edward III did not see the infant until about 10 July when he returned to Ghent. The royal couple's second son Lionel of Antwerp remained in Ghent with his mother.[2] Edward III gave £200 to Philippa's damsels Amice of Gloucester, Alice Betyngfield and Margery St Maur or Semor who brought him news of little John's birth, and the same Margery was John's first nurse, replaced some years later by Isolde or Isolda Newman. John's first wet-nurse was Margery Tilsthorpe.[3] He was perhaps named in honour of his father's late brother John of Eltham, earl of Cornwall, who had died in September 1336 three and a half years before John was born. Chronicler Jean Froissart says, however, that he was named after his godfather Jan III, duke of Brabant, who was a grandson of Edward I of England and thus Edward III's cousin. When Queen Philippa attended her first mass after giving birth to John, she received a gift of three expensive cloths, one brown, one red and one parti-coloured.[4]

Edward and Philippa's third son should be known as 'John of Ghent,' but 'John of Gaunt' has become standard in English thanks in great part to Shakespeare, who called him 'Old John of Gaunt, time-honour'd Lancaster' in the first line of his play about John's nephew Richard II (reigned 1377 to 1399). In his own lifetime, John was usually referred to on record as 'John de Gandavo', the Latinised form of the name. John of Gaunt sits alongside his legendary eldest brother the 'Black Prince' as the most famous of Edward III and Philippa of Hainault's many children, largely as a result of Anya Seton's enduringly popular novel *Katherine* about John and his long-term mistress, later his third wife, Katherine Swynford. Eight of John of Gaunt's children lived into adulthood. His eldest surviving son was Henry IV, who ruled from 1399 to 1413, and his eldest daughter Philippa and third daughter Catalina became queen of Portugal and queen of Castile respectively.

On 3 May 1340, Edward III attempted to arrange the future marriage of his eldest son to Margarethe of Brabant, second daughter of Duke Jan III of Brabant, Edward of Woodstock's second cousin, and the younger sister of the countess of Hainault and Holland. Born in 1323, Margarethe was seven years the boy's senior. Although Edward III granted the rights to his eldest son's marriage to Duke Jan and promised that if the wedding to Margarethe did not go ahead he would repay her dowry twofold, it never took place. In 1344 Pope Clement VI refused to grant a dispensation for consanguinity on the grounds that Edward of Woodstock's marriage into the French royal family would be more useful to 'make peace between the two crowns'. Clement told Jeanne of Burgundy, wife of Philip VI and the queen-consort of France, in December 1344 that he was still pondering whether or not to grant the dispensation for Edward of Woodstock to marry a daughter of the duke of Brabant, and that he tended to favour Philip and Jeanne's daughter Blanche for a marriage to one of the duke's sons instead. He also thanked Queen Jeanne for the 'excellent cheeses' she had sent him, perhaps as a kind of bribe to ensure the failure of the proposed England-Brabant union.[5]

Queen Philippa was also doing her utmost to persuade the pope to favour her husband over her uncle Philip VI during their struggle over the French throne: Clement VI thanked her in early September 1343 for sending him a 'ring set with precious diamonds'. Philippa's mother-in-law the dowager queen Isabella of France also sent the pope an unspecified jewel, perhaps also intended as a bribe so that he would favour her son over her cousin Philip VI and the French.[6]

In September and October 1338, Philippa paid a minstrel called Gerard the very generous sum of eighteen pence a day – in an era when labourers earned about two pence a day on average and master craftsmen six pence – to travel to Paris on her and her husband's behalf. Gerard was instructed to 'investigate secretly the actions of Lord Philip de Valois' for forty days.[7] Sending a minstrel as a spy was a clever idea, as they often travelled around Europe from royal court to royal court, and hence the presence of an English minstrel in Paris was unlikely to arouse much suspicion. After Edward III claimed the French throne in 1337, neither he nor Philippa referred to her uncle as king, but only as 'Philip de Valois' or 'Philip, count of Valois'. There is no doubt whatsoever that Philippa supported her husband loyally and whole-heartedly against Philip VI. The king of France was of course her own uncle, but whether they had much of a relationship is unclear. It is certainly possible that Philip and Philippa only ever met a handful of times and did not know each other very well.

Edward III struck a mighty blow against the French when his fleet won a great victory over Philip VI and his forces at the sea battle of Sluis on 24 June 1340. Nobody dared to tell the French king the outcome, except his jester, who informed the king that the cowardly English clung to their ships while the brave Frenchmen flung themselves into the sea. The English, for their part, joked that if the fish in Sluis harbour could speak, they would speak French, owing to the number of French bodies they had nibbled at. Bodies from the battle washed up on shore for the next few days and supposedly somewhere in the region of 17,000 Frenchmen drowned during the battle (though medieval estimates of the size of armies and of the number of casualties suffered are often gross exaggerations).[8] Queen Philippa hastened from Ghent to meet and congratulate her husband, and spent time with him on his ship, the *Thomas*.[9] Edward III sent a letter to 'Philip, count of Valois' in the aftermath of the battle, demanding the throne of France and stating that Philip had stolen his inheritance from him. A stunned Philip could only respond that he knew of no-one with the name 'Philip de Valois'.[10]

The following September, Edward received a visit from his mother-in-law Jeanne de Valois, dowager countess of Hainault and nun of Fontenelle. She had already visited her brother Philip, and now begged Edward to cease the fighting between them. The king of England did consent to send envoys to treat with Philip, and agreed to a truce between the two kingdoms to last until the following midsummer.[11]

In the summer of 1340, Edward III and Queen Philippa set up a household for their four younger children Isabella of Woodstock, Joan of Woodstock, Lionel of Antwerp and John of Gaunt. The French noblewoman Isabella de la Mote was appointed as its *maistresce*, 'mistress' or 'governess', the woman in overall charge of the household. A few years previously, 'the wife of Sir William de St Omer' was said to be in charge of the household of the royal children, then Edward of Woodstock, Isabella and Joan.[12] Isabella of Woodstock, as the eldest royal daughter, had three damsels or female attendants and her younger sister Joan had two, while Lionel and John had one nurse and one wet-nurse each and a *maistresce* for the two of them. Other senior staff of the royal children's household included a controller, two chaplains and a clerk of the chapel, and they had their own minstrel, Gerard le Gaeyt. Queen Philippa remained on the continent with her husband for the time being, but their children were sent back to England at the beginning of August 1340 or a little earlier: evidently there were fears for their safety, especially that of the two little boys, who were potential targets for kidnap by French forces.[13]

Until the establishment of the royal children's household in 1340, Philippa and Edward's second daughter Joan of Woodstock had been in the official custody of Marie de St Pol, dowager countess of Pembroke, beginning sometime before April 1338.[14] Lady de la Mote, the royal children's *maistresce*, had already been put in charge of Joan of Woodstock's household in July 1337 or earlier, under the overall control of the countess of Pembroke. Countess Marie, born *c.* 1303/4, was the daughter of the count of St Pol in northern France and was a great-granddaughter of Henry III of England, making her a second cousin of Edward III. Her older sister Mahaut (*c.* 1293-1358) was the much younger third wife of the late Charles de Valois, and was thus Queen Philippa's step-grandmother.

From 1321 to 1324, Marie was married to the decades-older Aymer de Valence, earl of Pembroke, never remarried, and outlived him by fifty-three years: she died in May 1377 in her seventies, just a few weeks before Edward III himself. Marie founded Pembroke College, originally called the Hall of Valence Marie, at the University of Cambridge in 1347, and herself had no children. The royal daughters Isabella and Joan were considered old enough to accompany their parents to tournament by 1342, when they were ten and eight respectively, probably accompanied by Marie de St Pol and Isabella de la Mote.[15]

In August and September 1340, before he decided on a temporary truce with Philip VI after the visit of his mother-in-law Jeanne, Edward III besieged the French-controlled town of Tournai. Queen Philippa became pregnant with her seventh child probably in September 1340, only about six months after John of Gaunt's birth. That November, Edward III quarrelled with John Stratford, formerly bishop of Winchester and now archbishop of Canterbury, and sent a long and emotional letter to Pope Clement VI complaining about Stratford. The king received no money at all from England throughout his siege of Tournai, and exclaimed afterwards 'I believe that the archbishop wished me, by lack of money, to be betrayed and killed.' He added the remarkable statement that Stratford 'spoke apart [i.e. separately] of me to my wife, and apart of my wife to me, in order that, if he were listened to, he might provoke us to such anger as to divide us forever.'[16]

What Stratford had said to the royal couple is unknown, but obviously, given Edward's reaction that it was likely to drive him and Philippa apart forever, it must have been deadly serious. Edward's biographer Ian Mortimer has pointed out that Edward and Philippa's seventh child, born on or a little before 5 June 1341, must have been born prematurely, as the king did not return to his wife at Ghent after the two-month siege of Tournai until 28 September 1340, and had left Philippa in the town on 16 July 1340. That is a short pregnancy for a child born on 5 June and perhaps even in late May 1341. It is possible, though only possible, that Stratford had made some accusation of adultery on Queen Philippa's part.[17] If so, the king did not himself ever accuse her of any wrongdoing, nor did he disavow their child, and their relationship evidently remained as strong and close as ever. The king's statement to the pope is, however, fascinating and intriguing: Archbishop Stratford talked to Edward and Philippa separately and told them something, or insinuated something, that might have destroyed their marriage forever had they believed him. It is telling that Edward made a point of saying 'if he were listened to', strongly implying that he refused to give any credence to whatever Stratford had told him about Philippa.

The queen was still in Ghent on 25 October 1340 when she granted lifelong custody of her Wiltshire castle of Devizes, its forest and all the lands around it to Sir Roger Beauchamp, father of her godson Philip.[18] She and the king returned to England at the end of November, and the Christmas of 1340, when Philippa was several months pregnant, was spent at Reading. On 31 January 1341 Philippa was at Langley in Hertfordshire, where her latest child would be born a few months later, with Edward III, and she was still there on 15 March. It seems that Philippa lived at the palace of Langley – usually called 'Childerlangley' in the fourteenth century and formerly her father-in-law Edward II's and his mother Queen Leonor's favourite residence – for much of the first half of 1341, though on 18 March she had moved the twenty-five miles to Windsor Castle.[19] Philippa's second daughter Joan of Woodstock, now seven, was ill in April 1341, and Joan's concerned father sent his personal physician John Gaddesden to look after her.[20]

Duke John III of Brittany, a great-grandson of Henry III of England and thus Edward III's kinsman, died on 30 April 1341, in his mid-fifties. John had been married three times – his first wife was Isabelle de Valois, elder sister of Philip VI and Queen Philippa's mother Countess Jeanne – but left no legitimate children. His preferred heir was his niece Jeanne de Penthièvre (b. *c.* 1319), daughter of his late full brother Guy and married to Philippa's cousin Charles of Blois. Duke John's younger half-brother John de Montfort (b. *c.* 1295), however, also claimed the duchy, and the long struggle between the Montfort faction and the Penthièvre/Blois faction is called the War of the Breton Succession. Philip VI of France took the Penthièvre/Blois side, as Charles of Blois was his nephew; Edward III of England took the Montfort side. The Penthièvre/Blois faction struck an important blow in November 1341 when they captured John de Montfort. Montfort was married to Joan of Flanders, and their son John de Montfort the younger was born in late 1339; he would later become Queen Philippa's son-in-law.

Edward III, meanwhile, assigned the income from the lands in England formerly held by Duke John III of Brittany, as earl of Richmond, to Queen Philippa 'for the sustenance of the king's children Lionel, John, Isabella and Joan.'[21]

In 1341, Philippa's chaplain Robert de Eglesfeld or Eaglesfield founded the 'Hall of the Queen's Scholars' at the University of Oxford, and named it in her honour. Edward III granted a licence for Robert to 'found a hall of scholars, chaplains and others ... under the name of the Queen's Hall' on 18 January 1341. It later became known as Queen's College, and still exists. Robert came from the village of Eaglesfield in the county of Cumberland (modern-day Cumbria), and intended the foundation to educate poor boys from Cumberland and Westmorland and to enable the boys to return there as clergymen. A grant by Queen Philippa, dated 23 July 1341, calls her 'patroness of a hall of scholars in Oxford, newly founded by Robert de Eglesfeld, king's clerk, which is called Queen's Hall, Oxford.' She gave Eaglesfield the advowson of a church in Westmorland, and a 'licence for them to appropriate the church to augment the number of scholars by six scholars, chaplains, to dwell in the hall and celebrate divine service daily, according to an ordinance to be made, for the good estate of the king, the said queen and their children, for their souls after death, and for the souls of the king's ancestors and the faithful departed.'

The provost and scholars of the new hall, however, had to petition the king in July 1342, stating that they were only 'moderately endowed' and 'have nothing whereof to live' except for one village in Cumberland 'now destroyed by the Scots'. The men pointed out that 'his [the king's] consort is their founder and patron,' and Edward III, 'desiring to be a partaker in the pious work of the foundation of such a house', agreed to help them. Edward also granted the provost and scholars his hospital of St Julian in Southampton, called 'God's House,' in March 1344.[22] The fourteenth century was a great age of college foundations at Oxford and Cambridge. Among others, Philippa's father-in-law Edward II founded Oriel at Oxford in 1326 and the King's Hall at Cambridge (later incorporated into Trinity College) in 1317, the bishop of Exeter founded Exeter College at Oxford in 1314, Edward III's first cousin Elizabeth de Burgh née de Clare re-founded Clare Hall, later Clare College, in 1338 (originally established in 1326), and Marie de St Pol, dowager countess of Pembroke, founded Pembroke College at Cambridge in 1347. Queen Philippa was also a patron of St Stephen's chapel at Westminster and the hospital of St Katherine by the Tower in London. In late 1351, Philippa issued letters patent for the 'regulation of the hospital' of St Katherine, which had been founded by her husband's great-grandmother Eleanor of Provence, Henry III's widow, on 5 July 1273. The hospital staff and residents consisted of a master, three brethren, three sisters, six poor clerks and eighteen poor women. By 1380, eleven years after Queen Philippa's death, the hospital of St Katherine by the Tower was in urgent need of repair throughout and the roof was falling down.[23]

Philippa gave birth to her seventh child at the royal palace of Langley on or before 5 June 1341. It was a boy, the fifth son Philippa had borne and the fourth who would survive childhood.[24] The king and queen named their son Edmund, probably in honour of Edward III's late uncle Edmund of Woodstock, earl of Kent, executed in March 1330. The boy would always be known as 'Edmund of Langley', usually spelt *Esmon de Langele* in contemporary documents. His nurse was Joan of Oxford and the rocker of his cradle was Maud Plumpton, both of whom had previously looked after Edmund's much older brother Edward of Woodstock. Joan was later replaced by Agnes Markaunt.[25]

Edward III again assigned custody of all the late Duke John III of Brittany's lands in England to Philippa on 25 June 1341 to the value of 2,000 marks yearly, of which £1,000 was set aside for 'the sustenance of Lionel, John and Edmund, the king's sons, and Isabella and Joan, his daughters'.[26] He had previously made this grant to Philippa for the sustenance of their children a few weeks before, and altered the wording of the grant so that it now referred to Edmund as well.

Edmund of Langley remained in Queen Philippa's custody until the end of September 1354 when he was thirteen, when he 'withdrew from her keeping'.[27] That is in fact much longer than one might normally expect; royal and noble sons of the era tended to remain in the household of one or both parents until the age of seven, when they were sent to live elsewhere. A record dating to sometime between 1349 and 1351 details payments made by Queen Philippa for the oblations (offerings made to God or the saints) of Edmund of Langley and his eldest sister Isabella of Woodstock, eleven years his senior, indicating that they both lived in the queen's household.[28] The year he left his mother's household, 1354, Edmund petitioned his father regarding some lands in Yorkshire, calling himself his 'little son Edmund' (*son petit fuiz Esmon*).[29] He was, then, still the youngest son of the king and queen.

John de Warenne, the elderly earl of Surrey (he was born in 1286) and Surrey's nephew and heir Richard Fitzalan, earl of

Arundel (born *c.* 1313), were chosen as little Edmund of Langley's godfathers in 1341. For all that the earl of Surrey was her fifth son's godfather and her second son William of Hatfield had been born at one of his manors in early 1337, Philippa did not approve of the earl's private life. Surrey had married Jeanne de Bar, a granddaughter of Edward I and thus Edward III's first cousin, all the way back in May 1306 (six and a half years before Edward III was even born), but the marriage had been a disaster. By 1313 or even before, the couple lived apart, and over the next few years Surrey made attempts to have his marriage annulled and to have his illegitimate sons with his mistress Maud Nerford made his heirs. In the 1340s, Maud Nerford was dead, and Surrey had begun another long-term extramarital relationship with the young Isabella Holland (b. 1310s or early 1320s), sister of the knights Robert, Thomas and Otto Holland.

The earl of Surrey made another bid to have his marriage of thirty-five years annulled so that he could marry Isabella Holland, and even pretended to have had an affair with his wife Jeanne's late aunt Mary (1279-1332), one of Edward II's sisters who was veiled as a nun of Amesbury Priory in childhood, before he married Jeanne de Bar. He hoped that this would persuade the pope to annul his and Jeanne's marriage on the grounds of incest. He chose Mary as she was a close relative of his wife, was conveniently dead and thus unable to refute the story, and had no children to take offence at his claims. Queen Philippa sent an indignant letter to Pope Clement VI, probably in 1343 or early 1344, asking him to order the earl of Surrey to treat Jeanne de Bar with the marital affection she deserved. By birth, Jeanne de Bar was French – her mother Eleanor (1269-1298) was Edward II's eldest sister and her father Henri III (d. 1302) was count of Bar in eastern France. The queen of France, Philip VI's wife Jeanne of Burgundy, also took an interest in her plight. Queen Jeanne wrote to the pope to complain about the earl of Surrey's shabby treatment of his countess.[30] Clement VI obliged the two queens and ordered Surrey to treat his wife with marital affection, but although Surrey and Jeanne de Bar remained married, the pope's appeals had no effect and Surrey continued to live with his mistress.

John de Warenne, earl of Surrey, died in late June 1347 the day before his sixty-first birthday, and left a crystal goblet ornamented with silver-gilt and a tripod to his then six-year-old godson Edmund of Langley, whom he called *Sire Esmon de Langele*. He also left items to his many illegitimate children and pointedly called his mistress Isabella Holland his *compaigne*, meaning consort or wife. To Jeanne de Bar, his royal wife of forty-one years, the earl left nothing. She outlived him by fourteen years and died in 1361, and Surrey's primary heir was his nephew the earl of Arundel.[31]

The King and the Countess
of Salisbury

A shadow may have been cast over Philippa's pregnancy with Edmund of Langley in 1340/41, thanks to the interference of the archbishop of Canterbury, though if Edward had ever entertained the suspicion that Edmund was not his son, he never acted on it. It does seem to be the case, however, that Edward showed more favour to his and Philippa's three eldest sons than to their youngest two, Edmund of Langley and Thomas of Woodstock (who was not born until 1355). Edward of Woodstock the eldest son was made earl of Chester when he was a baby, John of Gaunt was made earl of Richmond in January 1342 before he turned two, and Lionel's marriage to the heiress Elizabeth de Burgh was arranged in May 1341 when he was two and a half. Edmund did not gain a title until November 1362 when he was twenty-one years old and was the only one of the five royal brothers not to marry an heiress, though in fairness his father tried for years to arrange his marriage to Margarethe of Flanders, which would have brought Edmund control of the continental counties of Flanders, Artois, Nevers and Rethel on her father's death. When this fell through, however, Edmund was persuaded to marry Isabel of Castile, younger sister of his elder brother John of Gaunt's second wife Constanza, daughter and heir of King Pedro 'the Cruel'. Edmund's marriage strengthened English ties to the deposed royal line of Castile but brought Edmund himself no benefits whatsoever. Edward III arranged Thomas of Woodstock's marriage to a great heiress, Eleanor de Bohun, but did not give him a title. Thomas was already twenty-two when Edward died.

Edward III and Philippa of Hainault's middle three sons were close in age: Lionel of Antwerp born on 29 November 1338, John of Gaunt born on 6 March 1340, and now Edmund of Langley, less than fifteen months younger than John. The royal couple's eldest and youngest sons, by contrast, were much older and much younger than their brothers: Edward of Woodstock was eight and a half years older than Lionel, and the fifth and youngest surviving son, Thomas of Woodstock, was thirteen and a half years younger than Edmund of Langley. The births of the three royal sons between November 1338 and May 1341 must have made the king breathe much more easily, as the succession to his throne had been made secure.

From June 1330 until January 1337 the king had only one son and heir, then William of Hatfield was born but, sadly, almost immediately died. The little boy's death meant that, until Lionel was born in late 1338 eight and a half years after Edward of Woodstock's birth, Edward III still had only one son. The death of Edward III's only brother John of Eltham in September 1336, leaving no children, had made the situation potentially even more precarious, and meant that Edward of Woodstock was the king's only male heir. Edward of Norfolk (b. sometime in the 1320s), the only son of Edward III's half-uncle Thomas of Brotherton, earl of Norfolk (d. August 1338), died as a child in or before 1334, and Edward III's other half-uncle Edmund of Woodstock (d. March 1330) left only one surviving son, John of Kent, born in April 1330 shortly after his father's execution. Until Lionel of Antwerp was born, followed soon afterwards by his brothers John of Gaunt and Edmund of Langley, there was a disturbing lack of male children in the English royal family.

On 5 May 1341 a few weeks before Edmund of Langley's birth, Edward III and Queen Philippa's second son Lionel of Antwerp was betrothed to the great heiress Elizabeth de Burgh. Lionel was under two and a half years old at the time, and Elizabeth, born on 6 July 1332, was almost six and a half years his senior. She was the only child and heir of the late William de Burgh, earl of Ulster (1312-1333) and was also the heir of her paternal grandmother the senior Elizabeth de Burgh, née de Clare (1295-1360), Edward III's cousin and the founder of Clare College, Cambridge.

The young Elizabeth was one of the greatest heiresses of the fourteenth century, and Edward III, as he had perhaps been planning to do since she was born, snapped her up for his and Philippa's second son. The king held a jousting tournament at Dunstable in Bedfordshire in February 1342 to celebrate the engagement of the two young children.[1]

The king went on campaign to Scotland again at the end of 1341. Chronicler Jean le Bel gives a detailed but almost certainly untrue story of how, during this campaign, Edward III raped the countess of Salisbury. Le Bel claims that Edward had conceived a 'passionate love' for the countess when he rescued her from a castle which the Scots were besieging, and that when the countess knelt in front of him, she was so glorious and stunning that Edward instantly became smitten and could not control his lust. What follows next, according to le Bel, is unspeakably horrible: Edward is said to have gone to the countess's chamber, gagged her and raped and beaten her so savagely that she was left bleeding and battered.

There are many reasons, however, to reject the story, not least because Jean le Bel names the countess of Salisbury as 'Alice' when in fact she was called Katherine (née Grandison). She was the wife of Edward's closest friend William Montacute and had brought Edward news of the birth of his son Edward of Woodstock in June 1330, so evidently was very close to Queen Philippa, and had named her third daughter Philippa Montacute after the queen.[2] Whether Edward III was completely faithful or not to Philippa of Hainault throughout the first thirty years of their marriage is unknown, but it seems almost certain that he had no long-term mistress until the early 1360s when Philippa was very ill and in pain for the last few years of her life. There seems no reason to accuse the king of the crime of rape. Le Bel naming the countess of Salisbury as 'Alice' perhaps represents a confusion with Edward III's first cousin Alice of Norfolk, younger daughter and co-heir of the late Thomas of Brotherton, earl of Norfolk, who was beaten to death by her husband and his retainers in 1351. Alice's husband was the earl of Salisbury's younger brother, Edward Montacute.

Queen Philippa gave birth to her eighth child and third daughter Blanche in 1342, either in March or June, at the Tower of London.[3]

If Blanche of the Tower was born in March 1342, it cannot have been a full-term pregnancy, as Philippa gave birth to her son Edmund of Langley at the end of May or early June 1341, and would have been 'off-limits' to her husband for at least thirty days after birth, probably forty, until she was churched. She and Edward therefore cannot have resumed intimate relations until the end of June 1341 at the earliest.

The name Blanche was an unusual one in both their families, and was not found on Philippa's side of the family and only several generations back on Edward's: one of his great-grandmothers was Blanche of Artois (*c.* 1245/48-1302), queen of Navarre by her first marriage and countess of Lancaster by her second. The little Blanche of the Tower may therefore have been named in honour of the newly-born second daughter of Henry of Grosmont, earl of Derby and Isabella Beaumont: Blanche of Lancaster, who was born on 25 March 1342 and who would later marry John of Gaunt. Blanche of Lancaster may have been named after her father's eldest sister Blanche, Lady Wake, who was perhaps her godmother, and Blanche of Artois was her great-grandmother as well as Edward III's.[4] Blanche of the Tower was, sadly, another of Philippa's children who died young, and she was buried at Westminster Abbey in early February 1343 a few months after birth. If she was born prematurely, as seems likely given that she was born so soon after her brother Edmund, this might explain why she did not live very long.

In October 1341 Henry of Grosmont had gone to Scotland as the king's lieutenant and remained there until April 1342, so must have missed the birth of his younger daughter Blanche of Lancaster in March that year.[5] Almost certainly he had hoped for a son who one day would come into the vast Lancastrian inheritance of his father the elder Henry, earl of Lancaster and Leicester, who was still alive in 1342 and was now over sixty. Grosmont's elder daughter Maud, named after his mother Maud Chaworth (d. 1322), was not quite two years old when her sister Blanche was born, and at the end of 1344, aged only four, she married for the first time. Her wedding took place in her grandfather Henry of Lancaster's town of Leicester, and her father Grosmont held a jousting tournament there to celebrate the event.[6] The bridegroom was little Ralph

Stafford (b. *c.* late 1330s or early 1340s), son and heir of the king's friend Sir Ralph Stafford (made first earl of Stafford in 1351), and heir also of his maternal grandfather Hugh Audley, earl of Gloucester. The marriage of the two young children did not last long: Ralph Stafford died before November 1347, leaving his younger brother Hugh Stafford as heir.[7]

Edward III, like his cousin Grosmont, was also in Scotland, and was at Melrose and Roxburgh for Christmas 1341 and New Year 1342. At the end of January and beginning of February 1342 he was far to the south, at Castle Rising in Norfolk visiting his mother the dowager queen Isabella, with whom he seems to have been on rather better terms as more time passed since her disastrous regency of 1327 to 1330.

Edward and Philippa's third son, John of Gaunt, not yet two years old, was made earl of Richmond on 21 January 1342, a title which had belonged to Duke John III of Brittany (d. 1341). John of Gaunt was officially confirmed as earl on 20 September 1342.[8] Queen Philippa was at Langley on 31 January 1342 when she sent a letter to the chancellor, Robert Parving, so did not travel to Castle Rising with her husband to visit her mother-in-law (perhaps she was too far gone with her daughter Blanche to be able or willing to travel in comfort).[9]

Edward III's great jousting tournament at Dunstable in Bedfordshire on 11 and 12 February 1342 was held to celebrate the betrothal of his son Lionel to Elizabeth de Burgh. Philippa was there. It was, even by the standards of Edward III's glittering and spectacular jousting tournaments, a magnificent occasion. All the 'armed youth' of England were said to be present, no foreigners were there (except of course the queen herself), and supposedly no fewer than 250 knights took part. Philippa's former ward Laurence Hastings, earl of Pembroke, not quite twenty-one years old, fought in the tournament, as did William de Bohun, earl of Northampton, Thomas Beauchamp, earl of Warwick, Robert Ufford, earl of Suffolk, and John de Vere, earl of Oxford. Edward III himself fought in the disguise of a 'simple knight', and the rather enigmatic motto he devised for the tournament was 'It is as it is,' in English rather than in French, the usual language of the English court and elite. Little Lionel of Antwerp, the possibly rather bewildered fiancé for whom the whole event was held – he was only three years old – was given a state bed powdered with silk roses, while the king and queen had one covered in green cloth embroidered with silk dragons. Edward III had twelve red hangings made, more than twenty feet long and more than ten feet wide, with the motto 'It is as it is' embroidered onto them.[10] Presumably Lionel's fiancée Elizabeth de Burgh and her mother Maud of Lancaster, her maternal grandfather Henry, earl of Lancaster and Leicester, and her paternal grandmother the elder Elizabeth de Burgh (b. 1295), were also present in the stands.

John, Lord Beaumont, who had accompanied the king and queen to the continent in 1338/39 and whose wife Eleanor of Lancaster gave birth to their son Henry in late 1339 in the duchy of Brabant, was killed at a jousting tournament held a little later in 1342, perhaps on 14 April when Edward III is known to have held a tournament at Northampton. Queen Philippa may have attended this tournament as well, depending how advanced she was in her pregnancy with Blanche of the Tower, or whether she had recovered after the birth. If the story told by chronicler Jean le Bel that John Beaumont was killed while jousting is true, Philippa may personally have witnessed the death of the young nobleman she and her husband liked so much and had spent much time with.[11] Edward III, who was obviously hugely fond of his cousin Eleanor of Lancaster, rather remarkably gave her all the lands her late husband had held as her dower, although it was usual for widows to receive only one-third of their late husbands' lands.[12]

Queen Philippa's brother Willem, count of Hainault and Holland, visited England in 1342, according to chronicler Jean le Bel. His stay would appear to have been a long one: he apparently attended a jousting tournament held at Eltham in Kent in May, and was still there for yet another great tournament that August. He may have been wounded at the Eltham tournament, but if so, it cannot have been a serious injury.[13] Willem was now about twenty-five years old, and it would be the last time brother and sister saw each other; Willem had only three more years to live.

Lionel of Antwerp married Elizabeth de Burgh on 15 August 1342 when he was three years old and she was ten. Edward III held a great banquet at the Tower of London to mark the occasion, and a piper called Libekin and his companions performed for the king and queen the evening before the wedding.[14] On the occasion of Lionel and Elizabeth's betrothal a year previously, the king commented that the wedding would go ahead when Lionel was 'old enough', and apparently he deemed his son to be old enough to marry at three years and eight and a half months. The abduction and forced marriage of heiresses was not uncommon in the fourteenth century, and perhaps Edward III was concerned that this dire fate might befall Elizabeth de Burgh as well, heir as she was to the earldom of Ulster and to her grandmother's third of the earldom of Gloucester.

Marrying off two children might seem bizarre or even revolting to modern sensibilities, but at least it would protect Elizabeth from abduction, forced marriage and what amounted to rape, a fate which befell her adolescent cousin Margaret Audley, heiress to another third of the earldom of Gloucester, in early 1336. Margaret Audley's abductor was Sir Ralph Stafford, a friend of Edward III who helped him arrest Roger Mortimer in 1330 and was later rewarded with the earldom of Stafford. He suffered no consequences whatsoever for abducting a noblewoman who was a close kinsman of the king himself. Elizabeth de Burgh's grandmother, the elder Elizabeth de Burgh, was abducted by her second husband Theobald de Verdon in early 1316, and the elder Elizabeth's sister Eleanor Despenser, widow of Hugh Despenser the Younger, was also abducted by her second husband William la Zouche in early 1329. The victim of yet another abduction in late 1335 or early 1336 was the twice-widowed Alice de Lacy, now in her mid-fifties and countess of Lincoln in her own right. Unmarried heiresses, whatever their age, were vulnerable to abductions at the hands of men keen to force themselves into ownership of the women's lands. It therefore seems plausible that Edward III wished the young Elizabeth de Burgh to be married to his son as soon as possible so that she would avoid this fate, and her large inheritance would not be snatched out of his son's hands.

Edward III gave Queen Philippa custody of all the lands in Ireland which their daughter-in-law Elizabeth de Burgh would inherit when she came of age on 10 May 1346. Elizabeth should have attained her majority – fourteen years old, as she was already married – on 6 July 1346, so the gift should only have been a very short-term one. The lands were still in the queen's hands in October 1349, however.[15] Elizabeth de Burgh often appears in the chancery rolls as 'the king's daughter Elizabeth', and evidently had some influence at court, as various intercessions she made to the king on behalf of others and grants made to her personally demonstrate.[16]

Her mother Maud of Lancaster's second husband Ralph Ufford, justiciar of Ireland and younger brother of the earl of Suffolk, died in 1346. Maud thereafter became a canoness at the house of Campsea Ashe in the county of Suffolk, fulfilling a wish she had had since childhood, and her daughter Elizabeth was looked after by Queen Philippa, always a woman with strong maternal feelings.[17] Maud of Lancaster's other daughter Maud Ufford, Elizabeth de Burgh's much younger half-sister, only a toddler when her mother entered a religious house, probably grew up in the household of John de Vere, earl of Oxford, and married his son and heir Thomas.

Jean le Bel gives an account of the splendid round of jousting and feasting which marked the celebration of Lionel of Antwerp and Elizabeth de Burgh's wedding in August 1342 (though he does not give the reason for the feasting, apparently unaware of the royal wedding taking place or not interested in it). The celebrations lasted for fifteen days, and, he says, were the most magnificent events anyone had ever seen in England, with numerous English magnates present. They included Henry of Lancaster and his son Henry of Grosmont, earl of Derby, Elizabeth de Burgh's grandfather and uncle; Queen Philippa and her brother Count Willem of Hainault and Holland, and their uncle-in-law Robert of Artois, who had made his home in England for the previous few years to the utter fury of Philip VI of France; Edward and Philippa's eldest son, twelve-year-old Edward of Woodstock; and the earls of Northampton, Gloucester, Warwick, Salisbury, Suffolk, Pembroke, Arundel, Oxford and Stafford (according to le Bel, though Ralph Stafford in fact was not made earl of Stafford until a few years later).[18] This represents most of the English earls alive in 1342 with the exception of the elderly earl of Surrey, John de Warenne, who was to die in 1347; Huntingdon, who was Edward III's friend William Clinton and who had excused himself; and Hereford, who was the elder brother of the earl of Northampton. Humphrey de Bohun, earl of Hereford and Essex, may have suffered from a long-term illness or disability, as he played no role in Edward III's wars in Scotland and France, never took part in jousting tournaments, and never married or had children. (John of Kent, heir to the earldom of Kent, another first cousin of the king, was still only twelve years old in 1342, and although he may have attended he did not compete.) According to le Bel, no fewer than 800 knights and 500 ladies 'of high lineage' attended the tournaments and banquets of August 1342, though the chronicler casts something of a shadow over his version of events by claiming that the countess of Salisbury, supposedly the victim of Edward III's obsessive violence and his brutal rape of her a few months earlier, was forced against her will to attend and spent most of her time trying to prevent the king staring at her and making a scene.[19]

Edward III hosted yet another banquet at Eastry in Kent in September 1342 for Philippa and their eldest son, and invited the earls of Derby, Warwick, Salisbury and Suffolk as well as unspecified other great magnates.[20] The king sent an armed force to the duchy of Brittany in the autumn of 1342 shortly after this great feast in aid of his preferred claimant to the duchy, John de Montfort. Edward's kinsman Edward Despenser (born *c.* 1310), second son of Edward II's notorious favourite Hugh Despenser the Younger and a great-grandson of King Edward I, fighting under the banner of his elder brother Hugh, lord of Glamorgan, was killed at the battle of Morlaix in Brittany at the end of September.

John de Montfort's wife Joan of Flanders, their son John de Montfort the younger, not yet three years old, and their baby daughter Jeanne withdrew to England. John de Montfort himself fled to England later and would die there in September 1345, having never managed to gain control of Brittany. His wife Joan of Flanders, a fiery and powerful woman who had done her utmost to help her husband gain his inheritance, apparently became seriously mentally ill in England and was confined at Tickhill Castle in Yorkshire for some years for her own safety. Historian Julie Sarpy argues, however, that it suited Edward III's foreign policy for Joan to be removed from London and sequestered at Tickhill, and that the story of mental breakdown was arguably a fiction. Queen Philippa subsequently took care of the little de Montfort boy, John the younger, and the younger John's sister Jeanne de Montfort, who was to spend the rest of her life in England and who often spent time with the English royal family over the next few years. She was known as the 'damsel of Brittany'.

In November 1342 Edward III gave Queen Philippa official custody of their five younger children, Isabella of Woodstock, Joan of Woodstock, Lionel of Antwerp, John of Gaunt and Edmund of Langley, and Lionel's new wife Elizabeth de Burgh also lived with them. The entries on the Patent Roll granting Philippa custody of her children name John of Gaunt in first place, as he was earl of Richmond and hence outranked his elder brother Lionel (called 'Leo' here) and his younger brother Edmund, as well as his older sisters Isabella and Joan.[21] The royal children thereafter spent much time with their mother, though they and their household also frequently lived at Chertsey Abbey in Surrey: in November 1347 the abbot of Chertsey petitioned Edward III pointing out that 'the abbey is very often burdened with diverse charges by frequent visits of the king's children and the lengthy stay of them and their households.'[22]

Edward of Woodstock, as the heir to the throne, lived with his own household at Berkhamsted in Hertfordshire, and both Edward's mother the queen and his grandmother the dowager queen Isabella often visited him there. During one of Philippa's visits, Edward of Woodstock bought himself a gold ring with diamonds to wear while she was there, and on another occasion when both the king and queen visited him, Edward of Woodstock spent over £37 playing games of chance with them. On another occasion when his grandmother Queen Isabella was with him, Edward of Woodstock spent the large sum of £51 on gifts for her squires, clerks, valets and grooms who came with her. The prince spent £9 on two girdles garnished with silver when the queen, presumably Philippa and not Isabella, stayed with him again at Berkhamsted.[23]

The Queen's Household

In November 1342, Philippa's uncle-in-law Robert of Artois, count of Beaumont-le-Roger, was killed while fighting at Vannes in the duchy of Brittany. Edward III sent a short letter to Philippa from Grand-Champ on 25 November (under his secret seal) about the arrangements which would be made for Robert of Artois's funeral. He addressed his wife three times as *douz cuer*, 'sweet heart', or *très douz cuer*, an endearment also used a few years earlier – perhaps rather surprisingly – by Edward's mother Queen Isabella when she wrote to her husband Edward II.[1]

Robert of Artois's body was taken to England and buried at the Blackfriars' or Dominicans' church in London in early February 1343 as Edward III wished, though was later moved to St Paul's Cathedral. The king had written to his chancellor and treasurer on 21 November 1342 ordering them to have Artois buried respectfully at the Blackfriars because of the 'affection' he had for his kinsman, and four days later asked his queen to ensure that this command was carried out; yet another indication of the king's trust in Philippa. Edward III dated this letter 'the sixteenth year of our reign of England, and the third of France'.

Twelve-year-old Edward of Woodstock, 'keeper of the realm' or official regent of England during his father's absence overseas – Edward III returned to England at the beginning of March 1343 after four and a half months away – represented his father at Robert of Artois's funeral. Edward of Woodstock's sister Blanche of the Tower, who had died soon after her birth a few months previously, was interred at Westminster Abbey at around the same time, and Woodstock's letter about the two funerals, dated 30 January 1343, survives. He referred to 'the interments of Lady Blanche, our much-loved sister [*dame Blaunche nostre tres amee soer*], and Sir Robert of Artois, our very dear cousin'.[2] The young man's reference to Blanche of the Tower as his 'much-loved sister' is probably not merely a form of words but an example of the love and affection the royal family felt for each other; both Edward and his siblings and parents must have felt Blanche's loss keenly.

Another indication of Queen Philippa's involvement in her husband's government and his trust in her, at least when Edward III was absent from England, appears on 28 November 1342. An entry on the Patent Roll states

> Whereas the prior of St. Bartholomew's, Smethefeld [Smithfield], London, by the king's command brought before the council at the Tower of London a chest delivered to his custody by James Gerard and Daniel de Burgham, sealed with their seals, the chest was opened in the presence of Queen Philippa, Robert Parvyng, the chancellor, and William de Cusancia, king's clerk, the treasurer, and then by command of the queen delivered to the said James.[3]

Unfortunately it is very difficult to ascertain exactly how Philippa wielded influence, and whether or to what extent she was responsible for making and implementing decisions. The same applies to her mother-in-law Queen Isabella during Edward III's minority from 1327 to 1330; although there is little doubt that the dowager queen was, to a great extent at least, in charge of her son's government, all commands, writs, letters and son were issued in the king's name. Although we know that Edward III trusted Philippa and her judgement, and knew that she would faithfully carry out his wishes, it is almost impossible to determine exactly how and on which occasions she did so.

Various letters sent from a family called the van Arteveldes (well-off Flemish merchants) and from the mayor of the town of Bruges, do reveal the queen's involvement in her husband's government. At the beginning of 1343, Jacques van Artevelde wrote to Philippa, addressing her as 'very excellent and dearest Princess', and asked her to help obtain the release of quantities of cloth belonging to two friends of his that had been confiscated in England. The mayor of Bruges also asked the queen twice to help obtain the release of a ship from Bruges captured and held in Portsmouth.[4] As Philippa herself came from the Low Countries, it seems that the Arteveldes and the mayor of Bruges assumed that she might take a special interest in their cases, and that therefore it would be worthwhile to ask for her help.

The king made his and Philippa's son Edward of Woodstock Prince of Wales at the parliament held at Westminster in late April and May 1343. Edward III himself had never held the title or the lands of the principality, although his father Edward II had received them from his own father Edward I in February 1301 when he was sixteen. It may be that Edward II considered his son too young to have such a splendid gift bestowed on him; the last time father and son ever saw each other, at least according to official record, was in September 1325 when the future Edward III was not yet thirteen years old. It may be that Edward II had it in mind to make his son Prince of Wales when he returned from paying homage to his uncle, Charles IV of France. As the young man only returned to England a year later with his mother's invasion force, however, there was no opportunity for him to become Prince of Wales before he succeeded as king of England on his father's abdication in January 1327. Until 1283, the princes of Wales had been the native rulers of the principality. Since 1301 to the present day the title and lands have almost always been bestowed on the heir to the English throne. Edward III hosted a great feast on 12 May 1343 to celebrate his son's new title, attended by the archbishop of Canterbury, other bishops and magnates, and the queen.[5]

Philippa was in Westminster on 28 February 1343, in Reading on 13/14 August 1343, 4 December 1343 and 30 January 1344, and in Langley on 4 November 1343.[6] The queen was surely hurt in 1343/44 when her brother Willem, count of Hainault and Holland, defected from the English cause and joined Philip VI. As Philip was Willem's uncle, his desire for an alliance with him and with the powerful kingdom of France is hardly surprising, however much it might have upset and offended his sister. In May 1347, Philippa's nephew-in-law Reynald III of Guelders (born in May 1333 and barely fourteen years old then), the elder son of Edward III's sister Eleanor of Woodstock, would also desert the English cause.[7] Reynald succeeded his father the elder Reynald as duke of Guelders in 1343, and in later years would quarrel violently with his younger brother Eduard (b. 1336).

In 1344, Edward III made strenuous efforts to shore up his alliance with his cousin Duke Jan III of Brabant, and asked the pope to grant a dispensation for consanguinity for his and Philippa's two eldest children, Edward and Isabella of Woodstock, to marry two of Jan's children.[8] The marriages never took place, however, perhaps due in part to Philip VI of France and his wife Jeanne of Burgundy lobbying the pope on the matter, and Duke Jan abandoned his commitment to marry his children into England.

On 28 April 1343, Pope Clement VI – elected on 7 May 1342 after the death of Benedict XII on 25 April – confirmed 'the foundation of a college of masters, students and chaplains, called "Queen's Hall", newly founded by Queen Philippa in the University of Oxford.'[9] Philippa sent a sergeant-at-arms called Thedesius or Tedecius Benedicti of Folchinello to Pope Clement in the summer of 1343 carrying a present of a ring set with precious diamonds (for what purpose, assuming the queen had an ulterior motive for sending the gift, was not recorded). Shortly afterwards the pope wrote to Edward III and his cousin William de Bohun, earl of Northampton, asking them to set free Ralph de Montfort and other French knights whom Northampton had taken captive. The earl's man Hugh de Wrotelesse (from Wrottesley in Staffordshire) and a group of unnamed other followers of his captured Montfort and his colleagues while they were asleep and naked, and carted them off to prison, still naked.[10]

In early 1344, Queen Philippa became pregnant again, and was perhaps attended by William of Exeter, master of theology and medicine and also chancellor of the city of Lincoln, who is named as her physician in the early and mid-1340s.[11] Edward III held another tournament at Windsor in January 1344. Wealthy citizens of London were specifically invited, 300 knights took part, and Edward III used the famous round table of Arthurian legend as the focal point of the tournament. Around this time or a little earlier,

Edward also took the opportunity to go hunting with Queen Philippa, his mother Queen Isabella (now close to fifty years old but seemingly as healthy and active as ever), and four countesses. The king bought mulberry-coloured Turkish cloth and taffeta for the ladies.[12]

Edward III's close friend William Montacute, earl of Salisbury, was killed while jousting at the tournament in January 1344: he suffered terrible wounds and died later, and possibly Queen Philippa witnessed it.[13] Salisbury's heir was his fifteen-year-old son William, born in June 1328, and he left his daughters Elizabeth Despenser, Sybil Arundel and Philippa Mortimer as well. William Montacute the younger was married to Edward III's cousin Joan of Kent (b. 1326/27), but some years later she caused a scandal by claiming to have married the knight Sir Thomas Holland at the beginning of the 1340s before she went through a wedding ceremony with William.

Queen Philippa was at her castle of Marlborough in Wiltshire on 20 March 1344, and still there on 26 May when she made Sir Roger Beauchamp, one of her most favoured retainers, keeper of her nearby castle of Devizes and its three forests for life (a confirmation of an appointment she had made in Ghent three and a half years before).[14] Edward III, meanwhile, made two visits to his mother the dowager queen Isabella at Castle Rising in Norfolk on the other side of the country: the first from 11 to 15 March, and the second from on or just before 29 April 1344 until 8 May. On 29 April, the king paid his mother's minstrel John Sautreour, a name which indicated a person who played a stringed instrument called a psaltery, for playing for them at Castle Rising. The king and Queen Philippa were seemingly apart for quite a few weeks this year, rather unusually.[15]

The queen's ninth child and fourth daughter Mary was born at Bishop's Waltham in Hampshire on 10 October 1344. Mary of Waltham may have been named in honour of the Virgin Mary, or perhaps in memory of Edward III's aunt Mary, one of Edward II's many sisters and a nun at Amesbury Priory. She may also have been named after a godmother, and perhaps it was Marie de St Pol, dowager countess of Pembroke. Her nurse was Joan de Stodeley.[16] Edward III was also at Bishop's Waltham on the day of his daughter's birth, and soon afterwards spent his thirty-second birthday, 13 November, with his mother the dowager queen Isabella at her favourite residence of Castle Rising in Norfolk.[17]

In the 1340s, the king made rather more visits to his mother than had previously been the case, apparently evidence of his thawing towards her, and this was the third time he had stayed with her in 1344 alone. He had also invited her to go hunting with him and his wife at the beginning of 1344 or somewhat earlier. Various grants by Pope Clement VI in the autumn of 1344 were made at the joint request of the king and his mother, and indicate that Edward and Isabella sometimes co-operated. One of the grants was the appropriation of a church in Kent, given to Leeds Priory also in Kent, the priory 'having suffered by the siege of the neighbouring castle in the time of Edward of famous memory, the king's father' (a reference to Edward II's siege of Leeds Castle in October 1321 after the garrison refused to admit Queen Isabella to the castle).[18]

In late 1344, Pope Clement VI granted Queen Philippa and some of the members of her household permission to choose a confessor who would give them plenary absolution at the time of death. This permission usefully records many of the names of people who served in the queen's household, some of them slightly Latinised, so we learn that the knights of Philippa's household included Edmund Vancy, John Ufford, John Beauchamp and Bartholomew and Gilbert Emworth or Imworth; that the damsels included Petronilla Pagham, Margery Dutton, Christiana de Ros, Katherine de Hekeneye, Emeline Bothel and Alice de Benfield; and that the *donsels* (the male equivalent of damsels, i.e. men not knighted) included Luke Alberti, Thomas de Sancto Audomaro, Peter de Scandeleone and Giles Pagham, presumably Petronilla Pagham's husband or brother.[19] Another damsel was given only a first name, and a most unusual one: Louecta. Possibly this was Lonota de Werthyngpole, named in the 1330s as one of the attendants of Philippa's second daughter Joan of Woodstock. A doctor of canon law in the queen's household was called Geoffrey de Croppo Sancti Petri, and another unusually named person was Tetana, position not specified, who worked for the queen with her husband Guy.

This list also gives a useful insight into the way attendants sometimes switched between households: the damsel Petronilla or

Pernel Pagham served in the households of Philippa's daughter-in-law Elizabeth de Burgh and Elizabeth's mother Maud of Lancaster, dowager countess of Ulster and a later a canoness in Suffolk, as well as the queen's.[20] The queen often arranged marriages between members of her retinue: to take just one of example of many, her valet Edmund Rose married her damsel Agnes Archer around July 1343.[21]

Marital Negotiations and Intercessions

On 5 February 1345 at Ditton in Buckinghamshire, Queen Philippa and Edward III attended the wedding of Richard Fitzalan, earl of Arundel, and his second wife Eleanor of Lancaster, dowager Lady Beaumont. Eleanor and her first husband John Beaumont had been closely associated with the king and queen on the continent in 1338/39, and both Edward and Philippa were hugely fond of Eleanor, so it is hardly surprising that they attended her wedding. Eleanor was almost certainly pregnant with her first child by Arundel in July 1345 when she wrote to the pope asking for the legitimisation of all their offspring present and future. Their eldest child, born in late 1345 or early 1346, was Joan, later countess of Hereford, Essex and Northampton, and their second was Richard's heir, also called Richard, earl of Arundel, born before 1 March 1347.[1]

The earl of Arundel had previously been married to Edward III's kinswoman Isabella Despenser, eldest daughter of Hugh Despenser the Younger (executed in 1326) and Edward II's niece Eleanor de Clare, but he had their marriage annulled in late 1344 and thereby made their son Edmund (born *c.* 1326) illegitimate. Edmund Arundel's petition to the pope protesting against this makes it apparent that Richard Fitzalan and Eleanor of Lancaster had deceived the pope and lied about Eleanor's true identity in an effort to avoid their own consanguinity (they were third cousins) and Eleanor's close familial relationship to Arundel's first wife Isabella Despenser (they were first cousins). They claimed that Eleanor was called 'Joan Beaumont' until after they were safely married, when they could openly refer to her as 'Eleanor, daughter of Henry, earl of Lancaster'.[2] The earl of Arundel and Eleanor of Lancaster took to calling Arundel and Isabella Despenser's son Edmund his 'illegitimate' son, and Arundel even referred to his own eldest child as 'that certain Edmund who claims himself to be my son.'[3]

Whether or to what extent Queen Philippa was aware of any of this is unclear, but her support of a couple who lied to the pope and who treated Arundel's son so callously seems rather unfortunate. Edward III also wrote to the pope on behalf of Eleanor of Lancaster and the earl of Arundel on 22 February 1345, asking him to confirm the dissolution of Arundel's first marriage to Isabella Despenser and to grant a dispensation for his marriage to Eleanor, two and a half weeks after they had already married.[4]

A marriage was on the cards for little John of Gaunt in June 1345, now aged five, when Edward III wrote to Maria of Portugal, queen of Castile, suggesting a marital alliance between John and her sister.[5] This presumably means Maria's youngest sister Leonor of Portugal, who was born in 1328 and was therefore a dozen years John's senior, and who in November 1345 and July 1347 was also put forward as a possible bride for his eldest brother Edward of Woodstock, a boy much closer to her own age. Matters advanced so far in 1347 that English envoys to Portugal were instructed to arrange a time and place for Leonor's arrival in England and for her wedding to Edward of Woodstock, but their journey there was so delayed that they arrived in Portugal too late, in November 1347, and found that Leonor had just married King Pedro IV of Aragon. She became one of the victims of the Black Death in 1348.[6]

In June 1345, in the month he turned fifteen, Edward of Woodstock gave his mother a horse called Bayard Roos.[7] The name Roos or Ros implies that the horse had been given to Edward of Woodstock by a member of the Ros family, lords of Helmsley in Yorkshire, in the first place.

The next month, Edward III once more opened negotiations for the marriage of his and Philippa's second daughter Joan of Woodstock, aged eleven, and King Alfonso XI of Castile's son and heir Pedro, who was almost exactly Joan's own age. The royal cousin Henry of Grosmont, earl of Derby, and Richard Fitzalan, earl of Arundel, had been sent to the Iberian Peninsula in 1344 to negotiate alliances with the kings of Castile, Portugal and Aragon.[8] The men perhaps discussed a potential English-Castilian royal marriage on this occasion. Edward III had proposed a marriage between their respective off spring to Alfonso XI as far back as June 1335, when Joan of Woodstock and the Infante Pedro were mere toddlers, but Alfonso had shown no interest back then.[9]

Castile had, for the most part, long been an English ally, since the marriage of Edward III's grandparents Edward I and Leonor of Castile in 1254, and Edward II had betrothed his son the future Edward III and his elder daughter Eleanor of Woodstock into Castile in 1324/25. Portugal and the Spanish kingdoms made useful allies for England against France, and Edward III in the 1340s was clearly making a great effort to bind them to him by arranging the marriages of their children.

The queen was with her husband at Westminster on or a little before 17 September 1345 when she interceded with him to spare the life of a woman called Cicely, wife of William le Clere of Haxby in Yorkshire. Cicely and William broke into a church in Huntington and stole items, and also committed theft in their native Haxby. They were indicted before King's Bench, and William was hanged. As Cicely was pregnant, however, the death sentence was deferred, and she was imprisoned until after she had given birth. 'Moved by pity and at the supplication of Queen Philippa,' Edward III pardoned her and set her free.'[10] Although a fairly sizeable number of intercessions Philippa made with her husband throughout her life in England are recorded in the chancery rolls, historian Lisa Benz St John has pointed out that her two predecessors as queen-consort of England, Edward II's wife Queen Isabella and Edward I's second wife Queen Marguerite, 'were more successful at taking advantage of their roles as intercessors than Philippa'.

Philippa's intercessions number between zero and four every year, a much lower number than Isabella achieved during her marriage to Edward II, and Philippa's successful interventions remained consistently lower than Isabella's or Marguerite's with the exception of the years 1331 and 1338. During the seventeen years of Isabella of France's marriage to Edward II, not counting the last two years of Edward's reign when the royal couple lived permanently apart – Isabella arrived in England in early February 1308 and departed for her homeland in early March 1325 – she made a total of seventy-nine acts of intercession. During the forty-one and a half years of Philippa of Hainault's marriage to Edward III, from her wedding in late January 1328 until mid-August 1369 when she died, she made a total of seventy-six acts of intercession. Marguerite of France, who married Edward I on 8 September 1299 (nine years after the death of his first queen, Leonor of Castile) and was widowed on 7 July 1307, made no fewer than fifty-six acts of intercession during that period of less than eight years. She interceded with her stepson Edward II between 1307 and her death in February 1318 on another seven occasions.[11] Given the frequent modern assumption that, in stark contrast to the happy partnership of Edward III and Philippa, Edward II and Isabella's marriage was little but a tragic disaster for many years and that the presence of Edward II's male favourites or lovers must necessarily have impeded the queen's access to her husband and made it almost impossible for her to make requests of him on behalf of others, this is surprising.

There is also often an assumption that Queen Philippa was a highly effective and frequent intercessor with her husband, though Lisa Benz St John's comparisons with the queen's two predecessors demonstrate otherwise. There is no doubt whatsoever that Philippa and Edward III's marriage was a close and contented one and that the royal couple spent considerable time in each other's company, so the queen's comparatively much lower recorded number of intercessions in proportion to her much longer marriage is also rather surprising. Seventy-six acts of intercession in forty-one and a half years gives Philippa an average of just 1.8 intercessions per year, whereas Marguerite of France managed an average of 7 intercessions during her short marriage to Edward I and Isabella an average of 4.6 with Edward II.

On 22 September 1345 in the town of Leicester, Edward III's great-uncle Henry of Lancaster, earl of Lancaster and Leicester, died at the age of about sixty-five. He was the last surviving grandchild of Henry III and his queen Eleanor of Provence, and left his only son Henry of Grosmont as his heir and his six daughters Blanche Wake, Isabella of Lancaster (prioress of Amesbury in Wiltshire),

Maud de Burgh, Joan Mowbray, Eleanor Fitzalan and Mary Percy. Henry of Grosmont, earl of Derby, was currently on campaign on Edward III's behalf in Gascony, covering himself in glory as he always did, when he succeeded as earl of Lancaster and Leicester. In October 1348, Grosmont's aunt-in-law the elderly Alice de Lacy – widow of Thomas of Lancaster, executed by his cousin Edward II in 1322 – died as well, and he was her heir. He succeeded to her earldom of Lincoln to add to all his others.

Just four days after Earl Henry of Lancaster's death, on 26 September 1345, Queen Philippa's younger brother Willem, count of Hainault and Holland, died as well. He was killed in battle near Staveren during a failed expedition in his own territory of Friesland, where a rebellion against his rule had broken out. Willem was the last of Philippa's four brothers; the other three had all died in infancy, and he was only in his late twenties at the time of his death. His marriage to Johanna of Brabant produced no surviving children, though the couple did have a son, inevitably also called Willem, who died young and was buried in the church of the Carmelites in Brussels (the capital of the duchy of Brabant). Count Willem did leave two illegitimate sons, Adam van Berwaerde and Willem van Henegouwen ('of Hainault'), lord of Vlissingen, but being illegitimate, they of course had no claim to his lands.[12] The important question therefore arose of who precisely the rightful heir or heirs to the territories of Hainault, Holland, Zeeland and Friesland should be.

Edward III believed that his wife had a claim to one-quarter of the lands, as one of Willem's four sisters. The king had heard of his brother-in-law's death by 20 October 1345, when he empowered Philippa's uncle Sir Jan van Beaumont to claim and take possession of Philippa's inheritance.[13] Edward talked on 20 April 1346 of the lands which descended by right to his queen as the sister and one of the heirs of Count Willem, and appointed two men to 'keep possession of the inheritance'. On 25 June 1346 he appointed 'Teodoricus, lord of Montjoye and Falkyngburgh' to act as the arbitrator between himself and Philippa, and her sisters and their husbands, regarding Philippa's rightful inheritance from her brother.[14]

Philippa's older sisters Margaretha and Johanna and her younger sister Isabella were still alive, and in England the law of primogeniture, where the eldest son inherited everything, did not apply to female heirs, who inherited equal portions. Had this rule applied in Hainault and Holland, Queen Philippa would have inherited a quarter of her late brother's lands in her own right. Laws and customs were different on the continent, however and in the end the lands of the late Count Willem passed entirely to Philippa's eldest sister, the Empress Margaretha. She became countess of Hainault and Holland in her own right, and passed the titles and territories to her German sons after her own death. The question of the Hainault inheritance became a bone of contention between Edward III and Margaretha's husband Emperor Ludwig and even between the two Hainault sisters, and Philippa met Margaretha at Ypres in October 1346 to try to put an end to their quarrel.[15]

The sisters' uncle Philip VI of France promoted the rights of his eldest Hainault niece Margaretha to the Hainault/Holland inheritance, presumably in the belief that the late Count Willem's counties being in the hands of the German emperor and his wife and sons was less of a threat to him than some of them falling into Edward III's hands by right of his wife Philippa.[16] The king and queen were at Woolmer Green in Hertfordshire on the day of her brother's death, and it was on this day that the king received news of his great-uncle Henry of Lancaster's demise four days earlier. He had previously granted Henry's son and heir Henry of Grosmont an annuity of 1,000 marks (£666) during the lifetime of Grosmont's father, and as this was no longer to be paid to him now that his father was dead, Edward used it to benefit Philippa instead. He gave her the whole amount to use 'for the sustenance and expenses' of their children Isabella, Joan, Lionel, John, Edmund and Mary, and their daughter-in-law Elizabeth de Burgh, who were all officially in Philippa's care.[17] (Edward of Woodstock, as the eldest son and heir to the throne, was not.)

Philippa was at Westminster with her husband on 10 October 1345, and wrote to the mayor and aldermen of London shortly before 18 October, asking them to 'grant her a certain little tower situated in the Thames near the Black Friars', the London residence of the Dominican friars, for her friend Sir Gilbert de Dyneworth. The letter was read out to a congregation of the mayor, aldermen and commoners in the Guildhall on 18 October, but the queen's request was politely declined.[18]

Edward III sent envoys to Portugal for further negotiations regarding the marriage of Edward of Woodstock and a daughter of King Afonso IV, presumably, though she is not named, his youngest daughter Leonor (b. 1328), on 8 November 1345.[19] Edward III was so keen on the Portuguese alliance that he offered any other of his and Philippa's sons in place of Edward of Woodstock if necessary, and earlier that year had offered John of Gaunt.

The festive season of 1345 was spent at the royal manor of Woodstock, and the queen sent a letter from there on Christmas Eve to her ministers in the forest of High Peak.[20] Philippa was about two months pregnant again that Christmas; their tenth child would be born on 20 July 1346. Edward and the pregnant Queen Philippa, and the king's mother Queen Isabella, attended the funeral of Isabella's uncle Henry of Lancaster in the town of Leicester on 15 January 1346. Edward bought black cloth for himself, his queen and their households for the sombre occasion.[21] Most probably all of Edward and Philippa's children attended, with the possible exception of the infant Mary of Waltham; Edward of Woodstock certainly did, and laid three cloths on his great-great-uncle's coffin.[22] The elderly and blind Henry of Lancaster had been something of a cipher in English politics for the previous dozen years or so, but he was the greatest of all English noblemen and was of royal descent via both his parents Edmund of Lancaster and Blanche of Artois, and so the king and queen, the dowager queen and the heir to the throne honoured him by attending his interment in his own town.

Eleanor, Lady Beaumont and now countess of Arundel, a close friend of both Edward III and Queen Philippa, was the fifth of Lancaster's daughters and was surely also present at the funeral, unless she had too recently given birth to her daughter Joan. Lancaster's only son and heir Henry of Grosmont, earl of Derby and now also earl of Lancaster and Leicester, was not present at his father's funeral, being absent in Gascony leading a military campaign against the French. On 6 May 1346 Edward III talked of 'the glorious success of the earl of Lancaster in parts beyond sea', and asked for prayers for Henry of Grosmont and for the continued success of his mission.[23]

Meanwhile, on the same day as Henry of Lancaster's funeral, Ludwig of Bavaria, as overlord of the territories of Hainault, Holland, Zeeland and Friesland, granted all these lands to his wife Margaretha of Hainault. She duly travelled to her territories to take the homage of her important vassals and to establish her authority there as countess. Edward III sent ambassadors to Germany and appointed an arbitrator between Queen Philippa and her sisters regarding his wife's claim to the inheritance, but it was too late and the empress had already secured her position. Wilhelm of Jülich, husband of the second Hainault sister Johanna, also had a good claim to the counties of Hainault and Holland, but as his brothers-in-law Ludwig and Edward were far more powerful than he and he did not wish to alienate them, he did not promote his and Johanna's claim to her late brother's lands.[24] The fourth and youngest Hainault sister, Isabella, was not yet married, and as she had no powerful husband to promote her interests, she had no chance of securing any of her late brother's lands from her sister Margaretha and brother-in-law Ludwig.

Although Ludwig of Bavaria extended his already enormous territories by right of his wife, the year 1346 proved disastrous for him in other ways. He was deposed as Holy Roman Emperor on 13 April, and five of the seven electors, with the support of Pope Clement VI, chose Karl of Luxembourg (b. 1316), son and heir of Johann 'the Blind', king of Bohemia, as an anti-emperor.

Probably on 23 February 1346, King Edward and Queen Philippa visited their son Edward of Woodstock at Berkhamsted, and the young prince spent the large sum of £37, 13/- 4d playing games with his parents.[25] (To put this sum in perspective, it was the equivalent of a few years' income for most people alive in England at the time.) The queen was with her husband at Guildford in Surrey on 1 May, when she sent a letter to the chancellor John Offord asking for her rights in the wardship of John Sinclair to be protected, and probably heard the news of her brother-in-law Ludwig's deposition around this time.[26]

Edward of Woodstock was with his father again at Byfleet in Surrey on 15 May and spent another £4 13/- playing games of chance, and was with his mother at Reading on 31 May.[27] On

10 June 1346, Philippa's eldest daughters Isabella of Woodstock (aged fourteen) and Joan of Woodstock (aged twelve) asked their father to pardon one William de Bekethwait for the death of John de Beryer, and he granted it.[28] The two girls were in their parents' company before their father and eldest brother left for the continent again, and their loving father allowed them to intercede with him on behalf of others.

The Burghers of Calais

Edward III left England again on 12 July 1346, with his and Philippa's eldest son, sixteen-year-old Edward of Woodstock, in tow. There was no question of Philippa accompanying them overseas on this occasion, as she so often did; she was due to give birth at any moment. The king and the Prince of Wales were together 'in a ship between London and Canterbury' on 21 June when they spent 113 shillings playing at dice and tables.[1] The young prince was a warrior cast in the mould of his father, and the king gave him the honour of commanding the vanguard when the English forces met Philip VI's army near the village of Crécy in the county of Ponthieu, northern France. Edward of Woodstock repaid his father's trust in him, and the battle of Crécy in August 1346 is remembered as one of England's most famous and impressive military victories. Queen Philippa's uncle Charles, count of Alençon (born in 1297, the full brother of Philip VI and Jeanne de Valois, dowager countess of Hainault and Holland) and her first cousin Louis de Châtillon, count of Blois (son of Philip VI's, Jeanne de Valois's and Charles of Alençon's full sister Marguerite de Valois, d. 1342) were among the French noblemen killed at Crécy, yet another reminder of how the war cut across the queen of England's family.

Louis, count of Flanders, whose son and heir Louis (b. 1330) had been proposed on various occasions as a husband for Philippa's eldest daughter Isabella and second daughter Joan, also fell at Crécy, as did Philippa's second cousin Johann 'the Blind', king of Bohemia. Johann had just passed his fiftieth birthday, and his daughter Jutta, who was renamed Bonne in her new home, was married to Philip VI's son and heir the future John II of France and was the mother of his many children. Pope Clement VI wrote a letter two weeks after the battle, on 8 September 1346, declaring his 'grief' that the English and French had not managed to reach a treaty of friendship. Clement added that he was relieved to hear that at least Philip VI had borne himself bravely during the battle (Pope Clement, real name Pierre Roger, was himself a Frenchman by birth).[2]

A few weeks before the battle, news came to Queen Philippa's ears that more than two dozen men had taken forty cows, twenty bullocks, twenty heifers and a thousand sheep from her common pasture at Iselham in Cambridgeshire and had impounded them, with the sad result that half of the cows, bullocks and heifers and two hundred of the sheep had died of hunger. Philippa ordered an investigation, and a few days later another one, when it transpired that a group of men had broken into her Berkshire manor of Cookham and assaulted one of her servants very badly.[3] On 14 July she was at Southwick in Sussex, and even though her pregnancy was close to term, she managed to move on the 58 miles to Windsor Castle.[4]

On 20 July 1346 a few weeks after her husband and eldest son sailed from England, Philippa gave birth to her tenth child and fifth daughter, Margaret, at Windsor Castle. The girl was often called 'Margarete de Wyndesore', 'Margaret of Windsor,' and her nurse was Agnes Pore.[5] On the day of Margaret's birth, the sum of £500 was set aside for the expenses of the queen's purification, to be held thirty or forty days later.[6]

After she had recovered from the birth, Philippa joined her victorious husband on the continent, and her eldest daughter Isabella of Woodstock also travelled there to be reunited with her father and elder brother. Members of the queen's retinue were given safe-conducts to accompany Philippa abroad on 10 September 1346, and her second daughter Joan of Woodstock followed her to the continent in late April 1347. The queen arrived in Calais around 21 September.[7] Sometime in 1346 or 1347, perhaps while they were in Calais, Isabella and Joan of Woodstock sent a letter to the chancellor John Offord, asking him to discharge several men who had served them and 'our very dear lady and mother the queen' from paying taxes.[8] The infant Margaret of Windsor and her sister Mary of Waltham, who was not yet two, stayed behind in England in the care of their nurses, and the second royal son Lionel of Antwerp was also left behind and was appointed as nominal 'keeper of the realm' on 25 June 1346.[9] He was only seven years old, and surely his mother the queen, his guardian, helped to take care of government affairs in her husband's absence before she too departed for the continent, though it is impossible to say for certain. Joan of Woodstock, now twelve, interceded on behalf of a Spanish sailor called Lupus Johannis on 8 November 1346, and he was given permission to buy wheat in the west country of England and take it back to his homeland.[10] Her father had been negotiating for her marriage into the royal family of Castile, and it seems that Joan took a keen interest in Spanish matters.

The king and queen and several of their children would remain in Calais until October 1347, and so for a few months the royal family was separated. While Lionel of Antwerp and some of the younger royal siblings who had also remained in England were living at the castle of Beaumys in Berkshire in March 1347, the heiress Margery, widow of Nicholas de la Beche, was abducted from the castle. The abductors were a group of knights including John Dalton, the ringleader, Robert Holland, Thomas Arderne and William Trussell. The nobleman Michael Poynings was killed while trying to defend Margery during the attack, and although Margery claimed that she was already married to Sir Gerald de Lisle, she was forced to wed Sir John Dalton. The attack took place on Good Friday, 'before the dawn ... to the terror of the said keeper [of the realm, Lionel] and the rest of the king's children then with him there'.[11] There is nothing to suggest that Philippa's young children were personally in any danger, but it must have been a distressing event for them, more so for the abducted and forcibly married noblewoman Margery de la Beche.

Meanwhile, England won another great victory in 1346 when Edward III's brother-in-law David II of Scotland was defeated at the battle of Neville's Cross on 17 October. A Scottish force invaded the north of England on 7 October, in response to Philip VI's pleas to the northern kingdom to aid him against the English, but William la Zouche, archbishop of York, raised a large force and with Henry, Lord Percy, and Ralph, Lord Neville, inflicted a massive defeat on the Scottish army. David II himself was captured and numerous Scottish noblemen were killed, including King David's illegitimate half-brother Niall Bruce and John Randolph, earl of Moray. The sheriff of Yorkshire took David south to the Tower of London. He was subsequently sent to Odiham Castle in Hampshire and would remain in English captivity for eleven years. Pope Clement VI wrote to David's wife Joan of the Tower, Edward III's sister, a few months after the battle, consoling her over her husband's capture and assuring her that he would do his utmost to secure David's freedom.

English success continued at the battle of La Roche-Derrien in June 1347, when Queen Philippa's first cousin Charles de Blois, younger brother of Louis de Châtillon, count of Blois, who had been killed at Crécy a few months before, was captured. Charles would spend a few years in English captivity, despite a series of letters from Pope Clement VI to Edward III, Queen Philippa and Edward's mother Queen Isabella pleading for his release.

Philippa of Hainault was not, contrary to some reports, present at the battle of Neville's Cross or in charge of the imprisonment of King David in its aftermath. The story that Philippa rallied the English army before the battle of Neville's Cross appears to have been invented in the sixteenth century, and was repeated in the middle of the nineteenth by the writer Agnes Strickland and in the early twentieth by Blanche Christabel Hardy in her biography of Philippa. Strickland claimed that the queen travelled to Newcastle-on-Tyne, drew up an army, and rode in front of the massed troops on a white charger urging them 'for the love of God to fight manfully'. After the victory Strickland says Philippa returned to the battlefield on her white palfrey – apparently, she had swapped horses – and personally took charge of the captive king of Scots.[12] This makes a lovely story but is inaccurate in every detail. The queen had already crossed the English Channel to join her husband on the continent, and was certainly in Calais on 21 September and 23 October 1346; the battle was fought near Durham, 350 miles to the north of Calais, on 17 October.[13]

Philippa met her eldest sister Empress Margaretha sometime in October 1346 in the Flanders town of Ypres. The queen of England was accompanied during this journey to Ypres by Thomas Beauchamp, earl of Warwick, born in February 1314 and thus exactly her own age, two hundred archers, and an unspecified number of knights and squires. It was the first time the sisters had met face to face for many years, though unfortunately the occasion was not a particularly happy one, as they had been feuding over the rights to their late brother Willem's inheritance. They did, at least, agree to end their quarrel.[14] Edward III and his forces remained in Calais, which he besieged for eleven months from September 1346 to August 1347.

On 6 January and 28 February 1347, Edward of Woodstock played tables with his mother in his chamber in Calais, and during their long stay there gave Philippa two furs of 'pured' miniver and four dozen studs of gold for a jess he had previously given her. A jess is a leather strap for tethering a falcon or hawk, which shows that the queen went hawking at this time.[15] Queen Philippa, Edward III and their daughter Isabella of Woodstock met Louis de Male, the new count of Flanders, at Bergues near Dunkirk – the only time the English royal family left the port of Calais for many months – on 1 March 1347, and discussed the possibility of Louis and Isabella's future marriage. Philippa accompanying her husband and her daughter to meet her potential future son-in-law probably indicates that she played a role in arranging and negotiating this particular match, and as she herself came from the Low Countries, Edward III may have appreciated her insights and her influence on this occasion. As Lisa Benz St John has pointed out, however, it is generally difficult to ascertain what, if any, influence Queen Philippa wielded regarding her children's marriages, and although her natal ties to the Low Countries were doubtless useful for her husband, they do not necessarily prove that she instigated the marriages Edward planned for their children there.[16]

Louis de Male, born in October 1330, was sixteen when his marriage into the English royal family was discussed and negotiated, and Isabella of Woodstock, born in June 1332, was fourteen. Louis promised to marry Isabella within a fortnight of Easter – by the middle of April 1347, only a few weeks later – and was put under pressure to recognise Edward III as king of France and to perform homage to him as such as his overlord for his county of Flanders. While out hawking not long afterwards, however, Louis took the opportunity to flee to Philip VI's court, declaring that he would never accept as his wife the daughter of the man who had slain his father at the battle of Crécy.[17] A few months later he married Margarethe of Brabant, second daughter of Duke Jan III of Brabant, instead of Isabella.

Born in 1323, Margarethe was seven years his senior, and Edward III had tried to arrange her marriage to Edward of Woodstock some years before, until the pope thwarted him by refusing to issue a dispensation for consanguinity. Louis and Margarethe had a daughter, also called Margarethe, born in April 1350, their only surviving child and a great heiress who one day would inherit the counties of Flanders, Nevers, Rethel and Artois. Edward III would also attempt to arrange the heiress Margarethe of Flanders' marriage to two of his and Philippa's sons in the 1360s, and again was unsuccessful.

One of the best-known stories about Queen Philippa, probably only second in fame to the often-repeated tale that Edward chose her as his wife in preference to her sisters in 1326, relates to her successful pleas to save the lives of the burghers of Calais at the beginning of August 1347, just after the town surrendered to Edward at the end of his eleven-month siege. (The port of Calais remained in English hands for the next 211 years, until 1558, in Mary I's reign.) This story is related in detail by the chroniclers Jean le Bel and Jean Froissart. The six men, including the mayor of Calais, Eustache de Saint-Pierre, knelt in front of the king with nooses around their necks in the presence of a number of English magnates and the 'heavily pregnant' (*durement enchainte*) Queen Philippa. They handed Edward the keys to Calais, and submitted themselves to his mercy, after holding out against his siege for the previous eleven months. Le Bel says that all the lords and knights present were moved to tears of pity on witnessing the six men's plight (which, given that the English magnates tended to be hard-bitten warriors, seems incredibly unlikely), but that Edward III's heart was hardened by anger. He immediately ordered the mayor and his five associates to be beheaded. All the weeping lords and knights present begged him to change his mind, but he refused. Philippa's countryman and Edward's friend Sir Walter Manny then added his voice to the chorus, telling the king 'If you refuse to have mercy, everyone will say you have a heart full of cruelty.' Edward merely replied that it was too late, that lots of Englishmen had died during the siege of Calais, and so the six men must die too. He told the executioner to come forward and make himself ready.

There was now no-one who could change Edward's mind except Philippa. Weeping bitterly, she fell to her knees in front of her husband and cried out 'Ah, my worthy lord! Since I crossed the sea – in great peril, as you know – I have asked for nothing. But now I beg and implore you with clasped hands, for the love of Our Lady's son [i.e. Jesus Christ], have mercy on them.' Hearing these words, Edward's heart softened a little, and he replied 'Lady, I wish you were anywhere but here! Your entreaties are so heartfelt that I dare not refuse you. Though it pains me to say it, take them: I give these men to you.' Le Bel says that he 'spared all the people of Calais out of love for her', and Philippa had the six men provided with new clothes and did her best to make them comfortable.[18]

Unfortunately, as with the story that Edward of Windsor chose Philippa as his bride over her sisters (a tale seemingly invented by Philippa herself and related to Jean Froissart), her pleading with her husband to spare the lives of the Calais burghers is unlikely to be true. Jean-Marie Moeglin's 2002 work 'Les Bourgeois de Calais: Essai sur un Mythe Historique' points out the lack of any supporting evidence and the fact that the story only appears in the works of Jean le Bel and Jean Froissart, who used le Bel as his primary source.[19] Philippa, supposedly not merely pregnant but 'heavily pregnant' at the time this occurred, in fact was not, as her next child was born *c*. late May 1348 and thus was conceived around late August or early September 1347, about a month after this event.[20] Even if the tale bears some resemblance to reality, and certainly it fits well with what we know of Philippa and her kind, compassionate personality, it is extremely doubtful that she genuinely did save the men's lives with her intervention, and far more likely that the king had already decided to spare them and created a piece of theatre showcasing his mercy and clemency to an impressed public. Edward III was a master of public relations, and his ploy worked; the story spread quickly around Europe and is still often repeated even today.

Another story one often sees in modern literature is that Queen Philippa gave birth to a son called Thomas of Windsor, born at Windsor Castle in the summer of 1347. Supposedly, this little boy died a year or so after his birth, during the first great outbreak of the Black Death. In fact, there is no reason to believe that 'Thomas of Windsor' ever existed. Philippa was in Calais and not in Windsor in 1347, and as Edward III's biographer Ian Mortimer has pointed out, if she had been at Windsor that summer and had given birth to a child, the child could not have been her husband's, given that the king had been on the continent since July 1346. There is no evidence that Philippa was purified in 1347 after giving birth to a child, and no evidence of any arrangements made for an infant's burial.[21]

Philippa did give birth at Windsor Castle in May 1348 to a son called William, who died not long afterwards; there is much evidence both for this little boy's birth and for the elaborate arrangements his father made after his death. It seems very hard to believe that the royal couple could have had another son who died in 1348 at about a year old and yet no evidence exists for his funeral or tomb, or for the queen's purification after his birth, or for any kind of celebration held to mark the birth of another royal child (and Edward III held celebratory jousting tournaments at the drop of a hat). The entire existence of 'Thomas of Windsor' in some modern books and websites appears to be based on the spurious story by two chroniclers that Philippa was heavily pregnant when she interceded for the Calais burghers in early August 1347. 'Thomas of Windsor' has evidently been confused with the queen's next child, William of Windsor (born and died 1348), and has been assigned the name of her youngest child, Thomas of Woodstock (b. January 1355). Supposedly, according to some modern writers and websites, 'Thomas of Windsor' was buried at Langley Priory in Hertfordshire, which probably represents a confusion with the queen's fifth (but fourth surviving) son, Edmund of Langley, who really was buried there in 1402. 'Thomas' therefore seems to be a fictional composite based on combining details of several of Queen Philippa's sons who really did exist.

Edward of Woodstock, who turned seventeen in June 1347, gave his mother a palfrey called Grisel Petit Watte during Philippa's long visit to Calais. *Grisel* means a grey horse and Watte was a contemporary nickname for Walter. A few months later, the prince gave his mother other horses called Dun Skelton and Morel Huwet – Morel meant black – and one called Bayard Juet to his brother Lionel, eight and a half years his junior. The prince also bought a pony called Lyard Hobyn ('dappled-grey hobby horse') for his illegitimate son, whom he had named Edward after himself, in 1349.[22] There are few if any other references to this boy, about whom nothing is known, and the identity of the mother is also not known. Nineteen is a young age for Edward of Woodstock to have fathered a child old enough to have a pony bought for him, so apparently the prince of Wales had been sexually precocious. Assuming little Edward, the prince's illegitimate son, was at least three or so years old when he was considered old enough to ride and to have a pony bought for him, he was born in 1345 or 1346, and thus Queen Philippa had become a grandmother in her very early thirties. The boy perhaps died young, as he is very obscure and does not appear in any other known record, and does not seem to have been known to his much younger legitimate half-brother, King Richard II.

Edward of Woodstock fathered another illegitimate son called Roger of Clarendon who certainly lived into adulthood and was known to Richard II, and whose mother was called Edith Willesford. Edward's legitimate sons Edward of Angoulême and Richard II were not born until 1365 and 1367 when he was well into his thirties and had married his cousin Joan of Kent, and Roger of Clarendon was almost certainly born before Edward wed Joan in 1361. Edward III wrote to King Afonso of Portugal on 7 July 1347, a few weeks before Philippa's presumed intervention on behalf of the Calais burghers, about Edward of Woodstock's marriage to Afonso's youngest daughter Leonor (b. 1328). The king told his envoys to arrange a time and place for Leonor to arrive in England, but the envoys were so delayed that by the time they finally arrived in Portugal near the end of 1347, they were too late and Leonor had just married Pedro IV of Aragon.[23] It is fascinating to speculate how different English history would be if the young Prince of Wales had married Leonor and had children with her.

On 5 September 1347, Edward III pardoned a man for an unusual crime. John le Taillour, vicar of a church in Lincoln, had excommunicated the former and present parsons of the church, and had been imprisoned for his violent language. Taillour had also committed some kind of libel against the king and queen, which was bad enough to render Edward III speechless: Taillour was guilty of 'greater excesses affecting the person of the king and of Philippa, queen of England, his dearest consort, whereof on account of the horror and scandal of them the king is at present silent.' Taillour spent an unspecified long period in prison and 'humbly submitted himself to the king's grace'. As he had suffered during his long detention, Edward decided graciously to pardon him.[24] Unfortunately, the nature of his allegations against Edward and Philippa was not recorded; it would be most interesting to know what he said about them, and one wonders if it had anything to do with Archbishop John Stratford's conversations with the royal couple some years earlier, which Edward III declared would have driven him and Philippa apart forever if they had listened to his allegations.

Queen Philippa's brother-in-law Ludwig of Bavaria, deposed as Holy Roman Emperor eighteen months previously but still a powerful political force to be reckoned with, died on 11 October 1347 at the age of sixty-five. Ludwig was out bear hunting in the district of Fürstenfeldbruck a few miles north-west of Munich – bears did, rather astonishingly, still roam the forests of Bavaria then – when he suddenly collapsed and died in the arms of one of his subjects. A memorial now stands in the field where he passed away, recording Ludwig's death 'in the arms of a farmer.' Ludwig was buried with his first wife Beatrix of Świdnica or Schweidnitz in the *Dom zu Unserer Lieben Frau* or 'Cathedral of Our Dear Lady' in Munich, where his tomb and black marble sarcophagus can still be seen. Philippa's sister Empress Margaretha was only thirty-seven and had been married to Ludwig for almost twenty-four years. She gave birth to her tenth and youngest child, another son called Ludwig, in the month of her husband's death – the little boy had not yet been baptised when the emperor died – but he died in infancy sometime before 1 June 1349. This is unlikely to have been a full-term pregnancy, as Margaretha had only given birth to her previous child, Otto, at the end of 1346 or beginning of 1347. Little Ludwig is likely to have been born prematurely, and did not thrive and died soon after birth.[25] The emperor Ludwig left six sons, not counting the short-lived infant born to his widow: Ludwig, margrave of Brandenburg, and Stephan, duke of Lower Bavaria, from his first marriage to Beatrix of Świdnica; and Ludwig the Roman, Wilhelm, Albrecht and Otto, from his second to Margaretha of Hainault.

Ludwig of Bavaria was succeeded as Holy Roman Emperor not by one of his many sons but by his rival Karl IV, often known as Charles of Luxembourg, son and heir of Johann, king of Bohemia, killed at the battle of Crécy. In January 1348, four of the seven electors chose Edward III of England as an anti-king in opposition to Karl IV, without even consulting Edward, but he wisely declined the offer.[26] Six German knights travelled to England to inform the king of his election, and although they went away disappointed as Edward had no intention of taking up the appointment, they did leave with six fine palfreys as gifts from Edward and Philippa's eldest son the Prince of Wales, and almost certainly with gifts from the king himself as well.[27] This decision by the German electors reveals how much the king of England was respected and admired around Europe. Edward III, still only in his mid-thirties (he turned thirty-five the month after Ludwig of Bavaria's death), was a colossal figure on the European stage.

At the beginning of February 1349, Edward III attempted to negotiate a marriage between Karl – who would be crowned as Holy Roman Emperor in Rome in April 1355 – and his and Philippa's eldest daughter Isabella of Woodstock, but nothing came of it.[28] Karl by then had been widowed for several months from his first wife Blanche de Valois, who was one of the many half-sisters of Philippa's mother Jeanne de Valois, though in fact was younger than Philippa herself. When the negotiations for his possible marriage to Isabella of Woodstock fell through – he seems not to have been interested in a marital alliance with Edward III and England – Karl married the German noblewoman Anna of the Palatinate instead, and after her death married the Polish noblewoman Anna of Świdnica and fourthly, in 1363, another Polish noblewoman, Elizabeth of Pomerania.[29]

Edward III and Queen Philippa returned to England on 12 October 1347, the day after Ludwig of Bavaria died near Munich, and travelled to London.[30] About fifteen months after giving birth to Margaret of Windsor, Philippa was a few weeks pregnant again for the eleventh time. She was with her husband at Westminster in early February 1348 when she successfully requested pardons for five men accused of murder and for several others accused of 'adherence to the Scots'.[31] On 3 April 1348, Pope Clement VI issued a dispensation for John, heir to the earldom of Kent and Edward III's first cousin, to marry Philippa's niece Elisabeth of Jülich.[32] John was the posthumous son of Edmund of Woodstock, earl of Kent, beheaded on 19 March 1330 after attempting to free his supposedly dead half-brother Edward II from captivity while Queen Philippa was pregnant with her eldest child the Prince of Wales. John of Kent was born on 7 April 1330 so was not quite eighteen when the dispensation for his marriage was issued, and had become his father's heir when his elder brother Edmund died in early childhood in 1331. In October 1346 when he was sixteen, he was apparently in the custody of his mother Margaret née Wake, Edmund of Woodstock's widow, as Edward III asked Margaret to send John to him with as many men as possible as a show of force against Philip VI of France (or 'Philip de Valois' as Edward called him).[33] John of Kent was heir to his maternal uncle Thomas, Lord Wake (1298-1349) as well to the father who was beheaded before he was born.

Elisabeth of Jülich, sometimes also known as Isabella or Isabelle, was one of the children of Philippa's sister Johanna of Hainault and Wilhelm, marquis of Jülich. Her date of birth is not known, but she was probably close to John of Kent's own age, and it is possible that she was the child whose birth had been announced to Edward III and Philippa when the queen was heavily pregnant with her own first child in May 1330. Alternatively, she may have been the child born in the spring or early summer of 1332, a few months after her parents visited her aunt and uncle in England.

Clement VI gave John of Kent and Elisabeth of Jülich a licence to marry 'with a view to ending the strife' between Elisabeth's father Wilhelm of Jülich and John's cousin Reynald III, duke of Guelders, elder son of Edward III's sister Eleanor of Woodstock. Reynald was not even fifteen years old in April 1348 – he was born in May 1333 – but apparently was already feuding with his decades-older neighbour in Jülich. Elisabeth and John probably married soon afterwards, though they were to have no children together and John died at the age of only twenty-two in late 1352, leaving his sister Joan as his heir. Elisabeth of Jülich, rather remarkably, outlived him by almost sixty years: she spent the rest of her long life in England and died there in June 1411.

'How many Valiant Men, how many Fair Ladies' – The Black Death

In 1348, probably the darkest year of the European Middle Ages, when the first great outbreak of the Black Death killed a huge percentage of the European population, Edward III instituted the famous chivalric order which he called the Knights of the Garter. Celebrations were to be held at Windsor every year on 23 April, the feast day of St George. The Prince of Wales was the first member of the prestigious new order, and the royal cousin Henry of Grosmont was the second. Ten years later, Edward III honoured his wife by making Philippa the first Lady of the Garter, and she was the only one until the appointment of her daughter Isabella of Woodstock, a few years after Philippa's death. Other close members of the queen's family, such as her daughters-in-law Joan of Kent and Constanza and Isabel of Castile, and several of her granddaughters, became Ladies of the Garter in the 1370s and 1380s as well. Some of the other original Knights of the Garter in 1348 included Roger Mortimer, the twenty-year-old grandson and heir of the Roger Mortimer, earl of March, whom Edward III had executed in 1330; the king was not a vindictive man and did not visit the sins of the father on his son or grandson, and clearly had a high opinion of the young Roger and allowed him to thrive at his court. Sir Hugh Despenser, son and heir of Edward II's great favourite Hugh Despenser the Younger, whose execution the king had attended when he was fourteen, also made an excellent career at his kinsman's court. This Hugh was not one of the initial members of the Knights of the Garter, though may well have been invited to join had he not died in early 1349, probably of the plague.

On 28 April 1348, Philippa was still at Windsor, though Edward III had left there on the 26th and travelled to Woodstock.[1] The king was at Lichfield in Staffordshire in early May, where he held one of his many jousting tournaments; although the heavily pregnant queen was unable to attend, her daughter Isabella of Woodstock and her niece Elisabeth of Jülich were there. Elisabeth had either just married Edward III's teenaged cousin John of Kent or was soon to do so, and had probably arrived in England very recently. Henry of Grosmont, earl of Lancaster, Leicester, Derby and (from 1349) Lincoln, was one of the participants at the Lichfield tournament, and Henry's niece Elizabeth de Burgh, the king and queen's daughter-in-law, was among those watching in the stands with her aunt, Grosmont's eldest sister Lady Wake.

Other tournaments in 1348 took place at Windsor (to celebrate Philippa's latest purification), Eltham, Reading, Bury St Edmunds and Guildford. At the Eltham tournament, Edward III had five hoods made of white cloth embroidered with men dancing in blue habits and buttoned in front with large pearls, for himself, Grosmont, Sir Hugh Courtenay, Sir John Grey of Rotherfield and Sir John Lisle of Rougemont, all founder members of the Order of the Garter. At the Lichfield tournament, the participants wore a blue robe and white hood, perhaps the same garb as at Eltham.[2]

At Windsor Castle sometime in the second half of May 1348, now aged about 34, Philippa of Hainault gave birth to her eleventh child and sixth son William, and was churched on 24 June 1348, the feast of the Nativity of St John the Baptist. Edward III paid a massive sixty pounds for twelve carpets for the rooms Philippa lived in during her confinement, and for his baby son the king purchased a great bed of green taffeta decorated with red roses and (for some reason) serpents, and with curtains and cushions. Also in 1348, Philippa was given a set of wall hangings made of red sindon stamped with the letter S. She owned a cloak 'powdered with gold roses of eight petals and bordered with white pearls, in the middle of each rose an S of large pearls'.[3] Philippa's son John of Gaunt and his Lancastrian descendants later made great use of the S symbol, though the origin and meaning of it are unclear.

The little boy born in 1348 was known as William of Windsor after his birthplace, and his given name must have been intended to honour Philippa's late father Count Willem or her late brother, also the count of Hainault and Holland. During the joust held at Windsor on 24 June 1348 to celebrate the birth, Edward III bought two suits of clothes for Philippa's purification. On the day before, she wore a mantle, cape, supertunic and tunic of dark blue velvet embroidered with gold birds, each bird surrounded by a circle of pearls, and for the purification itself she wore the same four garments in red velvet. These were embroidered with oaks and other trees, with a lion beneath each tree made of large pearls. Four hundred large pearls were purchased, and thirty-eight ounces of small pearls, thirteen pounds of gold plate, seven pounds of embroidery silks and nearly 2,000 bellies of miniver and sixty skins of ermine. The weight of the queen's garments must have been incredible. In addition, the ground on which she walked was covered by an embroidery with silks and more pearls.

Edward of Woodstock bought his mother a courser (a kind of horse used for hunting) during the Windsor tournament of 1348, which bore the name of Bauzan ('Piebald') de Burgh, which perhaps indicates that the horse had been a gift to Edward in the first place from his sister-in-law Elizabeth de Burgh. At some point in *c.* 1348, perhaps at the tournament of June 1348, Edward III devised the motto, in English, 'Hay, hay, the wythe [white] swan, by Godes soule I am thy man.' Philippa's other sons also attended this tournament, inevitably all dressed in velvet: Elizabeth de Burgh's husband Lionel of Antwerp (aged almost ten) in azure blue, and John of Gaunt (aged eight) and Edmund of Langley (seven) in purple. The summer of 1348 was an unusually chilly and wet one; under normal circumstances, one imagines that the queen and her sons, wearing so much velvet in late June, would have been excessively hot.[4]

Edward of Woodstock was always an affectionate and generous brother to his many younger siblings, and he was William of

Windsor's godfather as well. The prince of Wales purchased a large number of expensive silver-gilt cups, dishes, jugs, bowls, pots and salt-cellars for the little boy's household, and also bought a cup and a jug for William's nurse and a cup each for the three women or girls who looked after the little boy in his cradle. His brother is referred to as 'Sir William of Wyndesore' in his accounts.[5] William of Windsor died a few months after his birth and was buried at Westminster Abbey in early September 1348.[6] Edward and Philippa had now lost two sons called William; it was an unlucky name for their children, although all their other five sons, Edward, Lionel, John, Edmund and Thomas (b. 1355), lived into adulthood. The little William of Windsor must have died at Brentford in Middlesex a few miles outside London, as King Edward paid a shilling each to fifty 'poor persons' for 'carrying torches from Brentford to London with the body of William, the king's son'. The fifty people were dressed in black russet. The king also paid for cloth of gold to cover William's body, 170 wax candles and torches to burn around his tomb, and for sixty silk pennons with gold.[7] William was buried next to his older sister Blanche of the Tower, who had died in 1342 and was buried in early 1343.

In late 1344, Edward III had begun to conduct serious negotiations with the large and powerful Spanish kingdom of Castile, and these negotiations finally bore fruit when he arranged the marriage of his and Philippa's second daughter Joan of Woodstock to the heir to the Castilian throne, the Infante Pedro, only legitimate son of Alfonso XI. The kingdom of Castile would be a useful ally against France, and news of Edward III's arrangements was greeted with some alarm in that kingdom. Pope Clement wrote to Jeanne of Burgundy, queen-consort of France, on 15 January 1345, telling her that King Alfonso XI of Castile had sent a knight and a physician to assure himself of the 'condition and manners' of Edward III and Philippa's daughter (whom he did not name in the letter). Clement went on to inform Queen Jeanne that he and the king of Castile had exchanged three letters on the matter, and rather self-pityingly pointed out that he was 'burdened with diverse and difficult affairs', perhaps a veiled warning to Queen Jeanne and the French not to keep pressing him about the proposed England-Castile match.[8]

Alfonso XI of Castile was born in August 1311 and was fifteen months older than Edward III. In 1325, before Edward III married Philippa of Hainault, he had been betrothed to Alfonso XI's sister Leonor of Castile, while Alfonso himself was betrothed to Edward's younger sister Eleanor of Woodstock. Edward III was the grandson of another Leonor of Castile, queen of England (*c.* 1241-90), the first wife of Edward I and mother of Edward II, and English relations with the kingdom of Castile had, for the most part, long been cordial. Owing to the altered political climate after Edward II's deposition in early 1327, the planned English-Castilian royal marriages did not go ahead, and Alfonso XI married Maria of Portugal instead of Eleanor of Woodstock. Maria was his first cousin on both sides of the family: his father and her mother were siblings, and his mother and her father were siblings. Perhaps because he felt little sexual attraction towards a woman he was so closely related to, Alfonso much preferred the company of his mistress Leonor Guzman, and had ten children with her. King Alfonso and Leonor Guzman's eldest surviving son was Enrique of Trastamara, who was born in January 1334 and was therefore just seven months older than his legitimate half-brother the Infante Don Pedro, Queen Maria's only son.

Pedro's fury at his father's preference for his mistress Leonor over his queen, and Pedro's and his mother's treatment of Leonor Guzman after his father's death, and the implacable hostility this engendered between Pedro and his half-brother Enrique of Trastamara, would ultimately result in Pedro's assassination. In England, Edward III was well aware of the influential and important position Leonor Guzman held at the Castilian court, and on occasion wrote to her as well as to Queen Maria. On 20 August 1345, he asked if she would be willing to send one of her sons to England as a companion for the Prince of Wales, though ultimately nothing came of it. In March 1346, Edward thanked Leonor for promoting the future marriage of her lover's legitimate son Pedro and his own daughter Joan.

Pedro of Castile was born on 30 August 1334 and was about seven months younger than his fiancée Joan of Woodstock, and was not yet fourteen when his future marriage was arranged.

When he reached adulthood, Pedro cut an impressive figure: he was a good six feet tall, slender but muscular, and had very light blond hair, pale skin and blue eyes. These were features which he inherited from his father Alfonso XI, who was also pale, blond and blue-eyed, and passed on to his daughter and heir Constanza of Castile and his granddaughter Catalina of Lancaster (who was also Edward III and Queen Philippa's granddaughter, though not via Joan of Woodstock).[9] Physically at least, Pedro certainly sounds like a bridegroom Joan could have delighted in, although his character left far more to be desired and he is known to posterity as Pedro 'the Cruel' – though then again, his posthumous reputation was much traduced by his half-brother, usurper and killer Enrique of Trastamara together with Enrique's descendants, and he may not have been quite as appalling as he has been painted.

Edward III, keen to safeguard the position of his daughter and any children she might have, sent envoys to Alfonso XI on 1 February 1348 to obtain a guarantee from the Castilian king that any son Joan of Woodstock and Pedro had would succeed to the throne of Castile after the death of Pedro. One of the envoys, Andrew Offord, was described as a 'professor of civil law', and he and the other two were instructed to 'obtain before all things sufficient security' that a son born to Joan and Pedro 'shall in any event' become king of Castile and Leon on Pedro's death. Offord was also given protection to travel to Spain in the company of Joan herself.[10] Infante Pedro sent his minstrel Garcias to England to perform for his fiancée, a rather sweet gesture which shows that Pedro was thinking of Joan before their wedding, and which perhaps somewhat belies his later atrocious reputation as Pedro 'the Cruel'. Garcias was to travel back to his native Castile in Joan's company, so would also be able to entertain her and her retinue, who included a company of 130 archers from Somerset, Dorset and Devon, during the long sea journey south.[11] Joan's eldest brother Edward of Woodstock gave her three tuns of Gascon wine 'when she left for parts beyond sea'.[12]

Perhaps also on the occasion of her departure from England, Edward gave Joan a magnificent brooch with rubies, diamonds, emeralds and pearls.[13] Joan was in the company of her father the king on or just before 3 April 1348, a few weeks before her departure for Spain, when she successfully interceded with him on behalf of the prior and convent of Plimpton.[14]

Tragedy struck the English royal family and untold millions of other people in Europe in the year 1348. The Black Death reached England during the wet and chilly summer of 1348. It was already raging on the continent, and the unfortunate Joan of Woodstock became one its many victims. Just before 1 July 1348 on the way to Spain, she and her retinue broke their journey in her father's territory of Gascony, and she succumbed to the plague in Lormont outside Bordeaux. She died at the age of fourteen.[15] Edward III had ordered forty ships to take his daughter and her retinue to Spain as early as 27 December 1347, and told the Castilian royal family on 1 January 1348 that he was about to send her to them. Perhaps he decided that it was not a sensible idea for his daughter to sail to Spain in the middle of winter when the seas were often very rough, but had he sent her to her wedding this early, Joan would have arrived in the south of France and subsequently in Spain before the epidemic of bubonic plague reached those areas, in which case she would almost certainly have lived and would have married Pedro.[16] Queen Philippa was at Westminster with her husband on 15 and 17 July 1348 when she granted Piers de Routh or Routhe, usher of her chamber, custody of Sandal Castle in Yorkshire and various parks in the same county, in her hands since the death of John de Warenne, earl of Surrey, a year previously. The king had given the queen various goods belonging to 'condemned persons and fugitives' in Northamptonshire, but some of them to the value of £200 had been stolen, and Edward ordered an inquiry at this time. It may be that the news of their daughter's demise had not yet reached the royal couple; messengers would have needed a good few days to travel the hundreds of miles from the south of France to Edward and Philippa in or near London.[17]

Philippa of Hainault and Edward III suffered another tragedy in 1348 when their little son William of Windsor died soon after he was born (William was buried on 3 September 1348, probably a few weeks or months after his death), and now their third child died as well, far from home. There can hardly have been anyone in Edward III's kingdom who did not lose a loved one, or several, to the Black Death, and now the king and queen had also lost a child to the plague on top of losing their infant son. Other royal European victims of the plague in the late 1340s and beginning of the 1350s included the man who should have been Joan of Woodstock's father-in-law, Alfonso XI of Castile, in a rather later outbreak in 1350; the queen-consort of France, Jeanne of Burgundy; Jeanne of Burgundy and Philip VI's daughter-in-law Bonne of Bohemia, duchess of Normandy, who would have become queen-consort of France the following year if she had lived; Leonor of Portugal, queen of Aragon, who should have married Edward of Woodstock in 1347; and Edward III's first cousin Jeanne II (b. 1312), queen-regnant of Navarre, who was succeeded by her teenage son Carlos II (b. 1332), later known as 'the Bad'. Members of the English nobility who died in 1348/9, perhaps also of the plague, included Queen Philippa's former ward Laurence Hastings, earl of Pembroke (whose one-year-old son and heir John would become the king and queen's son-in-law a few years later), Hugh, Lord Despenser, and Thomas, Lord Wake and his sister Margaret, the dowager countess of Kent and the mother-in-law of Philippa's niece Elisabeth of Jülich.

The grieving King Edward sent a poignant letter to Alfonso XI of Castile on 15 September 1348, in Latin:

> ...after much complicated negotiation about the intended marriage of the renowned Infante Pedro, your eldest son, and our most beloved daughter Joan [*Johannam filiam nostram dilectissimam*] ... we sent our said daughter to Bordeaux, en route to your territories in Spain. But see – with what intense bitterness of heart we have to tell you this – destructive Death, who seizes young and old alike, sparing no-one, and reducing rich and poor to the same level, has lamentably snatched from both of us our dearest daughter (whom we loved best of all, as her virtues demanded). No fellow human being could be surprised if we were inwardly desolated by the sting of this bitter grief, for we are human too. But we give thanks to God that one of our own family, free of all stain, whom we have

loved with pure love, has been sent ahead to Heaven to reign among the choirs of virgins, where she can gladly intercede for our offences before God himself.[18]

As well as revealing the king's grief for his daughter and his deep love for her, which his wife Philippa surely shared, this letter also reveals how the royal couple comforted themselves with the belief that Joan was now in Heaven and with God himself. Edward also sent letters in similar vein to Joan's fiancé Pedro and his mother Queen Maria.[19] The dating of the letter, just a few days after Edward and Philippa had buried another child, little William of Windsor, makes it even more poignant. On 25 October 1348 the king paid John, bishop of Carlisle, five marks a day for conducting Joan to Gascony, which seems to mean a delayed payment for escorting her to her intended wedding, rather than a payment for returning her body to England as sometimes assumed. The bishop of Carlisle was one of the men appointed on 12 February 1348 to travel with Joan from England to Spain.[20] Where Joan was buried is not entirely certain, but presumably somewhere in or near Bordeaux.

Joan of Woodstock's elder sister Isabella of Woodstock must also have missed her terribly; even though the two sisters might never have seen each other again after Joan married Pedro and spent the rest of her life in Spain, at least they could have kept in touch via letter, and exchanged gifts. Isabella of Woodstock was exactly the same age as her sister-in-law Elizabeth de Burgh, countess of Ulster and Lionel of Antwerp's wife, but Isabella's other sisters Mary of Waltham and Margaret of Windsor, were twelve and fourteen years younger than she was, so they can hardly have provided much company for her. Joan of Woodstock, the third royal child, died aged fourteen, and William of Hatfield the fourth child died as an infant in 1337, which left a large gap between the royal siblings: Edward and Isabella of Woodstock, born in June 1330 and June 1332, were much older than Lionel, the next surviving child, who was born in late November 1338. Lionel, John of Gaunt and Edmund of Langley were all very close in age and formed the second 'group' of royal children; Mary of Waltham and Margaret of Windsor were born only twenty-one months apart and formed the third group (William of Windsor would also have been part of this group had he lived); and, stuck out on his own and many years younger than his siblings, would come Thomas of Woodstock, the twelfth and youngest child of Edward III and Queen Philippa, not born until early 1355 and only seven months older than the royal couple's eldest legitimate grandchild.

The Spaniards on the Sea

On 9 December 1348, Queen Philippa was at Otford in Kent while Edward III was in London, though he joined her there on 17 December, and they spent Christmas at Otford.[1] Various entries in the chancery rolls in the last few weeks of 1348 and early 1349 reveal that the royal couple spent most of their time together, and that despite the heart-breaking loss of two of her children that year, the queen interceded with her husband and asked him to grant favours, appointments or pardons to people who had petitioned her.[2] Edward's kinsman Sir Hugh Despenser, lord of Glamorgan, died at the age of forty on 8 February 1349, perhaps of the Black Death, though this is uncertain. Despenser had made an excellent career at his cousin's court and played a vital role in the Crécy campaign of 1346, and had spent the best part of two decades doing his utmost to restore his family's good name and reputation after the executions of his father and grandfather in 1326. His marriage to Elizabeth Montacute, eldest daughter of the king's late good friend the earl of Salisbury (d. 1344), remained childless, and Despenser was succeeded as lord of Glamorgan by his nephew Edward when the latter came of age in 1357; Edward Despenser married Elizabeth Burghersh, granddaughter and heir of the king's steward Bartholomew, Lord Burghersh. The widowed Elizabeth Montacute's brother William Montacute (b. 1328), their father's successor as earl of Salisbury, had married the king's first cousin Joan of Kent a few years previously when they were both barely even into their teens, but in 1349 the pope dissolved their marriage on the grounds that Joan had previously been married to Sir Thomas Holland but had kept this secret for a few years, and had gone through with a bigamous wedding ceremony to Montacute. Joan of Kent's eldest child with Thomas Holland, also called Thomas, was born in 1350 or 1351, and her former husband William Montacute married his second wife Elizabeth Mohun a few years later (born around 1340 or 1343, she was much his junior).

Edward, illegitimate son of Queen Philippa's son Edward of Woodstock, appears on record in 1349 when the prince bought a pony for him. The identity of little Edward's mother is not clear, and this is the only known reference to the boy, so sadly it seems that he must have died young. As well as buying a pony for his little son in 1349, Edward of Woodstock bought a horse called Morel Huwet for his mother Queen Philippa and one for his brother Lionel of Antwerp, who turned eleven in late November 1349. One of the queen's illegitimate half-brothers, 'Sir John, bastard brother of the lady queen,' appears in her eldest son's accounts around this time when he also received a gift of a horse from his nephew. The prince bought palfreys for his uncle-in-law Wilhelm of Jülich, Johanna of Hainault's husband, and for the count of Hainault, presumably meaning one of Edward of Woodstock's cousins, Empress Margaretha's sons.[3] Queen Philippa, meanwhile, was staying at her Wiltshire castle of Devizes on 1 July 1349 when the long-serving bishop of Salisbury, Robert Wyville – he held the position from 1330 to 1375 – sent her a black palfrey as a gift.[4] She was at the royal manor of Sheen, later Richmond Palace, on 8 and 13 October 1349, and with her husband at Orsett in Essex in early December. Philippa sent a letter from there to the abbot of Colchester, also in Essex, and spent Christmas with her family at her own manor of Havering-atte-Bower.[5]

The Black Death still raged in England and other European countries throughout 1349. In late February 1350, King Alfonso XI of Castile died in his late thirties, during another wave of the great plague. His only legitimate son Pedro, who was fifteen and a half years old, succeeded him on the throne, and had Queen Philippa's daughter Joan of Woodstock not died of the plague herself eighteen months earlier in the summer of 1348, she would have become queen-consort of Castile at this point. King Pedro's utter fury at his father's treatment of his mother Queen Maria revealed itself when he and Maria had the late Alfonso's long-term mistress Leonor Guzman imprisoned and killed soon after she had lost her lover's protection. This made Pedro a mortal enemy in the person of his eldest half-brother Enrique of Trastamara, Leonor Guzman's eldest son, and Enrique would bring Pedro down and kill him a few years later. Possibly Joan of Woodstock had had a lucky escape: King Pedro married the fourteen-year-old French noblewoman Blanche de Bourbon (a granddaughter of Charles de Valois, and thus Queen Philippa's first cousin) in 1353, but he imprisoned her within days of the wedding and went off with his mistress Maria de Padilla, with whom he had several children. Two of them, Constanza and Isabel, survived infancy, and in the early 1370s married Queen Philippa's sons John of Gaunt and Edmund of Langley. Pedro had resented his father Alfonso XI's behaviour and his treatment of Pedro's mother; by going off with his mistress and abandoning his wife he did exactly the same thing himself, but in fact behaved even more appallingly than his father had, as at least Alfonso had never imprisoned his queen and kept her in solitary confinement as Pedro did with the unfortunate teenager Blanche de Bourbon.[6] News of Alfonso XI's death must have reached England from Spain in early to mid-March 1350. Queen Philippa was in Croydon, Kent with Edward III on 3 March that year, and in Colchester, Essex on 22 May.[7]

On 29 August 1350, the sea battle known as the Battle of Winchelsea, or more colourfully as *Les Espagnols sur Mer* ('The Spaniards on the Sea') was fought in the English Channel. Don Carlos de la Cerda, scion of a cadet branch of the Castilian royal family and of partly Spanish, partly French origin, was a notorious soldier of fortune. He captured a number of English trading ships, robbed them, and threw their crews overboard to drown. The furious Edward III decided to deal with de la Cerda, and lay in wait for him as he returned from Flanders to Spain. Two of Queen Philippa's sons also took part in the battle of The Spaniards on the Sea: Edward of Woodstock, Prince of Wales, who was twenty, and John of Gaunt, who was only ten years old but who joined his brother Edward on his ship rather than remaining on the shore with his mother in safety. Many Spanish ships were sunk and thus the English were victorious, though they also lost a few of their ships. The great nobleman and the king's cousin, Henry of Grosmont, earl of Lancaster, Leicester, Derby and Lincoln, saved the lives of Edward of Woodstock and John of Gaunt just as their ship was about to sink. Both they and Philippa, who had waited six miles inland while the battle was fought, must have been exceedingly grateful.

Probably just before the battle of the Spaniards on the Sea, news must have reached England of the death of Queen Philippa's maternal uncle, Philip VI of France, on 22 August. Philip had lost his wife of more than thirty-six years, Jeanne of Burgundy, on 12 December 1349, during the great epidemic of the Black Death. Just a month later on 11 January 1350, he married his second wife, Blanca or Blanche of Navarre, daughter of Jeanne II and sister of Carlos II 'the Bad', who had succeeded their mother on the throne of Navarre a few months earlier. Blanche was about thirty-seven years Philip's junior. Their marriage lasted only seven months, and Blanche gave birth to Philip's posthumous daughter in May 1351, nine months after her husband's death. The new king of France was now John II, Queen Philippa's first cousin, born in 1319 and the father of four sons and five daughters from his marriage to the late Bonne of Bohemia (d. 1349).

Edward III's brother-in-law David II of Scotland, whom Edward refused to acknowledge as king and usually called 'David Bruce, prisoner in the Tower of London', and, after the younger man's return to his own kingdom, 'the king's brother David Bruce of Scotland', was still in captivity in England in the early 1350s. On 13 July 1354, his ransom was set at 90,000 marks. David sent a long petition to Pope Clement VI shortly before October 1350, part of it ran:

> For nearly four years he, together with some of his barons, knights, and others, has been kept in captivity by the king of England, and despoiled of their goods, and they have not wherewith to pay their ransom, nor have they friends to redeem and restore them, and he is deprived by the fortune of war of the help of the king of France. He prays the pope for assistance and counsel, and for letters to the king of France on his behalf, so that

if peace were made between the kings of France and England, he, with his people, would be set free... Also, if the king of Scotland die without a lawful heir, the king of England or his son would be king of Scots.[8]

David's heartfelt petition and the pope's intercession on his behalf failed to move Edward III, and David was to remain in England until 1357, which represented a total of eleven years in captivity. He finally returned to his kingdom on acknowledgement of a payment of 100,000 marks, even greater than the sum demanded in 1354. He soon alienated his barons, however, by his excessive attachment to his influential mistress Katherine Mortimer (probably no relation to the English Mortimers), who was assassinated on orders of some of the disgruntled Scottish magnates as a result of her influence. David's snubbed wife Joan of the Tower returned to her native England, where she spent much time with her mother Queen Isabella, brother Edward III and sister-in-law Queen Philippa, and the royal Scottish couple's marriage ended in all but name. Although the English king never called David II by his rightful title of king, he always referred to his sister Joan as queen of Scotland.

At the beginning of the 1350s, Edward III pursued another possible marriage for his and Philippa's daughter Isabella of Woodstock, who turned nineteen in June 1351 and had been jilted by Louis of Flanders in 1347. The bridegroom in question was Bérard or Bernard d'Albret, second son of the influential Gascon lord Bernard Ezi IV, lord of Albret. Bérard d'Albret was a few years Isabella of Woodstock's junior; his older brother Arnaud Amanieu, their father's heir, was born in 1338 and was six years younger than Isabella. On 1 May 1351, the king promised Isabella and Bérard a joint income of 1,000 marks yearly 'in consideration of the marriage to be contracted between them'.[9] Edward III ordered five ships to take Isabella of Woodstock from the port of Plymouth to Gascony for her wedding to Bérard d'Albret in mid-November 1351. Once again, however, a planned marriage for the king and queen's eldest daughter did not work out, Isabella did not depart for her wedding and remained in England, and it may well be that she herself refused the match.[10] The second son of a Gascon noble was, after all, rather a poor match for the king of England's eldest daughter, however useful the Albret family might have been to Edward III.

Queen Philippa's feelings on the matter are unrecorded; perhaps she was pleased that her daughter would stay in England with her for a while longer. Her known itinerary in 1350/51 reveals that she was with her husband almost all the time, or at least just a short distance from him: she was at Mortlake (a manor on the River Thames west of London which belonged to the archbishops of Canterbury) on 10 October 1350, at Reading on 12 January 1351, at Westminster on 25 February, at Henley on the Heath on 7 August, at Chertsey on 28 August and 30 September. Philippa and Edward had now been married for well over twenty years, and there is every indication that their relationship was as strong and close as ever.

Less happily, according to the *Brut* chronicle, written in Middle English, there was a great drought in England in 1351, which lasted from March until July.

> There fell no rain into the earth, wherefore all fruits, seeds and herbs for the most part was lost; in default whereof there came so great disease of men and beasts, and dearth of victuals in England, so that this land, that ever before was plenteous, had need that time to seek his victuals and refreshing out of other countries.[11]

The royal cousin Henry of Grosmont left England for a few months in 1352 and headed off on a crusade to Lithuania, though he was back in England by Christmas that year and spent the festive season with the king and queen. Usually the most courteous and affable of men, Henry managed to quarrel with the German duke of Brunswick while he was overseas, and came very close to duelling with him in Paris; only the tact of John II of France, who declared that Brunswick's words had been misreported to Henry and vice versa, prevented bloodshed.[12] Edward had made Henry of Grosmont the first duke of Lancaster in 1351; Henry was only the second English duke in history, after Queen Philippa's son Edward of Woodstock, an indication of how deeply Edward III valued his kinsman. Early in 1352 Philippa and Edward attended a wedding in the royal chapel of Westminster. The bride was Maud of Lancaster, not quite twelve years old, elder daughter and co-heir of Henry of Grosmont, and the widow of little Ralph Stafford (d. 1347 or before), elder son of Edward's friend the earl of Stafford. The groom was Philippa's nephew Wilhelm of Bavaria, aged twenty-one and the second son of her eldest sister the dowager empress. Wilhelm had been invited to England by Edward III on 12 November 1351, and his mother Margaretha of Hainault came with him; she was given a safe-conduct to depart from England on 16 March 1352.[13] The two Hainault sisters thus had a chance to spend time together, almost certainly for the last time before Empress Margaretha's death four years later.

Chronicler Jean le Bel says of Wilhelm of Bavaria that he was 'tall, strong, swarthy and agile, more fleet and dexterous than any man in his land ... but he was curiously distant and inscrutable: he wouldn't welcome or acknowledge people ... and took no pleasure in the company of ladies and damsels.'[14] Wilhelm evidently had a difficult relationship with Empress Margaretha, and feuded with his mother for years over the counties of Hainault and Holland. Edward III sent Henry of Grosmont, duke of Lancaster and Wilhelm's father-in-law, to negotiate between Margaretha and her son in October 1353.[15]

Maud of Lancaster left England not long after her wedding to reside with her husband. Given that she was too young to live with Wilhelm yet as his full wife, she presumably resided with his family, perhaps with his mother, until she was old enough for her marriage to be consummated. She saw her father the duke only once again, in the Low Countries at Christmas 1353, and probably never saw her mother Isabella Beaumont again after she left England. Maud bore a daughter to Wilhelm in 1356 when she was sixteen, who died not long after birth and who would be their only child.[16]

In about 1357, the unfortunate Wilhelm began showing signs of insanity and in 1358 had to be confined, 'bound hand and foot' as Jean le Bel puts it. Although he lived until 1389, poor Maud, still only in her teens, became a widow in all but name. She was, however, a capable and resilient young woman, and 'the two lands of Hainault and Holland were governed by the lady his [Wilhelm's] wife.'[17] Later his younger brother Albrecht, Empress Margaretha's third son, took over.

Queen Philippa lost her mother on 7 March 1352 when Jeanne de Valois, nun and perhaps abbess of Fontenelle, dowager countess of Hainault and Holland, and aunt of the reigning French king John II, died in her late fifties. She was buried in the middle of the 'ladies' choir' at the abbey where she had died, and her tomb was discovered there in 1977. On 7 September 2001, Jeanne was reburied in the church of Saint-Géry in the town of Maing, near Valenciennes and also near the abbey of Fontenelle. And another loss came at the end of the year when Edward III's cousin John, earl of Kent, died during the night of 26/27 December at the age of only twenty-two. He left his widow Elisabeth of Jülich, Queen Philippa's niece. As they had no children, John's older sister Joan was his heir, and she duly became countess of Kent and Lady Wake in her own right. It is possible that Earl John had been seriously ill and expected to die earlier in 1352: on 24 August that year, Edward III gave Joan of Kent and her husband Sir Thomas Holland an allowance of 100 marks a year from the Exchequer, but added that the payment would cease if the earl of Kent died without heirs of his body and if, as a result, Joan inherited all his lands.[18] Joan of Kent, now twenty-five or twenty-six, was raising a family with Sir Thomas Holland. As well as their elder son and heir Thomas Holland the younger, born in 1350 or 1351, they were to have a younger son, John, and daughters Maud and Joan Holland as well, and John Holland married Queen Philippa's granddaughter Elizabeth of Lancaster in 1386. Joan of Kent's sister-in-law the widowed Elisabeth of Jülich became a nun at Waverley Abbey in Kent, but some years later changed her mind, came out of her convent, and married Sir Eustace d'Aubrichecourt, a brilliant soldier from Hainault who was one of the founding members of the Order of the Garter, in September 1360. Elisabeth was widowed again in late 1372. In her will of 20 April 1411, Elisabeth requested burial in the Franciscan church in Winchester with her first husband the earl of Kent, whom she had outlived by so many years. The archbishop of Canterbury imposed a severe penance on Elisabeth in 1360 for breaking her vow of chastity and marrying again. She was to walk to the shrine of St Thomas Becket in Canterbury every year, would eat nothing but bread and pottage one day every week for the rest of her life, and would feed six poor people every day after she and Eustace d'Aubrichecourt had indulged in 'carnal copulation.'[19]

A Last Child and a Grandchild

In early May 1353, Pope Innocent VI granted a dispensation for the future marriage of Philippa's youngest daughter Margaret of Windsor (born July 1346) and Margaret's second cousin Jean de Blois, son and heir of Charles de Blois and Jeanne de Penthièvre, claimant to Brittany.[1] Jean's father Charles had been a prisoner in England since he was captured in 1347, and he offered his son's marriage to Edward III's daughter as a means of securing his own release. Edward seems seriously to have considered the marriage, and duly freed Charles of Blois on promise of a large ransom to be paid, but ultimately the English king decided to stick to his alliance with the other faction claiming the duchy of Brittany. Margaret of Windsor later married John de Montfort (b. 1339), son and heir of the rival claimant, John de Montfort (c. 1295-1345).

Edward III was ill in the summer of 1353, perhaps seriously ill: when he and Philippa were at the Wiltshire palace of Clarendon at the end of July, the king paid over sixteen pounds to his apothecary John of Lucca (in Italy) for providing various medicines for him.[2] Edward had turned forty on 13 November 1352. Whatever the illness was that he suffered a few months later, he recovered and was to live for almost another quarter of a century. The royal couple spent the festive season of 1353 at Eltham in Kent, and Philippa must have watched her eldest son compete in a jousting tournament held there to mark the feast of the Epiphany, 6 January 1354. The Prince of Wales and his fellow jousters, including Sir John Chandos and Sir James Audley, looked splendid in armour covered with red and black velvet.[3]

Queen Philippa was at Colchester in Essex on 6 March 1354, when she wrote a letter appointing Piers de Routh, usher of her chamber, as master forester at Knaresborough in Yorkshire (a few years previously, she had also made him custodian of her castle at Sandal). Philippa called herself 'Philippe by the grace of God queen of England, lady of Ireland and duchess of Aquitaine'.[4] The queen probably turned forty around late January, February or March 1354, and it must have been in early or mid-April this year that she and Edward conceived their youngest child. It was surely much to the royal couple's surprise that Philippa found herself pregnant again six years after the birth of their last child, William of Windsor, in May 1348. Her youngest child would be born at the palace of Woodstock at the beginning of 1355.

At the parliament held at Westminster in late April and May 1354, Edward III restored Roger Mortimer the younger, namesake grandson and heir of the Roger Mortimer whom the king had had executed in November 1330, to the contentious earldom of March the elder Roger had created for himself in October 1328. Edward III, never a vindictive man (unlike both his parents), clearly saw much to admire in the younger Roger, and had made him a founder member of the Order of the Garter in April 1348 when the young man was not even twenty years old. The younger Roger Mortimer was born in November 1328 and was just past his second birthday when his grandfather was executed, and his father Edmund Mortimer, the elder Roger's eldest son, was 'seized by a sudden infirmity and went the way of all flesh' in early 1331, only a few weeks after his father's execution.[5] The younger Roger was married to Philippa Montacute, third daughter of the late William, earl of Salisbury (d. 1344) and Katherine née Grandisson. Philippa Mortimer née Montacute may have been Queen Philippa's goddaughter. Roger and Philippa Mortimer's son and heir Edmund Mortimer, born in early 1352, would become the queen's grandson-in-law some years later. After the older Roger Mortimer's downfall in 1330, Edward III had granted Roger's manor of Stratfield Mortimer in Berkshire to his queen. In 1354 he restored it to the younger Mortimer, and compensated Philippa with fifty-two pounds a year at the exchequer in cash or in land.[6]

The queen was with her husband at Westminster on 23 May 1354 when she requested a licence for the priory of Saint Frideswide in Oxford, a priory in which she always took an interest, to enlarge their house.[7] Philippa sent Richard of Lancaster and Robert of Rotherhithe to Nottingham that autumn, and while the two were 'engaged in furthering some difficult business of the said queen' they were assaulted by eight men and one woman, and imprisoned, 'whereby the said business remained undone'.[8]

The heavily pregnant queen spent Christmas 1354 with her husband at Hamstead Marshall in Berkshire, and the king most probably went hunting while they were there (Philippa also enjoyed the hunt whenever she could, but was surely too pregnant on this occasion). This year, Edward III had temporarily imprisoned his cousin Margaret of Norfolk – also often called Margaret Marshall, daughter and ultimate heir of Edward II's half-brother Thomas of Brotherton – at Somerton Castle in Lincolnshire after he found out that she had married her second husband without his permission. Margaret had been unhappily married to John, Lord Segrave, and left England, also without the king's permission, to seek an annulment from the pope in Avignon. Segrave, conveniently for Margaret, died anyway in 1353, and she soon married Sir Walter Manny, the Hainaulter who had come to England with Queen Philippa in late 1327. Margaret gave birth to her and Walter's only surviving child, Anne Manny, future countess of Pembroke, two days before her cousin ordered her arrest as 'quietly and honourably' as possible (to be fair to Edward, he probably did not realise that Margaret had just given birth when he issued this order). It was hardly a harsh incarceration, however; Margaret had all her household servants with her, and her new husband was allowed to make conjugal visits whenever they wished. In December 1355, the king officially pardoned Margaret of Norfolk and Walter Manny 'of all rancours and wraths conceived against them by the king for any causes'.[9] Margaret was, like the king himself, a grandchild of Edward I, and Walter was one of the king's most loyal and courageous lieutenants; he could not stay angry with the two for long.

On 7 January 1355 at the palace of Woodstock, Queen Philippa gave birth to Thomas. She was now probably almost forty-one, and the infant was a full quarter of a century younger than his eldest brother the Prince of Wales. Inevitably, Edward III held a jousting tournament at Woodstock to mark the queen's purification a few weeks later, and Henry of Grosmont, duke of Lancaster, Richard Fitzalan, earl of Arundel, Thomas of Hatfield, bishop of Durham, and Lords Neville and Percy all brought destriers (war-horses) to Woodstock for the occasion. Philippa's eldest son the prince took part in the tournament, and sometime that year spent time with his elderly grandmother, the dowager queen Isabella, whom he had made a great-grandmother in the mid-1340s or thereabouts when his illegitimate son Edward was born.[10] Little Thomas of Woodstock's nurse was called Alesia, wife of Marmaduke Vang, and she looked after him until he was about eighteen months old. Alesia was replaced by Christiana, wife of John Enefeld or Enfield.[11] The little boy seems to have remained in his mother's household for the first few years of his life, and was set up in his own household in 1366 or earlier.[12] Thomas of Hatfield, bishop of Durham, was one of the little boy's godfathers, and another was Thomas de la Mare, abbot of St Albans. Presumably Thomas of Woodstock was named after both godfathers, though perhaps Edward III had his late uncle Thomas of Brotherton, earl of Norfolk (1300-38) in mind as well.[13]

Queen Philippa was still at the palace of Woodstock on 1 February and 25 February 1355, when she granted a licence to the earl of Warwick's brother John Beauchamp to purchase the manor of Silham. Edward III's great tournament to celebrate his son's birth and the queen's purification was held at Woodstock on 22 February, and the queen must have watched it.

The king and queen received news in late April or early May 1355 that Edward's sister Eleanor of Woodstock, duchess of Guelders, had died, aged not yet thirty-seven. Eleanor had, like her younger sister Joan of the Tower, endured an unhappy marriage, and things hardly improved after her husband's death in 1343: she quarrelled with her elder son Duke Reynald III during his minority, and died in poverty. She was buried at Deventer Abbey. Her two sons Reynald and Eduard both became duke of Guelders, warred against each other after their mother's death and Eduard imprisoned Reynald. Both failed to father any legitimate children (though Reynald left at least two illegitimate ones). Both brothers died in 1371, and the duchy of Guelders passed to their eldest half-sister Mathilde and later to Queen Philippa's nephew Wilhelm of Jülich, duke of Jülich, husband of their second half-sister.

At not quite six months old, on 1 July 1355, Thomas of Woodstock was appointed as official guardian of the realm when his father and four much older brothers left the country on another military campaign to France (though in the end, the king did not depart from his kingdom until late October, and the campaign was a very short one).[14] Richard, earl of Arundel, and both English archbishops were among the men appointed as the real rulers of the kingdom during the king's absence, and perhaps the queen also involved herself in the running of her husband's government. In early July 1355, Philippa, her daughter Isabella of Woodstock (now twenty-three) and Edward III's cousins Henry of Grosmont, duke of Lancaster, and William de Bohun, earl of Northampton, worked together to request a pardon for a knight called John de Lyle, who had killed another knight called John de Goys. Edward III duly granted the pardon.[15]

Just seven months after the birth of her twelfth and last child, on 16 August 1355, Philippa's eldest legitimate grandchild (Edward of Woodstock having already fathered at least one and possibly several of the illegitimate kind) was born. The new grandchild was Philippa, the first and, as it turned out, only child of Lionel of Antwerp and Elizabeth de Burgh, and she was inevitably named after her paternal grandmother the queen, as several of Queen Philippa and Edward III's granddaughters would be. The queen attended her granddaughter's baptism at the palace of Eltham in Kent on the day of her birth and, with her daughter-in-law Elizabeth, countess of Ulster, 'lifted her from the sacred font'. This means that the queen was the little girl's godmother as well as her grandmother. William Edington, bishop of Winchester and chancellor of England (d. 1366), conducted the baptism ceremony. When little Philippa proved that she had come of age fourteen years later, three local men remembered her date of birth because the River Thames 'broke the pool called "Le Brech" at Grynewych [Greenwich] and flooded a very great number of acres of arable land' there in the summer Philippa was born.[16]

Lionel of Antwerp, born on 29 November 1338, was still only sixteen years old when his daughter was born, and his wife Elizabeth de Burgh was twenty-three. Little Philippa was in fact born thirty-seven weeks after her father's sixteenth birthday on 29 November 1354, so perhaps Lionel and Elizabeth had finally consummated their marriage because he had turned sixteen, more than twelve years after their wedding. If this was the case, Elizabeth became pregnant immediately, but although she was still only twenty-three years old in 1355 and lived for another eight years, she and Lionel never had another child. Perhaps her daughter's birth was a difficult one, and in 1356 the year after giving birth to Philippa, Elizabeth was ill, and her father-in-law the king paid a physician called Master Pascal for finding a cure for her.[17]

Lionel's elder brother Edward of Woodstock promised a gift of twenty pounds to the messenger, John Prior, who brought him news of his niece Philippa's birth, though John had to wait quite a long time to receive his money: he was finally given ten pounds of it in May 1358.[18] On 5 March 1356 when she was a few months old, Edward III sent his baby granddaughter to live at the priory of Campsea Ashe in Suffolk. Here she would join her other grandmother, Elizabeth de Burgh's mother Maud of Lancaster (*c.* 1310/12-1377), widow of William de Burgh, earl of Ulster and of Ralph Ufford, justiciar of Ireland, and now a canoness there.[19] A few years later, Lionel of Antwerp founded a priory for his mother-in-law at Bruisyard a few miles from Campsea Ashe, and Maud moved there.

Queen Philippa was at Westminster on 13 October 1355, the feast day of St Edward the Confessor, and still at Westminster on 24 November.[20] Edward III spent late October and early November in Calais, then travelled to the north of England and spent Christmas at Newcastle-upon-Tyne. Philippa's uncle Jan van Beaumont died on 11 March 1356, well into his sixties; his four sons all entered the Church and became canons, and Jan's heir was his late daughter Johanna's son Jean, count of Blois. Philippa's eldest sister the dowager empress died soon after their uncle, on 23 June 1356, probably the day before her forty-sixth birthday, at the castle of Le Quesnoy in Hainault. Margaretha was buried in Valenciennes, probably in the same church as her father Willem in

1337. She left her four sons Ludwig the Roman, Wilhelm, Albrecht and Otto, and five daughters: Anna and Agnes both became nuns and Agnes died as a teenager, Beatrix married King Erik of Sweden but died at the age of fifteen, Elisabeth was lady of Verona and countess of Württemberg by her two marriages and lived into the fifteenth century, and the empress's eldest child Margarethe of Bavaria was duchess of Slavonia in modern-day Croatia and the daughter-in-law of the king of Hungary. Margaretha of Hainault's second son Wilhelm of Bavaria, who had already gained control of the county of Holland in 1354 after a years-long power struggle against his mother, also gained control of Hainault after her death.

Wilhelm of Bavaria was married to Maud of Lancaster, and began showing signs of insanity the year after his mother's death and had to be confined in the castle of Le Quesnoy for his own safety and everyone else's.[21] The unfortunate Maud gave birth to a daughter in 1356 when she was sixteen, in the year of her mother-in-law's death, but the little girl soon died, and Maud then had to endure her husband's severe illness and incarceration.[22]

Edward of Woodstock left England in 1356 and won a startling victory over the French at the battle of Poitiers on 19 September that year. King John II of France himself was captured during that battle in what was one of the most extraordinary events of the English Middle Ages, a remarkable moment. Edward of Woodstock, with the captive John II of France in tow, arrived back in England on 5 May 1357, and on 24 May entered London.[23] The aged Queen Isabella, now over sixty but obviously still healthy and able to travel, was one of the many people who attended her grandson's victory parade in London.

John II lived at various places in England during his long captivity, though mostly at the Savoy Palace in London, rebuilt on a magnificent scale by the almost impossibly wealthy Henry of Grosmont, duke of Lancaster, which later passed to his younger daughter Blanche and her husband, Queen Philippa's son John of Gaunt. King John also lived at Somerton Castle in Lincolnshire for a while, and was destined to die in England without seeing his homeland again. He was treated with respect and honour and had a large retinue in England, including a man called the *comes de la March* in the extant household accounts of the dowager queen

Isabella, written in Latin.[24] This man dined with Isabella three times in 1357/58, and has often been wrongly identified as the English earl of March, the younger Roger Mortimer (1328-60), namesake grandson and heir of the dowager queen's executed favourite. The *comes de la March* was, in fact, the French count of La Marche, Jacques de Bourbon, a second cousin of Queen Isabella and a direct male-line ancestor of Henri de Bourbon (b. 1553), who became the first Bourbon king of France in 1589, succeeding the Valois. Queen Isabella's niece-in-law Jeanne de Bar, dowager countess of Surrey (1295/96-1361), and their kinswoman Marie de St Pol, dowager countess of Pembroke, were both also French by birth, and like the dowager queen regularly received and entertained the members of the captive king's retinue in England.[25]

Royal Marriages

Edward III and Queen Philippa spent the period of Advent in 1357 in Bristol and the festive season at Marlborough in Wiltshire. With them were their youngest child Thomas of Woodstock, who was almost three, their daughters Mary of Waltham and Margaret of Windsor, aged thirteen and eleven respectively, their daughter-in-law Elizabeth de Burgh, countess of Ulster, and Jeanne de Montfort, daughter of the late John de Montfort, claimant of the duchy of Brittany.

One member of the countess of Ulster's household in the late 1350s was merely a teenager at this time, and would later become one of the most famous English writers of all time: the poet Geoffrey Chaucer. Money was paid to choristers for singing before the royal children on the eve of St Nicholas, 5 December, and on the feast of the Epiphany, 6 January 1358, the royal family attended a great mass in Queen Philippa's chapel at Bristol. They kept in touch with the dowager queen Isabella at Hertford Castle via messengers, and exchanged gifts with her on the Feast of the Circumcision, 1 January, as was customary.[1]

The festivities held at Windsor in April 1358 for the annual celebrations of St George and the Order of the Garter were even more splendid than usual. The captive John II of France attended, though the other king until recently also captive in England, David II of Scotland, had returned to his kingdom to arrange the massive ransom he owed to Edward III. Queen Philippa of course was also there, with her sister-in-law Joan of the Tower, David II's wife and

Edward III's sister, and her mother-in-law Isabella of France, taking part in the last great public event of her long life. Isabella, now about sixty-two or sixty-three, was finally nearing the end of her life over three decades after leading a revolution which deposed a king of England for the first time in history and put her teenaged son on the throne. The king, perhaps realising that his mother did not have much longer to live, visited her on 26 October 1357 and in March, April and May 1358. He was also at Hertford, one of Isabella's favourite residences, on 12 July 1358, presumably visiting her again, and it would be the last time he saw her. Queen Philippa, meanwhile, was at Westminster with her husband on 22 February 1358, and was at Marlborough in Wiltshire on 7 and 12 July while Edward was at Hertford, so she did not visit her mother-in-law on that occasion, and would never see her again.[2] In July 1358, Philippa was preoccupied with having numerous necessary repairs carried out on the houses, walls and other buildings of several of her manors in the county of Sussex, and her son Edmund of Langley, now seventeen, was busily repairing his Yorkshire castle of Conisbrough, which had formerly belonged to his godfather the earl of Surrey.[3]

Philippa and her eldest son had, however, accompanied the king to visit Isabella on 26 October 1357 at Isabella's home on Lombard Street in London, and four minstrels entertained them as they dined. The dowager queen was active in the last months of her life and evidently not suffering from a debilitating illness. Although she paid an apothecary for medicines in February 1358, Isabella went on pilgrimage to Canterbury in October 1357 before she travelled to London and spent time there with her son and daughter-in-law, and she attended the Garter celebrations at Windsor in April 1358 and went to Canterbury again in June 1358, so was certainly still not unwell enough to be unable to travel. As well as receiving her son the king and daughter-in-law the queen, Isabella was visited by her grandsons Edward of Woodstock and Lionel of Antwerp and her first cousin Henry of Grosmont, duke of Lancaster. As well as visiting his mother on several occasions, Edward III wrote to her and sent her gifts of wine, caged birds and wild boar meat.[4]

Queen Isabella died at Hertford Castle on 22 August 1358. She had outlived two of her four children, John of Eltham, earl of

Cornwall, and Eleanor of Woodstock, duchess of Guelders, and several of her grandchildren. Her embalmed body lay in the chapel at Hertford Castle for three months until 23 November, watched over day and night by fourteen 'poor persons' who each received two pence per day for their services, plus food. Her son the king and daughter-in-law Philippa met her funeral cortège when it arrived in London on 24 or 25 November, and a man called John le Galeys ('the Welshman') received ten pounds for the use of his house at Mile End 'for the time the body of Isabella, late queen of England, remained there with the king and his household'.[5] The dowager queen's interment took place on 27 November – a long delay between death and burial was customary in the royal family in the thirteenth and fourteenth centuries – and in the presence of her family she was buried at the Greyfriars or Franciscan church in London, where her aunt Marguerite of France, half-sister of Philip IV of France and second wife of Edward III's grandfather Edward I, had been buried in March 1318. It is merely a romantic myth, still sometimes repeated today, that Isabella was buried next to her long-dead lover Roger Mortimer, first earl of March. Mortimer was buried at the Greyfriars in Coventry, not in London, and his body may have been moved to his family's main seat at Wigmore in Herefordshire at the request of his widow Joan Geneville (who died in 1356). Even if Isabella had requested burial next to Mortimer, and there is absolutely no evidence that she did or indeed that she ever wanted to be, Edward III would never have permitted his royal mother to lie for eternity next to a man he had had executed for treason.

Neither Roger Mortimer himself nor any of his family are, contrary to popular modern belief, mentioned in Isabella's household accounts, which fortuitously survive for the last year of her life: the countess of Pembroke who visited her and with whom she corresponded, sometimes assumed to be Mortimer's daughter Agnes (widow of Laurence Hastings, d. 1348, and mother of his heir John, b. 1347) was in fact Marie de St Pol, widow of the previous earl of Pembroke, Aymer de Valence (d. 1324). Isabella was buried, as she had certainly requested, with the clothes she had worn to her wedding with Edward II half a century previously (her body was, however, probably not dressed in the clothes, unless they were altered and let out, given that she was only twelve at the time of her wedding in 1308 and must have been rather larger half a century later). According to a later tradition, she was also buried with a silver casket on her chest containing Edward II's heart and though this may not be true, if it is, separate heart burial was common in medieval royal burials and her request does not imply anything sinister or morbid. Edward II's mother Leonor of Castile, queen of England (d. 1290), for example, was buried with the heart of her third son Alfonso of Bayonne (1273-84). Isabella's youngest child Joan of the Tower, queen of Scotland, would be buried in the same church as her mother four years later.

Finally, thirty years and a few months after she had married Edward III, Philippa of Hainault was the only queen in England. Soon afterwards, Philippa had an accident and for the remaining years of her life would suffer from considerable pain as a result: she fell from a horse while hunting with Edward III in the summer of 1358, and seems never to have really recovered. According to the *Eulogium Historiarum*, she shattered her shoulder-blade, which must have been terribly painful, and certainly she was never able to go hunting again.[6]

On 16 September 1358 a few weeks after her mother-in-law died and shortly after she fell from her horse while hunting, Queen Philippa was at Marlborough in Wiltshire, her own castle, with her husband.[7] She and the king were in London in the last week of November 1358 for Queen Isabella's funeral, and in that month or the next the royal couple attended a wedding. The bride was their granddaughter Philippa, child of Lionel of Antwerp and Elizabeth de Burgh. She was only three years old. Her groom was Edmund Mortimer, and he was six.[8] Edmund was the son and heir of Roger Mortimer, second earl of March, and the earl of Salisbury's sister Philippa Montacute, and the great-grandson of Roger Mortimer executed in 1330.[9]

This marriage would give the Mortimer family a strong claim to the throne later in the century as well as giving them the earldom of Ulster and the third of the earldom of Gloucester which Elizabeth de Burgh was set to inherit from her grandmother Elizabeth de Burgh the elder, Edward III's first cousin (who was still alive in late 1358 when her great-granddaughter Philippa married Edmund

Mortimer, and lived for another two years). As Edward III gave his granddaughter a marriage portion of 5,000 marks, evidently the king did not expect that Philippa would be her parents' only child and heir. Lionel was only twenty when his daughter married, his wife Elizabeth de Burgh twenty-six, and Edward III must have expected them to produce more children and to leave a son as their heir. As it happened, they did not have more children and the Mortimer family thus benefited hugely both from a large payout and the marriage of a great heiress, whose lands duly passed into Mortimer possession. Had the king expected that Philippa would be her parents' heir, he would not have felt the need to give the Mortimers such a large marriage portion.[10]

Young Philippa's four Mortimer children, born between 1371 and 1376, and their own children and grandchildren would be descended from Edward III and Queen Philippa's second son, a fact which would become vitally important in the fifteenth-century struggles for the English throne which later became known as the Wars of the Roses.

Rather remarkably, Edward III had arranged and overseen the marriage of his only legitimate grandchild before he oversaw the marriages of any of his and Philippa of Hainault's children except Lionel, little Philippa's father (who, like his daughter, had married when he was only three years old). This was of course not entirely a deliberate choice: had Joan of Woodstock not died in southern France in 1348, she would now be the queen-consort of Castile as the wife of King Pedro, and had the English envoys made better haste to the Iberian Peninsula in 1347, Edward of Woodstock would probably be married to Leonor of Portugal. Had Edward III put his foot down as most royal medieval fathers surely would have done, Isabella of Woodstock would have been married to one of her several fiancés years previously. In 1359, with eight living children (Edward, Isabella, Lionel, John, Edmund, Mary, Margaret and Thomas) yet only one legitimate grandchild and only one married child, the king decided it was high time to see to the marriages of several more of his offspring.

For his and Philippa's third son John of Gaunt, the king arranged a brilliant match with John's third cousin, Blanche of Lancaster (b. 1342), younger daughter and co-heir of Henry of Grosmont, duke of Lancaster. Blanche's elder sister Maud (b. 1340) had married Queen Philippa's nephew Wilhelm of Bavaria in 1352 and had lived on the continent ever since, though as noted above, endured a hopelessly awful situation when her husband became insane.

Blanche of Lancaster fared much better in the marital stakes than her sister in marrying John of Gaunt in Reading on 19 May 1359; the ceremony was performed by a clerk of Queen Philippa's chapel called Thomas Chynham.[11] John was nineteen and Blanche, according to the evidence of her father's Inquisition Post Mortem two years later, was seventeen, born on 25 March 1342. A dispensation for consanguinity had been issued by Pope Innocent VI on 6 January 1359, and the couple must have known each other all their lives.[12] John's parents attended the wedding, as did, presumably, Blanche's parents Duke Henry and his wife Isabella Beaumont. The king's sister Joan of the Tower (b. 1321), queen of Scotland, whose husband David II had until recently been a prisoner in England, was also there. Blanche and her father visited Duke Henry's town of Leicester before the wedding, and the sum of three shillings and eight pence was spent on minstrels who performed at their arrival. The townspeople gave Blanche and her lady attendants a generous gift of twenty-five pounds.[13]

Edward III paid thirty pounds for two silver buckles for his and the queen's eldest daughter Isabella of Woodstock to give to her new sister-in-law. A membrane still exists in the National Archives detailing other gifts given to the bride (referred to as *dame Blaunch*, 'Lady Blanche') the day after her wedding. Those who gave her gifts were her new husband, father-in-law, aunt-in-law Joan of the Tower, brothers-in-law Lionel (*Lyonel*), Edmund and four-year-old Thomas, sisters-in-law Isabella of Woodstock, Mary of Waltham and Margaret of Windsor, and Lionel's wife Elizabeth de Burgh, countess of Ulster. For some rather curious reason, Queen Philippa and her eldest son Edward of Woodstock are not mentioned on the list of gift-givers, though it would have been odd if they, alone of all the family, did not give Blanche wedding presents. John of Gaunt bought his new wife a gold brooch with a balas ruby (not actually a ruby but a rose-tinted aluminium/magnesium mineral, though no less beautiful for that) and pearls, and a gold and diamond ring, and Elizabeth de Burgh gave her first cousin Blanche a silver cup and a ruby ring. Blanche received three more silver cups, which were presented to her in the name of four-year-old Thomas of Woodstock and his sisters Mary of Waltham and Margaret of Windsor.[14]

Both the poet Geoffrey Chaucer (born *c.* 1340 or 1342 and thus exactly the same age as John and Blanche) and the chronicler Jean Froissart (just a little older) commented on Blanche of Lancaster's beauty. She was tall and fair, had wide hips and round breasts – Chaucer perhaps sharing too much information there – and was 'fattish and fleshy'. This was a definite positive in fourteenth-century England when few people enjoyed an abundance of food, and was a clear sign of wealth.

Blanche was indeed born to virtually limitless wealth and privilege, yet despite this did not grow up conceited and unapproachable, but had a delightful personality. Froissart admired Blanche of Lancaster enormously: she was 'light-hearted, happy, fresh, amusing, sweet, guileless, of humble manner', and he jocularly requested a plaster to be placed over his heart at the memory of her many years later.[15] Blanche was not only a great heiress but beautiful and kind, a courteous, humble person who, like her father the duke, was adored by everyone who met her. Her new husband John of Gaunt must have found it very easy to fall deeply in love with her. Their first child was born ten months and twelve days after their wedding.

Most probably Blanche's mother Isabella Beaumont attended the wedding and spent time with the king and queen in Reading during the great occasion, though Duchess Isabella is an oddly obscure figure who played very little role in the life of her charismatic and famous husband. In his long and remarkable *Book of Holy Medicines*, which Duke Henry wrote in 1354, he admitted to having 'kissed' (a euphemism) a number of low-born women, and he is known to have fathered at least one illegitimate child, a daughter named Juliane who spent her life in Henry's town of Leicester and married there.[16] Duchess Isabella may already have been dying at the time of her younger daughter's wedding in May 1359. That month, the pope granted Duke Henry, regarding an indult previously granted that his chaplains should give him and

Isabella plenary remission at the time of their death, an extension 'to another wife, if he takes one after the death of Isabella'.[17]

Queen Philippa's youngest daughter Margaret of Windsor also married in Windsor, her birthplace, on 19 May 1359; her bridegroom was John Hastings, heir to the earldom of Pembroke. The king spent well over £200 on 2,000 pearls for his daughter's wedding.[18] Margaret, born in July 1346, was twelve going on thirteen when she wed, and her husband John was eleven. He was born on 29 August 1347, and lost his father Laurence, earl of Pembroke, on 30 August 1348 when he was one year and one day old.[19] Via his mother Agnes Hastings née Mortimer, John Hastings was a grandson of Roger Mortimer, the first earl of March executed in November 1330, and as Agnes lived until 1368 she almost certainly attended her son's wedding. Laurence Hastings himself, the groom's late father, had been a ward of Queen Philippa in the early 1330s when he was about twelve, and Philippa must have known the whole family very well; little John himself spent much time with the king and queen's offspring as they were growing up. John Hastings' paternal grandmother Juliana, dowager Lady Hastings and countess of Huntingdon by her third marriage to Edward III's late friend William Clinton, was still alive, and probably also attended the royal wedding.[20]

The king and his four eldest sons Edward, Lionel, John and Edmund took part in a jousting tournament at Smithfield in London from 27 to 29 May, held in honour of John of Gaunt's new wife. They dressed as the mayor and aldermen of London. Thomas of Woodstock the youngest royal son, at only four, surely watched, as did his new brother-in-law John Hastings aged eleven, both too young to compete personally. Edward III paid forty pounds to William Volaunt, king of heralds, to distribute among the minstrels who had entertained the royal family and the watching crowds during the Smithfield tournament.[21]

Queen Philippa was still in Reading on 6 June 1359, or perhaps had returned to the town after watching the jousting tournament in London, when she sent a letter to the chancellor William de Edington appointing an attorney.[22] The queen's new daughter-in-law Blanche became pregnant around late June or early July

1359. Edward III demonstrated his anxiety for Blanche's well-being on 9 January 1360 by commenting that she was pregnant and 'because of the concern that we feel for her condition' he wished her to stay with Queen Philippa for the last month or two before her delivery.[23] Blanche's mother Isabella Beaumont, duchess of Lancaster, probably died while she was expecting her first child, thus increasing the king's concern for her. This might explain why Edward wished his wife, a woman with strong maternal feelings, to look after her. The king's letter is yet more evidence of the affection the royal family felt for each other.

John of Gaunt was out of England from late October 1359 until 10 May 1360, so missed the last few months of his wife's first pregnancy and his daughter's birth. Edward III had extended a truce with France until 14 June 1359, then demanded greater territorial concessions from his foes, which the French, not surprisingly, rejected. The king therefore set off on yet another military campaign in France in October 1359, accompanied by his sons Edward, Lionel, John and Edmund, and John of Gaunt's father-in-law Henry of Grosmont. Queen Philippa remained in England with Blanche of Lancaster and the rest of her family, and Thomas of Woodstock, still only four, was appointed as nominal keeper of the realm in his father's absence.[24] It is not clear where Philippa spent the festive season of 1359, but almost certainly Blanche was with her, and in the New Year of 1360 the queen must have received the sad news that her fifteen-year-old niece, Beatrix of Bavaria, Empress Margaretha's youngest daughter, and Beatrix's twenty-year-old husband Erik Magnusson, king of Sweden, had both died on Christmas Day. Although foul play was suspected, it seems more likely that the young couple died of natural causes, perhaps the plague. To compound the tragedy, Queen Beatrix had only recently given birth to a stillborn son.

Blanche of Lancaster, countess of Richmond, gave birth to her daughter, the future queen-consort of Portugal, on 31 March 1360, and the girl was, inevitably, named Philippa after her paternal grandmother. Most probably Queen Philippa attended the baptism of her granddaughter soon after her birth. Perhaps she was also her godmother, as was the case with her second son Lionel's daughter

Philippa in 1355, but Philippa of Lancaster was not her parents' heir as she had a younger brother, Henry, and such details were therefore not recorded. John of Gaunt had just turned twenty when his daughter was born, and Blanche of Lancaster had probably just turned eighteen. Little Philippa of Lancaster would be the only grandchild Henry of Grosmont, duke of Lancaster, would see; he died just under a year later.

Serious Debt

Queen Philippa was, as usual, in dire financial straits at the end of the 1350s, and pawned one of her crowns to the enormously wealthy earl of Arundel for £300.[1] On 26 June 1359, her husband granted her for life, 'beyond the lands already assigned to her in dower which are insufficient for the necessary expenses of her household and chamber,' another £2,000 annually in land.[2] Although Philippa now had one of the highest incomes in the country, the extra £2,000 (the equivalent of several million pounds today) still proved inadequate for her spending.

In May 1360 a few days after his return from his latest journey to France, Edward III took the decision to merge his and Philippa's households, presumably in an attempt to curtail the queen's endlessly spiralling costs. By 26 May 1360, she would seem to have accumulated debts of more than £5,850, or at least this was the sum she was to receive from the exchequer to pay to her creditors, mostly jewellers, embroiderers, tailors, furriers and goldsmiths. She appears to have spent something in the region of £2,000 annually on her own clothes, a huge amount even in an age when royalty did spend profligate sums on clothes and jewels, and an amount she continued to spend even after the merger of her household with her husband's and his attempts to rein in her debts. An ordinance of the royal council in February 1363 stated:

For six years from Michaelmas [29 September] last all the issues of the lands which Queen Philippa holds in dower, except £10 a day to be delivered to the treasurer of the household of the king and queen for the expenses of that household, and except 4,000 marks a year which shall be delivered to the queen for the expenses of her chamber, shall be reserved for payment of ancient debts still outstanding for expenses of the household of his said consort [Philippa] before the king took upon himself the charge of the expenses of the household of himself and his consort.[3]

Philippa's debts were so enormous that from September 1362 until 1368, therefore, all her annual income from her dower lands, saving 4,000 marks (£2,666) for her personal expenses and £10 a day for the expenses of her household, had to be given over to settling all the debts she had accumulated before 1360.

On 23 August 1360, Philippa was at her manor of Havering-atte-Bower in Essex, and the king was almost certainly there with her; he had been at the manor from 5 to 12 August.[4] Philippa was still at Havering on 8 October when she asked the chancellor, William de Edington, to appoint a new coroner of Norfolk.[5] Edward III sailed to Calais the following day with his and Philippa's sons including twenty-year-old John of Gaunt, proud father since March 1360 of the little Philippa of Lancaster. The king returned to his kingdom at the beginning of November 1360 after only a short sojourn abroad, having ratified the Treaty of Brétigny near Chartres a few days previously. This, at least in retrospect, marked the end of the first phase of the Hundred Years War, and gave Edward III control over much of the territory of the kingdom of France as well as setting the ransom of King John III as three million écus. Meanwhile in Germany, Philippa's nephew Gerhard of Jülich, count of Berg and Ravensberg, her sister Johanna's eldest child, was killed jousting in Düsseldorf on 18 May 1360. He would have succeeded his father Wilhelm as count of Jülich, but Wilhelm outlived his son by nine months, and his successor was his and Johanna of Hainault's second son, also Wilhelm. Gerhard of Jülich's sister Elisabeth, dowager countess of Kent, married her second husband Eustace d'Aubrichecourt four months after her brother's death.

A record of Edward III and Queen Philippa's Christmas clothes of 1360 still exists, and reveals that they were made of a fabric called *marbryn*, apparently meaning 'marble-like' and implying a cloth with two or more different colours weaved together. Edward III had a tunic, two supertunics (or over-tunics), a long cloak and two hoods, and twenty-six skins of ermine fur. Philippa's own clothes were lined with miniver and she had 106 ermine skins as well. The king's sister Joan of the Tower, queen of Scotland, estranged from her husband David II and living in England, received the same cloth for her Christmas garments as Philippa, but fewer furs. Thirty-year-old Edward of Woodstock received five ells more cloth and a little more ermine than his father, which might imply that he was a little taller than Edward III (who stood five feet ten and a half inches; Edward of Woodstock's height is not known, but an investigation in the late eighteenth century revealed that his son Richard II was six feet). The three surviving royal daughters Isabella of Woodstock, Mary of Waltham and Margaret of Windsor were with their parents at Christmas, and so were their sisters-in-law Elizabeth de Burgh and Blanche of Lancaster, and Mary's soon-to-be husband, John de Montfort of Brittany.[6]

Just after Christmas 1360, Sir Thomas Holland died, in his mid-forties, and was buried at Stamford in Lincolnshire. He was the husband of Edward III's first cousin Joan of Kent, with whom he had four children, and was one of the great knights of the era, a dashing and courageous soldier who had lost an eye most probably while taking part in one of Edward III's military campaigns in France. His death proved significant for the royal family, as it brought Holland's royal widow Joan, countess of Kent and Lady Wake in her own right, back onto the marriage market. Joan was still only in her early thirties, and as a well-off and demonstrably fertile royal cousin and heiress, was in great demand as a bride. At some point over the next few months, Joan's cousin Edward of Woodstock asked her to marry him, and she accepted.

That she retained strong feelings for Thomas Holland, however, is revealed by her wish twenty-five years later to be buried with him at Stamford in Lincolnshire, in preference to being interred with her royal husband who was the father of her youngest son the king of England, Richard II. Edward III also lost two of his first cousins in 1360: William de Bohun, earl of Northampton, on 16 September, and Elizabeth de Burgh, lady of Clare in Suffolk, on 4 November. Like the king, they were both grandchildren of Edward I.[7]

Elizabeth's namesake granddaughter and her husband Lionel of Antwerp finally took possession of all the lands they inherited from her.

On 23 March 1361 came a great loss for the English royal family. Henry of Grosmont, duke of Lancaster, father-in-law of Queen Philippa's son John of Gaunt, died in his town of Leicester at the age of barely fifty. Henry was the king's kinsman and one of his most loyal supporters for decades, and was a brave soldier and excellent military commander. Chronicler Jean le Bel called him 'exceedingly valiant' and 'the worthiest knight in the world'. The French author of the *Chronique des quatre premiers Valois* called him 'one of the best warriors in the world'.[8] A thoughtful and intelligent man as well, in 1354 Henry completed a long and remarkable text in French called *The Book of Holy Medicines*, in which he discussed the seven deadly sins and the wounds they inflicted on body and soul at length.

Henry revealed a lot of himself in the process: his love of fine clothes, dancing, eating salmon, the smell of flowers, gossiping, and being intimate with 'lowborn women', though he admitted that noblewomen smelled better.[9] Queen Philippa, Edward III, all their sons and their eldest daughter Isabella of Woodstock – and most probably their younger daughters Mary of Waltham and Margaret of Windsor – attended his funeral at the Newarke in Leicester in April (the Newarke was a hospital founded by Duke Henry's father in 1330, which the duke had considerably extended). In his will, Henry had requested burial three weeks after death, and was indeed interred twenty-two days after he died.

The duke of Lancaster's two daughters, Maud, duchess of Lower Bavaria and Queen Philippa's niece-in-law, not quite twenty-one years old, and Philippa's daughter-in-law Blanche, who turned nineteen two days after her father died, were his heirs to his vast lands. Maud was given Duke Henry's lands in the south of England, and Blanche those in the north, which made good sense as John of Gaunt was earl of Richmond and already owned lands in the north of England. Maud of Lancaster returned to England for the first time, as far as is known, since her marriage in 1352 in order to perform homage to Edward III for her lands; her husband Wilhelm would normally have done so, but the unfortunate man was still incarcerated. John of Gaunt performed homage to his father for his and Blanche's half of the inheritance, which included the duchy of Lancaster as well as the earldoms of Leicester, Derby and Lincoln.

Possibly in March 1361 – though the date is not recorded, and it might have taken place around 3 July that year – John de Montfort the younger, claimant to the duchy of Brittany, married Edward III and Queen Philippa's fourth daughter, Mary of Waltham. John was born in November or December 1339, so was some years older than Mary, born in October 1344 and sixteen at the time of her wedding. Mary of Waltham's husband would successfully assert his rights over Brittany and become its duke, but only after Mary's death, so she never became duchess of Brittany. Her marriage would prove to be a tragically short one. Mary died only months after her wedding, and to compound Queen Philippa and Edward III's grief, their youngest daughter Margaret of Windsor, married to young John Hastings of Pembroke, died as well. The girls were only teenagers, and their deaths must have caused their parents intense shock and grief. They had survived childhood, the most dangerous phase of life in the fourteenth century, only to die in adolescence and early adulthood. Neither young woman left any children.

And as well as losing two of her children and her husband's beloved kinsman Henry of Grosmont in 1361, Philippa lost three other close members of her family. Her youngest sister Isabella, lady of Renaix and Beaufort-sur-Meuse, passed away, leaving the queen of England and her elder sister Johanna, duchess of Jülich and countess of Cambridge, as the only surviving Hainault siblings. Isabella of Hainault had no children and her widower Robert of Namur had none with his second wife either, though had several illegitimate children (Robert did not remarry until 1380, nineteen years after Isabella of Hainault's death). Isabella was buried at the abbey of Fontenelle near Valenciennes, where her mother Countess Jeanne had been interred nine years before. Philippa and Isabella's niece Anna of Bavaria, second daughter of Empress Margaretha and a nun of Fontenelle, soon followed her aunt to the grave and was also buried at the abbey. And Duchess Johanna was widowed when Wilhelm, duke of Jülich and earl of Cambridge, one of Edward III's most faithful allies for decades, also died in 1361 in his early sixties.

Mary of Waltham's widower John of Brittany, who became Duke John IV of Brittany in 1364, married his second wife in May 1366: she was Joan Holland, daughter of Edward III's first cousin Joan of Kent and her husband Sir Thomas Holland, and the stepdaughter of Queen Philippa's eldest son Edward of Woodstock. The couple had no children, and all of Duke John's children came from his third marriage to Juana of Navarre, daughter of Carlos II the Bad and a future queen of England (after the duke's death she married Queen Philippa's grandson Henry IV, John of Gaunt and Blanche of Lancaster's son, in 1403). Margaret of Windsor's young widower John Hastings, heir to the earldom of Pembroke, was still only fourteen when Margaret passed away so it seems unlikely that their marriage had ever been consummated. Some years later John married his second wife, Walter Manny and the countess of Norfolk's only child, Anne, born in 1354 just days before the king had the countess temporarily imprisoned for marrying Walter without his permission.

Of Queen Philippa's five daughters, only Isabella of Woodstock, the eldest, was still alive. Joan of Woodstock died at age fourteen on her way to her wedding in Spain, Blanche of the Tower died not long after her birth, and now both Mary of Waltham and Margaret of Windsor were dead in their teens as well. The early 1360s saw another mass outbreak of the Black Death across Europe, and many fell victim; perhaps the king and queen's daughters, and the queen's sister Isabella and niece Anna, were among them.

A much happier event occurred on 10 October 1361, when, at his father's birthplace of Windsor, Edward of Woodstock, one of the most eligible bachelors in Europe, married at last, at the age of thirty-one. His bride was his cousin Joan of Kent, who was some years his senior: she was born either in September 1326 or September 1327. They were first cousins once removed – Edward of Woodstock was a great-grandson of Edward I (d. 1307) by his first marriage and Joan was Edward I's granddaughter by his second – which meant that they needed a papal dispensation for consanguinity. In addition, Edward was the godson of Joan's two Holland sons, Thomas and John, which created a spiritual affinity between them that also required a papal dispensation. The dispensation was formulated incorrectly and had to be reissued a year later, and there is evidence that their son King Richard II fretted about the legality of their union, as in the 1390s he owned a box of documents relating to their marriage and to the dissolution of his mother's bigamous marriage to William Montacute (b. 1328), earl of Salisbury.[10] Edward of Woodstock and Joan of Kent must have known each other for most of their lives; in the late 1340s he affectionately referred to her as Lady Jeannette.[11]

One chronicler stated that the marriage of the Prince of Wales 'greatly surprised many people', as well it might.[12] Presumably Edward and Joan's marriage was a love-match, though Edward could hardly have guessed that Thomas Holland would die at the age of only about forty-five in late 1360 and leave Joan free to marry him. One wonders if he would have waited many more years for her had Holland not died, or whether he would eventually have given up and married another woman. Although she brought Edward lands in England – the earldom of Kent she inherited from her brother John of Kent (d. 1352) and their father Edmund, and the important lordship of Wake she inherited from her maternal uncle Thomas Wake (d. 1349) – Joan brought him no powerful in-laws or political influence, nor did their marriage bring any diplomatic advantages regarding English foreign policy. Edward and Joan were, however, seemingly a devoted couple: in 1367 Edward addressed a letter to his wife as his 'very dear and very loyal heart, beloved consort' (*trescher et tresentier coer, bien ame compaigne*).[13] Even so, in 1385 Joan chose to be buried with Thomas Holland, the father of her oldest four children, rather than with her royal husband, which perhaps indicates that she had been happier in her previous marriage. After her wedding to Edward of Woodstock in 1361, she often appears in English government record as 'the king's daughter Joan, princess of Wales'.[14] Philippa must have known Joan of Kent for almost all the younger woman's life: Joan was only a baby when Philippa arrived in England at the end of 1327, and two or three years old when her father Edmund of Woodstock was beheaded after attempting to free his half-brother Edward II from captivity. She may, according to chronicler Jean Froissart, have have grown up at least part of the time in Philippa's household, though direct evidence of this claim is rather difficult to find.

Although Edward III and Queen Philippa surely wished their eldest son to be happy, and had not forced the heir to the throne into a marriage that would have benefited England, they were perhaps not entirely thrilled about his choice of bride. Still, they accepted it with good grace, and there is no evidence whatsoever of a rift between Edward and his parents or of any conflict between the royal couple and their new daughter-in-law, or even of any anger on Edward III's part. The happiness of their children seems to have been paramount to both king and queen, and they were especially indulgent towards their two eldest children Edward and Isabella. They both attended Edward of Woodstock and Joan of Kent's wedding, and so did most or all of their other surviving children and their children's spouses.

It is remarkable how close Edward III and Philippa of Hainault were to all their children and their husbands and wives, even well into their offspring's adult lives. The queen had a warm, loving, kind personality and strong maternal instincts, and her many children, sons- and daughters-in-law, godchildren and grandchildren benefited greatly.

John of Gaunt's sister-in-law, Maud of Lancaster, duchess of Lower Bavaria and countess of Hainault and Holland, died on 9 or 10 April 1362, a year after her father Henry of Grosmont, at the age of only twenty-two. Although born into endless wealth and privilege as the elder daughter and co-heir of the partly royal and immensely rich duke of Lancaster, Maud's life was a short and sad one. Her sudden death left her younger sister Blanche – and Blanche's husband John of Gaunt – as the sole heir to the Lancastrian fortune. Although her son and daughter-in-law benefited enormously by Maud's death, Philippa must have mourned for the young woman who had married her nephew and whose life had been so sadly cut short. The cause of Maud's death is not known; perhaps it was plague, or perhaps a sudden illness or infection.

'Blanche, queen of France' was in England in the spring of 1362; this presumably means the late Philip VI's decades-younger second wife Blanche of Navarre, born in 1330, sister of Carlos II 'the Bad', king of Navarre. (The widowed Philip and Blanche wed in January 1350 and had been married for only seven months when

233

Philip died.) Felipe of Navarre, another of the dowager queen of France's brothers, came to England with her. Queen Philippa was at Windsor Castle on 23 April that year for the annual St George and Order of the Garter celebrations, and probably Blanche of Navarre was there with her as well.

Apparently there was another drought in England in 1362, with 'great bareness of corn and fruit', and around late May a strange rain 'almost like blood' fell. It was, a contemporary believed, a year of great wonders and signs: there was an eclipse of the sun, a cross which also looked like it was made out of blood was seen in the sky from dawn until dusk in northern France that summer, and numerous people in England, France and other countries supposedly witnessed a peculiar apparition. Two castles appeared out of thin air, and great armies rode out of each, one dressed all in white and the other in black, and engaged each other in battle. After the army dressed in black overcame the army in white, they all vanished and were never seen again. The 'great and huge pestilence' which swept Europe at this time, another terrible outbreak of the Black Death following the first catastrophic pandemic of 1348/50, supposedly affected men disproportionately (though may have killed two of Queen Philippa's daughters, her sister Isabella of Hainault, niece Anna of Bavaria and niece-in-law Maud of Lancaster). The male victims' widows, 'out of governance' now that their husbands were dead, took 'lewd and simple' men as their husbands instead, and 'coupled ... with them that were of low degree and little reputation.'[15]

In the early summer of 1362, Edward III made Edward of Woodstock, prince of Aquitaine, and he went there to rule, accompanied by his wife Joan of Kent, on 9 June 1362. Queen Philippa would not see her eldest son again. Edward of Woodstock's behaviour as prince of Aquitaine seems rather exaggeratedly high and mighty even by the standards of the era: he kept Aquitainian lords waiting for days to see him, and when they were finally allowed to enter his exalted presence, he made them kneel to him for hours. His son Richard II later emulated his behaviour. Edward and Joan of Kent lived in magnificent, extravagant splendour, and not everyone approved: one observer stated that the princess of Wales and Aquitaine wore great furred gowns and low-cut bodices in the style usually worn by the mistresses of freebooters: 'I am disgusted by those women who follow such a bad example, particularly the Princess of Wales.'[16] Even so, not a word of condemnation came from Edward's parents the king and queen.

Queen Philippa's sister-in-law, Joan of the Tower, queen of Scotland, died at the age of forty-one in September 1362. She had been estranged from her husband David II for a considerable time and spent the last few years of her life in England, until August 1358 in the company of her elderly mother Queen Isabella, with whom she was extremely close. Queen Joan was buried at the Greyfriars church in London, where Queen Isabella had been interred four years previously and where Isabella's aunt Queen Marguerite, second wife of Edward III's grandfather Edward I (and the grandmother of Joan of Kent, princess of Wales and Aquitaine), had also been buried in 1318. All of Edward III's siblings were now dead – his two sisters Eleanor of Woodstock and Joan of the Tower, his brother John of Eltham, and his father's illegitimate son Adam, who had died as far back as September 1322 when he was an adolescent – and of them all, only Eleanor of Woodstock left children.

The grieving king marked his sister Joan's exequies every year, paying twenty-four pounds for 'banners and diverse other things' on the second anniversary of Joan's death in September 1364.[17] As for David II, he married his second wife Margaret Drummond in early 1364, had no children with her either, and died in February 1371 to be succeeded by his half-nephew Robert II, the first Scottish king of the House of Stewart. In the 1360s, there were even plans for John of Gaunt to succeed his childless uncle-in-law David II. This had first been put forward as a possibility in 1350/51 when John was only ten, and in November 1363 it was discussed again when David met his brother-in-law Edward III at Westminster.

The idea that the king of England himself would succeed David after the latter's death was mooted, and John of Gaunt was chosen as the best candidate of the five royal sons to succeed his father in turn. He was already duke of Lancaster and earl of Richmond, with vast estates in the north of England, and thus had a vested interest in maintaining peace and cordial relations with Scotland on the other side of the border. In the end, the Scottish parliament rejected the idea and upheld the rights of David II's Stewart relative, and Scotland would be ruled by the Stewart (later Stuart) dynasty for centuries.

To mark his fiftieth birthday on 13 November 1362, the king raised his and Philippa's middle three sons to peerages. Lionel of Antwerp was made the first duke of Clarence. John of Gaunt became the second duke of Lancaster, the title previously held by his father-in-law Henry of Grosmont. Edmund of Langley became earl of Cambridge, a title formerly held by his uncle, Queen Philippa's brother-in-law Wilhelm, duke of Jülich, who had died the year before. The evidence of Lionel of Antwerp's will a few years later reveals that the ceremony which made him a duke, and the ceremony which made his eldest brother prince of Wales in 1343, involved placing circlets made of gold on their heads.[18]

The King's Mistress

Queen Philippa, not yet fifty years old, began to suffer very badly with her health in the early 1360s. The nature of her illness is not entirely clear, but she was obviously often in great pain and immobile. Perhaps, like her father, she suffered from gout, or edema (dropsy), or perhaps the injuries she sustained when she fell from her horse in 1358 when, according to one chronicler, she broke her shoulder-blade, never healed properly. By 1365 and probably earlier, she was only able to travel by barge and litter.[1] The suffering Philippa endured as a result of her physical condition is made apparent by numerous grants she made in the 1360s, which include the phrases 'if the queen predecease' the grantor or 'if he survive the queen'. The first of such grants with this phrasing dates to November 1361, when Philippa gave a manor in Wiltshire to John Woderowe for a term of ten years, and added 'if the queen die within the said term, the said John shall retain the manor until the end of the ten years.' This gives some indication when Philippa first became seriously ill, and such phrasing became more common in and after 1363, perhaps indicating that her condition worsened.[2]

Evidently, Philippa believed that there was a strong possibility that she might die imminently, and wanted to ensure that the grants of land, income, appointments and favours she made would not be rendered void by her death. She was at Rockingham Castle in Northamptonshire on 16 August 1363, when one such grant, giving Robert atte Hethe the custody of her park of Odiham in Hampshire, was made.[3] Philippa also seems to have made preparations for her tomb even earlier, in 1362. On 15 July that year, there is a reference on the Patent Roll to 'six carts which Queen Philippa by her yeoman Stephen de Hadleye caused to be laden at Tutbury [in Staffordshire] with stones of alabaster, which Stephen brought to London'.[4] In fact she lived on for a few more years than she perhaps expected, though whether she had much quality of life throughout the 1360s is uncertain.

Sometime probably in the early 1360s, a woman entered the life of Philippa's husband, and for the rest of Philippa's life and long afterwards would be an important presence.[5] This was Alice Perrers, Edward III's mistress, who at least after Philippa's death in 1369 became notorious because of the endless favours, appointments and money the king piled on her and because she used her position to enrich herself and flaunted herself in public as the king's lover. The frequently vitriolic chronicler Thomas Walsingham of St Albans wrote in the late fourteenth century that Alice was 'a shameless impudent harlot, of low birth... She was not attractive or beautiful but knew how to compensate for these defects with the seductiveness of her voice.'[6] This seems unnecessarily malicious (and is all too typical of Walsingham's sneering, sardonic attitude), and certainly Edward III found Alice extremely attractive and desirable.

Little can be said about Edward and Alice's relationship early on or how and when it began in the first place, but Alice bore the king a son in or before 1364, and they had two daughters together as well. The son was called John de Southeray or Surrey, and the daughters were, not very creatively, named Jane and Joane. In her will of 15 August 1400 (written at Upminster under the name 'Lady Wyndsore', as she was then the widow of Sir William Windsor), Alice named Joane as the younger of her two daughters, and appointed her as one of the two executors of the will. Her son John de Southeray was married in early 1377, when he was probably about twelve or a little more, to Mary Percy (b. 1368), daughter of Lord Percy, granddaughter and heir of Lord Oreby and much younger half-sister of the first earl of Northumberland, and John was knighted by his father in April that year a few months after his wedding. Unfortunately for John, Mary Percy rejected him as 'plebeian' after Edward III's death, and, with the aid and support of her powerful Percy relatives, their marriage was annulled.[7]

It seems doubtful that Edward III had been entirely faithful to Queen Philippa for the previous thirty-five or so years of their married life – she would not have expected him to be – but there were no long-term mistresses and no illegitimate children whose existence has ever been discovered. Queen Philippa had grown up with at least eight illegitimate half-siblings from her father's extra-marital relationships, and must have known that her father himself also had at least five illegitimate half-siblings born to her grandfather Jan's mistresses, and that her younger brother Willem (*c.* 1317-45) also had two illegitimate children. Her own son Edward of Woodstock fathered an illegitimate son called Edward, and later another called Roger of Clarendon as well (Roger's date of birth is not known, but it is virtually certain that he was born in Queen Philippa's lifetime). Philippa's third son John of Gaunt is also commonly supposed to have fathered an illegitimate daughter called Blanche, whose mother was one of the queen's own attendants, Marie de St Hilaire from Philippa's native Hainault. The queen would therefore have found it entirely normal for royal and noble men to have mistresses and relationships with them that resulted in children, and would not have expected men to be held to the same standards of fidelity and monogamy as their wives.

Although we cannot know her innermost feelings on the matter, Philippa is unlikely to have been overly hurt by any affairs her husband may have had. Whomever he might have slept with, she was his adored wife, his precious queen, his companion, the mother of his heir and his other royal children. No other woman could touch Philippa's position, or oust her from the place she held in the king's heart, and she knew it. Thomas Walsingham claimed that 'while the queen was still alive, the king loved this woman [Alice Perrers] more than he loved the queen,' but this seems unlikely; although Edward III was doubtless hugely attracted to and aroused by Alice, he probably did not 'love' her more than he loved his wife.[8] It is possible, perhaps even likely, that the queen's deteriorating physical condition in the 1360s made it almost impossible for her to engage in intimate relations with her husband, and although we can never know for sure, it may be that Edward III undertook his relationship with Alice with his queen's knowledge and even with her blessing. In August 1373, four years after the queen's death, Edward gave a selection of jewels which has once belonged to his queen to his mistress. Of course Edward was not unfeeling enough to give away his wife's treasured belongings in Philippa's own lifetime, and as Ian Mortimer points out, Philippa herself had previously given the items to Euphemia, wife of Walter Hasleworth, and they were not in her possession at the time of her death.

Alice Perrers worked as one of Queen Philippa's damsels, or female attendants (the word means either an unmarried woman or a woman married to a man who was a knight, and has nothing to do with the woman's age). This, presumably, was how she came to Edward III's attention, though by 1366 the king may tactfully have removed her from Philippa's retinue. She does, however, appear on the list of Philippa's damsels for whom black cloth was purchased when they attended the queen's funeral in early 1370, as Aliccon (or Aliceon) Perrers. The date of Alice's appointment to the queen's household is uncertain but had occurred by 1359 at the latest. She was the wife or widow of one Janyn Perrers ('Janyn' or 'Janin' was a pet form of the extremely common name John).[9] Later, she married her second husband, William Windsor, and was widowed from him by the time she wrote her will in 1400.

John of Gaunt and Blanche of Lancaster's second child, the king and queen's latest grandchild, was born in February 1363, and, rather unusually, was named Elizabeth. This was not a name borne by any of John's sisters, and it may be that little Elizabeth of Lancaster's godmother was her aunt-in-law Elizabeth de Burgh, the new duchess of Clarence, and that she was named after her. It is also possible, though, that John and Blanche named their daughter after Elizabeth, Lady Audley, née Beaumont, one of Blanche's numerous aunts (her late father Henry of Grosmont had six sisters and her late mother Isabella Beaumont had at least three, perhaps five). Blanche of Lancaster spent much of her marriage to John of Gaunt pregnant; although only three of her children, Philippa, Elizabeth and Henry, outlived her, she gave birth to another two and perhaps even three sons and perhaps to another daughter as well, who did not survive.

Elizabeth de Burgh herself, duchess of Clarence and countess of Ulster, daughter-in-law of the king and queen, died in December 1363 when she was only thirty-one years old. She died in Dublin, and her body was brought back to England and buried at Bruisyard Abbey in Suffolk, at Edward III's expense.[10] Lionel of Antwerp was left a widower with an eight-year-old daughter, and had only just turned twenty-five. He himself founded Bruisyard Abbey for the benefit of his mother-in-law Maud of Lancaster, dowager countess of Ulster, who had become a canoness at nearby Campsea Ashe in 1347 or 1348. Maud, one of the six sisters of the late Henry of Grosmont and thus one of Blanche of Lancaster's numerous aunts, outlived her daughter by many years and died in 1377. Her younger daughter Maud de Vere née Ufford, countess of Oxford, would be buried at Bruisyard with her half-sister Elizabeth de Burgh when she died in 1413, and Lionel of Antwerp's remains would be taken there after he died in Italy in 1368.

Judging by various entries on the Patent Roll when she interceded with him on behalf of others, Philippa spent much or most of the year 1363 in her husband's company. On 15 January 1363 and supposedly for a whole week afterwards, it would seem that there was a hurricane in England and perhaps even an earthquake as well; a ferociously strong wind destroyed houses, churches and all manner of other buildings, and those buildings that withstood the wind were shaken badly and weakened. As though this were not bad enough, heavy rains and bad floods followed later in the year as well, and in Edward III's thirty-ninth regnal year, January 1365 to January 1366, there was a 'strong and huge frost' that lasted until the middle of March and made it impossible for anyone to till the hard, frozen ground.

At the parliament of October 1363, Edward III passed a series of regulations relating to clothes which people of different ranks were allowed to wear, the sumptuary laws. 'Various people of various conditions wear various apparel not appropriate to their estate,' it was announced, and a long set of regulations followed, including that the wives and daughters of servants must not wear veils which cost more than twelve pence, craftsmen must not wear clothes which cost in excess of forty shillings in total, and that the wives and children of squires or gentlemen below the rank of knight must not wear 'adornments, crimpings or knick-knacks, or any manner of apparel of gold, silver or precious stones'.[11]

The Christmas of 1363 was spent at Windsor, and Philippa was at the palace of Eltham in Kent on 12 January 1364.[12] Her cousin King John II of France died at her son John of Gaunt's palace of the Savoy in London on 9 April 1364, and his body was returned to his homeland and interred at the basilica of St-Denis in Paris, burial site of most French kings for many centuries. Edward III appointed an English knight called Sir Nicholas Damory, steward of his and Philippa's eldest daughter Isabella of Woodstock's household, to lead John's funeral cortege from London to Dover. Edward spent a rather less than munificent six shillings and eight pence in oblations on 19 April during a Mass said for John at St Paul's Cathedral, though the celebrations themselves were magnificent, with John's body carried into the cathedral accompanied by a hundred torch-bearers. Edward, Philippa and their children attended. The eldest of John II's four sons from his marriage to his late first wife Bonne of Bohemia, Charles V, now twenty-six years old, succeeded him as king.

Rather astonishingly, there were no fewer than five kings in England in 1364, counting Edward III and John II. The other three visitors were Edward's brother-in-law David II of Scotland, Pierre de Lusignan, king of Cyprus, and Valdemar IV, king of Denmark.[13]

Edward III bought two robes for Philippa in 1364, embroidered with Philippa's own mottoes, in English: *Ich wyndemuth* ('I twine myself', i.e. around her husband) and *Myn biddeneye* ('my bidding'). *Ich wyndemuth* was embroidered with coloured silk and pearls onto black cloth.[14] Another motto claimed to be hers, *ich wrude muche*, might be a misunderstanding of *ich wyndemuth*. *Ich wrude muche* appears to mean 'I work hard' or 'I wrought much', presumably in medieval Dutch or Flemish. Philippa was at Windsor Castle, Edward III's birthplace, on 1 December 1364, and her husband was almost certainly also there with her: he was at the palace of Sheen a few miles away on the 3rd and at Windsor from 18 to 30 December.[15] In the 1360s, it is unfortunately rather difficult to say very much about Queen Philippa and what she was doing. The records are certainly not silent, but they are not particularly illuminating. The queen's physical condition did not make it impossible for her to travel, and to some extent her itinerary can still be constructed, but it seems likely that she spent a great deal of her time bedridden and in pain. The queen probably turned fifty around February 1364.

Philippa's daughter-in-law Joan of Kent, princess of Wales and Aquitaine, gave birth to her first son in the town of Angoulême on 27 January 1365, and inevitably (and rather confusingly) called him Edward after his father and grandfather. Joan wrote to the mayor and aldermen of London sharing the good news of her son's birth on 4 February.[16] Pierre de Lusignan, king of Cyprus, who was travelling around Europe promoting a crusade and had been in England a few months before, attended the celebrations in Aquitaine held for the boy's birth.[17] Little Edward of Angoulême immediately became heir to the English throne after his father, and in England, the birth of the next heir to the throne was celebrated with ten days of feasts and jousting tournaments supposedly attended by a thousand lords and knights.

Queen Philippa was surely also present, and must have been delighted that her eldest son, now getting on for thirty-five years old, finally had a legitimate son to succeed him and her husband. Edward III rewarded John Delves, the messenger who had brought him 'the pleasing news' of Edward of Angoulême's birth, with a very generous income of forty pounds a year.[18] Edward of Woodstock held the greatest jousting tournament of his period of rule over Aquitaine in Angoulême in late April 1365 to celebrate the birth, and in May sent his father a gift of a lion and a leopard, which presumably were intended to join the menagerie in the Tower of London.[19] Although Philippa could not have known it, little Edward of Angoulême would never succeed as king, as he died in late 1370 or early 1371 at the age of five or six, leaving his younger brother Richard of Bordeaux as the heir of her husband and their eldest son.

On 27 July 1365, Queen Philippa's only living daughter Isabella of Woodstock married at last, the month after her thirty-third birthday; her husband was Enguerrand (also sometimes called Ingram or Ingelram) de Coucy, a French lord in the retinue of the captive John II in England until John's death the year before. Coucy was about eight or perhaps even ten years Isabella's junior, and evidently a rather dashing and handsome young nobleman. The king and queen spent extraordinarily large sums on Isabella and Enguerrand's wedding: at least £4,500 was paid out to goldsmiths for jewels and brooches given to Isabella. Edward III also spent a hundred pounds on the many minstrels who entertained the guests.[20] Two children were born rather quickly to Isabella of Woodstock: Marie, later countess of Soissons, born in France in April 1366 about nine months after her parents' wedding, and Philippa, born at the royal palace of Eltham in Kent in 1367 or 1368, named after her maternal grandmother the queen, who was probably also her godmother.

Philippa de Coucy later became countess of Oxford and duchess of Ireland as the wife of Richard II's notorious favourite, Robert de Vere (b. 1362).[21] On 26 November 1365, Edward III granted a licence 'for Ingram, lord of Coucy, and the king's daughter Isabel, his wife, to visit their lands and possessions in France; and grant that all children begotten between them, wherever born, shall enjoy their inheritance in England as if born in the realm'.[22] Edward III made Coucy the first earl of Bedford in May 1366.

In the summer of 1366, the king was ill, and his physician bought medicines from an apothecary to treat him. Curiously and rather intriguingly, Edward and Philippa received a visit this summer from 'the son of the king of India'. The identities of this king and his son are not clear.[23] By 12 September 1366, Geoffrey Chaucer's wife Philippa had joined the queen's household as one of her damsels, and Edward III promised her an annuity of ten marks (six pounds and sixty-six pence) from the Exchequer. Queen Philippa's son John of Gaunt granted Geoffrey an annuity of ten pounds for life on 13 June 1374, five years after the queen's death, because of Geoffrey's excellent service to him personally and because of his wife Philippa Chaucer's excellent service to 'our very honoured lady and mother, whom God pardon'.[24] Philippa

Chaucer and her sister Katherine, wife of the Lincolnshire knight Sir Hugh Swynford, were of Hainaulter origin, and Philippa must have been named after the queen.

In December 1366, Edward III hired a man called Edward Palmer to instruct his and Philippa's then almost twelve-year-old son Thomas of Woodstock 'in the science of grammar'. A few weeks later Edward and Philippa received a gift of thirty wild boar from Charles V of France.[25]

Philippa's daughter-in-law Joan of Kent, princess of Wales and Aquitaine, gave birth to her and Edward of Woodstock's second son on 6 January 1367, the feast of the Epiphany, in the city of Bordeaux. He was given the unusual name of Richard, which had not been used in the royal family since the death of Henry III's brother Richard, earl of Cornwall (b. 1209) in 1272. Richard of Bordeaux's three godfathers were, remarkably, all kings: certainly Jaime IV, titular king of Majorca though he never in fact gained control of his own kingdom, most probably Pedro 'the Cruel' of Castile, and Carlos II 'the Bad' of Navarre. It is possible, though, that Gosdantin or Constantine of Armenia may have been one of Richard's godfathers, and as he was called Richard in western European sources, he may have been the inspiration for the little boy's name. Richard of Bordeaux became heir to the English throne behind his father when his elder brother died.

The queen was probably seriously ill in January 1367, the month of her grandson Richard of Bordeaux's birth, when her husband paid two hundred marks to a craftsman for making her tomb within Westminster Abbey.[26] Although it was not altogether uncommon for tombs to be commissioned well before someone's death, in combination with the queen's ill health throughout much of the 1360s, it seems likely that Philippa was thought to be close to dying. If so, she rallied.

On 20 August 1367, mention is made of Queen Philippa's 'bastard sister' Elisabeth of Holland, who was given an annuity of twenty pounds from the Exchequer at the queen's request.[27] Elisabeth seems to have become a nun of Stratford-le-Bow by 1356, and might have come to England decades earlier. She settled in England, dying there in 1375. Despite the dire state of her health in 1367, Philippa still found the time to remember her half-sister and to request an income for her. One of the queen's letters, dated to 17 September in an uncertain year, was written at Stratford-le-Bow, so she may have been visiting her half-sister then.[28]

On 15 April 1367 just three months after Richard of Bordeaux's birth, another grandson of Queen Philippa's was born at Bolingbroke Castle in Lincolnshire: Henry of Lancaster, only surviving son of John of Gaunt and Blanche of Lancaster, and heir to the great Lancastrian fortune from the moment of his birth. John of Gaunt was in Spain at the time his son was born, and with his brother Edward of Woodstock and Pedro the Cruel won a great victory over Pedro's half-brother and enemy Enrique of Trastamara at the battle of Najera on 3 April 1367. The campaign against Trastamara proved successful, but had a serious long-term consequence: the great Prince of Wales and Aquitaine came down with some serious recurrent illness during the hot Spanish summer of 1367, from which he never recovered. Edward of Woodstock spent much of the remaining nine years of his life as an invalid.

Philippa's widowed second son Lionel of Antwerp left England for Italy in April 1368; Philippa never saw him again either (she had not seen her eldest son since Edward left for the south-west of France in 1362). Lionel travelled with a large retinue including his kinsmen Edward, Lord Despenser (b. 1336) and Despenser's younger brother Hugh, grandsons of Edward II's notorious favourite Hugh Despenser the Younger. They travelled through Paris, where they were greeted and feted by King Charles V and his brothers the dukes of Berry and Burgundy, the queen Jeanne de Bourbon and her brother the duke of Bourbon (the Bourbon siblings were Queen Philippa's much younger first cousins), and Lionel's brother-in-law Enguerrand, lord of Coucy and now earl of Bedford.[29] Duke Lionel married Violante Visconti in Milan on 28 May (or possibly on 5 June) 1368; he was twenty-nine and she was about fourteen, and was the daughter of Galeazzo Visconti, lord of Milan and Pavia. This marriage had been on the cards since July 1366, when Edward III sent his first cousin Humphrey de Bohun, earl of Hereford, and Sir Nicholas Tamworth to 'treat with Galeazzo, lord of Milan, of a marriage between Lionel, duke of Clarence and earl of Ulster, and Violanta, daughter of the said lord'. Lionel's brother Edmund of Langley, born in June 1341 and then twenty-five, was to be offered as a substitute bridegroom. The earl of Hereford was still outside England, presumably negotiating the marriage or on his way back to England from Italy, on 16 January 1367, and three days later Galeazzo Visconti drew up an agreement for the marriage and for his daughter's dowry.[30]

The End

Lionel, duke of Clarence and earl of Ulster, died on 17 October 1368, a few weeks before his thirtieth birthday and less than five months after his magnificent Italian wedding. He was buried in the church of St Peter in the Sky of Gold (*San Pietro in Ciel d'Oro*) in Pavia, though his body was later returned to England and buried at Bruisyard, the Augustinian priory in Clare, Suffolk, which Lionel himself founded some years before. Lionel was laid to rest with his first wife Elizabeth de Burgh, as he had requested. He left his thirteen-year-old daughter Philippa Mortimer, countess of March, as his sole heir, and his widow Violante later married Secondotto, marquis of Montferrat and thirdly her cousin Ludovico Visconti. Pope Urban V and some of Lionel's kinsmen and followers, including Edward, Lord Despenser, came to believe that Lionel had been poisoned. Jean Froissart recorded their suspicions, and pointed out how odd it was that such a young, healthy knight had died so suddenly. It seems far likelier, however, that Lionel died of an illness or infection. He wrote his will two weeks before he passed away, and as people in the fourteenth century tended only to make their wills when they thought they were dying, it seems that he was already seriously ill. In fact, Lionel was apparently already ill in August 1368 two months before his death, when Pope Urban V wrote to Lionel's kinsman Sir Hugh Despenser, asking Despenser to aid the papal chaplain Robert Stratton whom he had sent to Lionel to inquire after the royal duke's health.[1]

In his will, the duke left two coursers (horses) called Maugeneleyn and Gerfaucon to two of his household knights, and three breviaries (books of prayers), two with musical notes, to his chaplains. To a man called Thomas Waleys ('Welshman'), Lionel left 'a circle of gold with which my brother and lord [Edward of Woodstock] was created Prince [of Wales]', and to Edmund Mone 'the circle with which I was created duke'. Lionel also left valuable items – his gold coronets – to his wife Violante in his will and, despite her youth, appointed her as one of his executors. This would seem to argue against the notion that he believed her family had had him killed, as would the fact that he was staying in the house of his father-in-law the lord of Milan in Alba when he made his will.[2] His kinsman Edward, Lord Despenser, however, seems to have seriously believed that Lionel's death was the result of foul play by the Viscontis, and in revenge he and his brother Hugh Despenser joined Pope Urban V's ongoing war against Galeazzo Visconti and the city of Milan.

Queen Philippa had now outlived seven of her twelve children, all but one of her five daughters and three of her seven sons, and of the four sons who remained, Edward of Woodstock was already seriously ill. In late 1368, the only children Philippa had borne who remained alive and in good health were Isabella of Woodstock, John of Gaunt, Edmund of Langley and the adolescent Thomas of Woodstock.[3] Rather sadly, when one of Edward III's clerks made a list in December 1368 of all the members of the royal family and their retinues for whom cloth was to be purchased to make garments for the forthcoming Christmas season, he absently-minded wrote 'the duke of Clarence' after the king and queen and before their third son the duke of Lancaster, and had to cross the name out.

As Lionel had died overseas, his inquisition post mortem was not held until June 1369, and reveals that he owned lands in ten counties in the south of England as well as across Ireland, a lot of them by the 'courtesy of England'. This was a medieval custom whereby a man who married an heiress and outlived her had the right to hold her entire inheritance for the rest of his own life, as long as they had at least one child together who lived long enough to take a breath. Lionel had thus held all the lands of the late Elizabeth de Burgh since her death in late 1363.[4]

The royal family suffered another loss in September 1368 when Blanche of Lancaster, John of Gaunt's wife and the duchess of Lancaster, died aged only twenty-six, and was buried at Westminster Abbey. John outlived her by more than thirty years and was buried next to her in 1399, though he had been married to two other women in the meantime. As he and Blanche had children together, John, like his elder brother Lionel, had the right to keep all his late wife's enormous inheritance in his own hands by the 'courtesy of England', and thus their son and heir Henry did not hold them until after John's death in 1399. Although it was once believed that Blanche died of plague in 1369, the year has been corrected by more recent historians, and she possibly died during a difficult pregnancy or after childbirth (if she did bear a child in 1368, there is no certain record of the infant).[5] Blanche left three surviving children: eight-year-old Philippa, five-year-old Elizabeth, and one-year-old Henry, her heir and the future King Henry IV of England.

Queen Philippa sent an envoy, Sir Richard de Stury, to Louis, count of Flanders, on 1 December 1368, and Stury returned with Louis's reply on Christmas Day. Philippa had proposed a marriage between her recently widowed son John of Gaunt, whom Louis in his letter to Philippa called 'our dearest cousin, the duke of Lancaster, your son' and Louis's only surviving child and heir, Margarethe of Flanders (b. 1350). The demands of politics at the highest levels, and the decades-long wish of both Queen Philippa and Edward III to secure the counties of Flanders, Nevers, Rethel, Artois and Burgundy for one of their children (either Isabella of Woodstock in the 1340s via marriage to Louis himself, or John of Gaunt or Edmund of Langley in the 1360s via marriage to Louis's only child), meant that John would be given little time to grieve for the loss of his wife, though one assumes that the queen did not press ahead with a possible second marriage for her son against his will or without his knowledge. Louis of Flanders replied via Richard de Stury, however, that he had already consented to his daughter's marriage to Philip 'the Bold' (1342-1404), duke of Burgundy, youngest of the four sons of the late John II of France and Charles V's brother, and the couple duly wed in June 1369.[6] Ultimately, John of Gaunt did not remarry for three years after

Blanche's death, and wed the seventeen-year-old Constanza of Castile, King Pedro the Cruel's elder daughter and heir from his relationship with his mistress Maria de Padilla, in September 1371. Probably in 1372, John began his famous long-term relationship with his mistress Katherine Swynford, mother of four of his children, the Beauforts, and much later his third wife.

Although the proposed England-Flanders match in late 1368 failed, it is interesting to note that even near the end of her life, it was Queen Philippa, not Edward III, who sent the envoy Richard de Stury to Louis of Flanders to put forward the suggestion to him; Louis's reply was addressed to his 'dearest lady' (*treschere dame*), not to Philippa and her husband the king jointly. As previously noted, it is frustratingly difficult to ascertain from the extant records how involved the queen was in her husband's government and foreign policy, or even in the marriage negotiations for her children. Louis of Flanders' letter makes it apparent that Philippa did assume responsibility for appointing and sending an envoy to him on this occasion, and she may have done the same thing on numerous other occasions as well, but we have no record of it. Richard de Stury was a knight of the king's chamber, so clearly Edward allowed his wife to issue commands to his own household staff, though there is no record in the chancery rolls of the queen's appointment of him to negotiate a marriage for her son in 1368. We are fortunate to have Louis of Flanders' letter to Philippa in December 1368 and its revelation that, even near the end of her life, she was actively involved in politics.

Given the loss of both Lionel of Antwerp and Blanche of Lancaster in 1368, the Christmas festivities were perhaps rather muted in the royal family that year, though they did purchase new robes for the season so perhaps tried to make the best of it. Although they could not have known it, 1368 was to be the last Christmas of Queen Philippa's life as well, and despite the losses she had suffered and despite her ill-health, she was surely delighted to be surrounded by the remaining members of her family.

The festive season was spent at Windsor (where Philippa seems to have spent most or all of the last year or so of her life), and although Edward of Woodstock was in Aquitaine with his wife Joan of Kent and their two infant sons, the king and queen's other four surviving children were there with them: Isabella of Woodstock, countess of Bedford, aged thirty-six, perhaps with her two young Coucy daughters, though her husband Enguerrand is not mentioned as being present; John of Gaunt, duke of Lancaster, aged twenty-eight; Edmund of Langley, earl of Cambridge, aged twenty-seven and not yet married; and Thomas of Woodstock ('Lord Thomas de Wodestoke'), the baby of the family, not yet fourteen.

John Hastings, earl of Pembroke, widower of Philippa's youngest daughter Margaret of Windsor, was evidently still considered a member of her family – Edward III continued to refer to John as 'the king's son' for the rest of the young earl's life and even after his early death in 1375 – and was also at Windsor that Christmas. Earlier in 1368, John, now twenty-one, had married his second wife Anne Manny, daughter and co-heir of the king's first cousin Margaret, countess of Norfolk and her second husband the Hainaulter knight Walter Manny. Anne was only fourteen in 1368, and their only child, John Hastings the younger, was not born until November 1372. Also present at Windsor were the young earl and countess of March and Ulster, Edward III and Queen Philippa's granddaughter and grandson-in-law, sixteen-year-old Edmund Mortimer and his thirteen-year-old wife Philippa of Clarence, and the earl of Oxford, Thomas de Vere (born *c*. 1336). Oxford's son and heir Robert, who was six years old in 1368, would become the notorious and hated favourite of Queen Philippa's grandson Richard II in the 1380s. Oxford's wife Maud Ufford was the much younger half-sister of the late Elizabeth de Burgh, duchess of Clarence, and may, as a member of the extended royal family, also have been present.

Alice Perrers, who had certainly borne the king a son called John de Southeray well before 1368 and perhaps had already given birth to their two daughters Jane and Joane as well, is not mentioned in the long list of Queen Philippa's attendants this year. One of the queen's damsels was named, rather oddly, as 'Billion Quarret' and one of the knights serving in the household of the king and queen was Sir Gilbert Despenser, now around fifty years old and the only surviving son of the long-dead Hugh Despenser the Younger. Gilbert was the uncle of Edward, Lord Despenser and his younger brother Sir Hugh, warring against the Visconti lords of Milan because they believed the Viscontis had murdered the queen's second son Lionel. The two eldest sons of the earl of Arundel and his second wife Eleanor of Lancaster, Richard (b. 1346/7) and John (b. *c*. 1350) Arundel, appear in the list of royal household knights but without 'Sir' in front of their names like all the others, so had apparently not been knighted yet. Another household knight was Sir William Windsor, the future second husband of Alice Perrers. Geoffrey Chaucer and his wife Philippa, sister of Katherine Swynford who would become John of Gaunt's long-term lover in the early 1370s, are also named in the long list of royal household members. Three heralds appear whose names are recorded as Vaillant, Haveryge and Wyndesores, i.e. 'Windsor,' and the steward of the queen's household is named as Sir Johan Delues. Her *henstman* or *henxman*, meaning an attendant or trusted follower (modern English 'henchman', but without the sinister connotations) was called Rauf or Ralph, and her husband's own *henstman* bore the odd name of Solace or Solas.

Philippa loved having her own family around her, and even at the end of her life she kept in touch with her natal family as well. Before 30 May 1369, Philippa received a visit from Peter, the butler of her nephew Albrecht (b. 1336), duke of Lower Bavaria and count of Hainault and Holland, and before he left England she gave Peter twelve pounds in cash and a gift of a horse. Duke Albrecht, the third son of the late Empress Margaretha, sent a servant of his called John Hake to his aunt in England with 'a ship laden with wines' for her. At the same time, Philippa sent a goldsmith called John Lyndowe to 'the duchess of Holland', which probably means her brother Willem's widow Johanna, duchess of Brabant, giving him a generous ten pounds in cash and a horse for the journey.[7]

The queen's fourth son Edmund of Langley, earl of Cambridge, and her son-in-law John Hastings, earl of Pembroke, left England in January 1369. They travelled to the duchy of Aquitaine with a sizeable army of men, intending to strengthen the forces of Edmund's eldest brother the Prince of Wales and Aquitaine. John of Gaunt also left England in June 1369; Edward III appointed him his captain and lieutenant in France, and John set off for Picardy to forestall a French invasion of the south coast of England.[8] Of all the queen's sons, only Thomas of Woodstock, who turned fourteen in early 1369, remained in England in the summer of that year.

Even in the last weeks of her life, Queen Philippa continued to intercede on behalf of others, and on 22 June 1369 asked her husband to grant a pardon to Alice Marchant of Somerset. Alice had stolen goods to a value of twenty-seven shillings and eight pence from William Deuyas of Maidenhead, and was sentenced to death, but was pregnant. The judgement was therefore delayed until after she had given birth, but the queen successfully begged her husband to let Alice go free. On the same day, Philippa asked for a pardon for Margaret, wife of Henry Melbury, who had broken into the house of Walter Knyght during the night and stolen a pot, a pan, some cloths and thirty-five shillings in cash. Margaret Melbury was also pregnant when she was sentenced to death, and again, Edward III respited the punishment and set Margaret free.

Edward III agreed to give an annuity of a hundred shillings to Philippa's damsel Alice of Preston for the rest of Alice's life, also on 22 June.[9] That all these intercessions occurred on the same day argues that Philippa had perhaps not been well enough or lucid enough to respond to any petitions for several months – these are her first recorded intercessions since 26 November 1368, though she appointed Sir Richard de Stury to travel to Flanders on or just before 1 December as well – and now that she was well enough to do so, made up for lost time. At the end of her life, after years of pain and suffering, Queen Philippa retained her compassion, her kindness and her desire to help those less fortunate than herself. Philippa was lucid again on 13 July 1369 when she appointed one John of Ypres as the forester of Whittlewood, and on 3 August when she made another grant to the keeper of her forest of Kingswood.[10]

On 15 August 1369 (the feast of the Assumption of the Virgin Mary) at Windsor Castle, her husband's birthplace, Philippa of Hainault, queen of England, finally slipped away after a decade of pain and serious illness. She was probably fifty-five years old.

The queen had known much tragedy: she outlived seven of her twelve children including four of her five daughters, and her eldest child Edward of Woodstock had been ill since his Spanish campaign of 1367. Although Edward survived his mother by almost seven years, he spent much of the last nine years of his life as an invalid, and did not outlive his father. Nor had Philippa seen her eldest child for some years when she died. The queen was also outlived by her elder sister Johanna of Hainault, dowager duchess of Jülich and countess of Cambridge, who died in 1374 in her early sixties, and their illegitimate half-sister Elisabeth of Holland, nun of Stratford-le-Bow, who wrote her will in September 1375 and probably died not long afterwards. Possibly, some of Philippa's other illegitimate half-siblings survived her as well. She left her grandchildren Philippa of Clarence, countess of March and Ulster; the three Lancaster children Philippa, Elizabeth and Henry; the little Coucy girls Marie and Philippa; and Edward of Woodstock's sons Edward of Angoulême and Richard of Bordeaux (and his illegitimate son Roger of Clarendon). Queen Philippa never knew her many other grandchildren who would be born after her death, and had she lived for just another eighteen months she would have seen her first great-grandchild Elizabeth Mortimer, born in February 1371 and the eldest child of Philippa of Clarence.

Chronicler Jean Froissart puts a long and rather flowery deathbed speech in Philippa's mouth, making three requests of her husband: that he will pay off all her debts to merchants in England and on the continent, that he will fulfil all her obligations to charities, and that one day he will be laid to rest next to her. A tearful Edward III agrees. A much later story claimed that the queen confessed on her deathbed to the bishop of Winchester, William Wykeham, that her son John of Gaunt was a lowborn child of Ghent. Supposedly, Philippa related to the bishop how she had borne a daughter in Ghent in 1340 but suffocated the little girl by accident, and persuaded a local woman to give up her newborn son to her and promised the woman that she would raise the boy as her own son.[11] There is not, it hardly needs to be said, the slightest reason to give this tale any credence whatsoever, and one wonders whether the long-suffering Queen Philippa was in any state to be making deathbed speeches, let alone tortured confessions that one of her children was not in fact her and Edward's son.

It is possible that Philippa's physicians – such as Master Peter of Florence, who attended her in the 1360s – believed her to be dead on 14 August, the day before she truly did pass away. Unless a royal clerk repeatedly recorded the date incorrectly on the Patent

Roll, on 14 August 1369 Edward III re-confirmed numerous grants and appointments Philippa had previously made to members of her household and retainers, such as reappointing Adam Forester as porter of the queen's houses in La Réole, London, and re-granting an income of two pence a day to William White, one of Philippa's palfreymen. These entries all refer to 'the late queen' and to the 'death of the queen'. She was not, in fact, dead on 14 August.

If Queen Philippa ever made a will (as a married woman she would have required her husband's permission to do so), it has not survived. Her mother-in-law Isabella made hers while heavily pregnant with her eldest child Edward III in October 1312, and perhaps Philippa did the same in 1330 while she was carrying Edward of Woodstock. Queen Isabella's will no longer survives either, though the will of Philippa's third son John of Gaunt, made in early February 1399 on the day he died, is still extant. It reveals that sometime before her death, Philippa left John 'a gold fastening of the old kind, with the name of God written in each part of the same fastening, which my very honoured lady and mother the queen, whom God absolve, gave to me, commanding me to keep it, with her blessing'. John in turn bequeathed it to his eldest son and heir, Henry of Lancaster, duke of Hereford and earl of Derby, who became King Henry IV a few months later. John's surviving register also shows that Philippa gave him a gold cup with foot and cover decorated with oak-trees and letters of the alphabet. Like his father, who broke up and gave away the queen's 1328 wedding gift of a book to him, John of Gaunt was not particularly sentimental about presents, even ones given to him by his late mother: at Christmas 1372, he gave the gold cup to the countess of Salisbury.

No doubt Philippa left items to her other children, and perhaps to her grandchildren and godchildren as well. Her namesake granddaughter and goddaughter Philippa Mortimer (or Philippa of Clarence as she is sometimes also called), countess of March and Ulster, proved that she had come of age – fourteen, as she was already married – five days after the queen's death on 20 August 1369, at her birthplace of Eltham in Kent.[12] The jurors who confirmed Philippa's date of birth recalled how Queen Philippa had raised the infant from the font during her baptism in August 1355.

On 23 August 1369, Philippa's third son John of Gaunt encountered a French army led by Philip, duke of Burgundy, at Tournehem-sur-la-Hem a few miles from Calais. No battle took place, as John held a strong defensive position, and after two weeks Burgundy withdrew. John's younger brother Edmund of Langley was also in France in the summer of 1369 with their brother-in-law the earl of Pembroke, leading a siege of La Roche-sur-Yon south of Nantes, and John and Edmund's eldest brother Edward of Woodstock was in his duchy of Aquitaine. Philippa's only surviving daughter Isabella of Woodstock may also have been in France with her Coucy husband, and it is entirely possible that of all the dozen children the queen had borne, only the youngest, the adolescent Thomas of Woodstock, was in England at the time of her death. He, and his father the king, were with Philippa until the end.

Seventeen days after Philippa's death, on 1 September 1369, Edward III sent a letter in French to his clerk Henry Snayth or Snaith, keeper of the great wardrobe. He ordered vast quantities of black cloth and fur to be purchased to provide mourning clothes for the royal family and for the queen's household. John of Gaunt, duke of Lancaster, was named first in the letter, being the eldest and highest-ranking of the royal sons who would be able to attend Philippa's funeral. He was followed by the king and queen's grandson-in-law Edmund Mortimer, earl of March (called their 'son' as was customary) and another son of theirs, called the 'earl of Oxford'. This is possibly a clerical error for the earl of Cambridge, Philippa's fourth son Edmund of Langley, who is not otherwise mentioned in the letter. Although the earl of Oxford, Thomas de Vere, most probably did attend Philippa's funeral and had been named as one of the queen's retainers at Christmas 1368, he was not a son, son-in-law or grandson-in-law of the king and queen (unless this means that he was Edward III's or Philippa's godson).[13]

The queen's granddaughters were mentioned next: Philippa of Clarence, countess of March and Ulster, who had recently taken possession of her late parents' many lands after proving her age; Philippa and Elizabeth of Lancaster, aged nine and six; and one of Isabella of Woodstock's two Coucy daughters, either Marie or Philippa, who were born in 1366 and 1367 or 1368, so were only tiny children in 1369. The little Coucy girl was to be accompanied by two nurses and three other female attendants, for whom more black cloth was purchased. All the members of Edward and Philippa's family were to receive twelve ells of black cloth (an ell was forty-five inches), with the sole exception of Jeanne de Montfort, called 'the damsel of Brittany', who was to receive thirteen.[14] As Jeanne was given more cloth even than the adult male members of the royal family who attended Philippa's funeral, this would seem to suggest that she was of imposing stature.

Queen Philippa's illegitimate half-sister 'Lady Elizabeth [of] Holand, sister of our said consort', was also given twelve ells of black cloth, a length of expensive miniver, and two hats, also of miniver. The king and queen's other sons Edward of Woodstock and Thomas of Woodstock were not named on the list of royal family members for whom cloth was purchased, and although her little Coucy daughter was certainly there, neither was the only surviving royal daughter, Isabella of Woodstock. Edward of Woodstock and his wife Joan of Kent were far away in Aquitaine, which explains their absence, and perhaps Isabella of Woodstock was in France with Enguerrand de Coucy; the absence of Thomas of Woodstock, however, seems rather odd. He was named as a member of the royal family and was bought special robes for the Christmas festivities a few months earlier.[15] The fourth royal son Edmund of Langley was not named either, unless the 'earl of Oxford' listed was an error for 'earl of Cambridge'.

Philippa's ladies-in-waiting were named in the list as Lady Ferrers, Lady Mohun, Philippa Zouche, Margaret Seyncler or Sinclair, and Luce atte Wode. The queen had sixteen damsels, or perhaps some of them were former damsels, including Geoffrey Chaucer's wife Philippa and the king's mistress Alice Perrers, named as 'Aliccon Perrers' (or possibly 'Aliceon') and appearing third in the list of sixteen. The two young daughters of John of Gaunt, duke of Lancaster, were accompanied by three damsels, Agnes Falconer, Eleyne Gerberge and Blanche Swynford, whose mother Katherine Swynford née Roet would begin a famous long-term relationship with John of Gaunt a couple of years later and would become his third wife and duchess in 1396.

Blanche Swynford was probably about the same age as the Lancaster daughters, and was the niece of the queen's damsel Philippa Chaucer, Katherine Swynford's sister. As well as their three damsels, Philippa and Elizabeth of Lancaster had no fewer than ten 'under-damsels' (*souzdamoiselles*) looking after them during their grandmother's funeral; one of them was Philippa Picard, who had also worked in the household of their grandmother the queen on occasion. An Elizabeth Breton, 'damsel to the said sister of our said consort', Elisabeth of Holland, is also mentioned and was given six ells of black cloth. Over thirty knights of the queen's household and a few dozen squires are named; one of the squires was Geoffrey Chaucer.[16]

Edward III sent another letter on 5 December 1369 probably to the abbot of Westminster, stating that he wished the solemnities of the queen's funeral to last for a full six days.[17] Philippa was finally interred at Westminster Abbey on 9 January 1370, almost five months after her death. A long delay between the death of a royal person and their funeral was usual in the fourteenth century (Edward III himself in 1377 being a notable exception): Edward II supposedly died on 21 September 1327 and was buried on 20 December; Edward's widow Queen Isabella died on 22 August 1358 and was buried on 27 November; and Isabella's uncle Henry, earl of Lancaster, died on 22 September 1345 and was buried on 15 January 1346. Philippa's funeral took even longer than usual to arrange and was intended by her widower to be a great state occasion. The six days which Edward III wished the solemnities to last began with the departure of the funeral procession from Windsor, and ended with its arrival at Westminster Abbey and the queen's interment there.[18] The *Anonimalle* chronicle says that her funeral procession went from Windsor, to Kingston-upon-Thames, to Saint Mary Overy in Southwark, to St Paul's Cathedral in London, and finally to Westminster Abbey. It also says Philippa's coffin was surrounded by a large quantity of wax candles during this procession.[19] An entry on the Patent Roll, dated to 10 January 1370, perhaps in error, is an order to a number of men in Southwark to 'compel all men of the said town to have the streets thereof cleansed and of all dung and other filth and the pavement repaired where necessary', and to imprison any who refused, 'for the coming of a great number of prelates, earls, barons and magnates of England through the town with the body of Philippa, late queen of England'.[20]

The king paid a stonemason named John Orchard five pounds for making 'diverse images in the likeness of angels' and six angels made of copper for Philippa's tomb, and images of alabaster 'upon a small marble tomb for an infant son and daughter of the queen'.[21] This was Philippa's third daughter Blanche of the Tower, who was born and died in 1342, and her sixth son William of Windsor, born and died in 1348. Her tomb, which the king had had made in January 1367 by a Frenchman named Hawkin Liège at a cost of two hundred marks, and alabaster effigy still exist in Westminster Abbey, though the tomb has been altered since the fourteenth century. Philippa's effigy lies atop a chest which originally had numerous statues in niches carved around all four sides, though only two of them still exist.

At the head of the chest stood statues of Philippa's most important male relatives: Edward III in the middle, with Philippa's brother-in-law the emperor Ludwig of Bavaria to his immediate left and Edward of Woodstock to Ludwig's left, and to Edward III's immediate right, Philippa's cousin John II of France (or possibly his son Charles V), with Philippa's father Willem, count of Hainault and Holland, to the French king's right. At the foot of the chest stood five kings, identified as Pedro I 'the Cruel', king of Castile (who almost became Philippa's son-in-law), Philippa's great-uncle Robert 'the Wise', king of Naples (*c.* 1277-1343), Edward III's brother-in-law David II of Scotland, and probably Johann the Blind's son Karl IV, king of Bohemia and Holy Roman Emperor (1316-78), and Edward III's kinsman Carlos II 'the Bad', king of Navarre (1332-87).

On the left side of the tomb stood statues of Philippa's other four sons Lionel of Antwerp, John of Gaunt, Edmund of Langley and Thomas of Woodstock, Lionel and John's wives Elizabeth de Burgh and Blanche of Lancaster, Edward of Woodstock's wife Joan of Kent, Philippa's eldest daughter Isabella of Woodstock (there was no statue of her husband Enguerrand de Coucy, however), and Edward III's siblings John of Eltham and Joan of the Tower.

Finally, on the right side of the chest were depictions of the queen's continental and maternal relatives: her mother Jeanne de Valois, brother Count Willem (d. 1345) and Willem's wife Johanna of Brabant (d. 1406), Edward III's other sister the duchess of Guelders and her husband Reynald II, the queen's eldest sister Margaretha the empress and Margaretha's second son Wilhelm of Bavaria, Philippa's youngest daughters Mary of Waltham and Margaret of Windsor (though her second daughter Joan of Woodstock is not there), probably her paternal grandfather Jan II, count of Hainault – though this is uncertain – and certainly her maternal grandfather Charles, count of Valois. The statues alternated by sex on each side of the chest, a lord next to a lady, though are also in a vague hierarchical order; Joan of the Tower, queen of Scotland, stands closer to Philippa's head than her older brother John of Eltham, earl of Cornwall, for example, while Thomas of Woodstock, the youngest royal son, stands farthest from his mother's head.[22]

The effigy on the queen's tomb looks remarkably lifelike and realistic, and shows her with a kindly, amicable expression. Philippa looks heavy and plump around the middle, and has a thin upper lip, a broad forehead, and a straight nose. Her face is also rather broad. She is depicted wearing a very tight garment called a *cotehardie* which laces up the front and which is decidedly unflattering to her figure, fastened with a narrow and very long hip belt, and also wears an elaborate, reticulated head-dress which covers all her hair. (A reticulated head-dress was a common style of the era, where the wearer's hair was encased in net bags made of gold or silver thread set on either side of the head.) It is hardly surprising that the queen had become plump in late middle age after giving birth to a dozen children, and owing to her medical condition, she had been mostly immobile for the last few years of her life.

Rather than commissioning a stylised, idealised image of a queen, it seems that Edward III wished for and ordered a genuine portrait of the woman who, while she may not have been beautiful and was perhaps not even particularly pretty, was nevertheless the woman he had loved for more than four decades and who had been his rock, his support, his faithful companion through everything. Philippa and Edward's marriage, arranged by his mother in 1326 as a means of bringing down his father's (probable) lover, developed into one of the great royal love affairs of the English Middle Ages.

Numerous grants from the king to the queen's former household staff are recorded in the months and years after her death as Edward III rewarded the women who had served and looked after his beloved wife. Sometime before April 1365, Philippa had arranged the marriage of two members of her household: her damsel Stephanetta and the usher of her chamber, John of Olney, and she granted them twenty-five marks a year. Edward III raised this by another ten marks annually a few months after Philippa's death.[23] At the end of her life, Philippa was attended by close to twenty damsels, who a few months after her death were also given annuities from the Exchequer. As well as Stephanetta Olney (whose name appears on record as Estevene or Estephene, the usual fourteenth-century female form of the name Stephen), the women were Alice of Preston, Maud Fisher, Joan Kanley, Elizabeth Pershore, Joan Cosin, Philippa Picard or Pycard, Philippa Chaucer, wife of the poet Geoffrey (and named separately to Philippa Picard, so not the same person as sometimes assumed), Agatha Lyngeyn, Maud Radescroft, Agnes of Saxilby, Katherine Spigurnell, Marie Saint Hillaire, Margaret Ellerton, Luce or Lucetta atte Wode, and others. Philippa had also arranged the marriage of her attendant Luce, formerly called Luce of Gainsborough (in Lincolnshire) to her valet John atte Wode. Six months after Philippa's death, Edward III gave Luce an annuity of twenty marks for life; she had previously received ten marks a year.[24] A Joan Caulee, presumably the same former damsel of Queen Philippa also known as Joan Kanley, was granted ten marks a year by Philippa's eighteen-year-old grandson Richard II in 1385 because she was 'broken with age and cannot work'.[25] 'Aliccon Perrers' is also mentioned as one of the queen's damsels for whom black cloth for Philippa's funeral was purchased, even though Alice had not otherwise been named in the lists of the queen's attendants since before 1366.[26] Now that the queen was dead, Edward III's relationship with Alice became gradually more public, and in 1375 he held a jousting tournament where Alice openly appeared as Lady of the Sun.

King Edward also demonstrated concern for his late wife's immortal soul: Philippa's Franciscan confessor Brother John de

Malberthorp was granted forty marks yearly from the Exchequer a few months after her death 'to celebrate divine service and pray for the soul of the said queen'.[27] Her son John of Gaunt's extant registers refer to Philippa as *ma dame la Roine Philippe qi Dieux assoille*, 'my lady Queen Philippa, whom God absolve', a conventional and respectful way of talking about a person who had died. John also called her *nostre tres honure dame et miere Philippe nadgaires Roine d'Engleterre, qi Dieux pardone*, 'our very honoured lady and mother Philippa, late queen of England, whom God pardon' (again, a conventional way of respectfully referring to the dead, not an indication that John believed his mother needed pardoning by God). An inquisition post mortem held in York 'in the fourth week of Lent' in 1370 intended to 'enquire as to the lands [in Yorkshire] and date of death of Queen Philippa' estimated the date completely incorrectly: the jurors claimed that she died 'at the feast of the Nativity of St Mary last', which was 8 September 1369, three and a half weeks after the correct date.[28]

Queen Philippa was greatly missed by her husband's subjects when she passed away, and for forty years she had impressed the people of England with her kindness, dignity, faithfulness and piety. Thomas Walsingham, monk and chronicler of St Albans, put aside his usual snide and arch manner when he spoke of Philippa as the 'most noble woman and constant lover of the English'.[29] A monk of Westminster wrote a moving poem in Latin, commemorating the queen:

Let the whole of England have time for prayers
Because Queen Philippa lies dead, closed up in death.
While she flourished she was full of grace to the English.
The people were not in want; neither was her country in need
    of grain.
It is clear to everyone now that she was successful.
She would call upon Christ while she lived so that the kingdom
    should not lack for its harvest.

The poem makes it apparent that the overwhelming priority of people who lived in the fourteenth century was having enough food, though sadly the year of the queen's death saw another mass outbreak of the plague, with 'great falling of waters' and therefore 'great hindering and destroying of corn' in the floods.[30] Despite their suffering and hunger, the people of England found time to mourn their queen. The chancellor of England pointed out how 'No Christian king or other lord in the world ever had so noble and gracious a lady for his wife or such children – princes, dukes or others – as our lord the king has had.'[31] Jean Froissart called Philippa 'the most courteous, noble and liberal queen that ever reigned in her time,' and had stated on an earlier occasion how the English exclaimed 'Long live the good Philippa of Hainault [*la bonne Phelippe de Hainnau*], queen of England, our dear and dread lady, who brought to us and to England honour, profit, grace and tranquillity.' The author of the *Brut* wrote that Philippa was 'a full noble and good woman'. He tended to refer to her as 'the good lady and queen'.[32]

Philippa died one week before the eleventh anniversary of her mother-in-law Queen Isabella's death in August 1358, and the death dates of the two queens were so close – 15 and 22 August – that Edward III held joint commemorations for his mother and his wife for the remaining few years of his life. The king, however, spent far more on his wife's obsequies than on his mother's. The combined cost of the two queens' anniversaries cost the king about £50 a year, which included payments to paupers, wine, candles and alms to prisoners in the gaol of Newgate in London.[33]

Philippa's widower died eight years after she did, on 21 June 1377 at the age of sixty-four, six months into the fifty-first year of his reign. On 3 April 1377 just two and a half months before his death, Edward promised to pay the order of Dominicans (the Black Friars, or Friars Preacher) twenty pounds annually from the Exchequer to mark the anniversary of Philippa's death every year. Philippa and Edward's then eighteen-year-old grandson Richard II confirmed this annuity in February 1385, and added a request that as well as celebrating the anniversary of his grandmother's death, the Dominicans would say prayers for himself and his queen Anne of Bohemia (daughter of the emperor Karl IV) while living, and for their souls after death.[34]

Edward III was laid to rest next to Queen Philippa in Westminster Abbey, according to her own request, foregoing his former wish forty years previously to be buried in Cologne Cathedral in Germany in fulfilment of a prophecy. (Possibly Edward had never intended to be buried in Cologne, but the prophecy was politically useful to him in the late 1330s.) The first few decades of the king's reign had been glorious, but after Philippa's death, Edward lapsed into a long and slow decline. He lost all the companions of his youth: William Clinton, earl of Huntingdon, died in 1354, Robert Ufford, earl of Suffolk, in November 1369 two and a half months after the queen, Ralph Stafford, earl of Stafford, in 1372, and the Hainaulter lord and husband of the king's cousin Margaret of Norfolk, Walter Manny, also in 1372. Chronicler Thomas Walsingham of St Albans narrated a story that Edward's influential mistress Alice Perrers stripped the rings from his fingers when she realised that he was having a major stroke and abandoned him to die alone. This is implausible – other chroniclers relate that the king was surrounded by his loving family when he died – but that the tale existed in the first place perhaps reveals something of his subjects' attitude to Edward III at the end of his life and indicates that he had lost some of the respect, love and admiration he had built up over the previous few decades.

Edward III and Queen Philippa's eldest son died on 8 June 1376 a week before his forty-sixth birthday and a year before Edward III's own death, and Edward of Woodstock, born as the heir to the throne in June 1330, never ruled as king. His only surviving legitimate son Richard of Bordeaux succeeded him as Prince of Wales, and in June 1377 became King Richard II of England at the age of only ten. Philippa of Hainault was, therefore, not the mother of a king of England, and although her third son John of Gaunt named himself king of Castile and Leon by right of his second wife Constanza of Castile in early 1372, he never reigned as such and never controlled or governed his wife's kingdoms. Philippa's mother Countess Jeanne de Valois had expressed a wish in 1330, on hearing that her three eldest daughters Margaretha, Johanna and Philippa were all pregnant, that she might become a grandmother of kings. In fact, this wish never came true. Empress Margaretha's four sons who lived into adulthood were all dukes, but none reigned as kings (let alone succeeded their father as emperor); Johanna's sons were a count and a duke; and Philippa's five sons were prince of Wales and dukes of Clarence, Lancaster, York and Gloucester, John of Gaunt's claimed title of king of Castile and Leon being merely an empty one.

Richard II of England reigned for twenty-two years and in 1399 was deposed by another of Queen Philippa's grandsons, John of Gaunt and Blanche of Lancaster's son Henry of Lancaster, who became King Henry IV. Henry displaced Edmund Mortimer, great-grandson of Philippa's second surviving son Lionel of Antwerp, who was only eight years old in 1399 and in no position to be able to push his own claim to the throne. Edmund did, however, pass on his claim to his nephew Richard, duke of York (b. 1411), who was also the great-grandson of Philippa's fourth eldest surviving son Edmund of Langley and was the father of two kings, Edward IV and Richard III. The descendants of Philippa of Hainault's sons would battle for the English throne in the fifteenth century.

Philippa of Hainault's Children

1. **Edward of Woodstock**, prince of Wales 1343, prince of Aquitaine 1362, duke of Cornwall 1337, earl of Chester 1331, known to posterity as 'the Black Prince' (not a fourteenth-century appellation). Edward was born on 15 June 1330, died on 8 June 1376 a year before his father, and was buried in Canterbury Cathedral in Kent. After numerous attempts over the years to find a bride for him, he married his father's first cousin Joan of Kent (b. September 1326 or September 1327) in October 1361. Their first son Edward of Angoulême (b. January 1365) died young, and Edward's and his father's heir was his second son Richard of Bordeaux (b. 6 January 1367), who succeeded his grandfather as king in June 1377. An illegitimate son called Roger of Clarendon also lived into adulthood and was executed by his cousin Henry IV in 1402, but Edward of Woodstock's legitimate line ended with the death of his son Richard II in February 1400, as Richard had no children, legitimate or otherwise. Edward's widow Joan of Kent lived until August 1385 and was buried with her first husband Sir Thomas Holland in Stamford, Lincolnshire.

2. **Isabella of Woodstock**, Lady Coucy, countess of Bedford, born *c.* 16 June 1332, died 5 October 1382* and buried at the Franciscan church in London. She married Enguerrand or Ingelram, Lord Coucy, later earl of Bedford (born *c.* 1340) in July 1365, and had daughters Marie de Coucy, countess

of Soissons (1366-1405), and Philippa de Coucy, duchess of Ireland and countess of Oxford (1367/8-1411). Philippa de Coucy, married to Richard II's notorious 'favourite' Robert de Vere (1362-92), had no children; Marie de Coucy's son Robert of Bar was killed at the battle of Agincourt in 1415, fighting against his kinsman Henry V of England (Edward III and Queen Philippa's great-grandson). Isabella of Woodstock was the only daughter of Philippa of Hainault and Edward III who had children, and, via her daughter Marie de Coucy, was an ancestor of the Bourbon kings of France and Spain and of Mary, Queen of Scots. Her widower Enguerrand de Coucy married Isabelle of Lorraine as his second wife and had another daughter, and died in 1397.

* For the evidence demonstrating that Isabella died in 1382, not 1379 as commonly stated, see Jessica Lutkin's article 'Isabella de Coucy, Daughter of Edward III: The Exception who Proves the Rule' in *Fourteenth Century England VI*, ed. Chris Given-Wilson and Nigel Saul, pp. 132-3.

3. **Joan of Woodstock** was probably born around 21 January 1334, although the exact date is uncertain, and she may have been born at the end of 1333 or in early February 1334. She was sometimes wrongly called Joan of the Tower in her own lifetime, a confusion by royal clerks with her aunt the queen of Scotland, and almost certainly she was, like her two older siblings, born at the palace of Woodstock. Joan died of the plague near Bordeaux in late June or on 1 July 1348, aged fourteen, on her way to marry Pedro, heir to the throne of Castile, later King Pedro 'the Cruel' (born August 1334, reigned 1350 to 1369). Her burial place is unknown. Pedro married Blanche de Bourbon (whose sister Jeanne later became queen-consort of France as the wife of Charles V) instead in 1353, but imprisoned her days after their wedding. His daughters with his mistress Maria de Padilla, Constanza (b. *c*. 1354) and Isabel (b. *c*. 1355), were legitimised in 1362 after Blanche de Bourbon's death and married Joan of Woodstock's younger brothers John of Gaunt and Edmund of Langley in 1371 and 1372.

4. **William of Hatfield**, born *c.* early January 1337, died in or before early February 1337, buried in York Minster. Named after Philippa's father the count of Hainault and Holland, and the first of her two sons named William who died in infancy.

5. **Lionel of Antwerp**, first duke of Clarence 1362, earl of Ulster, born at the abbey of St Michael in Antwerp in modern-day Belgium on 29 November 1338, died in Alba, Italy on 17 October 1368. Lionel was initially buried in the church of St Peter in the Sky of Gold in Pavia, Italy, though his remains were later returned to England and interred with his first wife at Bruisyard, the Augustinian house he himself had founded in Suffolk. Married (1) August 1342 Elizabeth de Burgh, heiress of Ulster (b. July 1332, d. December 1363); (2) late May or early June 1368 Violante Visconti of Milan (*c.* 1353/4-1386). One daughter from his first marriage, Philippa Mortimer, countess of March and Ulster (1355-80), who was the great-great-grandmother of Edward IV (r. 1461-70 and 1471-83) and Richard III (r. 1483-85).

6. **John of Gaunt**, titular king of Castile and Leon 1372, second duke of Lancaster 1362, duke of Aquitaine 1390, earl of Richmond, Leicester, Lincoln and Derby, born in Ghent in modern-day Belgium on 6 March 1340, died 3 February 1399, buried in St Paul's Cathedral, London with his first wife. Married (1) May 1359 Blanche of Lancaster (1342-September 1368), younger daughter and (from April 1362) sole heir of Henry of Grosmont, first duke of Lancaster; (2) September 1371 Constanza of Castile, King Pedro's elder daughter and heir, rightful queen of Castile and Leon (*c.* 1354-March 1394); (3) January 1396 Katherine Swynford (*c.* 1345-May 1403), his long-term mistress and mother of his four Beaufort children. Had eight children who lived into adulthood, including Henry IV, king of England, Philippa of Lancaster, queen of Portugal, and Catalina of Lancaster, queen of Castile, and had more than forty grandchildren. Great-grandfather of Edward IV and Richard III; great-great-grandfather of the first Tudor king, Henry VII (r. 1485-1509); grandfather of Duarte I of Portugal

(r. 1433-38) and Juan II of Castile (r. 1406-54); grandfather of Joan Beaufort (*c.* 1404-45), queen-consort of Scotland; great-grandfather of Isabel the Catholic (1451-1504), queen-regnant of Castile and queen-consort of Aragon.

7. **Edmund of Langley**, earl of Cambridge 1362, first duke of York 1385, born 5 June 1341 or a little earlier, died 1 August 1402, buried at Langley Priory in Hertfordshire next to his first wife. Married (1) July 1372 Isabel of Castile (*c.* 1355-December 1392), daughter of King Pedro and younger sister of his sister-in-law Constanza, duchess of Lancaster; (2) *c.* November 1393 Joan Holland (*c.* 1375/80-April 1434), granddaughter of his sister-in-law Joan of Kent from her first marriage. Three children from his first marriage: Edward, second duke of York, killed at the battle of Agincourt in 1415 fighting for Henry V; Constance, Lady Despenser; and Richard of Conisbrough, earl of Cambridge, executed for treason by Henry V in 1415. Edmund of Langley was the great-grandfather of Edward IV and Richard III via his younger son Richard of Conisbrough, and his daughter Constance Despenser (d. 1416) was the great-grandmother of Richard III's queen Anne Neville (1456-85). He was the last surviving of Queen Philippa's children, and the only one to live past 1400.

8. **Blanche of the Tower**, born March or June 1342, died shortly after birth, buried in Westminster Abbey in early February 1343.

9. **Mary of Waltham**, born 10 October 1344, died after 1 October 1361; married John of Brittany (1339-99), later Duke John IV; no children. Her widower married her brother Edward of Woodstock's stepdaughter Joan Holland (1350s-1384), and thirdly Juana of Navarre (*c.* 1370-1437), one of the daughters of King Carlos II 'the Bad,' who was the mother of all eight or nine of his children. Duke John IV died in 1399, and his widow Juana married Mary's nephew Henry IV (1367-1413), king of England, John of Gaunt's son and heir, in 1403.

10. **Margaret of Windsor**, born 20 July 1346, died after 1 October 1361; married John Hastings, heir to the earldom of Pembroke (b. 29 August 1347, d. 1375) in May 1359; no children. Margaret of Windsor's widower married secondly Anne Manny (1354-84), daughter and co-heir of Margaret, countess of Norfolk and her second husband the Hainaulter knight Walter Manny, who was the mother of his son and heir John (1372-89). The younger John Hastings (b. 1372) married firstly Margaret of Windsor's niece Elizabeth of Lancaster (1363-1425), John of Gaunt's second daughter (the marriage was annulled before consummation), and secondly Margaret's great-niece Philippa Mortimer (1375-1400), younger daughter of Philippa of Clarence (1355-80) and granddaughter of Lionel of Antwerp.

Thomas of Windsor, who was supposedly born at Windsor Castle in the summer of 1347, died of the Black Death in the summer of 1348 and was buried at Langley Priory in Hertfordshire, is a son sometimes ascribed to Philippa by modern writers, but he did not exist. Philippa was in Calais, not Windsor, at the time that Thomas was allegedly born, and his entire existence appears to be based on the spurious story by chroniclers Jean le Bel and Jean Froissart that Philippa was heavily pregnant when she pleaded for the lives of the Calais burghers at the beginning of August 1347. 'Thomas of Windsor' has been given the name of Philippa's seventh son Thomas of Woodstock, the birthplace of her sixth son William of Windsor and the burial site of her fifth son Edmund of Langley, and is thus a fictional composite of her three youngest sons.

11. **William of Windsor**, born *c.* mid or late May 1348 at Windsor Castle, died in Brentford, Middlesex before 5 September 1348, buried in Westminster Abbey. He was the second of Queen Philippa's sons named William who died in infancy, and his eldest brother Edward of Woodstock, eighteen years his senior, was his godfather. Unlike his fictional brother 'Thomas of Windsor', there is much evidence proving William's existence.

12. **Thomas of Woodstock**, earl of Buckingham 1377, first duke of Gloucester 1385, born 7 January 1355. After his sisters Mary of Waltham and Margaret of Windsor died in 1361, his nearest surviving sibling was Edmund of Langley, who was thirteen and a half years older than he, and he was only seven months older than his niece Philippa of Clarence, his parents' eldest legitimate grandchild. Thomas was murdered on the orders of his nephew Richard II in Calais in September 1397. In 1376 he married Eleanor de Bohun (1366-99), co-heir, with her younger sister Mary, of her father Humphrey, earl of Hereford, Essex and Northampton. Thomas and Eleanor had one child, Anne of Gloucester (1383-1428), countess of Stafford and Eu, who married and had children; their other children, including their only son Humphrey, died in their teens or younger. Via Anne of Gloucester, Thomas of Woodstock was the ancestor of the fifteenth-century dukes of Exeter and Buckingham and the earls of Essex.

Some Original Sources

1. *The printed English translation of Bishop Walter Stapeldon's description of a Hainault girl in 1319, who can be assumed to be Philippa's eldest sister Margaretha, later the Holy Roman Empress, from the late nineteenth century:*

The lady whom we saw has not uncomely hair, betwixt blue-black [*sic*; *bloy* almost certainly means 'blonde' not 'blue'] and brown. Her head is clean-shaped; her forehead high and broad, and standing somewhat forward. Her face narrows between the eyes, and the lower part of her face is still more narrow and slender than the forehead. Her eyes are blackish-brown and deep. Her nose is fairly smooth and even, save that it is somewhat broad at the tip and somewhat flattened, yet it is no snub nose. Her nostrils are broad, her mouth fairly wide. Her lips somewhat full, and especially the lower lip. Her teeth which are fallen and grown again are white enough, but the rest are not so white. The lower teeth project a little beyond the upper, yet this is but little seen. Her ears and chin are comely enough. Her neck, shoulders and all her body and lower limbs are reasonably well shapen; all her limbs are well set and un-maimed; and nought is amiss so far as a man may see. Moreover, she is brown of skin all over, and much like her father; and in all things she is pleasant enough, as it seems to us. And the damsel will be of the age of nine years on St John's day next to come, as her mother saith. She is neither too tall nor too short for such an age; she is of fair carriage.[1]

2. *Jean Froissart's account of how Edward III allegedly chose Philippa as his bride over her sisters in 1326, as seemingly narrated to him many years by Philippa herself:*

Now Count Willem had four daughters, Margaretha, Philippa, Johanna and Isabella. Of them, the young Edward, who later became king of England, was most dedicated to Philippa, and his regard and his love were more inclined to Philippa than to the others – and also the young girl knew him better and kept him greater company than her sisters. So I have heard for truth from the good lady who became queen of England.'

In the French original: '*Adont avoit li contes Guillaumes IIII filles, Margerite, Phelippe, Jehanne et Ysabiel. De quoy li jones Edouwars qui fu puis roys d'Engleterre s'adonnoit le plus et s'enclinoit de regart et d'amour sus Phelippe que sus les autres, et ossi la jone fille le cognoissoit plus et lui tenoit plus grant compaignie que nuls de sereurs; ainssi l'ay-je oy depuis recorder la bonne dame qui fut royne d'Engleterre.*'[2]

3. *A letter by Queen Philippa, dated at Colchester, 6 March 1354, in French in the original and typical of her letters:*

Philippe by the grace of God queen of England, lady of Ireland and duchess of Aquitaine, to all those etc [who see or hear these present letters], greeting. Know that, of our special grace and for the good and agreeable service that our dear servant Piers de Routh, usher of our chamber, has done for us for a long time past and still does from day to day, we have granted him the office of master forester of our forest of Knaresborough, which John de Staunford, who has been called to God, had of our grant, for the said Piers to have for the term of his life, taking for it as much as the said John had and as much as it is reasonable that he should take. In witness of this, we have had these our letters made. Given under our privy seal at Colchester the sixth day of March in the twenty-eighth year of the reign of our dearest lord the king of England.[3]

4. *A letter sent to Philippa by Louis, count of Flanders, in December 1368, which makes it apparent that even at the end of her life, the queen was involved in her husband's government, foreign policy and marital negotiations for her children:*

Dearest lady, I have received your gracious letters of credence via Sir R[ichard] de S[tury], whom it has pleased you to send to me; and I have listened to his inquiry, most courteously presented to me on your behalf, as to whether I would be prepared to enter into negotiations for the marriage of my dearest cousin the duke of Lancaster, your son, and my daughter [Margarethe of Flanders], now that the marriage previously arranged between her and your other son, Sir Edmund [*monsieur Esmon*], can no longer take place, owing to the lack of dispensation. I thank you as much as I can for the honour and the great love you have shown to me and my said daughter. But, dearest lady, you must remember how the king [Edward III], to fulfil his obligation for the said dispensation, sent away for it to our very holy father [the pope], and what followed from this. And recall that afterwards the king sent to me to inform me that he had been unable to obtain it. Nevertheless, because above all things I desired the said marriage to take place, I myself sent letters to our said holy father on several occasions, beseeching him that it may please him to issue the said dispensation. And even after he refused, I waited another two years in the hope that our said holy father might reflect that all this has been quite hard for me, considering that I have only one daughter and no other heir, and she is old enough to marry, and that I desire with all my heart to see my line continued, as is right.

'But recently, because there was no longer any hope that the first negotiation [for Edmund and Margarethe] might prove successful, owing to the said causes, thanks to the diligent action and at the request of my lord the king [of France] and at the command of my dearest and dread lady and mother, I agreed to negotiate a marriage between the duke of Burgundy and my daughter. If I had known of your present proposal, I would have been able to give you a more satisfactory reply, and if you may, dearest lady, may it please you to excuse me for not entering into other negotiations during this one that I have agreed to. When our own negotiations were taking place, I refused to enter into discussion with anyone else, though I was asked to on numerous occasions. And this is what I have replied to the said Sir R. and he will tell you this on my behalf. Dearest lady, if you wish anything else from me, let me know it and I will do it willingly and from the heart. May the Holy Spirit have you in his keeping.[4]

Endnotes

Abbreviations
CCR: Calendar of Close Rolls
CChR: Calendar of Charter Rolls
CFR: Calendar of Fine Rolls
CPR: Calendar of Patent Rolls
TNA: The National Archives

Chapter 1: The Hainault Girl

1. Charles de Valois and Marguerite of Anjou-Naples were second cousins twice over: they had four of their eight great-grandparents in common, Louis VIII and Blanche of Castile, king and queen of France, and Ramon-Berenger of Provence and Beatrice of Savoy, count and countess of Provence. Marguerite of Anjou-Naples' paternal grandfather, Charles the Lame's father Charles of Anjou (1227-85), king of Sicily, was the posthumous son of Louis VIII of France and the youngest brother of Louis IX (Charles de Valois's grandfather). Charles of Anjou's wife Beatrice of Provence (d. 1267), countess of Provence in her own right and Marguerite of Anjou-Naples' grandmother, was the youngest sister of Marguerite of Provence (d. 1295), queen of Louis IX of France, Charles de Valois's paternal grandmother.

2. Janet van der Meulen, 'Sche Sente the Copie to her Doughter: Countess Jeanne de Valois and Literature at the Court of Hainault-Holland', *I Have Heard About You: Women's Writing Crossing the Dutch Border*, ed. Suzan van Dijk, translations by Jo Nesbitt (Hilversum: Uitgeverij Verloren, 2004), p. 67, note 25.

3. Isabelle de Valois died in the lifetime of her father-in-law Arthur II, duke of Brittany (1262-1312), and never became duchess of Brittany. Her widower, later Duke John III, married his second wife Isabel of Castile in 1310 and his third, Joan of Savoy, in 1329, but left no legitimate children. The younger Jeanne de Valois, b. 1304, Isabelle and Jeanne's half-sister, was the second daughter of Charles de Valois and his second wife Catherine de Courtenay, and married Robert of Artois (b. 1287), claimant to the county of Artois.

4. Henry Stephen Lucas, *The Low Countries and the Hundred Years War, 1326-1347* (University of Michigan: Ann Arbor, 1929), p. 43. The Battle of the Golden Spurs in 1302 is also sometimes called the Battle of Courtrai, or Kortrijk in Dutch. Three of Willem of Hainault's uncles, his father Count Jan's younger brothers, were bishops: Bouchard, bishop of Metz, Guy or Gwijde, bishop of Utrecht, and Willem, bishop of Cambrai. The final brother, Floris or Florent, was prince of Achaea in Greece by right of his wife, Isabella of Villehardouin.

5. F. W. D. Brie, ed., *The Brut or the Chronicles of England,* part 1 (London: Early English Text Society, 1906), p. 293; *Oeuvres de Froissart,* ed. Kervyn de Lettenhove, vol. 7 (Brussels: Comptoir Universel d'Imprimerie et de Librairie, 1869), p. 428. The *Anonimalle* chronicle, written in England in French, calls her *dame Philippe: The Anonimalle Chronicle 1307 to 1334, from Brotherton Collection MS 29,* ed. W. R. Childs and J. Taylor (Yorkshire Archaeological Society Records Series 147, 1991), pp. 138, 146.

6. Lucas, *The Low Countries and the Hundred Years War,* p. 580.

7. The count of Holland who married Edward I's daughter Elizabeth in January 1297 was Jan I, who died childless in November 1299, aged fifteen. Holland thus passed to his father Floris V's (1254-96) cousin, Queen Philippa's grandfather Jan II, already count of Hainault since 1280, and then to Philippa's father Willem in 1304 on Jan II's death.

8. King Stephen's daughter Mary (d. 1182), countess of Boulogne, had a daughter Mathilde (d. 1210), who married the duke of Brabant and was Philippa's ancestor. Edward III of England was also a descendant of Harold Godwinson and Harold's daughter Gytha of Wessex via his mother Isabella of France, but was not descended from King Stephen.

9. Her English Wikipedia page often gives 24 June 1314 as her date of birth, though it is sometimes edited to state 1313, or sometime between 1310 and 1315, and her Dutch Wikipedia page (accessed 20 January 2019) gives 24 June 1314. The German Wikipedia page for Philippa states that she was born on 24 June 1311, and the one for her father (both accessed 20 January 2019) says that Margaretha was born in 1310, Philippa in 1311, Isabella in 1314 and Johanna in 1315. This birth order is wrong, and the dates are mere inaccurate guesses. The English Wikipedia page for Philippa's brother Willem currently states that Willem was born in 1307, which, given that their mother Jeanne de Valois was herself almost certainly born in 1294/5, seems extremely unlikely. Jeanne's own Wiki page repeats that she was born in 1294 and gave birth to Willem in 1307, that Philippa was her second daughter and born on 24 June 1314, and claims further that her eldest two sons Willem and Jan were her eldest children overall.

10. *Willelmi, Capellini in Brederode, Postea Monachi et Procuratoris Egmondensis Chronicon,* ed. Cornelis Pijnacker Hirdijk (Amsterdam: Müller, 1904), pp. 145, 244. The *secunda filia* was not specifically given the name Johanna in the chronicle, but was stated to be the Hainault daughter betrothed and then married to the son of the count of Jülich, so her identification as Johanna is clear.

11. *Urkundenbuch für die Geschichte des Niederrheins oder des Erzstifts Cöln, der Fürstenthümer Jülich und Berg, Geldern, Meurs, Kleve und Mark, und der*

Reichsstifte Elten, Essen und Werden, aus den Quellen in dem Königlichen Provinzial-Archiv zu Düsseldorf und in den Kirchen- und Stadt-Archiven der Provinz, vollständig und erläutert, Band III: Von dem Jahr 1301 bis 1400 einschliesslich, ed. Theodor Joseph Lacomblet (Düsseldorf: H. Voss, Im Commission der Schaub'schen Buchhandlung, 1853), no. 161, pp. 120-21. I owe this reference to the Foundation for Medieval Genealogy website, www.fmg.ac.

12. *Foedera, Conventiones, Litterae et Cujuscunque Acta Publica*, vol. 2.1, 1307-1327 (London: Thomas Rymer, 1818), p. 381.

13. *Foedera 1307-27*, p. 405.

14. *Foedera 1307-27*, pp. 437, 446.

15. A. W. E. Dek, *Genealogie der Graven van Holland* (Zaltbommel: Europeese Bibliotheek, 1969), p. 40; Van der Meulen, 'Sche Sente the Copie to her Doughter', p. 76.

16. Dek, *Genealogie der Graven van Holland*, p. 40. The sons were: Jan van de Poel, with Willem's mistress Trude, ancestor of the lords of de Poel; Jan Aelman; Claas van de Gheijne, with Alida, ancestor of the lords of Cronenburg; Jan van Dolre; Willem, with Doedijn; Jan Zuurmond.

17. François Lemaire, *Notice Historique sur la Ville de Nivelles, et sur les Abbesses qui l'ont Successivement Gouvernée depuis sa Fondation jusqu'à la Dissolution de son Chapitre* (Nivelles: F. Cuisenaire, 1848), p. 111.

18. *Calendar of the Patent Rolls 1367-70*, p. 6, calling her 'Elizabeth de Holand' and 'bastard sister' of the queen; *Life-Records of Chaucer*, Parts I-IV, ed. Walford D. Selby, F. J. Furnivall, Edward A. Bond and R. E. G. Kirk (London: Chaucer Society, 1900), p. 172.

19. *Excerpta Historica, Or, Illustrations of English History*, ed. Samuel Bentley (London: printed by and for Samuel Bentley, 1831), pp. 23-25; John Matthews Manly, *Some New Light on Chaucer: Lectures Delivered at the Lowell Institute* (Gloucester, Mass: Peter Smith, 1959), pp. 205-9. I am grateful to Judy Perry for bringing Elisabeth's will to my attention.

20. George Frederick Beltz, *Memorials of the Order of the Garter From Its Foundation to the Present Time* (London: W. Pickering, 1841), p. 385 (in Latin); *Register of Edward the Black Prince*, vol. 4, ed. M. C. B. Dawes (London: HMSO, 1933), p. 73.

21. Dek, *Genealogie der Graven van Holland*, p. 39; the illegitimate children were Simon, Willem, Hendrik, Aleid and Ida. Willem's legitimate sisters included the duchess of Bourbon and the countesses of Artois and Norfolk.

22. The dictionary at anglo-norman.net (accessed 28 February 2019) translates the word *bloy/blu/bloi/bloe* (and numerous other possible variant spellings) as blue when referring to cloth and textiles and to the colour blue in certain other contexts, azure when referring to heraldry, and fair or tawny or golden when referring to colour in various other contexts. Confusingly, the word can also mean ashen and grey, or discoloured, or dark, or gloomy, or livid. It therefore requires a degree of interpretation to ascertain its correct meaning in any given context. Michael Prestwich also translates *entre bloy et brun* as 'between blonde and brown' in his *Plantagenet England 1225-1360* (Oxford: Oxford University Press, 2005), p. 215. For Walter Stapeldon's description of the Hainault girl, almost certainly Margaretha, in 1319, see Appendix 2.

23. http://www.100greatblackbritons.com/bios/queen_phillipa.html (accessed 28 February 2019); Stuart Jeffries, 'Was this Britain's first black queen?' *The Guardian*, 12 March 2009. A Google search for Philippa of Hainault brings up 'Philippa of Hainault was black' and 'Philippa of Hainault African' as auto-fills (and does the same for Queen Charlotte), so the strange notion has become quite widespread.

24. David Hughes, *The British Chronicles*, vol. 2 (2007).

25. *True Chronicles of Jean le Bel, 1290-1360*, trans. and ed. Nigel Bryant (Woodbridge: The Boydell Press, 2011), pp. 107-8.

26. For the Cumans, see Ion Grumeza, *The Roots of Balkanization: Eastern Europe C. E. 500-1500* (Lanham: University Press of America, 2010), p. 36. The description of the Hainault girl, most probably Margaretha, is in C. Hingeston-Randolph, *The Register of Walter de Stapledon, Bishop of Exeter, A. D. 1307-1326* (London: George Bell and Sons, 1892), p. 169; see Appendix 2.

27. Henry V was Queen Philippa's great-grandson, and the great-nephew of Edward of Woodstock. Shakespeare's play refers to 'Edward the Black Prince' and 'Edward, Black Prince of Wales' on two occasions. *Grafton's Chronicle*, vol. 1 (re-published in London in 1809), p. 332, states that Edward of Woodstock '...was in his dayes accompted the flower of all chiyualrye throughout all the worlde, and also some writers name him the black prince.' The 'some writers' are not specified, nor the source Grafton used for the nickname, though he and other, rather later writers appeared to be under the impression that the nickname was widely known and commonly used. The notes of the antiquarian John Leland (d. 1552) in his *Collectanea* seem also to refer to the name.

28. W. Mark Ormrod, *Edward III* (New Haven and London: Yale University Press, 2011), p. 567.

Chapter 2: Meeting Edward

1. *CPR 1324-7*, pp. 171, 193; *Calendar of Close Rolls 1323-7*, pp. 505-6, 508, 527-8, 540-41, 569; *Calendar of Chancery Warrants Preserved in the Public Record Office, 1244-1326* (London: His Majesty's Stationery Office, 1927), pp. 549-50.

2. Malcolm Vale, *The Princely Court: Medieval Courts and Culture in North-West Europe* (Oxford: Oxford University Press, 2001), pp. 160-61.

3. J. G. Smit, 'De Verblijfplaatsen van de Graven van Holland en Zeeland in de Late Middeleeuwen', *Regionaal-Historisch Tijdschrift*, 24 (1992), p. 125.

4. Vale, *The Princely Court*, p. 176.

5. Vale, *The Princely Court*, pp. 272-3, 368-9.

6. Van der Meulen, 'Sche Sente the Copie to her Doughter', pp. 75-6.

7. Peter H. Wilson, *The Holy Roman Empire: A Thousand Years of Europe's History* (London: Allen Lane, 2016), p. 257.

8. *Calendar of Entries in the Papal Registers Relating to Great Britain and Ireland: Papal Letters*, vol. 2, 1305-1341, ed. W. H. Bliss (London: HMSO, 1895), p. 459.

9. *Calendar of Papal Letters 1305-41*, pp. 485, 489, 490, 492.

10. *Urkundenbuch für die Geschichte des Niederrheins*, ed. Lacomblet, nos. 180, 236.

11. Van der Meulen, 'Sche Sente the Copie to her Doughter', p. 65; Lucas, *The Low Countries and the Hundred Years War*, p. 94.

12. *1299, Één Graaf, Drie Graafschappen: De Vereniging van Holland, Zeeland en Henegouwen*, ed. Dick Edward Herman de Boer, Erich H. P. Cordfunke and Herbert Sarfatij (Hilversum: Uitgeverij Verloren, 2000), p. 129.

13. Lucas, *The Low Countries and the Hundred Years War*, p. 94.

14. *Calendar of Chancery Warrants 1244-1326*, pp. 549-50.

15. *CCR 1323-7*, pp. 505-6, 527-8, 569; Lucas, *The Low Countries and the Hundred Years War*, pp. 53-4.

16. Carla Lord, 'Queen Isabella at the Court of France', *Fourteenth Century England II*, ed. Chris Given-Wilson (Woodbridge, 2002), p. 49, for the Hainault visit and velvet; Pierre Chaplais, ed., *The War of Saint-Sardos (1323-1325): Gascon Correspondence and Diplomatic Documents*, Camden third series, vol. LXXXVII (London: Offices of the Royal Historical Society, 1954), p. 189, for the date of Charles IV and Jeanne of Evreux's wedding (which in modern writing is often wrongly stated to have taken place in 1325).

17. Lord, 'Queen Isabella at the Court of France', pp. 50-51.

18. Van der Meulen, 'Sche Sente the Copie to her Doughter', p. 65; Vale, *The Princely Court*, p. 273.

19. Catherine de Valois (b. 1303) was married to Philippa of Hainault's great-uncle Philip of Taranto (b. *c.* 1278), despot of Romania, king of Albania and prince of Achaea, one of the younger siblings of her grandmother Marguerite of Anjou-Naples.

20. Their itinerary is in Vale, *The Princely Court*, p. 339.

21. Society of Antiquaries of London, Manuscript 122 (Edward II's chamber account of 1325/26), p. 45: the messenger was Percival Simeon, and Valois was called 'Sir Charles de Valeis, uncle of my lady the queen'.

22. Cited in Malcolm Vale, *The Origins of the Hundred Years War: The Angevin Legacy 1250-1340* (Oxford: Clarendon Press, 1990, reprinted 2004), p. 196.

23. Chaplais, *Gascon Correspondence and Diplomatic Documents*, p. 16. A letter to Edward II from Ralph, Lord Basset in January 1324 states that Valois wished to send envoys to England 'to discuss and negotiate the marriages of my ladies your two daughters, that is, for one daughter the son of the said Sir Charles who is the issue of his third wife, and for the other, one of the sons of the son of his first marriage' (my translation). John, b. 1319, was the only son of Philip de Valois until his brother Louis, who died young, was born in 1329.

24. Chaplais, *Gascon Correspondence and Diplomatic Documents*, p. 270.

25. *CCR 1323-7*, p. 577.

26. *Vita Edwardi Secundi Monachi Cuiusdam Malmesberiensis*, ed, N. Denholm-Young (London: Thomas Nelson and Sons, 1957), pp. 144-5. The letter or proclamation does not exist, but a letter sent to Isabella by all the English bishops was recorded by the clerk who wrote the *Vita Edwardi Secundi*, and they wrote: 'But as for what you have written, that what your brother the king of France and your other friends of that country intend to do on your behalf,

will turn out not to the prejudice of the lord king [Edward II] or anyone else, but to the destruction of Hugh alone...'.

27. Chaplais, *Gascon Correspondence*, p. 72.

28. *Foedera 1307-27*, pp. 617-8 (Edward's letter); *Calendar of Papal Letters 1305-41*, p. 260 (dispensation).

29. Leonor of Castile was born in *c.* 1307 as the daughter of King Fernando IV of Castile and Constança of Portugal. In 1319 she married the Infante Jaime of Aragon, eldest son and heir of King Jaime II, but soon after the wedding Jaime renounced his claim to his father's throne and became a monk, and their marriage was dissolved. In February 1329, Leonor married Infante Jaime's younger brother Alfonso IV of Aragon instead, as his second wife.

30. *Historiae Anglicanae Scriptores Decem*, ed. Roger Twysden (1652), column 2767-8.

31. *CCR 1323-7*, p. 577.

32. Lucas, *The Low Countries and the Hundred Years War*, p. 55. Edward and Philippa's marriage contract still exists, and was offered for sale by the London auction house Bonham's in March 2019. It begins *Nous Edwars Dux de Guyane, ainsnels filz de tresexcellent Prince monseigneur Edward par la grasce de dieu Roy Dengletere*, 'We, Edward, duke of Guyenne [i.e. Aquitaine], eldest son of the most excellent prince, my lord Edward, by the grace of God king of England'. Edward of Windsor promised *que nous prenderons a femme et a espeuse demiselle Phelippe, fille monsigneur Guillaume Conte de Haynau, de Hollande de Zéelande et signeur de Frize, dedens deus ans de la date de ches presentes lettres*, 'that we will take as our wife and our bride the damsel Philippa, daughter of my lord Willem, count of Hainault, Holland and Zeeland, and lord of Friesland, within two years from the date of these present letters'.

33. *CCR 1323-7*, pp. 556-7, dated 15 April 1326. The daughter Afonso and Beatriz had in mind as a bride for Edward of Windsor was probably Maria of Portugal, born *c.* 1313, who ultimately married her first cousin Alfonso XI of Castile (fiancé of Edward of Windsor's sister Eleanor of Woodstock in 1325/26) and in 1334 became the mother of Pedro I of Castile, who would have married Edward III and Philippa of Hainault's daughter Joan in 1348, but she died on the way to their wedding.

34. *Oeuvres de Froissart Publiées avec les Variantes des Divers Manuscrits*, vol. 2, 1322-1339, ed. M. le Baron Kervyn de Lettenhove (Brussels: Comptoir Universel d'Imprimerie et de Librairie, 1867), p. 54. In the French original, Froissart wrote: *Adont avoit li comtes Guillaumme IIII fillez: Margerite, Phelippe, Jehanne et Ysabiel. De quoy li jones Edouwars qui fu puis roys d'Engleterres'adonnoit le plus et s'enclinoit de regart et d'amour sus Phelippe que suz les autres – et ossi la jonne fille le cognoissoit plus – et tenoit plus grant compaignie que nulle de sessereurs. Ainsi ay je oy depuis recorder de la bonne damme qui fu royne d'Engleterre.* See also *Oeuvres de Froissart*, ed. Lettenhove, vol. 17, p. 26.

35. *True Chronicles of Jean le Bel*, ed. Bryant, pp. 50-51.

36. *The Chronicle of Iohn Hardyng, Containing an Account of Public Transactions from the Earliest Period of English History to the Beginning of the Reign of*

Edward IV, ed. Henry Ellis (London: F. C. and J. Rivington et al, 1812), p. 317.

37. *Foedera 1327-44,* p. 712 (*'nuptiali foedere inter nos & filiam nobilis viri, W. Hanon', Holand' & Seland comitis'*); *Issues of the Exchequer; Being a Collection of Payments Made out of His Majesty's Revenue, From King Henry III to King Henry VI Inclusive,* ed. Frederick Devon (London: John Murray, 1837), p. 140; *True Chronicles of Jean le Bel,* pp. 11, 50-51, 191; *Adae Murimuth Continuatio Chronicarum,* ed. E. M. Thompson (London: Eyre and Spottiswoode, 1889), p. 56.

Chapter 3: Queen in Name Only

1. *Calendar of Papal Letters 1305-41,* p. 260.
2. Lucas, *The Low Countries and the Hundred Years War,* p. 62.
3. Vale, *The Princely Court,* p. 193.
4. Vale, *The Princely Court,* p. 294.
5. De Boer, Cordfunke and Safartij, *1299, Één Graaf, Drie Graafschappen,* p. 44.
6. Lucas, *The Low Countries and the Hundred Years War,* pp. 56-7, 63-4.
7. Lucas, *The Low Countries and the Hundred Years War,* pp. 65-7.
8. Vale, *The Princely Court,* p. 273.
9. Lucas, *The Low Countries and the Hundred Years War,* pp. 70-71, 73; *CPR 1327-30,* p. 179.
10. Van der Meulen, 'Sche Sente the Copie to her Doughter', p. 76, my translation.
11. Cited in van der Meulen, 'Sche Sente the Copie to her Doughter', p. 76, my translation.
12. The National Archives, E 101/399/12; Ormrod, *Edward III,* pp. 127, note 38, 130; for the 1331 visit, see also below.
13. Willem was granted a safe-conduct on 6 October 1327, and two days later the bishop of Coventry and Lichfield was authorised to 'treat for a marriage between the king and Philippa': *CPR 1327-30,* pp. 176, 179.
14. *CPR 1327-30,* p. 190; *Anonimalle Chronicle 1307 to 1334,* p. 138; *Annales Paulini 1307-1340,* in W. Stubbs, ed., *Chronicles of the Reigns of Edward I and Edward II,* vol. 1 (London: Rolls Series, 1882), pp. 338-9.
15. Devon, *Issues of the Exchequer,* p. 140.
16. Devon, *Issues of the Exchequer,* p. 140; *CPR 1327-30,* p. 231; David Anthony Harding, 'The Regime of Isabella and Mortimer 1326-1330', University of Durham MPhil thesis (1985), pp. 279, 291-2.
17. Ian Mortimer, *The Perfect King: The Life of Edward III, Father of the English Nation* (London: Vintage, 2006), p. 67; Michael A. Michael, 'A Manuscript Wedding Gift from Philippa of Hainault to Edward III', *The Burlington Magazine,* vol. 127, no. 990 (September 1985); W. M. Ormrod, 'The Personal Religion of Edward III', *Speculum,* 64 (1989), p. 857. The psalter in the British Library is called the 'Psalter of Queen Philippa', MS Harley 2899, and there is also Dr Williams's Library MS Ancient 6, another psalter which belonged to the queen. It is possible but not certain that one of the psalters was a wedding gift from Edward, as on stylistic grounds it can most probably be dated to the late 1320s. For more information, see https://dwl.ac.uk/view.php?page=278. The other psalter dates to sometime between 1328 and 1340.

Endnotes

See also Anne Rudloff Stanton, 'The Queen Mary Psalter: A Study of Affect and Audience', *Transactions of the American Philosophical Society*, new series, vol. 91, no. 6 (2001), p. 196.

18. Ormrod, *Edward III*, p. 70.
19. The National Archives SC 8/258/12857; SC 8/46/2263.
20. Ormrod, *Edward III*, pp. 71, 74.
21. Natalie Fryde, *The Tyranny and Fall of Edward II 1321-1326* (Cambridge: Cambridge University Press, 1979), pp. 209, 213-6, 223-4.
22. Fryde, *Tyranny and Fall*, pp. 224, 273 note 94.
23. Cited in Ormrod, *Edward III*, p. 71 note 91.
24. Lucas, *The Low Countries and the Hundred Years War*, pp. 96-8; *Adae Murimuth Continuatio Chronicarum*, p. 61.
25. K. A. Muffat, 'Feststellung der Geburtsdaten von Kaiser Ludwigs des Bayern Söhnen', *Sitzungsberichte der Philosophisch-Philiologischen und Historischen Classe der K. B. Akademie der Wissenschaften zu München*, Band 3 (1873), pp. 890, 893-6.
26. Ormrod, *Edward III*, p. 81; *Foedera 1327-44*, p. 743.
27. Lucas, *The Low Countries and the Hundred Years War*, p. 80.
28. SC 1/36/107. Her husband Edward was at Sempringham in Lincolnshire over 100 miles away, which tends to confirm that the young couple did not live together at first, though in July 1328 they were together in Staffordshire and were together again at Westminster that November.
29. *CPR 1327-30*, pp. 257, 328, 337, 382.
30. *CPR 1327-30*, pp. 270, 389, 453.
31. *CPR 1327-30*, pp. 413, 453, 510. John Dene was one of Isabella's household staff who returned to England from France in late 1325 and early 1326 when Isabella refused to do so, and joined Edward II's household instead: Society of Antiquaries MS 122, pp. 41, 56, 64.
32. E 101/380/4, fo. 22r; *CCR 1323-7*, pp. 517, 645; *CPR 1327-30*, p. 552. Emma Prior retired again on or shortly before 31 July 1330: *CPR 1327-30*, p. 544.
33. *CPR 1327-30*, p. 544; *CPR 1330-4*, pp. 244, 306, 414, 457, 541;*Calendar of Memoranda Rolls (Exchequer): Michaelmas 1326–Michaelmas 1327* (London: HMSO, 1968), no. 2270 (p. 373); C. M. Woolgar, *The Senses in Late Medieval England* (New Haven and London: Yale University Press, 2006), p. 238.
34. *Memorials of London and London Life in the XIIIth, XIVth and XVth Centuries*, ed. H. T. Riley (London: Longmans, Green, 1868), p. 198.
35. *CCR 1327-30*, for example, contains only one reference to Philippa: p. 534, when her servant John of Odiham retired and was sent to the abbey of Wilton on 23 March 1329.
36. *Calendar of Papal Letters 1305-41*, 291, 294, 296, 297, 319, 323, 406 etc; *Calendar of Entries in the Papal Registers Relating to Great Britain and Ireland: Petitions to the Pope, vol. 1, 1342-1419*, ed. W. H. Bliss (London: HMSO, 1896), pp. 68, 381.
37. *Calendar of Papal Letters 1305-41*, p. 489.
38. Riley, *Memorials of London and London Life*, pp. 170-71.

39. Henry of Lancaster's mother Blanche of Artois, countess of Lancaster (d. 1302) was queen-consort of Navarre by her first marriage, and the mother of Jeanne I (1273-1305), queen-regnant of Navarre and queen-consort of France, who was the mother of Louis X, Philip V and Charles IV of France and of Queen Isabella, and was Henry of Lancaster's older half-sister.

40. *Calendar of the Plea and Memoranda Rolls of the City of London*, vol. 1, 1323-1364, ed. A. H. Thomas (London: HMSO, 1926), pp. 77-83.

41. Ormrod, *Edward III*, pp. 77-8.

Chapter 4: Deposing the King of Folly

1. *Foedera 1327-44*, p. 763; Harding, 'The Regime of Isabella and Mortimer', p. 295.

2. *Foedera 1327-44*, p. 765; *Oeuvres de Froissart*, vol. 17, p. 37. The king of Bohemia (*Behaigne*) was Johann 'the Blind' of Luxembourg, and the king of Majorca was Jaime III. By 'the king of Navarre' Froissart presumably means Philip of Evreux, cousin and husband of Jeanne II (b. 1312), queen of Navarre in her own right and a first cousin of Edward III.

3. Ormrod, *Edward III*, p. 83; *Annales Paulini 1307-1340*, pp. 352-3.

4. *Foedera 1327-44*, pp. 736, 766.

5. *CPR 1327-30*, pp. 500-1, 508, 512, 541; *CFR 1327-37*, p. 161; *CCR 1330-3*, pp. 5, 37.

6. Riley, *Memorials of London and London Life*, p. 186.

7. Mortimer, *Perfect King*, p. 76, for the clothes at Philippa's coronation; Ian Mortimer, *The Time Traveller's Guide to Medieval England: A Handbook for Visitors to the Fourteenth Century* (London: The Bodley Head, 2008), pp. 105-6, citing TNA E 101/385/4, membrane 28, and E 101/386/18, membrane 59, for her hood and hat.

8. Ormrod, *Edward III*, p. 84.

9. *Adae Murimuth Continuatio Chronicarum*, ed. Thompson, pp. 253-7.

10. For more information on Edward II's possible survival, see Kathryn Warner, *Long Live the King: The Mysterious Fate of Edward II* (Stroud: The History Press, 2017); Ian Mortimer, *Medieval Intrigue: Decoding Royal Conspiracies* (London: Continuum, 2010), 61-173, and his books *Perfect King* and *The Greatest Traitor: The Life of Sir Roger Mortimer, Ruler of England 1327-1330* (London: Vintage, 2003).

11. Brie, *The Brut or the Chronicles of England*, part 1, pp. 261-2.

12. *CPR 1327-30*, p. 523.

13. Van der Meulen, 'Sche Sente the Copie to her Doughter', p. 64.

14. Devon, *Issues of the Exchequer*, p. 141.

15. Roger's itinerary in Mortimer, *Greatest Traitor*, p. 317, reveals that he was at Woodstock on many days from the end of March onwards; and TNA SC 1/38/193 (Isabella was at Woodstock on 30 May, and every other piece of evidence for her itinerary in 1330 places her with her son with the king).

16. *CPR 1330-4*, p. 16.

17. *CPR 1330-4*, pp. 16, 74; *Issues of the Exchequer*, pp. 143-4. By the mid-1340s, Thomas had joined Philippa's own household: *Petitions to the Pope 1342-1419*, p. 84. Probably he was related to her damsel Emma Prior.

A Thomas Prior, possibly the same man, is named as a King's Scholar at the University of Cambridge in 1332 and 1333: *Admissions to Trinity College, Cambridge*, ed. W. W. Rouse Ball and J. A. Venn, vol. 1 (London: MacMillan and Co. Ltd., 1916), pp. 90, 92, 94.

18. *Issues of the Exchequer*, p. 144, for the 200 marks to Katherine. Katherine and William Montacute's eldest daughter, Elizabeth, married Hugh Despenser the Younger's eldest son and heir Hugh and was named after her paternal grandmother Elizabeth Montfort, and their second was Sybil, named after her maternal grandmother Sybil Tregoz, who married the earl of Arundel's son Edmund.

19. *Calendar of Papal Letters 1305-41*, p. 497.

20. *CPR 1330-4*, p. 2.

21. *Calendar of the Charter Rolls*, vol. 4, 1327-41 (London: HMSO, 1912), pp. 199, 210.

22. *CPR 1334-8*, p. 243.

23. Ormrod, *Edward III*, pp. 88, 128; Stella Mary Newton, *Fashion in the Age of the Black Prince: A Study of the Years 1340-1365* (Woodbridge: The Boydell Press, 1980), p. 21.

24. Woolgar, *The Senses in Late Medieval England*, p. 126.

25. Vale, *The Princely Court*, pp. 129-30.

26. Van der Meulen, 'Sche Sente the Copie to her Doughter', p. 65.

27. Ormrod, *Edward III*, p. 128.

28. Woolgar, *The Senses in Late Medieval England*, p. 240.

29. *Calendar of Papal Letters 1305-41*, pp. 498-9.

30. *CCR 1330-3*, pp. 161-2; *The Parliament Rolls of Medieval England 1275-1504*, ed. Chris Given-Wilson et al (Woodbridge: Boydell, 2005), November 1330 parliament.

31. Lisa Benz St John, *Three Medieval Queens: Queenship and the Crown in Fourteenth-Century England* (New York: Palgrave Macmillan, 2012), p. 127.

32. *CCR 1330-3*, pp. 65, 99.

33. *CPR 1330-4*, p. 20.

34. Ormrod, *Edward III*, p. 125.

35. Ormrod, *Edward III*, p. 125.

36. *CPR 1330-4*, pp. 36, 37.

37. Ormrod, *Edward III*, pp. 96, 103.

38. Richard Rastall, 'Secular Musicians in Late Medieval England', Manchester University PhD thesis (1968), pp. 76-7, 84; *CPR 1361-4*, p. 346; *CPR 1364-7*, p. 29; Ormrod, *Edward III*, pp. 316-17.

39. Woolgar, *The Senses in Late Medieval England*, p. 236.

Chapter 5: Queen at Last

1. *CPR 1330-4*, pp. 55-6, 420, 512.

2. *CPR 1334-8*, pp. 61-2, 79, 84, and also *CCR 1330-3*, pp. 212, 257, 291; *CCR 1333-7*, p. 10.

3. TNA E 43/664; *CCR 1337-9*, p. 231.

4. Ormrod, *Edward III*, p. 128.

5. TNA SC 8/265/13210; E 43/520.

6. *CPR 1330-4*, pp. 78, 523.

7. *CFR 1327-37*, p. 216.

8. TNA SC 8/171/8543.

9. *CPR 1330-4*, pp. 41-2, 48; *Foedera 1327-44*, pp. 805-6; TNA E 101/310/24.

10. *CPR 1330-4*, pp. 48, 90.

11. Rastall, 'Secular Musicians', p. 77.

12. Ormrod, *Edward III*, p. 103.

13. TNA E 101/380/4, fos. 11v, 16r, 24v.

14. Ormrod, *Edward III*, p. 103.

15. Ormrod, 'Personal Religion of Edward III', pp. 855-6.

16. *Calendar of Papal Letters 1305-41*, p. 531; *Calendar of Papal Letters 1342-62*, p. 252.

17. *CCR 1330-3*, p. 262; *Foedera 1327-44*, p. 824; Lucas, *Low Countries and the Hundred Years War*, p. 95.

18. *Anonimalle 1307 to 1334*, p. 146; Ormrod, *Edward III*, p. 130; Antonia Gransden, *Historical Writing in England*, vol. 2, c. 1307 to the Sixteenth Century (London: Routledge and Kegan Paul, 1982), p. 63; and see also Richard Barber, *Edward III and the Triumph of England: The Battle of Crécy and the Company of the Garter* (London: Allen Lane, 2013). For Eleanor of Woodstock at the tournament and her impending marriage, see A. K. McHardy, 'Paying for the Wedding: Edward III as Fundraiser, 1332-3', *Fourteenth Century England IV*, ed. J. S. Hamilton (Woodbridge: The Boydell Press, 2006), pp. 43-4.

19. *Anonimalle 1307 to 1334*, p. 146; and see also Kenneth Fowler, 'Henry of Grosmont, First Duke of Lancaster 1310-1361', University of Leeds PhD thesis (1961), p. 19.

20. *Anonimalle 1307 to 1334*, p. 146; *Oxford Dictionary of National Biography*, entry for Philippa of Hainault. In July 1314, Nicholas Farndon informed Edward II that the goods of the countess marshal, i.e. Queen Philippa's aunt Alix of Hainault, widow of the earl of Norfolk and earl marshal of England, had been seized by pirates: TNA SC 1/34/116.

21. Fowler, 'Henry of Grosmont, First Duke of Lancaster', p. 19.

22. Rastall, 'Secular Musicians', p. 78, for the details in this paragraph.

23. Lucas, *Low Countries and the Hundred Years War*, p. 95.

24. *Foedera 1327-44*, p. 829; *CCR 1330-3*, p. 380.

25. *CPR 1330-4*, pp. 223-4.

26. *CPR 1330-4*, p. 414.

27. Mortimer, *Perfect King*, pp. 96-7.

28. Ormrod, *Edward III*, p. 129.

29. *CPR 1330-4*, p. 266.

30. Malcolm Vale, *The Princely Court*, pp. 312-13; *CFR 1327-37*, p. 308; Constance Bullock-Davies, *A Register of Royal and Baronial Domestic Minstrels 1272-1327* (Woodbridge: The Boydell Press, 1986), p. 205.

31. Bullock-Davies, *Register of Minstrels*, pp. 5, 38, 121, 191.

32. Kathryn Warner, *Long Live the King: The Mysterious Fate of Edward II*, p. 159; Roy Martin Haines, *Death of a King* (Lancaster: Scotforth Books, 2002), p. 111.

33. *CPR 1330-4*, pp. 223, 340, 422, 474 (wedding expenses); *CPR 1330-4*, p. 250 (marriage to Reynald arranged). See also McHardy, 'Edward III as

Fundraiser', pp. 44-6; Edward III sent out literally hundreds of letters asking for money to help pay for his sister's wedding.

34. *CPR 1327-30*, pp. 482, 509, 534; *CPR 1330-4*, p. 7.
35. Mortimer, *Perfect King*, pp. 97, 433.
36. Ormrod, *Edward III*, p. 131 note 62; *Foedera 1327-44*, p. 829.
37. Ormrod, *Edward III*, p. 130.
38. https://medievalroyalwardrobelexis.wordpress.com/2016/04/05/fit-for-a-queen-the-wardrobe-of-philippa-of-hainault-c-12323/.
39. Ormrod, *Edward III*, p. 128; Mortimer, *Perfect King*, pp. 97-8; Woolgar, *Senses in Late Medieval England*, pp. 235-6.
40. *CCR 1333-7*, p. 5.
41. J. Munby, R. Barber and R. Brown, *Edward III's Round Table at Windsor: The House of the Round Table and the Windsor Festival of 1344* (Woodbridge: The Boydell Press, 2007), p. 35.
42. Fowler, 'King's Lieutenant', p. 28.
43. *CPR 1330-4*, pp. 494-5.
44. Woolgar, *Senses in Late Medieval England*, p. 236.
45. TNA SC 1/39/15; *CPR 1330-4*, pp. 399, 403, 557.
46. *CPR 1330-4*, p. 425.
47. Ormrod, *Edward III*, p. 129; B. C. Hardy, *Philippa of Hainault and her Times* (London: John Long Limited, 1910), pp. 85-6.
48. *CCR 1333-7*, p. 33.
49. Hilda Johnstone, *Edward of Carnarvon 1284-1307* (Manchester: Manchester University Press, 1946), p. 24.
50. See Ormrod, *Edward III*, pp. 159-60, for the battle.
51. TNA SC 8/32/1566; SC 1/39/33; *CCR 1333-7*, pp. 50, 154.
52. Devon, *Issues of the Exchequer*, p. 143; *CPR 1330-4*, p. 490; *CPR 1334-8*, p. 31; *CPR 1338-40*, pp. 21, 305, 458; *CCR 1337-9*, 85; TNA SC 8/80/3971.
53. *CPR 1330-4*, pp. 498, 582.
54. Ormrod, *Edward III*, pp. 162, 615.
55. Ormrod, *Edward III*, p. 104.

Chapter 6: Building a Family

1. Joan was called 'Joan de la Tour' in November 1347 and 'Joan de Wodestok' in April 1338 and May 1342: *CPR 1338-40*, p. 53; *CPR 1340-3*, p. 462; *CPR 1345-8*, p. 430; Edward III's itinerary is in Ormrod, *Edward III*, p. 615. Joan was also often simply called 'the king's daughter Joan.'
2. Devon, *Issues of the Exchequer*, pp. 144-5.
3. *CPR 1330-4*, p. 523; *CPR 1340-3*, p. 529; CCR 1333-7, p. 94; Hardy, *Philippa of Hainault*, p. 93.
4. *CPR 1334-8*, pp. 157, 191. In March 1334 Edward had also sent envoys to arrange a marriage between John of Eltham and Marie, daughter of Guy, count of Blois and one of Queen Philippa's first cousins: *CPR 1330-4*, p. 534.
5. *CPR 1334-8*, p. 420; *CPR 1338-40*, pp. 193, 378, 398.
6. See *Collectanea Topographica et Genealogica*, vol. 4, eds. F. Madden, B. Bandinel and J. G. Nichols (London: John Bowyer Nichols and Son, 1837), pp. 389ff.

7. J. Munby, R. Barber and R. Brown, *Edward III's Round Table at Windsor*, p. 35.

8. Rastall, 'Secular Musicians', p. 82.

9. E. A. Bond. 'Notices of the Last Days of Isabella, Queen of Edward the Second, drawn from an Account of the Expenses of her Household', *Archaeologia*, 35 (1854).

10. *Galfridi le Baker de Swinbroke Chronicon Angliae Temporibus Edwardi II et Edwardi III*, ed. J. A. Giles (London: James Bohn, 1846), p. 106; A. R. Myers, *English Historical Documents 1327-1485* (London, 1969; reprinted 1996), p. 52; *Chronicon Henrici Knighton, vel Cnitthon, monachi Leycestrensis*, vol. 1, ed. J. R. Lumby (London: Eyre and Spottiswoode for HMSO, 1889), p. 460.

11. Rastall, 'Secular Musicians', p. 82.

12. *The Anonimalle Chronicle 1333-81*, ed. Vivian Hunter Galbraith (Manchester: Manchester University Press, 1927; reprinted 1970), pp. 3-5, 12; Rastall, 'Secular Musicians', pp. 83.

13. Riley, *Memorials of London and London Life*, p. 190.

14. *CPR 1334-8*, pp. 174, 207. Ogerston is now a deserted village. John de Laundes is variously described in the chancery rolls as a merchant of Paris and a merchant of Genoa (Italy).

15. *CPR 1334-8*, p. 455.

16. Benz St John, *Three Medieval Queens*, p. 136, citing TNA E 101/387/19, mem. 5.

17. Lucas, *The Low Countries and the Hundred Years War*, pp. 191-3.

18. Mortimer, *Perfect King*, p. 131, which also discusses the story that Edward stabbed his brother to death.

Chapter 7: Surviving Loss

1. For John's funeral, see Paul Dryburgh, 'Living in the Shadows: John of Eltham, Earl of Cornwall (1316-36)', *Fourteenth Century England IX*, ed. James Bothwell and Gwilym Dodd (Woodbridge, 2016), p. 45; also Ormrod, 'Personal Religion of Edward III', pp. 867-8.

2. Riley, *Memorials of London and London Life*, p. 198.

3. Ormrod, *Edward III*, p. 617, for Edward's location.

4. Ormrod, *Edward III*, p. 174 note 113, citing the register of William Melton, archbishop of York (d. 1340).

5. *CPR 1345-8*, p. 16.

6. Rastall, 'Secular Musicians', p. 85.

7. Malcolm Vale, *Princely Court*, pp. 341-2.

8. Vale, *Princely Court*, p. 291.

9. *1299, Één Graaf, Drie Graafschappen*, ed. de Boer, Cordfunke and Safartij, p. 129.

10. The 2008 French comedy film *Bienvenue Chez Les Ch'tis*, called 'Welcome to the Sticks' in English, pokes gentle fun at the tendency of people from northern France and Belgium to pronounce an 's' sound as 'sh' to this day.

11. A scan of Willem's will can be seen on the website of the Nationaal Archief (National Archive) of the Netherlands, at www.gahetna.nl, and is printed in M. Léopold Devillers, 'Sur la Mort de Guillaume le Bon, Comte de Hainaut, de Hollande, de Zélande, et Seigneur de Frise', *Compte-Rendu*

des Séances de la Commission Royale d'Histoire, Deuxième Série, Tome 5 (Brussels, 1878), pp. 426-36. His funeral arrangements are on pp. 411 and 417 onwards, and the recipients of alms on pp. 424-5. For Willem's burial at the church of the Cordeliers, see also Jean-Baptiste de La Curne Sainte-Palaye, *Mémoires sur l'Ancienne Chevalerie: La Voeu du Heron. La Vie de Gautier de Mauny. Le Roman des Trois Chevaliers & de la Canise. Mémoires Historique sur la Chasse* (Paris: Chez la Veuve Duchesne, 1781), p. 77.

12. Janet van der Meulen, 'Sche Sente the Copie to her Doughter', pp. 67-9; Charles Potvin, *Panégyriques des Comtes de Hainaut & de Hollande, Guillaume I et Guillaume II. Li dis dou boin Conte Willaume. Graf Wilhelm von Holland: Un Poème Flamand du XIVe Siècle. La Mort du Conte de Henau* (Mons: Masquillier & Dequesne, 1863).

13. Devillers, 'Sur la Mort de Guillaume le Bon', p. 410 note 3; Oxford Dictionary of National Biography, entry for Queen Philippa; Ardis Butterfield, *The Familiar Enemy: Chaucer, Language, and Nation in the Hundred Years War* (Oxford: Oxford University Press, 2009), p. 120.

14. TNA SC 1/39/50.

15. Ormrod, 'Personal Religion of Edward III', p. 867.

16. *True Chronicles of Jean le Bel*, p. 92.

17. J. G. Smit, 'De Verblijfplaatsen van de Graven van Holland en Zeeland in de Late Middeleeuwen', *Regionaal-Historisch Tijdschrift*, 24 (1992), p. 124 note 48.

18. ODNB, 'Philippa of Hainault'; Van der Meulen, 'Sche Sente the Copie to her Doughter', pp. 78-80.

19. Devon, *Issues of the Exchequer*, p. 147; CCR 1333-7, p. 599; CPR 1334-8, p. 537; Riley, *Memorials of London and London Life*, pp. 189-90, 198.

20. Ormrod, *Edward III*, p. 190 (twenty-fifth birthday); CCR 1333-7, p. 94; CPR 1334-8, pp. 427, 478-9, 487.

21. *True Chronicles of Jean le Bel*, p. 92.

22. CPR 1334-8, p. 486.

23. CCR 1333-7, p. 252.

24. ODNB entry for Isabella of Woodstock, countess of Bedford.

25. Rastall, 'Secular Musicians', p. 86; *Calendar of Fine Rolls 1337-47*, p. 55.

26. Ormrod, 'Personal Religion of Edward III', p. 866; *Calendar of Papal Letters 1342-62*, pp. 151, 176, 478; *Petitions to the Pope 1342-1419*, p. 239; CPR 1334-8, p. 394; CPR 1348-50, p. 571; CPR 1374-7, p. 397.

Chapter 8: A Long Sojourn Abroad

1. *Foedera 1327-44*, pp. 1024, 1044; TNA SC 1/50/189. Edward and Philippa were also at Langley on 8 March 1341, but dating the letter to 1338 seems to make more sense, as they did travel abroad that year. See Ormrod, *Edward III*, p. 200 note 95.

2. TNA SC 1/54/28 (in French in the original; my translation).

3. Lucas, *The Low Countries and the Hundred Years War*, p. 283; Mortimer, *The Perfect King*, p. 149 (silver basins).

4. Mortimer, *Perfect King*, p. 149; Ormrod, *Edward III*, p. 201; Hardy, *Philippa of Hainault*, p. 104.

5. Constance Bullock-Davies, *A Register of Domestic Minstrels*, p. 165; *Chronique Métrique de Godefroy de Paris*, ed. J.-A. Buchon (Paris: Verdière, 1827), pp. 196-7, and see Kathryn Warner, *Isabella of France: The Rebel Queen* (Stroud: Amberley, 2016), pp. 78-9.

6. Sara Cockerill, *Eleanor of Castile: The Shadow Queen* (Stroud: Amberley, 2014), p. 304.

7. Hardy, *Philippa of Hainault*, p. 104.

8. *The Complete Peerage by G. E. C.*, vol. 9, p. 85 note c; *CPR 1361-4*, p. 36. Alice was already dead by 16 November 1351 when she was called 'late the wife of' Edward Montacute and two of her daughters were sent to live in the custody of their paternal grandmother Elizabeth Montacute, née Montfort: *CPR 1350-4*, p. 181.

9. Hardy, *Philippa of Hainault*, pp. 109-10.

10. Hardy, *Philippa of Hainault*, p. 109.

11. *CPR 1340-3*, p. 569; *CPR 1343-5*, p. 42; *The Brut or the Chronicles of England*, part 2, pp. 306, 309; *Oeuvres de Froissart*, ed. Lettenhove, vol. 7, pp. 246-7.

12. *CPR 1338-40*, p. 313.

13. *The Chronicle of Iohn Hardyng*, p. 334.

14. Rastall, 'Secular Musicians', p. 88.

15. *CPR 1334-8*, pp. 189, 347; *CPR 1338-40*, pp. 519, 521; *CPR 1340-3*, p. 345; *CCR 1339-41*, p. 407.

16. Mortimer, *Perfect King*, pp. 20-21.

17. Rastall, 'Secular Musicians', p. 88. The very pro-Lancastrian *Brut* claims that in 1359, the tomb of Thomas, earl of Lancaster, beheaded by his cousin Edward II in 1322, was opened and his blood was found to be as fresh as on the day he died (the author wished Thomas to be canonised and indeed often calls him 'Saint Thomas of Lancaster', and this was one of the miracles the author claims Thomas performed). Edward III and Philippa's son John married Blanche of Lancaster, great-niece and ultimate heir of Thomas, in 1359. Soon afterwards, claims the author, Edward III made arrangements for his own burial in Westminster Abbey, and chose the location of his tomb, near the chapel of Saint Edward. *The Brut or the Chronicle of England*, part 2, p. 309.

18. Rastall, 'Secular Musicians', p. 88.

19. Balduin was the brother of the late Henry of Luxembourg (d. 1313), Ludwig of Bavaria's predecessor as Holy Roman Emperor, and the uncle of Henry of Luxembourg's son Johann 'the Blind', king of Bohemia (another of the seven electors and the only one not present in Koblenz). For Margaretha, *Oeuvres de Froissart*, ed. Lettenhove, vol. 2, p. 360.

20. Ormrod, *Edward III*, pp. 206-7.

21. *The Wardrobe Book of William de Norwell: 12 July 1338 to 27 May 1340*, ed. Mary Lyon et al (Brussels: Palais des Académies, 1983), pp. 212, 214.

22. Hardy, *Philippa of Hainault*, p. 110; Rastall, 'Secular Musicians', p. 89.

23. *CPR 1340-3*, pp. 72-3.

24. *CPR 1340-3*, pp. 72-3; *CPR 1350-4*, p. 63; *Calendar of Inquisitions Post Mortem 1347-52*, no. 415.

25. *CPR 1338-40*, pp. 358-9.

Chapter 9: Founding a College

1. Lucas, *Low Countries and the Hundred Years War*, p. 364; *Oeuvres de Froissart*, ed. Lettenhove, vol. 2, pp. 474, 476, 479.

2. Ormrod, *Edward III*, pp. 212, 225, 618; Lucas, *Low Countries and the Hundred Years War*, p. 376.

3. *CCR 1341-3*, p. 467; W. M. Ormrod, 'The Royal Nursery: A Household for the Younger Children of Edward III', *English Historical Review*, 120 (2005), p. 414.

4. Lucas, *Low Countries and the Hundred Years War*, p. 377.

5. *Foedera 1327-44*, pp. 1122, 1140; *CPR 1338-40*, pp. 510, 511; *Calendar of Papal Letters 1342-62*, 13, 14. The pope's letters to Edward III and Edward of Woodstock name the duke of Brabant's daughter as Joan or Johanna rather than Margarethe, perhaps in error; Johanna was Duke Jan's eldest daughter, born 1322, married to Queen Philippa's brother Willem, count of Hainault. Duke Jan III of Brabant's mother Margaret of England (1275 - c. 1333) was a daughter of Edward I of England and sister of Edward II. Jeanne of Burgundy, Philip VI's queen, born c. 1293 and one of the daughters of the duke of Burgundy, was a different person from Jeanne of Burgundy (d. 1330), Philip V's queen and the heiress of the county of Artois and the county palatinate of Burgundy.

6. *Calendar of Papal Letters 1342-62*, pp. 3, 32.

7. Rastall, 'Secular Musicians', p. 87.

8. Ormrod, *Edward III*, p. 224; Michael Prestwich, *Plantagenet England 1225-1360*, p. 312; Mortimer, *Perfect King*, pp. 177-8; Lucas, *Low Countries and the Hundred Years War*, p. 403.

9. Lucas, *Low Countries and the Hundred Years War*, p. 403.

10. Mortimer, *Perfect King*, pp. 177-8.

11. Lucas, *Low Countries and the Hundred Years War*, p. 420; Mortimer, *Perfect King*, pp. 179-80.

12. Riley, *Memorials of London and London Life*, p. 190.

13. Ormrod, 'The Royal Nursery', pp. 402-5.

14. *CPR 1338-40*, p. 53; *CPR 1340-3*, p. 462.

15. Ormrod, *Edward III*, p. 144.

16. *Calendar of Papal Letters 1305-41*, p. 585.

17. Mortimer, *Perfect King*, pp. 183-5, 434.

18. *CPR 1340-3*, p. 115.

19. TNA SC 1/39/163; *CPR 1340-3*, p. 180; *CPR 1343-5*, p. 129; *CPR 1361-4*, p. 3.

20. Ormrod, 'Royal Nursery', p. 407.

21. *CPR 1340-3*, p. 198. The duke of Brittany was the nephew and heir of John of Brittany, earl of Richmond (c. 1266-1334), who spent most of his life in England.

22. *CPR 1340-3*, pp. 73, 249, 491; *CPR 1343-5*, pp. 215, 239-40.

23. *Calendar of Papal Letters 1342-62*, p. 88; *CPR 1377-81*, pp. 507-8.

24. The infant would be the last of Philippa's twelve children to die, and was the only one of them who lived into the 1400s; he died at his birthplace of Langley in August 1402.

25. *CCR 1349-54*, p. 299; *CPR 1345-8*, p. 72; *CPR 1348-50*, p. 108; *CPR 1358-61*, p. 168; *CPR 1364-7*, p. 185.

26. *CPR 1340-3*, p. 236.

27. *CPR 1358-61*, p. 117.

28. Lisa Benz, 'Queen Consort, Queen Mother: The Power and Authority of Fourteenth-Century Plantagenet Queens', University of York PhD thesis (2009), p. 168.

29. TNA SC 8/246/12284.

30. *Calendar of Papal Letters 1342-62*, pp. 116, 169, 173.

31. Frederick Royston Fairbank, 'The Last Earl of Warenne and Surrey', Yorkshire Archaeological Society', 19 (1907); and see http://www.warrenfamilyhistory.com/Download/Earls%20Willl.pdf for a translation.

Chapter 10: The King and the Countess of Salisbury

1. *CPR 1340-3*, p. 187; Munby, Barber, Brown, *Edward III's Round Table at Windsor*, p. 36.

2. *True Chronicles of Jean le Bel*, pp. 124-6, 146-7; Mortimer, *Perfect King*, pp. 191-8.

3. Mortimer, *Perfect King*, p. 199, gives March; Ormrod, *Edward III*, p. 130, gives June.

4. *Calendar of Inquisitions Post Mortem 1361-5*, no. 118, gives Blanche of Lancaster's date of birth. Blanche of Artois's first marriage to Enrique I, king of Navarre (d. 1274), produced Jeanne I, queen-regnant of Navarre and queen-consort of France, wife of Philip IV of France and mother of Edward III's mother Isabella; her second to Edward I's brother Edmund of Lancaster (d. 1296) produced Henry of Lancaster, earl of Lancaster and Leicester, Henry of Grosmont's father.

5. *Complete Peerage*, vol. 7, p. 404.

6. *Knighton's Chronicle 1337-1396*, ed. Geoffrey Haward Martin (Oxford: Clarendon Press, 1995), vol. 2, p. 30; *CPR 1343-5*, pp. 366, 384; TNA DL 25/2184.

7. *Calendar of Inquisitions Post Mortem 1347-52*, no. 56; *CCR 1346-9*, pp. 344-5.

8. *Calendar of Charter Rolls 1341-1417*, pp. 9, 12.

9. TNA SC 1/39/163.

10. Ormrod, *Edward III*, p. 316, and see Mortimer, *Perfect King*, pp. 199-200, for the tournament and for his interpretation of the motto as a reference to Edward II's real death in *c.* 1341 many years after his reported death in September 1327.

11. *Adae Murimuth Continuatio Chronicarum*, p. 124; Munby, Barber and Brown, *Round Table*, pp. 35, 36, for the tournament. However, there is an entry on the Patent Roll dated 10 May 1342, which gave John Beaumont royal permission to settle three of his own manors on himself and his wife Eleanor jointly. *CPR 1340-3*, p. 428. Either this permission was only recorded by royal clerks a few weeks after John was already dead, or the date of his death given by Adam Murimuth is wrong.

12. *CCR 1341-3*, pp. 578, 622, 626. Edward also made Eleanor official custodian of the lands in England of Fécamp Abbey and the lands of the late Sir John Botetourt together with the marriage rights of his heir, in part payment of

the debts he owed to her late husband, and granted the marriage rights of her toddler son Henry Beaumont to her. *Calendar of Fine Rolls 1337-47*, pp. 141, 347, 386; *CPR 1338-40*, p. 312; *CPR 1343-5*, p. 557; *CPR 1348-50*, pp. 483-4; *Calendar of Inquisitions Post Mortem 1336-46*, no. 381.

13. *True Chronicles of Jean le Bel*, p. 147; Munby, Barber and Brown, *Round Table*, p. 35, and ODNB, entry for Queen Philippa.

14. Ormrod, *Edward III*, pp. 130, 140; Ormrod, 'Royal Nursery', p. 411 note 74; *Calendar of Plea and Memoranda Rolls 1323-64*, p. 153; Rastall, 'Secular Musicians', p. 92.

15. *CPR 1345-8*, p. 87; *CPR 1348-50*, p. 40.

16. *CPR 1350-4*, p. 495; *CPR 1354-8*, pp. 531, 601; *CPR 1358-61*, pp. 237, 352, 456.

17. Maud left another daughter, Maud Ufford, who was born shortly before or after her father Ralph died in 1346 and was about thirteen and a half years younger than her half-sister Elizabeth de Burgh. Maud Ufford married Thomas de Vere, heir to the earldom of Oxford, when she was only four years old (*CPR 1348-50*, p. 511), and probably grew up with the de Veres. Her only son Robert de Vere, earl of Oxford and duke of Ireland (1362-92) was the great favourite and perhaps lover of Queen Philippa's grandson Richard II in the 1380s.

18. *True Chronicles of Jean le Bel*, p. 147.

19. *True Chronicles of Jean le Bel*, pp. 146-7.

20. Ormrod, *Edward III*, p. 141.

21. Ormrod, 'Royal Nursery', p. 402; *CPR 1340-3*, p. 569; *CPR 1343-5*, pp. 42-3.

22. *CPR 1345-8*, p. 431.

23. *Register of Edward the Black Prince Preserved in the Public Record Office*, ed. M. C. B. Dawes, part IV (London: HMSO, 1933), pp. 69, 74, 165, 428.

Chapter 11: The Queen's Household

1. TNA SC 1/56/79 is Edward III's letter, cited in E. Déprez, 'La Mort de Robert d'Artois', *Revue Historique*, 94 (1907), p. 65; Queen Isabella's to Edward II dated 31 March 1325, calling him *mon tresdoutz cuer* or 'my very sweet heart' five times, is in Pierre Chaplais, ed., *The War of Saint-Sardos (1323-1325): Gascon Correspondence and Diplomatic Documents*, pp. 199-200.

2. Déprez, 'La Mort de Robert d'Artois', pp. 65-6.

3. *CPR 1340-3*, p. 572.

4. TNA SC 1/56/57; SC 1/56/62; Napoléon de Pauw, *Cartulaire Historique et Généalogique des Artevelde* (Brussels: Académie Royale de Belgique, Commission Royale d'Histoire, Documents Inédits, 1920), pp. 622-3.

5. Ormrod, *Edward III*, pp. 140-41.

6. *CPR 1343-5*, pp. 111, 140, 195, 235, 262.

7. Ormrod, *Edward III*, p. 289.

8. *Foedera 1344-61*, p. 25.

9. *Calendar of Papal Letters 1342-62*, p. 87.

10. *Calendar of Papal Letters 1342-62*, p. 3.

11. *Calendar of Papal Letters 1342-62*, p. 110.

12. Munby, Barber and Brown, *Round Table*, p. 48 onwards; Hardy, *Philippa of Hainault*, pp. 144-5; Mortimer, *The Perfect King*, pp. 211-12, for the cloth.
13. *Adae Murimuth Continuatio Chronicarum*, ed. E. M. Thompson, p. 323; ODNB entry for William.
14. *CPR 1343-5*, p. 270; *CPR 1348-50*, p. 443; *CPR 1377-81*, p. 182.
15. Rastall, 'Secular Musicians', p. 91; Ormrod, *Edward III*, p. 620.
16. *CPR 1348-50*, p. 130.
17. Ormrod, *Edward III*, p. 254.
18. *Petitions to the Pope 1342-1419*, pp. 85, 86.
19. *Petitions to the Pope 1342-1419*, p. 85.
20. *Petitions to the Pope 1342-1419*, p. 74; *CPR 1350-4*, p. 307.
21. *CPR 1343-5*, p. 111.

Chapter 12: Marital Negotiations and Intercessions

1. Their younger children were Alice, countess of Kent, John, marshal of England, and Thomas, archbishop of York and Canterbury. *CFR 1413-22*, pp. 166-7, lists the siblings in what must be birth order: Joan, Richard, Alice, John and lastly Thomas, who is known to have been twenty years old when he became bishop of Ely in August 1373. Eleanor of Lancaster was the fifth of Henry, earl of Lancaster's six daughters; Maud, mother of Queen Philippa's daughter-in-law Elizabeth de Burgh, was his third.
2. *Calendar of Papal Letters 1342-62*, pp. 164, 254.
3. Michael Burtscher, *The Fitzalans, Earls of Arundel and Surrey, Lords of the Welsh Marches (1267-1415)* (Woonton Almeley: Logaston Press, 2008), p. 43.
4. *Calendar of Papal Letters 1342-62*, pp. 164, 188, 254; *Petitions to the Pope 1342-1419*, pp. 75, 81, 99; *Foedera 1344-61*, pp. 30-31; *Complete Peerage*, vol. 1, pp. 243-4.
5. *Foedera 1344-61*, p. 45.
6. *CPR 1345-8*, pp. 12, 357; Richard Barber, *Edward, Prince of Wales and Aquitaine: A Biography of the Black Prince* (Woodbridge: The Boydell Press, 1978, reprinted 1996), p. 82.
7. *Register of the Black Prince*, vol. 4, p. 67.
8. Fowler, *King's Lieutenant*, pp. 45-7.
9. *CPR 1343-5*, p. 508; Lucas, *The Low Countries and the Hundred Years War*, 188; *CCR 1333-7*, p. 649.
10. *CPR 1343-5*, p. 549.
11. Lisa Benz, 'Queen Consort, Queen Mother', PhD thesis, pp. 66-7, 71, 74-5, 85, 270-71.
12. Dek, *Genealogie der Graven van Holland*, p. 41. Adam Murimuth, English royal clerk and chronicler, noted Count Willem's death: *Adae Murimuth Continuatio Chronicarum*, pp. 188-9.
13. *Foedera 1344-61*, p. 61; *CPR 1343-5*, p. 555.
14. *CPR 1345-8*, pp. 26, 70-1, 150.
15. Ormrod, *Edward III*, p. 288 and note 72.
16. Lucas, *Low Countries and the Hundred Years War*, pp. 539-40.
17. *CPR 1343-5*, p. 552.

18. CPR *1345-8*, p. 19; *Plea and Memoranda Rolls of the City of London 1323-1364*, mem. 25b.
19. *CPR 1345-8*, p. 12.
20. *CPR 1345-8*, p. 23.
21. Mortimer, *Perfect King*, p. 217; Ormrod, *Edward III*, p. 268.
22. *Register of the Black Prince*, vol. 4, p. 73.
23. *CPR 1345-8*, p. 87.
24. Lucas, *Low Countries and the Hundred Years War*, pp. 542-3, 591.
25. *Register of Edward the Black Prince*, vol. 4, p. 74.
26. TNA SC 1/40/31.
27. *Register of Edward the Black Prince*, vol. 4, p. 74.
28. *CPR 1345-8*, p. 124.

Chapter 13: The Burghers of Calais

1. *Register of Edward the Black Prince*, vol. 4, p. 74.
2. *Calendar of Papal Letters 1342-62*, p. 29.
3. *CPR 1345-8*, pp. 178, 183.
4. TNA SC 1/42/101.
5. *CPR 1348-50*, p. 468; *CPR 1350-4*, p. 294.
6. *Foedera 1344-61*, p. 86.
7. *Foedera 1344-61*, pp. 90, 118; *CPR 1345-8*, p. 200.
8. TNA SC 1/40/5; Benz, 'Queen Consort, Queen Mother: The Power and Authority of Fourteenth-Century Plantagenet Queens', pp. 172-3.
9. *CPR 1345-8*, p. 142.
10. *CPR 1345-8*, p. 213.
11. *CPR 1345-8*, pp. 310-12, 318-19, 344, 427, 436, 460, 543-4.
12. Strickland, *Lives of the Queens of England*, vol. 2, pp. 188-9. Hardy's 1910 biography of Philippa repeats the tale, pp. 159-62, and cites the sixteenth-century writer Raphael Holinshed (d. *c*. 1580).
13. *CPR 1345-8*, pp. 200, 477.
14. Lucas, *Low Countries and the Hundred Years War*, pp. 558-9.
15. *Register of Edward the Black Prince*, vol. 4, pp. 70, 74-5.
16. *Foedera 1344-61*, pp. 111-12; Benz, 'Queen Consort, Queen Mother', pp. 174-5. See, however, Chapter 20 below for an occasion when Philippa corresponded with Louis de Male regarding a possible marital alliance between England and Flanders in late 1368, near the end of her life.
17. ODNB; Lucas, *Low Countries and the Hundred Years War*, pp. 562-5.
18. *True Chronicles of Jean le Bel*, pp. 202-3.
19. See Nicholas Offentstadt's article 'History refuses to look kindly upon the good burghers of Calais' in *The Guardian*, 14 August 2002; and Laurent Avezou's review of Moeglin's article in *Bibliothèque de l'école des chartes*, 2003, tome 161, livraison 1, pp. 349-351.
20. See Mortimer, *Perfect King*, pp. 252-3, and John Carmi Parsons, 'The Pregnant Queen as Counsellor and the Medieval Construction of Motherhood', *Medieval Mothering*, ed. John Carmi Parsons and Bonnie Wheeler (New York: Garland Publishing, 1996), pp. 40-41.
21. Mortimer, *Perfect King*, pp. 434-5.

22. Beltz, *Memorials of the Order of the Garter*, pp. 383-4; *Register of Edward the Black Prince*, pp. 67-8, 71, also references the horses, though here the identity of Edward (*dominum Edwardo filiolo suo*, 'his son') is stated to be the prince's 'godson'.
23. *Foedera 1344-61*, pp. 128-9.
24. *CPR 1345-8*, p. 402.
25. Muffat, 'Feststellung der Geburtsdaten von Kaiser Ludwigs des Bayern Söhnen', pp. 897-9.
26. Wilson, *The Holy Roman Empire*, p. 216.
27. *Register of Edward the Black Prince*, vol. 4, p. 72.
28. *CPR 1348-50*, p. 251.
29. Karl's daughter Anne of Bohemia, born in 1366 when Karl was fifty years old, three years into his fourth marriage to Elizabeth of Pomerania, would marry Queen Philippa's grandson Richard II in 1382 and become queen of England.
30. *Foedera 1344-61*, p. 139.
31. *CPR 1348-50*, p. 20.
32. *Calendar of Papal Letters 1342-62*, p. 268.
33. *Foedera 1344-61*, p. 91.

Chapter 14: 'How many Valiant Men, how many Fair Ladies' – The Black Death

1. TNA SC 1/40/30.
2. Kenneth Fowler, 'Henry of Grosmont, First Duke of Lancaster 1310-1361', pp. 541-4.
3. Devon, *Issues of the Exchequer*, pp. 153-4; C. M. Woolgar, *The Great Household in Late Medieval England* (New Haven and London: Yale University Press, 1999), p. 100; Arthur P. Purey-Cust, *The Collar of SS: A History and Conjecture* (Leeds, 1910), p. 199.
4. Woolgar, *Great Household in late Medieval England*, p. 100, and Newton, *Fashion in the Age of the Black Prince*, p. 34, for Philippa's clothes; *Register of Edward the Black Prince*, vol. 4, p. 67, for the horse; Ormrod, *Edward III*, p. 316, and Mortimer, *Perfect King*, p. 259, for the tournament and motto; Kathleen Pribyl, *Farming, Famine and Plague: The Impact of Climate in Late Medieval England* (Springer International Publishing, 2017), p. 131, for the weather.
5. *Register of Edward the Black Prince*, vol. 4, pp. 72, 150.
6. Mortimer, *Perfect King*, p. 434.
7. Devon, *Issues of the Exchequer*, p. 153; Woolgar, *Great Household*, p. 100.
8. *Calendar of Papal Letters 1342-62*, p.24.
9. *Foedera 1344-61*, pp. 59, 74, for Edward III's letter to Leonor Guzman. For Pedro of Castile's appearance, see John Pohl and Garry Embleton, *Armies of Castile and Aragon 1370-1516* (2015), p. 44; Clara Estow, *Pedro the Cruel of Castile 1350-1369* (2005), p. 30; Magaretta Jolly, ed., *Encyclopedia of Life Writing: Autobiographical and Biographical Forms* (2013), p. 698; Robert Folger, *Generaciones Y Semblanzas: Memory and Genealogy in Medieval Iberian Historiography* (2003), p. 187. Catalina of Lancaster was the daughter of Pedro's daughter Constanza and Queen Philippa's son John of Gaunt.

10. *Foedera 1344-61*, p. 151; *CPR 1348-50*, pp. 24, 26.
11. *Foedera 1344-61*, p. 155; *CPR 1348-50*, p. 40.
12. *Register of Edward the Black Prince*, vol. 4, p. 68.
13. *Register of Edward*, vol. 4, p. 69.
14. *CPR 1348-50*, p. 57.
15. Ormrod, 'Royal Nursery', pp. 412-13, for the date and location.
16. *Foedera 1344-61*, pp. 146-7.
17. *CPR 1348-50*, pp. 121, 167.
18. *Foedera 1344-61*, p. 171, cited and translated by Rosemary Horrox, *The Black Death* (Manchester: Manchester University Press, 1994), p. 250.
19. *Foedera 1344-61*, p. 172.
20. *Foedera 1344-61*, pp. 151, 176. Joan of Woodstock's Wikipedia page, accessed 27 September 2018, states wrongly that the bishop's mission was to return Joan's body to England.

Chapter 15: The Spaniards on the Sea

1. TNA SC 1/40/32.
2. *CPR 1348-50*, pp. 195, 199, 217, 237, 248, 254 etc.
3. Beltz, *Memorials of the Garter*, p. 385; *Register of Edward the Black Prince*, vol. 4, p. 71.
4. *Life-Records of Chaucer*, Parts I-IV, ed. Walford D. Selby, F. J. Furnivall, Edward A. Bond and R. E. G. Kirk, pp. xi-xii.
5. TNA SC 1/41/84; CPR 1348-50, p. 423; Rastall, 'Secular Musicians in Late Medieval England', 95.
6. Blanche, born 1339, was one of the daughters of Isabelle de Valois, much younger half-sister of Philippa's mother Jeanne, countess of Hainault and Holland. Blanche de Bourbon's sister Jeanne married their cousin Charles V of France and was the mother of Charles VI.
7. TNA SC 1/56/26; SC 1/42/102.
8. *Foedera 1344-61*, pp. 250, 281, 285, 286; *CPR 1360-4*, p. 435.
9. *CPR 1350-4*, p. 114.
10. *Foedera 1344-61*, p. 235; *CPR 1350-4*, pp. 184-5; Jessica Lutkin, 'Isabella de Coucy, Daughter of Edward III', *Fourteenth Century England VI*, pp. 135-6.
11. TNA SC 1/40/116; SC 1/41/82; *CPR 1350-4*, pp. 120, 152, 319, 345; *CPR 1358-61*, p. 32 (Philippa's itinerary); *The Brut or the Chronicles of England*, part 2, p. 304..
12. Kenneth Fowler, *The King's Lieutenant: Henry of Grosmont*, pp. 106-9.
13. *Foedera 1344-61*, pp. 235, 241; *Knighton's Chronicle 1337-1396*, ed. Martin, vol. 2, p. 69. Ralph Stafford was born in the late 1330s or thereabouts, and was the elder son and heir of the earl of Stafford and the grandson and heir of Hugh Audley, earl of Gloucester (d. 1347). Ralph's death in or before 1347 left his younger brother Hugh Stafford as the Stafford/Audley heir.
14. *True Chronicles of Jean le Bel*, pp. 107-8.
15. *Foedera 1344-61*, p. 263.
16. Fowler, 'Henry of Grosmont, First Duke of Lancaster', p. 453; Brad Verity, 'The First English Duchess: Isabel de Beaumont, c. 1318- c.1359',

Foundations (2004), vol. 1.5, pp. 315, 319 (journal of the Foundation for Medieval Genealogy).

17. *True Chronicles of Jean le Bel*, p. 108.
18. For Jeanne's reburial in 2001, see http://www.lavoixdunord.fr/204305/article/2017-08-14/la-comtesse-jeanne-de-valois-repose-dans-l-eglise-saint-gery-de-maing and https://fr.wikipedia.org/wiki/Abbaye_de_Fontenelle, accessed 12 March 2019; *CIPM 1352-60*, no. 46, and *CPR 1350-4*, p. 312, for John and Joan of Kent.
19. *Testamenta Vetusta: Illustrations from Wills*, vol. 1, p. 179.

Chapter 16: A Last Child and a Grandchild

1. *Calendar of Papal Letters 1342-62*, p. 513.
2. Mortimer, *The Perfect King*, p. 306.
3. Mortimer, *The Perfect King*, p. 308.
4. *John of Gaunt's Register*, vol. 1, no. 758, pp. 282-3.
5. *Calendar of Inquisitions Post Mortem 1327-36*, no. 387 (Edmund's inquisition post mortem); *Calendar of Inquisitions Post Mortem 1347-52*, no. 247 (Roger's proof of age); *CPR 1350-4*, p. 540 (quotation).
6. *CPR 1354-8*, p. 7.
7. *CPR 1354-8*, p. 45.
8. *CPR 1354-8*, p. 161.
9. *CPR 1354-8*, pp. 93, 325; *CCR 1354-60*, p. 27; TNA C 49/7/27; *CIPM 1370-73*, no. 148 (she was 'aged 17 on the eve of St James last' in January 1372).
10. *Register of Edward the Black Prince*, vol. 4, p. 165.
11. *CPR 1354-8*, p. 425; *CPR 1358-61*, p. 337.
12. *Oxford Dictionary of National Biography*, entry for Thomas of Woodstock.
13. *CPR 13254-8*, pp. 186, 258; *Oxford Dictionary of National Biography*, entry for Thomas of Woodstock.
14. *CPR 1354-8*, p. 269.
15. *CPR 1354-8*, p. 263.
16. *Calendar of Inquisitions Post Mortem 1365-69*, no. 385.
17. Devon, *Issues of the Exchequer*, p. 164.
18. *Register of the Black Prince*, vol. 4, p. 251.
19. *CPR 1354-8*, p. 352.
20. *CPR 1354-8*, p. 287; *CPR 1361-4*, p. 458.
21. This Maud of Lancaster, duchess of Lower Bavaria, was the niece of Maud of Lancaster the dowager countess of Ulster, Lionel of Antwerp's mother-in-law.
22. Brad Verity, 'The First English Duchess: Isabel de Beaumont, c. 1318- c.1359', *Foundations* (2004), vol. 1.5 (journal of the Foundation for Medieval Genealogy), p. 319, for Maud giving birth in 1356.
23. Michael Bennett, 'Isabelle of France, Anglo-French Diplomacy and Cultural Exchange in the 1350s', *The Age of Edward III*, ed. James Bothwell (York: York Medieval Press, 2001), p. 217. One of the French noblemen killed at Poitiers was Pierre, duke of Bourbon, married to Queen Philippa's half-aunt Isabelle de Valois and thus her uncle by marriage.
24. Bennett, 'Isabelle of France, Anglo-French Diplomacy', p. 219.

25. Bennett, 'Anglo-French Diplomacy', pp. 219-20. Marie was the daughter of the count of St Pol, and her mother Marie of Brittany was the daughter of Beatrice of England, daughter of Henry III and sister of Edward I; Jeanne de Bar was the daughter of Count Henri III of Bar (d. 1302), and her mother Eleanor (d. 1298) was Edward I's eldest daughter.

Chapter 17: Royal Marriages

1. Bennett, 'Anglo-French Diplomacy', p. 220.
2. TNA SC 1/42/100; SC 1/41/81; *CPR 1361-4*, p. 269.
3. *CPR 1358-61*, p. 62.
4. See E. A. Bond, 'The Last Days of Isabella, Queen of Edward the Second, Drawn from an Account of the Expenses of her Household', *Archaeologia*, 35 (1854).
5. F. D. Blackley, 'Isabella of France, Queen of England (1308-1358) and the Late Medieval Cult of the Dead', *Canadian Journal of History*, 14 (1980), p. 31.
6. Mortimer, *The Perfect King*, p. 360; Ormrod, *Edward III*, p. 314; *Eulogium Historiarum Sive Temporis*, vol. 3, ed. Frank Scott Haydon (London: Longman Green 1863), p. 227.
7. *John of Gaunt's Register*, vol. 1, no. 758, p. 283.
8. For the wedding date, see Devon, *Issues of the Exchequer*, p. 172; Ormrod, 'Edward III and his Family', *Journal of British Studies*, 26 (1987), p. 410 note 46. Edmund Mortimer was born on about 25 January or 2 February 1352, so was three and a half years older than his little wife Philippa: *CIPM 1352-60*, no. 640.
9. If Philippa Montacute was Queen Philippa's goddaughter, as seems possible given her name and the closeness of her parents William Montacute (d. 1344) and Katherine Grandisson to the royal couple, this would have created a spiritual affinity when Philippa Montacute's son married the queen's granddaughter which would have required a papal dispensation.
10. Bridget Wells-Furby, 'Marriage and Inheritance: The Element of Chance in the Development of Lay Estates in the Fourteenth Century', *Fourteenth Century England X*, ed. Gwilym Dodd (Woodbridge: The Boydell Press, 2018), p. 125.
11. *Issues of the Exchequer*, p. 170; Anthony Goodman, *John of Gaunt: The Exercise of Princely Power in Fourteenth-Century Europe* (London: Longman, 1992), pp. 34-5. The king's accounts talk of three marriages performed by Chynham in the royal chapel of Reading: John of Gaunt's, his sister Margaret's (who certainly also married at the same time), and 'the daughter of the earl of Ulster.' This is a reference to Lionel of Antwerp's daughter Philippa, who had married the previous December.
12. *Petitions to the Pope 1342-1419*, p. 337.
13. *Records of the Borough of Leicester*, ed. Mary Bateson, vol. 2 (London: C. J. Clay and Sons, 1901), pp. 108-9.
14. *Issues of the Exchequer*, p. 172; TNA E 101/393/10.
15. Cited in Goodman, *John of Gaunt: Exercise of Princely Power*, p. 34, though my translation is a little different.

16. For Juliane, see Douglas Richardson's post 'New Light on Juliane, wife of William Dannet, of Leicester, bastard daughter of Henry, Duke of Lancaster', dated 21 February 2009, in www.soc.genealogy.medieval.

17. *Calendar of Papal Letters 1342-62*, p. 607. Isabella was one of the sisters of John, Lord Beaumont, who with his wife Eleanor of Lancaster (the fifth of Henry of Grosmont's six sisters) spent time with Edward III and Philippa in Brabant in 1339/40, and was killed jousting in 1342. Via her paternal grandfather Louis Brienne – her father and several of his siblings used their mother Agnes Beaumont's name – Isabella Beaumont was the great-granddaughter of John Brienne (d. 1237), king of Jerusalem, Latin emperor of Constantinople and claimant to the throne of Armenia.

18. *Issues of the Exchequer*, p. 172.

19. *Calendar of Inquisitions Post Mortem 1347-52*, no. 118; *Calendar of Inquisitions Post Mortem 1365-69*, no. 266.

20. William Clinton himself died in 1354, leaving his nephew as his heir. Juliana died in 1367.

21. *Issues of the Exchequer*, p. 171; *The Brut or the Chronicles of England*, p. 309.

22. TNA SC 1/56/40.

23. Goodman, *John of Gaunt*, p. 35; TNA SC 1/50/124.

24. *CPR 1354-8*, p. 271.

Chapter 18: Serious Debt

1. *Issues of the Exchequer*, pp. 170-71.

2. *CPR 1358-61*, pp. 237-9.

3. See Chris Given-Wilson's article 'The Merger of Edward III and Queen Philippa's Households', *Historical Research*, 51 (1978), and Chapter 5 of his PhD thesis, 1976, pp. 105-10.

4. TNA SC 1/41/86; Ormrod, *Edward III*, p. 626.

5. TNA SC 1/56/78.

6. Newton, *Fashion in the Age of the Black Prince*, pp. 65-6.

7. Elizabeth's granddaughter and heir Elizabeth de Burgh the younger, countess of Ulster, was married to Edward III and Queen Philippa's second son Lionel. Remarkably, the elder Elizabeth had lived long enough to see the marriage of one of her great-grandchildren, little Philippa, in late 1358. William de Bohun's heir was his son Humphrey (b. 1342), also the heir to his father's childless elder brother Humphrey de Bohun the elder, earl of Hereford and Essex, who would die in October 1361. Humphrey de Bohun (b. 1342) was the half-brother of Roger Mortimer, second earl of March (b. 1328) via his mother Elizabeth Badlesmere.

8. *True Chronicles of Jean le Bel*, pp. 78, 88; *Chronique des quatre premiers Valois* cited in Clifford J. Rogers, 'The Bergerac Campaign (1345) and the Generalship of Henry of Lancaster', *Journal of Medieval Military History*, ed. Bernard S. Bachrach et al (2004), p. 89; and see also Nicholas A. Gribit, *Henry of Lancaster's Campaign to Aquitaine, 1345-46* (2016).

9. *The Book of Holy Medicine*s, by Henry of Grosmont, first Duke of Lancaster, ed. and trans. Catherine Batt (Tempe, Arizona, 2014).

10. A. K. McHardy, 'A Personal Portrait of Richard II', *The Reign of Richard II*, ed. Gwilym Dodd (Stroud: Tempus Publishing, 2000), p. 11.
11. Beltz, *Memorials of the Order of the Garter*, p. 385.
12. The *Polychronicon*, vol 8, p. 360, cited in Edward of Woodstock's entry in the *Oxford Dictionary of National Biography*.
13. A. E. Prince, 'A Letter of Edward the Black Prince Describing the Battle of Najera', *English Historical Review*, 11 (1926), p. 418.
14. *CPR 1361-4*, p. 126.
15. *CPR 1361-4*, pp. 203, 217-18; *The Brut*, part 2, pp. 313-14.
16. Cited in Barbara Emerson, *The Black Prince*, p. 171.
17. *Issues of the Exchequer*, p. 184.
18. *Testamenta Vetusta: Being Illustrations from Wills*, vol. 1, ed. Nicholas Harris Nicolas (London: Nichols and Son, 1826), pp. 70-71.

Chapter 19: The King's Mistress

1. Mortimer, *The Perfect King*, p. 360.
2. *CPR 1361-64*, p. 102; *CPR 1364-7*, pp. 109, 114, 235, 300, 383, 396, 421.
3. *CPR 1364-7*, p. 109. Edward III was fifty miles away at Newstead Abbey in Nottinghamshire at the time.
4. Mortimer, *The Perfect King*, p. 360; *CPR 1361-4*, p. 232.
5. For Edward III and Alice Perrers' relationship, see Laura Tompkins, 'Alice Perrers and the Goldsmiths' Mistery: New Evidence Concerning the Identity of the Mistress of Edward III', *English Historical Review*, 130 (2015), pp. 1361-91.
6. *Chronica Maiora*, cited in W. M. Ormrod, 'Who Was Alice Perrers?', *The Chaucer Review*, 40 (2006), p. 219.
7. Alice Perrers' will is in *Testamenta Vetusta*, vol. 1, ed. Nicolas, pp. 152-3. See Laura Tompkins, 'Mary Percy and John de Southeray: Wardship, Marriage and Divorce in Fourteenth-Century England', *Fourteenth Century England X*, ed. Gwilym Dodd (Woodbridge: The Boydell Press, 2018), pp. 133-56, for the Percy/Southeray marriage and annulment. Mary Percy, who was Lady Oreby in her own right as she was the heiress of her mother and grandparents, married secondly John, Lord Ros, and died childless in 1394. John de Southeray went to Portugal with his half-brother Edmund of Langley in 1381, and disappears from the record after 1384.
8. Mortimer, *The Perfect King*, p. 379; Walsingham cited in Ormrod, 'Who Was Alice Perrers?', 219.
9. Ormrod, 'Who Was Alice Perrers?', pp. 223-4, and see also his articles 'The Trials of Alice Perrers' and 'Alice Perrers and John Salisbury', and Laura Tompkins' article about her, cited in the bibliography. She appears among the damsels bought cloth for Philippa's funeral in *Life-Records of Chaucer*, p. 172, and was listed as the third name of the sixteen women.
10. TNA E 101/394/19 (Elizabeth's body).
11. *The Brut*, part 2, p. 315 (the weather conditions); *The Parliament Rolls of Medieval England*, October 1363 parliament (sumptuary laws); *CPR 1361-4*, pp. 334, 375, 388, 392, 408 etc (the queen's itinerary).
12. *CPR 1361-4*, p. 472.

13. *Issues of the Exchequer*, p. 183 (expenses for John); Ormrod, *Edward III*, p. 469; Sydney Armitage-Smith, *John of Gaunt, King of Castile and Leon, Duke of Aquitaine and Lancaster, Earl of Derby, Lincoln, and Leicester, Seneschal of England* (New York: Charles Scribner, 1904), p. 28 (the kings in England in 1364).

14. Newton, *Fashion in the Age of the Black Prince*, pp. 56-7.

15. TNA SC 1/63/249 (Philippa); Ormrod, *Edward III*, p. 627 (Edward's itinerary).

16. *Calendar of Letter-Books Preserved Among the Archives of the Corporation of the City of London, Letter-Book D, c. 1309-1314*, ed. Reginald R. Sharpe (London: John Edward Francis for HMSO, 1902), p. 310; the letter was recorded on the reverse of the folio on which Isabella of France's announcement of the birth of her son Edward III to the mayor and aldermen in November 1312 was recorded. It states 'Letter from Johanna, Princess of Wales, to the Mayor and Aldermen, announcing the birth of a son, 27 January, 39 Edward III', and is dated at the castle of 'Engolesme' (i.e. Angoulême) on 4 February.

17. John Harvey, *The Black Prince and His Age* (London: B. T. Batsford, 1976), p. 104.

18. Ormrod, *Edward III*, p. 421 (celebrations); *CPR 1364-7*, p. 180 (Delves).

19. Barber, *Black Prince*, p. 184; Frederick Devon, *Issues of the Exchequer*, p. 184.

20. Jessica Lutkin, 'Isabella de Coucy, Daughter of Edward III: The Exception who Proves the Rule', *Fourteenth Century England VI*, ed. Chris Given-Wilson and Nigel Saul (Woodbridge: The Boydell Press, 2010), p. 138; *Issues of the Exchequer*, p. 188.

21. The marriage of Philippa de Coucy and Robert de Vere was planned on 16 October 1371, when Enguerrand de Coucy and his wife Isabella of Woodstock were granted Robert's marriage 'in order to the contracting of matrimony between the said Robert and Philippa'; *CPR 1370-4*, p. 137.

22. *CPR 1364-7*, p. 190.

23. Mortimer, *The Perfect King*, p. 360.

24. *CPR 1364-7*, p. 311; *John of Gaunt's Register*, ed. Armitage-Smith, part 1, 1371-1375, no. 608.

25. *Issues of the Exchequer*, p. 189.

26. *Issues of the Exchequer*, p. 189.

27. *CPR 1367-70*, p. 6.

28. TNA SC 1/41/83.

29. Albert Stanborough Cook, *The Last Months of Chaucer's Earliest Patron* (New Haven, Connecticut, 1916), pp. 32-4.

30. *CPR 1364-7*, pp. 303, 304, 347; Stanborough Cook, *The Last Months of Chaucer's Earliest Patron*, pp. 26-9.

Chapter 20: The End

1. *Oeuvres de Froissart*, ed. Lettenhove, vol 7, p. 251; *Calendar of Papal Letters 1362-1404*, p. 27.

2. *Testamenta Vetusta*, vol. 1, ed. Nicholas Harris Nicolas, pp. 70-71.

3. On 25 June 1368, a few weeks after her son's splendid wedding in Italy, Philippa was at Windsor when she sent a letter to the chancellor William Wykeham: TNA SC 1/56/39.

4. *Life-Records of Chaucer*, p. 162; *Calendar of Inquisitions Post Mortem 1365-69*, no. 332.

Endnotes

5. J. J. N. Palmer's article 'The Historical Context of the "Book of the Duchess": A Revision', *The Chaucer Review*, vol. 8, no. 4 (1974), pp. 253-61, corrected the long-held misapprehension about the year of Blanche's death.

6. For Philippa's correspondence with the count of Flanders about John's marriage, see Palmer, 'Historical Context', pp. 253-5. TNA E 101/315/26 is a membrane of the envoy Richard de Stury's expenses travelling to Flanders on this occasion. See also Léon Mirot and Eugène Dupréz, 'Les ambassades anglaises pendant la guerre de Cent Ans. Catalogue chronologique (1327-1450)', part 2, *Bibliothèque de l'école des chartes* (Paris: A. Picard, 1899), tome 60, p. 185. Margarethe of Flanders had been widowed at the age of eleven in 1361 when Philippe de Rouvres, duke of Burgundy, count of Artois, Auvergne and Boulogne, a great-grandson of Philip V of France and stepson of John II, died as a teenager. For what follows about the Christmas celebrations, and those who were present, *Life-Records of Chaucer*, pp. 162-9.

7. *CPR 1367-70*, pp. 252, 255.

8. *Oxford Dictionary of National Biography*, entries for Edmund of Langley and John of Gaunt.

9. *CPR 1367-70*, pp. 274, 277, 285.

10. *CPR 1367-70*, pp. 317, 335.

11. *Sir John Froissart's Chronicles of England, France, Spain, and the Adjoining Countries*, vol. 4, ed. Thomas Johnes (London: Longman, Hurst, Rees and Orme, 1805), pp. 20-23; the John of Gaunt story is cited in Agnes Strickland, *Lives of the Queens of England*, p. 205.

12. *CPR 1367-70*, pp. 301-3, 322-5 (Edward III's grants supposedly after the queen's death); *Testamenta Eboracensia, Or Wills Registered at York*, part 1, ed. James Raine (London: J. B. Nichols and Son, 1836), p. 231 (John's will and the gold fastening); *John of Gaunt's Register*, ed. Armitage-Smith, part 1, 1371-1375, no. 1090, p. 93 (gold cup); *Calendar of Inquisitions Post Mortem 1365-9*, no. 385 (Philippa Mortimer's proof of age). Queen Philippa's entry in the *Oxford Dictionary of National Biography* states that she died a little before 14 August, presumably on the basis of the king's grants on that date recorded on the Patent Roll which say that she was dead, but the general consensus is that she died on 15 August, as given in Mark Ormrod's *ODNB* entry about Edward III.

13. Thomas's son and heir Robert, born January 1362, later married Edward III and Philippa's granddaughter Philippa Coucy, so perhaps the king named Thomas de Vere as his son because Thomas's own son would later become his grandson-in-law.

14. Jeanne, born *c.* 1341/2, was the sister of John de Montfort, who became Duke John IV of Brittany and was the widower of Queen Philippa's daughter Mary of Waltham. Jeanne later married Ralph, Lord Basset of Drayton, and died in 1402.

15. *Life-Records of Chaucer*, p. 162.

16. *Life-Records of Chaucer*, pp. 172-5. Lady Ferrers was Margaret née Ufford, daughter of the earl of Suffolk and wife of William, Lord Ferrers of Groby, who with her sister-in-law Elizabeth née Ferrers, countess of Atholl, was named as one of the queen's ladies at Christmas 1368); Lady Mohun was Joan née Burghersh, mother-in-law of the earl of Salisbury, who died in 1404 when she was over eighty.

17. The letter is cited in the original French in Ormrod, 'Personal Religion of Edward III', pp. 868-9 note 115.
18. Ormrod, 'Personal Religion', p. 868.
19. *Anonimalle Chronicle 1333-1381*, ed. Galbraith, p. 58.
20. *CPR 1367-70*, pp. 340-1.
21. *Issues of the Exchequer*, pp. 199-200.
22. *Issues of the Exchequer*, p. 189; Anne McGee Morganstern, *Gothic Tombs of Kinship in France, the Low Countries, and England* (University Park, Pennsylvania: Pennsylvania State University Press, 2000), pp. 96-100.
23. *CPR 1364-7*, p. 107; *CPR 1367-70*, p. 388; *CPR 1370-4*, pp. 133-4, 262; *CPR 1377-81*, p. 161.
24. *CPR 1354-8*, p. 200; *CPR 1358-61*, pp. 12, 101; *CPR 1364-7*, p. 225; *CPR 1374-7*, p. 12; *CPR 1377-81*, p. 122.
25. *CPR 1385-9*, p. 68.
26. *CPR 1367-70*, p. 342; *Life-Records of Chaucer*, pp. 162-70, 172.
27. *CPR 1367-70*, p. 432.
28. *John of Gaunt's Register*, vol. 1, ed. Sydney Armitage-Smith (London: Royal Historical Society, 1911), nos. 57, 608; *Calendar of Inquisitions Post Mortem 1365-69*, no. 434.
29. Walsingham, *Historia Anglicana*, vol. 1, p. 309, cited in Ormrod, 'Personal Religion of Edward III', p. 850, and in Philippa's entry in the Oxford Dictionary of National Biography.
30. The poem is cited in English translation in Ormrod, *Edward III*, p. 471, and in the Latin original in Ormrod, 'Personal Religion of Edward III', p. 850 note 7. *The Brut or the Chronicles of England*, part 2, p. 321, for the pestilence, floods and food shortages.
31. Cited in Ormrod, *Edward III*, p. 470.
32. *Sir John Froissart's Chronicles of England, France, Spain, and the Adjoining Countries*, vol. 4, p. 20; *Oeuvres de Froissart*, ed. Lettenhove, vol. 5, p. 141; *The Brut or the Chronicles of England*, ed. Brie, p. 321.
33. Ormrod, *Edward III*, p. 470; Ormrod, 'Personal Religion', pp. 868-9.
34. *CPR 1381-5*, p. 559.

Appendix 2

1. C. Hingeston-Randolph, *The Register of Walter de Stapledon, Bishop of Exeter, A. D. 1307-1326*, p. 169.
2. *Oeuvres de Froissart*, ed. Kervyn de Lettenhove, vol. 2, 1322-1339 (Brussels: 1867), pp. 54-5.
3. *John of Gaunt's Register 1371-1375*, ed. Armitage-Smith, no. 758; my translation.
4. The letter is cited in J. J. N. Palmer's article 'The Historical Context of the 'Book of the Duchess'', pp. 253-5, in the French original and in English translation; my own translation differs. Count Louis's mother, whom he refers to in the letter, was Marguerite of France (1310-82), a daughter of King Philip V (d. 1322) and Jeanne of Burgundy (d. 1330), and a first cousin of Edward III.

Select Bibliography

Primary Sources

Adae Murimuth Continuatio Chronicarum, ed. E. M. Thompson (London: Eyre and Spottiswoode, 1889)

Annales Londonienses 1195-1330, in W. Stubbs, ed., *Chronicles of the Reigns of Edward I and Edward II*, vol. 1 (London: Rolls Series, 1882)

Annales Paulini 1307-1340, in. Stubbs, ed. *Chronicles of the Reigns*, vol. 1

The Anonimalle Chronicle 1307 to 1334, from Brotherton Collection MS 29, ed. W. R. Childs and J. Taylor (Yorkshire Archaeological Society Records Series 147, 1991)

The Anonimalle Chronicle 1333-81, ed. Vivian Hunter Galbraith (Manchester: Manchester University Press, 1927; reprinted with minor corrections, 1970)

The Antient Kalendars and Inventories of the Treasury of His Majesty's Exchequer, three vols., ed. Francis Palgrave (London, 1836)

The Brut or the Chronicles of England, parts 1 and 2, ed. F. W. D. Brie (London: Early English Text Society, 1906-8)

Calendar of the Charter Rolls, one vol., 1341-1417 (London: HMSO, 1916)

Calendar of the Close Rolls, seventeen vols., 1307-1374 (London: HMSO, 1892-1911)

Calendar of Documents Relating to Scotland, vol. 3, 1307–1357, ed. Joseph Bain (Edinburgh: H. M. General Register House, 1887)

Calendar of Entries in the Papal Registers Relating to Great Britain and Ireland: Papal Letters, ed. W. H. Bliss and J. A. Twemlow, 3 vols. 1305-41, 1342-62, 1362-1404 (London: HMSO, 1895-1902)

Calendar of Entries in the Papal Registers Relating to Great Britain and Ireland: Petitions to the Pope, vol. 1, 1342-1419, ed. W. H. Bliss (London: HMSO, 1896)

Calendar of the Fine Rolls, seven vols., 1307-1377 (London: HMSO, 1912-24)

Calendar of Inquisitions Miscellaneous (Chancery), 2 vols. 1308-1348, 1348-1377 (London: HMSO, 1916)

Calendar of Inquisitions Post Mortem, six vols., 1327-69 (London, Public Record Office, 1909-38)

Calendar of Letter-Books Preserved Among the Archives of the Corporation of the City of London, Letter-Books D, E, F, G, 1309-1374, ed. Reginald R. Sharpe (London: John Edward Francis for HMSO, 1902-5)

Calendar of Memoranda Rolls (Exchequer): Michaelmas 1326–Michaelmas 1327 (London: HMSO, 1968)

Calendar of the Patent Rolls, twenty-one vols., 1307-1377 (London: HMSO, 1894-1916)

Calendar of the Plea and Memoranda Rolls of the City of London, vol. 1, 1323-1364, ed. A. H. Thomas (London: HMSO, 1926)

Croniques de London depuis l'an 44 Hen. III jusqu'à l'an 17 Edw. III, ed. J. G. Aungier (London, Camden Society, 1844)

Chronica Monasterii de Melsa, 3 vols., ed. Edward A. Bond (Cambridge: Cambridge University Press, 1867)

The Chronicle of Geoffrey le Baker of Swinbrook, ed. Richard Barber, trans. David Preest (Woodbridge: Boydell and Brewer, 2012)

Chronicon Galfridi de Baker de Swynebroke, ed. E. M. Thompson (Oxford: Clarendon Press, 1889)

Chronicon Henrici Knighton, vel Cnitthon, monachi Leycestrensis, 2 vols., ed. J. R. Lumby (London: Eyre and Spottiswoode for HMSO, 1889-95)

A Collection of All the Wills now Known to be Extant of the Kings and Queens of England, Princes and Princesses of Wales, and Every Branch of the Blood Royal (London: J. Nichols, 1780)

English Historical Documents, vol. 4, 1327-1485, ed. A. R. Myers (London: Eyre and Spottiswoode, 1969; reprinted by Routledge, 1996)

Eulogium Historiarum Sive Temporis, vol. 3, ed. Frank Scott Haydon (London: Longman Green 1863)

Excerpta Historica, Or, Illustrations of English History, ed. Samuel Bentley (London: printed by and for Samuel Bentley, 1831)

Flores Historiarum, ed. H. R. Luard, vol. 3 (London: Eyre and Spottiswoode for HMSO, 1890)

Foedera, Conventiones, Litterae et Cujuscunque Acta Publica, vols. 2.1, 1307-1327, vol. 2.2, 1327-1344, vol. 3.1, 1344-1361, vol. 3.2, 1361-1377 (London: Thomas Rymer, 1818-30)

Henry of Grosmont, First Duke of Lancaster, *Le Livre de Seyntz Medicines: The Book of Holy Medicines*, translated with notes and introduction by Catherine Batt (Tempe, Arizona: Medieval and Renaissance Texts and Studies, vol. 419, 2014)

Issues of the Exchequer; Being a Collection of Payments Made out of His Majesty's Revenue, From King Henry III to King Henry VI Inclusive, ed. Frederick Devon (London: John Murray, 1837)

Jean Froissart: Chronicles, translated and edited by Geoffrey Brereton (London: Penguin, 1968, reprinted with minor corrections 1978)

Gesta Edwardi de Carnarvon Auctore Canonico Bridlingtoniensi, in W. Stubbs, ed., *Chronicles of the Reigns of Edward I and Edward II*, vol. 2 (London: Rolls Series, 1883)

John of Gaunt's Register, vol. 1, 1371-1375, ed. Sydney Armitage-Smith (London: Camden third series, volume 20, 1911)

Select Bibliography

Knighton's Chronicle 1337-1396, ed. Geoffrey Haward Martin (Oxford: Clarendon Press, 1995)

The Chronicle of Lanercost 1272-1346, ed. Herbert Maxwell (Glasgow: James Maclehose and Sons, 1913)

Life-Records of Chaucer, Parts I-IV, ed. Walford D. Selby, F. J. Furnivall, Edward A. Bond and R. E. G. Kirk (London: Chaucer Society, 1900)

Le Livere de Reis de Britannie e le Livere de Reis de Engletere, ed. John Glover (London: Longman Green, 1865)

Memorials of London and London Life in the XIIIth, XIVth and XVth Centuries, ed. H. T. Riley (London: Longmans, Green, 1868)

Memorials of the Order of the Garter from Its Foundation to the Present Time, ed. George Frederick Beltz (London: W. Pickering, 1841)

The National Archives: C (Chancery), DL (Duchy of Lancaster), E (Exchequer), SC (Special Collections)

The Parliament Rolls of Medieval England 1275-1504, ed. Chris Given-Wilson, Paul Brand, Seymour Phillips, Mark Ormrod, Geoffrey Martin, Anne Curry and Rosemary Horrox (Woodbridge: Boydell, 2005)

Polychronicon Ranulphi Higden, Monachi Cestrensis, vol. 8, ed. J. R. Lumby (London: Longman Green, 1865)

Records of the Borough of Leicester, ed. Mary Bateson, 2 vols. (London: C. J. Clay and Sons, 1899-1901)

Register of Edward the Black Prince Preserved in the Public Record Office, ed. M. C. B. Dawes, parts I-IV, 1346-65 (London: HMSO, 1930-33)

The Register of Walter de Stapledon, Bishop of Exeter, A. D. 1307-1326, ed. C. Hingeston-Randolph (London: George Bell and Sons, 1892)

Scalacronica: The Reigns of Edward I, Edward II and Edward III as Recorded by Sir Thomas Gray of Heton, Knight, ed. Herbert Maxwell (Glasgow: James Maclehose and Sons, 1907)

Scalacronica: By Sir Thomas Gray of Heton, Knight. A Chronicle of England and Scotland From A. D. MLXVI to MCCCLXII, ed. J. Stevenson (Edinburgh: Maitland Club, 1836)

Sir John Froissart's Chronicles of England, France, Spain, and the Adjoining Countries, 10 vols., ed. Thomas Johnes (London: Longman, Hurst, Rees and Orme)

Testamenta Eboracensia, Or Wills Registered at York, part 1, ed. James Raine (London: J. B. Nichols and Son, 1836)

Testamenta Vetusta: Being Illustrations from Wills, vol. 1, ed. Nicholas Harris Nicolas (London: Nichols and Son, 1826)

The True Chronicles of Jean le Bel, 1290-1360, trans. and ed. Nigel Bryant (Woodbridge: Boydell and Brewer, 2011)

Urkundenbuch für die Geschichte des Niederrheins oder des Erzstifts Cöln, der Fürstenthümer Jülich und Berg, Geldern, Meurs, Kleve und Mark, und der Reichsstifte Elten, Essen und Werden, aus den Quellen in dem Königlichen Provinzial-Archiv zu Düsseldorf und in den Kirchen- und Stadt-Archiven der Provinz, vollständig und erläutert, Band III: Von dem Jahr 1301 bis 1400 einschliesslich, ed. Theodor Joseph Lacomblet (Düsseldorf: H. Voss, Im Commission der Schaub'schen Buchhandlung, 1853)

La Vie du Prince Noir by Chandos Herald, ed. Diana B. Tyson (Tübingen: Max Niemeyer Verlag, 1975)

Vita Edwardi Secundi Monachi Cuiusdam Malmesberiensis, ed. Noel Denholm-Young (London: Thomas Nelson and Sons, 1957)

The War of Saint-Sardos (1323-1325): Gascon Correspondence and Diplomatic Documents, ed. Pierre Chaplais, Camden third series, vol. LXXXVII (London: Offices of the Royal Historical Society, 1954)

The Westminster Chronicle 1381-1394, ed. L. C. Hector and B. F. Harvey (Oxford, 1982)

Willelmi, Capellini in Brederode, Postea Monachi et Procuratoris Egmondensis Chronicon, ed. Cornelis Pijnacker Hirdijk (Amsterdam: Müller, 1904)

Secondary Sources

Armitage-Smith, Sydney, *John of Gaunt, King of Castile and Leon, Duke of Aquitaine and Lancaster, Earl of Derby, Lincoln, and Leicester, Seneschal of England* (New York: Charles Scribner, 1904)

Barber, Richard, *Edward, Prince of Wales and Aquitaine: A Biography of the Black Prince* (Woodbridge: The Boydell Press, 1978, reprinted 1996)

Barber, Richard, *Edward III and the Triumph of England: The Battle of Crécy and the Company of the Garter* (London: Allen Lane, 2013)

Bennett, Michael, 'Isabelle of France, Anglo-French Diplomacy and Cultural Exchange in the 1350s', *The Age of Edward III*, ed. James Bothwell (York: York Medieval Press, 2001)

Benz, Lisa, 'Queen Consort, Queen Mother: The Power and Authority of Fourteenth-Century Plantagenet Queens', University of York PhD thesis (2009)

Benz St John, Lisa, *Three Medieval Queens: Queenship and the Crown in Fourteenth-Century England* (New York: Palgrave Macmillan, 2012)

Blackley, F. D., 'Isabella of France, Queen of England (1308-1358) and the Late Medieval Cult of the Dead', *Canadian Journal of History*, 14 (1980)

Bond, E. A., 'The Last Days of Isabella, Queen of Edward the Second, Drawn from an Account of the Expenses of her Household', *Archaeologia*, 35 (1854)

Bothwell, James, ed., *The Age of Edward III* (York: York Medieval Press, 2001)

Bothwell, James, and Dodd, Gwilym, *Fourteenth Century England IX* (Woodbridge: The Boydell Press, 2016)

Bullock-Davies, Constance, *A Register of Royal and Baronial Domestic Minstrels 1272-1327* (Woodbridge: The Boydell Press, 1986)

Burtscher, Michael, *The Fitzalans, Earls of Arundel and Surrey, Lords of the Welsh Marches (1267-1415)* (Woonton Almeley: Logaston Press, 2008)

Butterfield, Ardis, *The Familiar Enemy: Chaucer, Language, and Nation in the Hundred Years War* (Oxford: Oxford University Press, 2009)

De Boer, Dick Edward Herman, Erich H. P. Cordfunke and Herbert Sarfatij, eds., *1299, Één Graaf, Drie Graafschappen: De Vereniging van Holland, Zeeland en Henegouwen* (Hilversum: Uitgeverij Verloren, 2000)

Dek, A. W. E., *Genealogie der Graven van Holland* (Zaltbommel: Europeese Bibliotheek, 1969)

De La Curne Sainte-Palaye, Jean-Baptiste, *Mémoires sur l'Ancienne Chevalerie: La Voeu du Heron. La Vie de Gautier de Mauny. Le Roman des Trois Chevaliers & de la Canise. Mémoires Historique sur la Chasse* (Paris: Chez la Veuve Duchesne, 1781)

Select Bibliography

Déprez, E., 'La Mort de Robert d'Artois', *Revue Historique*, 94 (1907)

Devillers, M. Léopold, 'Sur la Mort de Guillaume le Bon, Comte de Hainaut, de Hollande, de Zélande, et Seigneur de Frise', *Compte-Rendu des Séances de la Commission Royale d'Histoire*, Deuxième Série, Tome 5 (Brussels, 1878)

Dodd, Gwilym, and Musson, Anthony, eds., *The Reign of Edward II: New Perspectives* (York: York Medieval Press, 2006)

Dodd, Gwilym, ed., *Fourteenth Century England X* (Woodbridge: The Boydell Press, 2018)

Emerson, Barbara, *The Black Prince* (London: Weidenfeld and Nicholson, 1976)

Fowler, Kenneth, 'Henry of Grosmont, First Duke of Lancaster 1310-1361', University of Leeds PhD thesis (1961)

Fowler, Kenneth, *The King's Lieutenant: Henry of Grosmont, First Duke of Lancaster 1310-1361* (London: Elek Books, 1969)

Fryde, Natalie, *The Tyranny and Fall of Edward II 1321-1326* (Cambridge: Cambridge University Press, 1979)

Galway, Margaret, 'Alice Perrers' Son John', *English Historical Review*, 66 (1951)

Given-Wilson, Chris, 'The Court and Household of Edward III, 1360-1377', Univ. of St Andrews PhD thesis (1976)

Given-Wilson, Chris, 'The Merger of Edward III and Queen Philippa's Households', *Historical Research*, 51 (1978)

Given-Wilson, Chris, and Curteis, Alice, *The Royal Bastards of Medieval England* (London: Routledge and Kegan Paul, 1984)

Given-Wilson, Chris, and Saul, Nigel, ed., *Fourteenth Century England VI* (Woodbridge: The Boydell Press, 2010)

Goodman, Anthony, *John of Gaunt: The Exercise of Princely Power in Fourteenth-Century Europe* (London: Longman, 1992)

Gransden, Antonia, *Historical Writing in England*, vol. 2, c. 1307 to the Sixteenth Century (London: Routledge and Kegan Paul, 1982)

Green, David, *Edward the Black Prince: Power in Medieval Europe* (London: Longman, 2007)

Haines, Roy Martin, *Archbishop John Stratford: Political Revolutionary and Champion of the Liberties of the English Church, ca. 1275/80-1348* (Toronto: Pontifical Institute of Mediaeval Studies, Studies and Texts, number 76, 1986)

Haines, Roy Martin, *King Edward II, His Life, His Reign and Its Aftermath, 1284-1330* (Montreal: McGill-Queen's University Press, 2003)

Hamilton, J. S., ed., *Fourteenth Century England VIII* (Woodbridge: The Boydell Press, 2014)

Harding, David Anthony, 'The Regime of Isabella and Mortimer 1326-1330', University of Durham MPhil thesis (1985)

Hardy, B. C. [Blanche Christabel], *Philippa of Hainault and her Times* (London: John Long Limited, 1910)

Harvey, John, *The Black Prince and His Age* (London: B. T. Batsford, 1976)

Holmes, G. A., *The Estates of the Higher Nobility in Fourteenth-Century England* (Cambridge: Cambridge University Press, 1957)

Horrox, Rosemary, *The Black Death* (Manchester: Manchester University Press, 1994)

Jones, Michael, *The Black Prince* (London: Head of Zeus, 2017)

Lemaire, François, *Notice Historique sur la Ville de Nivelles, et sur les Abbesses qui l'ont Successivement Gouvernée depuis sa Fondation jusqu'à la Dissolution de son Chapitre* (Nivelles: F. Cuisenaire, 1848)

Lord, Carla, 'Queen Isabella at the Court of France', *Fourteenth Century England II*, ed. Chris Given-Wilson (Woodbridge: The Boydell Press, 2002)

Lucas, Henry Stephen, *The Low Countries and the Hundred Years War, 1326-1347* (University of Michigan: Ann Arbor, 1929)

Lutkin, Jessica, 'Isabella de Coucy, Daughter of Edward III: The Exception who Proves the Rule', *Fourteenth Century England VI*, ed. Chris Given-Wilson and Nigel Saul (Woodbridge, 2010)

Manly, John Matthews, *Some New Light on Chaucer: Lectures Delivered at the Lowell Institute* (Gloucester, Mass: Peter Smith, 1959)

McFarlane, K. B., *The Nobility of Later Medieval England* (Oxford: Clarendon Press, 1973)

McHardy, A. K., 'Paying for the Wedding: Edward III as Fundraiser, 1332-3', *Fourteenth Century England IV*, ed. J. S. Hamilton (Woodbridge: The Boydell Press, 2006)

Meulen, Janet van der, 'Sche Sente the Copie to her Doughter: Countess Jeanne de Valois and Literature at the Court of Hainault-Holland', *I Have Heard About You: Women's Writing Crossing the Dutch Border*, ed. Suzan van Dijk, translations by Jo Nesbitt (Hilversum: Uitgeverij Verloren, 2004)

Mirot, Léon, and Eugène Dupréz, 'Les ambassades anglaises pendant la guerre de Cent Ans. Catalogue chronologique (1327-1450)', parts 1 and 2, *Bibliothèque de l'école des chartes* (Paris: A. Picard, 1898-9), tomes 59 and 60

Mitchell, Linda, *Portraits of Medieval Women: Family, Marriage and Politics in England, 1225-1350* (New York: Palgrave Macmillan, 2003)

Morganstern, Anne McGee, *Gothic Tombs of Kinship in France, the Low Countries, and England* (University Park, Pennsylvania: Pennsylvania State University Press, 2000)

Mortimer, Ian, *The Greatest Traitor: The Life of Sir Roger Mortimer, Ruler of England 1327-1330* (London: Vintage, 2003)

Mortimer, Ian, 'The Death of Edward II in Berkeley Castle', *English Historical Review*, 120 (2005)

Mortimer, Ian, *The Perfect King: The Life of Edward III, Father of the English Nation* (London: Vintage, 2006)

Mortimer, Ian, *The Fears of Henry IV: The Life of England's Self-Made King* (London: Vintage, 2007)

Mortimer, Ian, *The Time Traveller's Guide to Medieval England: A Handbook for Visitors to the Fourteenth Century* (London: The Bodley Head, 2008)

Mortimer, Ian, *Medieval Intrigue: Decoding Royal Conspiracies* (London: Continuum, 2010)

Muffat, K. A., 'Feststellung der Geburtsdaten von Kaiser Ludwigs des Bayern Söhnen', *Sitzungsberichte der Philosophisch-Philiologischen und Historischen Classe der K. B. Akademie der Wissenschaften zu München*, Band 3 (1873)

Munby, Julian, Barber, Richard, and Brown, Richard, *Edward III's Round Table at Windsor: The House of the Round Table and the Windsor Festival of 1344* (Woodbridge: The Boydell Press, 2007)

Newton, Stella Mary, *Fashion in the Age of the Black Prince: A Study of the Years 1340-1365* (Woodbridge: The Boydell Press, 1980)

Ormrod, W. M., 'Edward III and his Family', *Journal of British Studies*, 26 (1987)

Ormrod, W. M., 'The Personal Religion of Edward III', *Speculum*, 64 (1989)

Ormrod, W. M., 'The Royal Nursery: A Household for the Younger Children of Edward III', *English Historical Review*, 120 (2005)

Ormrod, W. M., 'Who Was Alice Perrers?', *Chaucer Review*, vol. 40, no. 3 (2006)

Ormrod, W. M., 'The Trials of Alice Perrers', *Speculum*, 83 (2008)

Ormrod, W. M., 'Alice Perrers and John Salisbury', *English Historical Review*, 123 (2008)

Ormrod, W. Mark, *Edward III* (New Haven and London: Yale University Press, 2011)

Ormrod, W. M., ed., *Fourteenth Century England VII* (Woodbridge: The Boydell Press, 2012)

Palmer, J. J. N., 'The Historical Context of the "Book of the Duchess": A Revision', *The Chaucer Review*, vol. 8, no. 4 (1974)

Parsons, John Carmi, 'The Pregnant Queen as Counsellor and the Medieval Construction of Motherhood', *Medieval Mothering*, ed. John Carmi Parsons and Bonnie Wheeler (New York: Garland Publishing, 1996)

Pauw, Napoléon de, *Cartulaire Historique et Généalogique des Artevelde* (Brussels: Académie Royale de Belgique, Commission Royale d'Histoire, Documents Inédits, 1920)

Potvin, Charles, *Panégyriques des Comtes de Hainaut & de Hollande, Guillaume I et Guillaume II. Li dis dou boin Conte Willaume. Graf Wilhelm von Holland: Un Poème Flamand du XIVe Siècle. La Mort du Conte de Henau* (Mons: Masquillier & Dequesne, 1863)

Prestwich, Michael, *Plantagenet England 1225-1360* (Oxford: Oxford University Press, 2005)

Pribyl, Kathleen, *Farming, Famine and Plague: The Impact of Climate in Late Medieval England* (Springer International Publishing, 2017)

Prince, A. E., 'A Letter of Edward the Black Prince Describing the Battle of Najera', *English Historical Review*, 11 (1926)

Rastall, Richard, 'Secular Musicians in Late Medieval England', Manchester University PhD thesis (1968)

Rens, F., 'Johanna van Valois, Gravin van Henegouwen (1340)', *Belgisch Museum voor de Nederduitsche Tael- en Letterkunde*, 4 (1840)

Sandqvist, T. A. and M. R. Powicke, eds., *Essays in Medieval History Presented to Bertie Wilkinson* (Toronto: University of Toronto Press, 1969)

Sarpy, Julie, *Joanna of Flanders: Heroine and Exile* (Stroud: Amberley Books, 2019)

Saul, Nigel, *Richard II* (New Haven and London: Yale University Press, 1997)

Saul, Nigel, *The Three Richards: Richard I, Richard II and Richard III* (London: Hambeldon, 2005)

Shenton, Caroline, 'Edward III and the Coup of 1330', *The Age of Edward III*, ed. J. S. Bothwell (York: York Medieval Press, 2001)

Smit, J. G., 'De Verblijfplaatsen van de Graven van Holland en Zeeland in de Late Middeleeuwen', *Regionaal-Historisch Tijdschrift*, 24 (1992)

Stanborough Cook, Albert, *The Last Months of Chaucer's Earliest Patron* (New Haven, Connecticut, 1916)

Strickland, Agnes, *Lives of the Queens of England from the Norman Conquest*, vol. 2 (Philadelphia: Lea and Blanchard, 1848)

Sumption, Jonathan, *Divided Houses: The Hundred Years War*, vol. 3 (London: Faber and Faber, 2009)

Tompkins, Laura, 'Alice Perrers and the Goldsmiths' Mistery: New Evidence Concerning the Identity of the Mistress of Edward III', *English Historical Review*, 130 (2015)

Tompkins, Laura, 'Mary Percy and John de Southeray: Wardship, Marriage and Divorce in Fourteenth-Century England', *Fourteenth Century England X*, ed. Gwilym Dodd (Woodbridge: The Boydell Press, 2018)

Turner, Marion, *Chaucer: A European Life* (Princeton, New Jersey: Princeton University Press, 2019)

Underhill, Frances A., *For Her Good Estate: The Life of Elizabeth de Burgh* (New York: St Martin's Press, 1999)

Vale, Juliet, *Edward III and Chivalry: Chivalric Society and Its Context, 1270-1350* (Woodbridge: The Boydell Press, 1983)

Vale, Malcolm, *The Origins of the Hundred Years War: The Angevin Legacy 1250-1340* (Oxford: Clarendon Press, 1990, reprinted 2004)

Vale, Malcolm, *The Princely Court: Medieval Courts and Culture in North-West Europe* (Oxford: Oxford University Press, 2001)

Ward, Jennifer, *English Noblewomen in the Later Middle Ages* (London and New York: Longman, 1992)

Warner, Kathryn, 'The Adherents of Edmund of Woodstock, Earl of Kent, in March 1330', *English Historical Review*, 126 (2011)

Warner, Kathryn, *Edward II: The Unconventional King* (Stroud: Amberley, 2014)

Warner, Kathryn, *Isabella of France: The Rebel Queen* (Stroud: Amberley, 2016)

Warner, Kathryn, *Long Live the King: The Mysterious Fate of Edward II* (Stroud: History Press, 2017)

Warner, Kathryn, *Richard II: A True King's Fall* (Stroud: Amberley, 2017)

Warner, Kathryn, *Blood Roses: The Houses of Lancaster and York Before the Wars of the Roses* (Stroud: History Press, 2018)

Waugh, Scott, *England in the Reign of Edward III* (Cambridge: Cambridge University Press, 1991)

White, Leila Olive, 'Philippa of Hainault, Queen of England', MA thesis, Univ. of Illinois, 1915

Wilson, Peter H., *The Holy Roman Empire: A Thousand Years of Europe's History* (London: Allen Lane, 2016)

Woolgar, C. M., *The Great Household in Late Medieval England* (New Haven and London: Yale University Press, 1999)

Woolgar, C. M., *The Senses in Late Medieval England* (New Haven and London: Yale University Press, 2006)

Index